Structuring Mass Higher Education

In response to the growth of mass higher education, many universities are rethinking their future roles within their national systems of higher education as well as in a global context. Expansion has invariably changed the experience of higher education for all the involved parties: from presidents, rectors, and vice-chancellors to first-term undergraduates, organized interest groups, government bureaucracies, policy-makers, and – of course – taxpayers and parents.

Providing an international comparative perspective, *Structuring Mass Higher Education* examines the impact of these changes upon national systems of higher education. In particular, this text explores how "elite" universities have sought to retain their national status and, in some cases, secure a "world-class ranking."

Extensively researched case studies covering a wide range of countries explore questions such as:

- What are the drivers of change in systems of mass higher education?
- Within mass systems of higher education, what are the links that bind the various institutions and groupings of institutions together?
- Is there global convergence in the structuring of systems of higher education?
- Do national and regional systems have the capacity to interpret global pressures for change in a manner that preserves national cultural traditions?

Structuring Mass Higher Education provides a timely and valuable discussion that will help higher education policy makers, researchers, and students to understand these critical issues in greater depth.

David Palfreyman is Director of the Oxford Centre for Higher Education Policy Studies (OxCHEPS), New College, University of Oxford.

Ted Tapper is a Visiting Fellow at the Oxford Centre for Higher Education Policy Studies (OxCHEPS), New College, University of Oxford, and the Centre for Higher Education Management and Policy at Southampton University (CHEMPAS).

International Studies in Higher Education
Series Editors:
David Palfreyman, OxCHEPS
Ted Tapper, OxCHEPS
Scott Thomas, Claremont Graduate University

The central purpose of this series of a projected dozen volumes is to see how different national and regional systems of higher education are responding to widely shared pressures for change. The most significant of these are: rapid expansion; reducing public funding; the increasing influence of market and global forces; and the widespread political desire to integrate higher education more closely into the wider needs of society and, more especially, the demands of the economy. The series will commence with an international overview of structural change in systems of higher education. It will then proceed to examine on a global front the change process in terms of topics that are both traditional (for example, institutional management and system governance) and emerging (for example, the growing influence of international organizations and the blending of academic and professional roles). At its conclusion the series will have presented, through an international perspective, both a composite overview of contemporary systems of higher education, along with the competing interpretations of the process of change.

Published titles:

Structuring Mass Higher Education
The Role of Elite Institutions
Edited by David Palfreyman and Ted Tapper

Forthcoming titles:

International Perspectives on the Governance of Higher Education
Alternative Frameworks for Coordination
Edited by Jeroen Huisman

Spring 2009

International Organizations and Higher Education Policy
Thinking Globally, Acting Locally?
Edited by Roberta Malee Bassett and Alma Maldonado

Spring 2009

Academic and Professional Identities in Higher Education
The Challenges of a Diversifying Workforce
Edited by George Gordon and Celia Whitchurch

Structuring Mass Higher Education

The Role of Elite Institutions

Edited by David Palfreyman and
Ted Tapper

Routledge
Taylor & Francis Group

NEW YORK AND LONDON

First published 2009
by Routledge
270 Madison Ave, New York NY 10016

Simultaneously published in the UK
by Routledge
2 Park Square, Milton Park, Abingdon, Oxon, OX14 4RN

Routledge is an imprint of the Taylor & Francis Group, an informa business

Transferred to Digital Printing 2010

© 2009 David Palfreyman and Ted Tapper

Typeset in Minion by Wearset Ltd, Boldon, Tyne and Wear

Library of Congress Cataloging in Publication Data
Sructuring mass higher education : the role of elite institutions / edited by David Palfreyman and Ted Tapper.
p. cm. – (International studies in higher education)
Includes bibliographical references and index.
1. Education, Higher–Cross-cultural studies. 2. Educational change–Cross-cultural studies. 3. School management and organization–Cross-cultural studies. 4. Education and globalization–Cross-cultural studies. I. Palfreyman, David, 1954- II. Tapper, Ted.
LB2322.2.S77 2008
378–dc22
2008018007

ISBN 10: 0-415-42604-9 (hbk)
ISBN 10: 0-415-88507-8 (pbk)
ISBN 10: 0-203-88972-X (ebk)

ISBN 13: 978-0-415-42604-6 (hbk)
ISBN 13: 978-0-415-88507-2 (pbk)
ISBN 13: 978-0-203-88972-5 (ebk)

Contents

Illustrations

Box

Series Editors' Introduction

International Studies in Higher Education

This Series is constructed around the premise that higher education systems are experiencing common pressures for fundamental change, reinforced by differing national and regional circumstances that also impact upon established institutional structures and procedures. There are four major dynamics for change that are of international significance:

1. Mass higher education is a universal phenomenon.
2. National systems find themselves located in an increasingly global marketplace that has particular significance for their more prestigious institutions.
3. Higher education institutions have acquired (or been obliged to acquire) a wider range of obligations, often under pressure from governments prepared to use state power to secure their policy goals.
4. The balance between the public and private financing of higher education has shifted – markedly in some cases – in favour of the latter.

Although higher education systems in all regions and nation states face their own particular pressures for change, these are especially severe in some cases: the collapse of the established economic and political structures of the former Soviet Union along with Central and Eastern Europe, the political revolution in South Africa, the pressures for economic development in India and China, and demographic pressure in Latin America.

Each volume in the Series will examine how systems of higher education are responding to this new and demanding political and socio-economic environment. Although it is easy to overstate the uniqueness of the present situation, it is not an exaggeration to say that higher education is undergoing a fundamental shift in its character, and one that is truly international in scope. We are witnessing a major transition in the relationship of higher education, state and society. What makes the present circumstances particularly interesting is to see how different systems – a product of social, cultural, economic and political contexts that have interacted and evolved over time – respond in their own peculiar ways to the changing environment. There is no assumption that the pressures for change have set in motion the trend towards a converging model of higher education, but we do believe that in the present circumstances no understanding of 'the idea of the university' remains sacrosanct.

Although this is a Series with an international focus it is not expected that each individual volume should cover every national system of higher education. This would be an impossible task. Whilst aiming for a broad range of case studies, with each volume addressing a particular theme, the focus will be upon the most important and interesting examples of responses to the pressures for change. Most of the individual volumes will bring together a range of comparative quantitative and qualitative information, but the primary aim of each volume will be to present differing interpretations of critical developments in key aspects of the experience of higher education. The dominant overarching objective is to explore the conflict of ideas and the political struggles that inevitably surround any significant policy development in higher education.

It can be expected that volume editors and their authors will adopt their own interpretations to explain the emerging patterns of development. There will be conflicting theoretical positions drawn from the multi-disciplinary, and increasingly interdisciplinary, field of higher education research. Thus we can expect in most volumes to find an intermarriage of approaches drawn from sociology, economics, history, political science, cultural studies, and the administrative sciences. However, whilst there will be different approaches to understanding the process of change in higher education, each volume editor(s) will impose a framework upon the volume inasmuch as chapter authors will be required to address common issues and concerns. Moreover, the volume editor(s) will write introductory and concluding chapters that set out the major themes to be addressed and which draw the arguments together comparatively. Furthermore, the Series Editors will also update this foreword as each volume appears, both to show how the new volume fits into the overall framework of the Series as well as to inform readers about related future texts. This, therefore, is not a Series that will bring together under one label a number of what are essentially 'stand alone' texts. A clear framework provided by both the Series and individual volume editors is designed to aid continuity and comparison.

David Palfreyman
Director of OxCHEPS, New College, University of Oxford

Ted Tapper
OxCHEPS, New College, University of Oxford and CHEMPAS, University of Southampton

Scott Thomas
Professor of Educational Studies, Claremont Graduate University, California

Contributors

Foreword

Sheldon Rothblatt is Emeritus Professor of History at the University of California, Berkeley, and sometime Director of the Center for Studies in Higher Education on that campus. He was educated at the University of California, Berkeley, and King's College, University of Cambridge. His academic publications are in the comparative history of universities, with translations into Italian, Spanish, Swedish and Japanese. In 2002 he gave the Bishop Waynflete Lectures at Magdalen College, University of Oxford, which, expanded and revised, were published in 2007 under the title *Education's Abiding Moral Dilemma: Merit and Worth in the Cross-Atlantic Democracies, 1800–2006* (Symposium Books, UK).

General Editors

David Palfreyman, is Bursar and Fellow, New College, Oxford, and also Director of OxCHEPS (The Oxford Centre for Higher Education Policy Studies), details of which can be seen on its website at http://oxcheps.new.ox.ac.uk. David is a General Editor for the seventeen-volume Open University Press–McGraw Hill series: *Managing Universities and Colleges* (within which he and David Warner contribute a volume on *managing crisis*).

Ted Tapper is Visiting Fellow at the Oxford Centre for Higher Education Policy Studies and at CHEMPAS, University of Southampton. Most of his research on higher education has been concerned with issues of governance with a particular focus on the changing relationship between the state and the universities in the British context. In recent years he has added a stronger comparative dimension to his research and this book reflects that development.

Scott L. Thomas is Professor in the School of Educational Studies at Claremont Graduate University. His work focuses on stratification in higher education with an especial interest in issues relating to college access and the secondary school achievement gap. Thomas also has a line of methodological work that focuses on multilevel models and social network analysis. His work in this area includes a book, *An Introduction to Multilevel Modeling* (with Ron Heck, published by Psychology Press), and related articles in a variety of refereed journals.

Authors

James Fairweather is Professor of Higher, Adult and Lifelong Education, and Director of the Center for Higher and Adult Education at Michigan State University. Fairweather is internationally known for his work in faculty roles and rewards as well as reform in engineering and science education. His book, *Faculty Work and Public Trust*, is a seminal work on faculty rewards. Among his honors is the Career Research Award from the American Educational Research Association (Division J). Currently Fairweather is co-principal investor for the Center for the Integration of Research, Teaching and Learning funded by the National Science Foundation. Prior to coming to Michigan State University Fairweather taught in the Center for the Study of Higher Education at Penn State University.

Peter Scott is Vice-Chancellor of Kingston University London. Previously he was Pro-Vice-Chancellor and Professor of Education at the University of Leeds and before that Editor of *The Times Higher Education Supplement*. He was a member of the board of the Higher Education Funding Council for England from 2000 until 2006. He is chair of the Universities Association for Lifelong Learning. His books include *The Meanings of Mass Higher Education* and, with Helga Nowotny and Michael Gibbons, *Re-Thinking Science*.

Agnete Vabø is a Senior Researcher at NIFU STEP Studies in Innovation, Research and Education, Oslo, Norway. Over a number of years she has undertaken research into the development of the academic profession particularly in the Nordic countries. Two of her most recent works in English are: Høstaker, Roar & Vabø (2008), Knowledge Society, Higher Education and the Society of Control. *Learning and Teaching*, 1(1): 122–154; Vabø (2007). The Principal–Agent Relationship and Its Impact on the Autonomy of the Academic Profession, in Locke and Teichler (Eds.), *The Changing Condition for Academic Work and Career in Select Countries*.

Per Olaf Aamodt is a Senior Researcher at NIFU STEP Studies in Innovation, Research and Education, Oslo Norway. His major research in higher education research is the student experience, access to higher education, learning outcomes and reasons why students fail to complete their studies. Two of his most recent works in English are: Aamodt and Kyvik (2005). Access to higher education in the Nordic countries in Tapper and Palfreyman (Eds.), *Understanding Mass Higher Education: Comparative Perspectives on Access*; and Aamodt (2005) Access to Higher Education within a Welfare State System: Developments and Dilemmas Teixeira in Johnson, Joao Rosa and Vossensteyn (Eds.), *A Fairer Deal? Cost-Sharing and Accessibility in Western Higher Education*.

Alma Maldonado-Maldonado is an assistant professor in the University of Arizona's Center for the Study of Higher Education. She earned her doctorate at Boston College. Her research focuses on comparative higher education, international organizations, and higher education policy with particular reference to Latin America. She is co-editor of two books, *Private Higher Education: An International Bibliography* and *Educación Superior Latinoamericana y Organismos Internacionales. Un Análisis Crítico.* Her current main research project is an examination of collaboration between universities on the Mexico–USA border. With Roberta Bassett she is editing a book for this series on the role of international organizations in shaping higher education policy worldwide.

N. Jayaram is Director of the Institute for Social and Economic Change, Bangalore, India. He is on the Steering Committee of the International Network on the Role of Universities in Developing Areas (INRUDA). He is the Managing Editor of *Sociological Bulletin* (Journal of the Indian Sociological Society). He has published extensively on the sociology of higher education in India, and his books include *Higher Education and Status Retention, Sociology of Education in India, Social Conflict* (co-edited with Satish Saberwal), *The Indian Diaspora* (ed.), *Keywords: Identity* (with Aziz Al-Azmeh, Wang Bin, David A. Hollinger, Mahmood Mamdani and Emmanuel Renault), and *On Civil Society: Issues and Perspectives* (ed.).

Barbara M. Kehm is Professor of Higher Education Research at the University of Kassel (Germany) and Managing Director of the International Centre for Higher Education Research (INCHER) also at Kassel. She has published numerous scholarly works on contemporary developments in higher education with a focus on issues of internationalization and the governance of higher education systems and institutions. She is also active in a number of international organizations devoted to monitoring and understanding policy change in higher education.

Peer Pasternack is Associate Professor of Higher Education Research and Research Coordinator at the Institute of Higher Education Research, Halle-Wittenberg (HoF Wittenberg). He has written widely on developments in European higher education and has particular expertise on the changing character of higher education in the former East Germany (German Democratic Republic – DDR)

Andre Kraak is Director of Research on Human Resources Development at the Human Sciences Research Council (HSRC), Cape Town, South Africa. Dr Kraak has been involved in several education and training policy development initiatives since the late 1980s. His interests and expertise span further and higher education, skills development, and science and technology policy studies.

Kai-Ming Cheng is Professor in Education and Senior Advisor to the Vice-Chancellor at the University of Hong Kong. He received his doctoral degree from the Institute of Education, University of London. From 1996 to 2006, he was Visiting Professor at the Harvard Graduate School of Education and taught there every spring. His research started with an analysis of educational trends in rural China, which he has extended to India. In recent years, he has concentrated on studying changes in the workplace and how they impact on education reform. In Hong Kong he is a member of the Education Commission and is also active in the comprehensive education reform movement there.

Yan Wang is currently (2007–2008) a Hubert H. Humphrey Fellow of the Fulbright Program sponsored by the State Department of the USA. She was Executive Director, Department for International Cooperation, Beijing Academy of Educational Sciences from 2002 to 2007. In this role she was extensively engaged in educational research and policy consultancy in the areas of basic education, vocational and technical education and training, and higher education. She holds a Master of Educational Economics and Administration, and a first degree in English Literature. She is now pursuing a doctoral program at the University of Hong Kong.

Su-Yan Pan is Research Assistant Professor at the Faculty of Education, University of Hong Kong. Her research is concentrated on the development of higher education in China. She has worked as an Associate Professor at the School of Education at the Huazhong University of Science and Technology, and the Institute of Higher Education, Shanghai Jiaotong University. She received her PhD from the University of Hong Kong.

Frans Kaiser is a Senior Research Associate at the Center for Higher Education Policy Studies (CHEPS) of the University of Twente in the Netherlands. As the co-ordinator of the International Higher Education Monitor he has a broad interest and insight into higher education policies and statistical trends in many Western higher education systems. His latest projects are on system steering mechanisms and the development of a European classification for higher education institutions.

Hans Vossensteyn has worked at the Center for Higher Education Policy Studies (CHEPS) of the University of Twente in the Netherlands since 1991. He is a Senior Researcher and Research Co-ordinator, and since 2007 he has also been a Professor at the MBA-Higher Education and Science Management Center at the Fachhochschule Osnabrück in Germany. Hans has covered many higher education research topics: internationalization; higher education indicators, both quantitative and qualitative; and international comparative analyses with a strong focus on financial matters – allocation models, tuition fees, student financial support and access and equity. In 2005 he completed with distinction his PhD on students' price-responsiveness. He is a member of several advisory and editorial boards and is involved in training and consultancy.

Ireneusz Białecki trained as a sociologist and has a particular interest in inequality of access to education. Currently he is a Professor at the University of Warsaw and Head of the Centre for Science Policy and Higher Education. He is Editor of the journal *Nauka I Szkolnictwo Wyższe* [Science and Higher Education], which is published at the Centre. He is also a member of the Editorial Board of the *European Journal of Vocational Training*. In 1994–1996 he served as National Study Manager for IALS (International Adult Literacy Survey, OECD), while in 2000–2003 he was a member of the Polish team for PISA (Program for International Student Assessment). His publications in English include: Bialecki and Heyns (1993). Inequality in Education in Post-war Poland in Hans-Peter Blossfield and Yossi Shavit (Eds.), *Persistent Inequality: Changing Educational Stratification in Thirteen Countries*. Boulder, Colorado: Westview Press, and Bialecki and Heyns (1991) Reluctant Vanguard and Makeshift Coalition. *American Political Sciences Review*, June.

Malgorzata Dąbrowa-Szefler is a Professor at the University of Warsaw. She is co-author of the recently published *Country Background Report* (2007) of the OECD review of Polish tertiary education. She is a specialist on the financing of higher education and her publications include: Dąbrowa-Szefler (2003) *System nauki i szkolnictwa wyższego: elementy funkcjonowania i zarządzania* [System of Science and Higher Education: aspects of functioning and management], Centre for Science Policy and Higher Education, Warsaw; Dąbrowa-Szefler (2001) *Kadry dla nauki w Polsce. Stan i perspektywy rozwoju* [Manpower for research and science in Poland: Present State and Perspectives], Centre for Science Policy and Higher Education, Warsaw.

Cécile Deer is a research fellow attached to a multidisciplinary research centre (SKOPE – the Centre of Skills, Knowledge and Organisational Performance) in the Department of Economics at Oxford University, and is also a lecturer at Balliol College, Oxford. She has written extensively on contemporary higher education issues including the evolution and political economy of the reform of higher education systems in the national, European and international contexts addressing, more specifically, questions of access. She is the author of *Higher Education in England and France since the 1980s* (Symposium Books, 2002).

Simon Marginson is a Professor in the Centre for the Study of Higher Education at the University of Melbourne, Australia. He is a Fellow of the Academy of Social Sciences Australia, and the Society for Research into

Higher Education, UK. He is active as a media commentator in Australia; a scholar in North America and Mexico, Western Europe, and East and Southeast Asia; and in writing policy papers for the OECD. Simon works in comparative and international education in the context of globalization. He is interested in problems of human freedom and academic creativity, and the trajectories of research universities, His latest book is *Prospects of Higher Education: Globalization, Market Competition, Public Goods and the Future of the University* (Sense Publishers, 2007).

Fumi Kitagawa holds a PhD in Urban and Regional Studies. In Japan her work at the Department of Higher Education, National Institute for Educational Policy Research (NIER) focused on the internationalization of higher education; the financing of higher education; university–industry links; and the contribution of universities to their regions. From January 2008, Fumi has been based at CIRCLE, Lund University in Sweden where she is an assistant professor.

Roger L. Geiger was embedded with the Institution for Social and Policy Studies, Yale University, from 1974 to 1987. He is currently Distinguished Professor of Higher Education, Pennsylvania State University. His study of universities and economic development, with co-author Creso Sá, *Tapping the Riches of Science: Universities and the Promise of Economic Growth*, was published by Harvard University Press in 2008. He is also an editor of *The Future of the American Public Research University* (2007). His study, *Knowledge and Money: Research Universities and the Paradox of the Marketplace* was published by Stanford University Press (2004). His other writings relevant to the Ivy League are cited in this contribution to this volume.

Foreword

If those interested in the fortunes of universities today have any doubts as to a national obsession with super-universities, let them plunge into the details provided by the expert contributions to this volume. Nation after nation, government after government, research university after research university, are committed to what is now called "the world-class university." Just mentioning the phenomenon summons up a dizzyingly competitive race for global standing measured by a number of different ranking methods. (I am almost reminded of an eighteenth-century parlor game called "the ranking of the arts." Which art form contributed most to civilization? Music, sorrowfully, as "merely" entertainment was last.) It does little good to complain that the rankings may distort educational priorities. As Ted Tapper and David Palfreyman (editors of this volume) along with other close observers of the rankings game say, they are here to stay; and it behooves those who care about the well-being of the university as a special cultural artifact to pay serious attention to what is happening.

The drive to create a colony of universities particularly distinguished by research excellence (teaching excellence is a more vexed question, much harder to measure), merit recruitment and by signal contributions to economic and social advancement is not just the natural desire of educational institutions to set themselves apart in order to achieve fame, although this is a tendency. The academic profession itself, as most professions, has always been reputation-minded. Historically, professional people were not likely to be the richest members of society, nor members of the leading social hierarchies (with exceptions), so their claim to attention was through educational competence and superiority. (In the case of England, as Robert Anderson explains, even "effortless superiority" (2006).) The late Harold Perkin (1969) noted that the academic profession had become even more important in our day. It was the "key profession" because it educated all the others. But what is particularly special about the present situation is that governments – admittedly not all – have taken a keen and decisive interest in encouraging – the word may be too mild – the further advance of elite research universities. Given the long if recent history of government efforts to promote more egalitarian educational opportunities and, with such actions, to mitigate the effects of social and historical privilege, the changing role of government is significant. Books have been written on the subject.

That role has shifted in many western countries from social democratic or welfare state objectives, variously pursued, to a friendlier view of the place of free markets in re-shaping the curricular emphases of the research university and, as a by-product, its internal structure and decision-making habits. That does not mean, it must be said, that the welfare state is in danger of becoming irrelevant. On the contrary, public expectations remain high. Environmental issues, job-retraining, aging populations, poverty, health, as well as the circulation of diseases either new or seemingly moribund remain important. New forms of financial and entrepreurial activity have renewed desires for regulation. The world is still a dangerous place, and citizens demand protection. Nevertheless, what has emerged after some fifty years of expansion in secondary and tertiary education (in some instances earlier), an expansion that has moved higher education from elite through mass to universal entry (using the terms made famous by the late Martin Trow, 2006), are the combined pressures of national and global markets and government. These are impossible to resist, although their advance is disputed by those with doubts. *Inter alia*, they charge that the drive for wealth and influence at bottom simply reflect values more congenial to market purchases than to inherited values of a higher order. The argument may be old-fashioned but hardly trivial.

The welfare state proved to be a reasonably effective instrument for distributing certain health and economic, as well as educational benefits. It proved to be less effective in encouraging the creative energies of nations committed to a particular historical definition of progress, or even in generating the resources needed for welfare state promises. European governments, having committed themselves, at least in principle, to egalitarian policies regarding the provision of post-secondary education, discovered that there too the costs were over-running their ability to maintain some degree of equity over what increasingly came to be seen as a national system of higher education requiring system policies.

In the newly developed and globally interconnected competitive environment, it seemed rational to concentrate public resources on select institutions as a form of grand seed money, so to speak. Various indicators of research productivity, "efficiency gains," value-added learning, quality assurance and audits were devised using intermediate agencies to force those universities to diversify their income streams through "privatization." In some cases research universities did not have to be forced, having already developed "multiversity" capabilities. Many academic observers concluded that such actions from the center were new forms of interference with institutional independence and academic freedom, although it was no longer clear that even the nation-state had primacy over the global university. Reluctantly, in some countries, but not in all, governments eased restrictions on charging tuition fees. From California's sometime "free" tuition universities to most universities elsewhere, the costs of attending a residential university, and especially one with a brand name, rose to unprecedented heights, easily out-racing inflation and raising anxieties about student loans, lending practices and payback schemes. After adverse media exposure, in 2008, the Croesus colleges and universities of the United States agreed to use more of their endowments for tuition discounting.

The model, or shall we say, the example of a world-class university is American, especially the handful of inordinately wealthy private research institutions. Through judicious portfolio investments, and the contributions of successful alumni – Stanford University tapped the huge resources of Silicon Valley, whose industries it helped establish – the "wealth gap" grew to a point where the famous state-established research universities began to talk about "a crisis of the publics." They wondered whether in the emerging future they could retain their own reputations as world-class institutions.

As the following essays so thoroughly demonstrate, the race for global pre-eminence has spread to newcomers such as China. India, another potential global player, is however still beset by educational rigidities. Established industrial economies like Japan have taken a further look at their configuration of universities, singling out the former Imperial University of Tokyo, the private university of Waseda and several others as candidates for the exclusive club. Latin American universities are still procrastinating whether they should compete for membership. In a different corner of the world, the University of Auckland, until a few decades ago more or less another of the university colleges in the solar system of the examining University of London (now losing its planets), has declared its desire to join the trend. Nearby Australia is well along in the process. Israeli universities have long since privatized.

It makes no sense for any nation not to urge its leading universities towards further excellence, towards discovery and its applications as the wellsprings of modern health, towards superb teaching and towards the education of potentially outstanding students as possibly leaders and shapers of tomorrow's governments and institutions. But money, high status and privilege also bring responsibilities. The great Dr. Johnson once said that superiors condescend to inferiors. In turn, inferiors defer to superiors. Such behavior is unacceptable in a democracy and certainly not acceptable in education. The world-class research university is underpinned by a great array of other types of tertiary educational institutions upon which its legitimacy, indeed its very success, depends. They serve an immense variety of public needs and provide the opportunities for upward mobility that any generous-minded and decent nation requires. Those institutions also possess talent – talent very often originating within the famous universities. They are engaged in the noble task of uncovering student ability where it might otherwise be neglected. Universities that have scaled the heights in a new environment of fierce rivalries retain an obligation to give creative thought as to how an entire national system can thrive without being partitioned into haves and have-nots, and riven by ruinous jealousies.

Here is another assignment worthy of the world-class university.

Sheldon Rothblatt
Emeritus Professor of History
University of California, Berkeley

References

Robert Anderson, *British Universities Past and Present* (London and New York: Hambledon Continuum, 2006), chapter four.

Harold Perkin, *Key Profession: the History of the Association of University Teachers* (London: Routledge and Kegan Paul, 1969).

Martin Trow, 'Reflections on the Transition from Elite to Mass to Universal Access: Forms and Phases of Higher Education in Modern Societies since WWII', reprinted in *International Handbook of Higher Education*, eds. James J.F. Forest and Philip G. Altbach (New York: Springer, 2006).

Preface

There has been a global shift towards mass higher education defined by expanding student numbers. The purpose of this, the first volume in the International Studies in Higher Education Series, is to see how this development has impacted upon the existing structures of higher education. How have national and, in some cases, regional systems of higher education responded to the rapid expansion of student numbers? Do existing institutions expand to take up the increased demand? Are new institutions created and, if so, how do these fit into the prevailing structures? What impact has the arrival of mass higher education had upon our understanding of the purposes, programs and processes of higher education? Critically, does mass higher education undermine institutional diversity (only one model of the university ultimately prevails)? Or, can national systems incorporate the presence of existing elite institutions, which may aspire to be 'world-class' universities? Perhaps the expansion of higher education is in fact an essential corollary to the perpetuation of an elite national stratum of universities: the mass base interlocking with the elite institutions to create a coherent whole?

Within this volume three different kinds of structural change are addressed through the presentation of appropriate case studies. Firstly, there are national systems (or segments within national systems) that are pressured by forces that are essentially global in scope: the expansion of participation in higher education, the emergence of higher education as an international commodity, the increasing impact of the regulatory state and managerial structures of governance, and the seemingly inexorable shift in the balance of funding from public to private resources.

Secondly, although all higher education systems have to respond to particular local pressures for change, for some those pressures are of such a magnitude that it is hard to imagine they will not impact significantly upon the established order. However, there are certain systems, for example those of the United States and the Nordic countries which, although very different in character, are in a position to make adjustments over time that are reflective of national traditions. Thus, the process of structural change is likely to be measured and controlled. It is more difficult to believe that this can be the case when global trends are reinforced by local political and economic turmoil. The intensity of pressures for change, therefore, is much more pronounced in some national and regional systems than others. Eastern and Central Europe, the former Soviet Union and South Africa have had to face more turbulent shockwaves than, for example, Australia, Canada and the Netherlands.

Thirdly, the book will explore how those institutions that have established international reputations are responding to the fact that there are now widely publicized league tables that claim to measure comparatively institutional excellence on a global basis. Assuming that they wish to sustain their reputations, how seriously do these institutions take such tables, and what steps do they follow to maintain their status? But this is not a matter for institutional strategies alone since national governments, as different in their relationship to electoral pressure as China and Germany, have announced their determination to pursue public funding strategies that will result in 'world-class' status for at least some of their universities. It is evident that the publication of league tables is exerting an impact both on how national governments structure their systems of higher education and on how higher education institutions order their affairs. This is regardless of how the tables may be evaluated in terms of their rigor in measuring status (their technical and methodological validity) or in terms of judgements on the merits of pursuing such a task (their meaningfulness, even their moral validity).

The debates, both academic and political, as to how systems of higher education should be structured are ongoing. However, we suggest that, over approximately the next ten years, the varying models of mass higher education will take their long-term shape and, once in place, it will be difficult within the national context alone to reformulate them. Therefore, one can expect this book to be central to the higher education policy agenda – with an international resonance – for at least the next decade. Moreover, it provides the context for the other volumes in the Series that will address more specific issues.

1

Structuring Mass Higher Education
Interpreting the Process of Change

Ted Tapper and David Palfreyman

Introduction: Defining the Focus

In the conclusion of our previous edited book (Tapper and Palfreyman, 2005) we posed the question: 'Whither Mass Higher Education?' In this text, through an analysis of contemporary developments in a range of very different higher education systems, we commence the task of answering that question. It is a critical consideration that national and regional systems of higher education will not only have followed different patterns of development but also be at contrasting stages in moving towards the mass model of higher education. For example, have participation rates in the first mass system of higher education, the United States, reached saturation point? Will that rate now stabilize or even decline (Douglass, 2007)? The question therefore is whether the expansion process itself has an independent impact upon system and institutional behaviour. If there is indeed participatory stagnation in the US will there be a political push to remove the apparent blockages to access? Or is higher education reaching the limits of expansion, and developments in the US represent the beginnings of a new model? Moreover, within the individual higher education institution it is easy to imagine a scenario in which initial expansion was embraced but then followed by subsequent self-doubts and policy change.

The point is that the development of mass higher education goes through different stages and can invoke policy changes that impact upon how it is structured. The somewhat chequered recent history of higher education expansion in Britain illustrates the point perfectly. The decision in 1965 to create a separate polytechnic sector ushered in the binary model, which was terminated by the 1992 Further and Higher Education Act with all higher education institutions becoming the responsibility of funding councils with national remits. Both decisions are embedded in the cultural and political context in which British higher education is enmeshed. Moreover, the political push specifically to broaden access has also had a structural impact. Scotland owes its high participatory rate in part to the expansion of higher education in its traditional non-university sector. England has belatedly followed suit by creating Foundation degrees as a channel into the university sector and a stage in the acquisition of a traditional undergraduate degree. Thus it is possible to construct programs of higher education not only independently of the universities but also outside of the higher education sector itself, which is structural innovation with a vengeance!

There is a broad acceptance of the proposition (which is reflected in all the contributions to this book) that systems of higher education are increasingly shaped less by national and local forces and more by pressures that are exerted at the global level, whether these be regional political structures, international economic organizations or institutional competition for scarce resources including students and faculty. But at the same time there is a general recognition of the fact that the process of change is composed of an interactive process in which local and national forces will interpret the global pressures to construct policy. Furthermore, Maassen and Stensaker (2005) argue that theories of change in higher education need to incorporate the idea of different institutional inputs (from government, from organized interests, from individual institutions and from academic disciplines) that draw upon established cultural traditions. And, moreover, there are some who are prepared to argue for the continuing importance of key individual actors (Watson and Bowden, 1999).

To look at patterns of expansion in higher education systems permits the construction of descriptive comparative maps: starting dates, differential rates of expansion, the penetration of the major social groups, contrasts in the access routes followed by those social groups, and retention (drop-out) rates. To explain these patterns, and to examine how established systems respond to them or even adjust their responses over time (our present task), undoubtedly requires theoretical understanding that incorporates national and local cultural values enshrined in the institutional contexts that envelop systems of higher education. However, within itself this does not progress the analysis of structural evolution very far if the intention is to explain why and how systems evolve in particular ways over time. Political analysis has to accompany cultural theory if this further step is to be taken. Moreover, it has to be a political analysis that recognizes the contrasts in the relationships between national systems and global forces. All models of higher education may be worthy but not all have the same ability to resist or negotiate an acceptable national compromise with the pressures for change. Within national systems the political influence of elite institutions may be sufficiently strong to encourage powerful government backing to enhance their international reputations or to permit them to define this as an acceptable institutional goal that they can then sustain through their own efforts.

Structural Change: The Key Pressures

Relating structural change to the emergence of mass systems of higher education is undoubtedly a consequence of the pervasive influence of Trow's (1973) characterization of the participatory base of contemporary models as either elite, mass or universal. We have been seduced by the implicit assumption that there is a universal trajectory, and the concept of 'mass' embraces the idea of very high participatory rates whilst we all know that 'universal' participation is simply unrealistic. Moreover, some concepts, and 'mass' is one of them, simply carry more resonance than others – like 'universal'.

However, in some systems of higher education – with the United States undoubtedly leading the way – there has always been a measure of structural differentiation. Indeed, it can be seen as *the* distinctive virtue of American higher education that it lacked a narrow understanding of the idea of the university; that it was a pluralist model, funded both privately and from the public purse, and purposely designed to meet very different needs and serve a range of interests. Furthermore, this was a model that, albeit in a controlled manner, was reinforced by planned state systems with California's Master Plan as the exemplar template. The implication, therefore, is that mass higher education per se is not the force that initiates structural change in systems of higher education and, consequently, there are critical further considerations that have to be built into the equation.

Although structurally differentiated systems of higher education may have diverse origins, there still remains the proposition that mass higher education itself inevitably results in a hierarchy of institutional status. Thus England has Oxbridge, Australia the Sandstones (or the Group of Eight), Japan the former Imperial Universities, the US the Ivy League and France the *grandes écoles*. In these cases there is of course a past tradition to take into account – these institutions have always constituted an elite stratum within their national systems and that legacy is slow to evaporate. But, of course, more than reputation alone is needed to sustain the legacy. The move towards mass higher education raises the inevitable question of how the costs of expansion are to be met. In publicly funded systems will the status of elite institutions be sustained by privileged access to the public purse (the more generous public funding of the *grandes écoles* as opposed to the French universities)? Or will the institutions themselves have sufficient resources to maintain, at least in the short run, their pre-eminence (as is arguably true of Oxford and Cambridge). An alternative scenario is the absence of marked differences in funding (with either public or private resources) and the outcome being either institutions with a widely shared high esteem (public funding is generous – arguably the Scandinavian model) or with an equally widely shared low esteem (uniformly low public funding – arguably the French and German universities in recent years, although clearly this situation is in the process of changing).

Inevitably, if higher education institutions are essentially publicly funded then governments will determine both the overall resource level and its pattern of distribution. They have it within their power to construct different models of higher education. It is clear that some governments (for example,

China, Japan and Germany) have made a conscious decision to use their control of funding to sponsor the development of a number of national universities that can compete effectively in 'the world-class league'. The English moves in the same direction are subtler. Public funding for research is distributed competitively which ensures that comparatively few universities are better resourced than others. Moreover, universities can now charge students variable fees, which will have a significant impact on resource patterns if the ceiling on fees is either raised or removed (a review is scheduled in 2009).

If funding issues and the inter-related role of the state are critical to the structuring of mass higher education, equally it has to be recognized that national systems of higher education, especially at their elite end, find themselves in a global marketplace. Higher education is a commodity that is traded internationally and increasingly there are pressures to remove those barriers – often constructed by national governments in response to local interests – that would restrict that trade. Whilst institutional reputations have been embedded at the national level, the emergence of international ranking lists – world league tables for universities – has widened the comparative scope. The movement has been from taken-for-granted reputations to ranking lists constructed from measured criteria. Assuming that institutions are keen to hold on to their rankings, or even to enhance them, then inevitably they must compete for the resources that constitute their basis: research funding, research outputs, and star faculty and graduate students (both recruited internationally) who will either undertake research and/or pursue professional degree programs. Moreover, there is also a potentially broader impact since, in the context of a relative decline in public funding, national systems (and not just particular institutions) may become financially dependent upon the recruitment of overseas students (a trend that is clearly evident in Australia, the UK and the US).

The current pressure therefore upon established systems of higher education does not come from expansion alone. The move towards mass higher education has been accompanied by an intensified role for both the state and the market. For the state there are key funding issues (the extent and manner in which it is prepared to fund a system of mass higher education) and the degree and form in which it will try to regulate that system, including the extent to which it will encourage institutional differentiation and niching. Interestingly the recent Spellings Report (US Department of Education, 2006: 20) raised the issue of institutional accountability. Although the recommendation was for higher education institutions to embrace and implement 'serious accountability measures', a natural British response (based on its own experience of such matters) would be to see this as the beginning of a move down the slippery slope towards some form of state (but clearly not federal) regulation – who, for example, will determine what constitutes 'serious accountability measures'? Equally for the market the issue is 'value-for-money'. For example, a fee-paying student (even if the fee is subsidized) is presumably interested in the quality of her/his experience of higher education. And, although one can hope for an altruistic corporate input into research funding, it is certainly advisable to work with the proposition that companies will be wondering what are their precise payoffs. With respect to both the market and the state the issue for institutions of higher education is how they respond to such pressures from either or each.

Structural Change: Degrees of Vulnerability

It is important to recognize at the outset that higher education systems have different strategic relationships to the pressures that have emerged from the interaction of state, market and the expansion of higher education. Furthermore, they are embedded in values that are more or less accommodating of the idea that the question of change needs to be addressed seriously. At first glance it would appear that the US model is especially privileged. It is large and diverse with no historical legacy of structural rigidity, which is reinforced by a mix of private and public funding coupled with the acceptance that institutions can both be founded and closed. With the exception of certain important state systems (perhaps California's Master Plan has run its course?), there is little need to think of the possibility of national structural change because of the overall flexibility of the general heritage. Certainly in terms of the relationship to the global market US higher education would appear very favoured – as displayed by trends in the movement of students and faculty and the dominance of the world league tables by American universities. And yet the Spellings Report is clearly a response to contemporary unease, and there is evidence that participation rates have stabilized, or are even in decline. Moreover, there is the question of whether 'middle America' can continue to meet the increases in tuition fees, especially those of the private colleges and universities.

But any doom and gloom interpretation of the malaise of US higher education needs to temper its analysis with a comparative perspective that goes much deeper than supposedly declining participatory rates. The reality is that the US model may need to adjust to evolving circumstances but it has the resources of time and space to make the necessary accommodations on the basis of internal negotiations. This is unlikely to be true for those national systems that are entwined with developments at the regional level (for example, the Bologna Process and the emergence of the European Higher Education Area), and even less for those national systems whose development is at least to some extent guided by international organizations (consider the role of the World Bank in several developing countries).

It is equally important to realize that just as national systems have differing relationship to the pressure for change so do national institutions. It is difficult to find a league table that fails to place Harvard at the top of the pecking order. This is underwritten by its resource base, and more especially the largesse of its endowment income. The adjustments that Harvard has to make to sustain its pre-eminence are minimal; it has the resources to prevent a possible clash between its core values and the decision to remain *the* leading university on the world stage. However, the position of the Universities of Oxford and Cambridge is clearly different. Both universities, at least in comparison to Harvard, are not well-resourced and, perhaps more significantly, they are committed to a collegiate model of the university which had valued highly the quality of undergraduate teaching. The issue is whether they have the resources and will to sustain that tradition while at the same time ensuring they can pursue those activities that ensure an elevated ranking in the league tables: providing a working base for Nobel Prize winners and Field Medallists, and ensuring a flow of research activity that guarantees publication in the leading scientific journals. There is a clash of values about what the purposes of the collegiate university should be, which is coming to a head (Tapper and Palfreyman, 2000: 200–206).

The *grandes écoles*, as elite publicly funded institutions, appear to be secure in their position not so much because of the resource base they generate themselves but more because of interesting tensions within the value system that underwrites French higher education, and which results in their continuing privileged access to public funding. On the one hand there is open access to the universities (those with the required entry qualifications are guaranteed a place), whilst entry into the *grandes écoles* is fiercely competitive, reflecting a belief that those destined for the highest ranks in state and society should be exposed to the most rigorous training. The French model, therefore, adjusts to the pressures for higher education (more students with the requisite qualifications coupled with the expanding demand of the bourgeoisie for access – two almost universal prerequisites of mass higher education) by permitting open access to universities (coupled with the creation of different degree tracks) whilst sustaining an elite stratum. The conundrum then for the French model is how to incorporate a flourishing research tradition.

However, it is important not to forget that there still remain national systems for which the broad long-term pressures for change, structural or otherwise, remain – *at least in the short-term* – of secondary importance. There are those countries experiencing revolutionary shifts in both their economic and political structures (for example, as different as South Africa and the nations of Eastern and Central Europe), which may embrace structural change but are driven more by local political pressures. Moreover, there are some countries (for example, the Gulf States) with the financial resources that can almost ensure their immunity from global pressures. They are in a position to respond to local values and internal political inputs, which is not to say that they may also look to international trends when determining policy development. And clearly there are a few nations that have strong political structures, underwritten by explicit values, where the drivers of change are likely to be controlled by the central state (with, in their very different ways, North Korea and Cuba providing models). Perhaps the most interesting case studies are those countries whose systems have been underwritten by broadly supported values (open access, high levels of public funding, and institutional parity), but which now find themselves under pressure in the global market from models with different values (institutional differentiation, a greater sharing of public and private funding, and structured access).

Structural Change: Understanding the Responses

How national and regional systems of higher education are actually respond- ing to the pressures for change is a matter that will be dealt with in the chap- ters that follow. And, of course, the final chapter will draw together comparatively the actual response patterns, how they are to be explained and what policy lessons they provide. The purpose now is to present an overview of the different possibilities that emerge out of the present context. The inten- tion is to construct a simple framework to guide the concluding comparative overview. Moreover, at least ingredients of the framework appear in the analysis of the individual national/regional systems and the elite institutions that follows. The intention is to offer some themes that will find resonance in those chapters.

With respect to higher education institutions, regardless of the size and origins of their resource base, the focus is very much upon models of gover- nance, the quality of leadership and the appropriateness and competence of managerial structures. If there is a history of institutional achievement then these variables are invariably perceived as being fit for purpose; if the reverse is the case then the search for new structures and personnel will sooner or later emerge. The emphasis in this chapter has been upon structural differen- tiation at the system level but it is equally true that in today's university there will often be internal structural cleavages (Fallis, 2007). The only defining feature that several branches of a university may share with one another is a limited amount of overlap in the addresses of their headed notepaper! Differentiation in degree programs (liberal arts degrees, vocational programs or professional training) may be contained within separate institutional boundaries but there is no reason why such boundaries should not exist within one multi-purpose institution. Even degree programs that have identical labels and lead to identically labelled formal qualifications may in fact describe different (if overlapping) experiences of higher education. So programs are restructured as departments grapple to hold on to their students.

In terms of those policy parameters that encapsulate national systems, the key consideration is the interaction between the market, the state and the higher education institutions. Will there be a command-and-control (*dirigiste*) state, which uses its authority (and invariably its control of funding) that attempts to determine both how universities operate and their pattern of development? Alternatively, will there be a regulatory state that steers through audit and risk management (Tapper, 2007)? With respect to both the control and regulatory (or steering) models, what will be the role of the higher education interests in shaping the functioning and the intended outcomes of these models? Will they be incorporated or marginalized in the policy-making process? If you work with the proposition that the purpose of system control or steering is to regulate institutional behaviour, then it is possible that within the confines of a regulatory framework more responsibility is delegated to institutional actors. However, whether this amounts to institutional autonomy is a more complex question. Do the institutions exercise managerial control rather than policy control (Shattock, 2006)? If higher education systems have generally moved from state control to state steering, then the strength of the steering mechanisms needs to be investigated. Moreover, are they enforced through a tight regulatory framework or by offering rewards in return for compliance (incentive schemes to induce conformity)?

Conclusion: Explaining Change

As befits an edited book, although the individual authors have been asked to address a common set of problems within the contexts provided by their national and regional settings, there has been no attempt to impose on them either a particular disciplinary approach or a defined explanatory framework. In other words as editors we have stated the problem and outlined the issues that we feel need to be addressed. But there is no theoretical or disciplinary straitjacket.

The central issue under examination – structural change in higher education with particular reference to the role of elite institutions – can be interpreted through different disciplinary perspectives: economics (the emergence of a global market and the perceived economic returns of investment in higher education), sociology (the seemingly universal middle-class pursuit of higher education), demographic and educational studies (shifts in social patterns and the expansion of demand for secondary education), political science (the political promotion of widening participation coupled with a desire to, at the very least, steer system goals), and management studies (how increasingly complex organizations can function effectively). And, of course, these various disciplinary perspectives have to be placed within the context of systems of higher education that are invariably the product of complex historical processes centered on the nation state.

However, underwriting many of the chapters is the realization that change in higher education, at both the system and institutional level, is invariably enveloped in political struggle. The responses to mass higher education, and the attendant pressures, will be politically negotiated at and between various levels – the international, the national, and the institutional. There is, therefore, a common interest in explaining the responses to the pressures for structural change, and thus an implicit political dimension to all the chapters. And the final chapter will draw together comparatively these response patterns.

References

Douglass, J. (2007) 'What Happened to America's Higher Education Advantage?', *Oxford Magazine*, 267, Michaelmas Term, 15–17.

Fallis, G. (2007) *Multiversities, Ideas and Democracy*, University of Toronto Press, Toronto.

Maassen, P. and B. Stensaker (2005) 'The Black Box Revisited: The Relevance of Theory Driven Research in the Field of Higher Education Studies', in I. Bleiklie and M. Henkel (eds), *Governing Knowledge: A Study of Continuity and Change in Higher Education: A Festschrift in Honour of Maurice Kogan*, Springer Press, Dordrecht, 213–226.

Shattock, M. (2006) *Managing Good Governance*, OUP/McGraw-Education, Maidenhead.

Tapper, T. (2007) *The Governance of British Higher Education: The Struggle for Policy Control*, Springer Press, Dordrecht.

Tapper, T. and D. Palfreyman (2000) *Oxbridge and the Decline of the Collegiate Tradition*, Woburn Press, London.

Tapper, T. and D. Palfreyman (2005) *Understanding Mass Higher Education: Comparative Perspectives on Access*, RoutledgeFalmer, London.

Trow, M. (1973) *Problems in the Transition from Elite to Mass Higher Education*, Carnegie Commission on Higher Education, OECD, Paris.

US Department of Education (2006) *A Test of Leadership: Charting the Future of US Higher Education* (Spellings Commission Report), US Department of Education, Washington DC.

Watson, D. and R. Bowden (1999) 'Why did they do it? The Conservatives and Mass Higher Education, 1979–97', *Journal of Education Policy*, 14 (3), 243–256.

Part I
Structural Change in Systems of Higher Education

2

U.S. Higher Education
Contemporary Challenges, Policy Options

James Fairweather

Introduction

Much comparative higher education research focuses on differences between national systems, particularly the historical and cultural milieu unique to each country. The presumption is that national systems must be understood in their own right, and that the differences between national settings and systems often make finding common solutions problematic. Yet today the problems each nation confronts in delivering higher education to its citizens have much in common. Every nation is trying to educate more of its citizens, not fewer of them. Every nation is trying to figure out how to pay for higher education, including how much it should cost and who should pay for it. Increasingly national systems share the goal of preparing citizens for participation in a global economy, not just a local or regional one. How to cope with and incorporate technology in instruction, meet the needs of increasingly diverse students, and maintain quality while expanding access are also goals shared by many, perhaps most, nations.

To promote a common understanding of the higher education policy problems facing all of us, in this chapter I discuss U.S. higher education in a way that individuals from different countries can understand and, I hope, use in assessing the usefulness of the approaches the U.S. is taking to solve these universal problems. I first describe the defining characteristics of American higher education. I then present a brief history of the evolution of U.S. higher education. Next I discuss the structure and function of American higher education, including the range of types of institutions, the roles of federal and state governments, the broader external environment, accreditation, quality, and standards, and financing.

Following this description I discuss the key challenges facing American higher education. I then discuss the potential role of the public elites (public research universities) in solving crucial policy problems by examining how one state, Michigan, views the role of its public elites in helping transform its economy from traditional manufacturing toward a knowledge-based economy.

Defining Characteristics

The U.S. has never had a Ministry of Education or national oversight of its colleges and universities. The U.S. Constitution grants the authority for all forms of education to state governments. The federal government has an indirect role in higher education, primarily through funding research and subsidizing student loans (Gladieux, Hauptman, and Knapp, 1994). In turn state governments have delegated to institutional boards of trustees the legal responsibility for managing American colleges and universities. These boards serve as buffers between colleges and universities and state and federal governments.

U.S. academic institutions have always responded in some way to markets, particularly markets for students. By "market" I mean not a profit-making motive, often described as "academic capitalism," (Slaughter and Leslie, 1997) but the willingness and ability to respond to the changing needs of constituents including students, state and federal governments, alumni, or other groups. Indeed, most American colleges and universities are not-for-profit institutions, required by law to invest revenues that exceed costs in the operation of the institution. This "market responsiveness" has been and will be a major factor in the ability of academic institutions to respond to changing national and local needs.

Market responsiveness is also a defining characteristic of American higher education, the competition between institutions for students, faculty members, research monies, and status (Jencks and Riesman, 1968). This competition is responsible in large part for the wide variation in size, internal structures and operations, sources of support, and standards between American colleges and universities (Trow, 1988). At the same time, a common credit structure, some standardization in curricula, and an emerging national labor market for faculty members permit easy mobility of students and faculty between institutions (Fairweather, 1995; Thelin, 2004).

Another defining characteristic of American higher education is the long-held tradition of requiring students and their parents to pay some portion of the cost of attending a college or university, most often through tuition (Johnstone, 1998). Students historically have contributed at least some portion of the costs of attending college in the U.S.

Finally, U.S. higher education incorporated and adapted competing traditions of higher education from abroad; it did not evolve from a single academic tradition. American higher education blends the liberal arts tradition of the UK with the German research and graduate education model. Along the way the U.S. incorporated the concept of public service into its overall model of higher education (Thelin, 2004). These characteristics may combine in ways that emphasize institutional differences – e.g., the private research university, the private liberal arts college – or they may be combined in a single "multiversity," such as the public land-grant research university (Geiger, 1986).

In this context, the U.S. is not a system as understood in centralized national models led by a Ministry of Education. Even members of supposedly homogeneous state "systems" can vary substantially (McGuinness, 1999). Rather, the U.S. is a market-driven aggregation of institutions competing for students, resources, and status. The evolution of this "system" is best viewed as an outcome of institutional competition rather than as a response to a centralized directive from a government agency (Trow, 2001).

A Brief History of U.S. Higher Education

The structure of American higher education cannot be understood without a discussion of the key events shaping it. This information is especially important for readers unfamiliar with the workings of market-based systems, which stand in stark contrast to Ministry-based, top-down, planned systems.

The origination of American higher education preceded the establishment of the U.S. as a nation. Harvard College in Massachusetts, now Harvard University and universally recognized for its intellectual and research stature, started as a small church-affiliated (Calvinist) institution in 1636 with very few students and even fewer faculty members. At about the same time Yale and William and Mary also opened their doors in affiliation with churches, the latter with the Church of England. The primary purpose of each college was to prepare selected males for the ministry by means of a traditional liberal arts curriculum (Geiger, 2005; Thelin, 2004).

Since the U.S. did not have a Constitution prior to 1776, no national or state guidelines existed to guide the operation and management of these colleges and the ones that followed over the next few decades. The roles of the church and the then colonial (now state) governments conflicted from the beginning. Harvard College was (and remains) run by a Board of Overseers. Yale, in contrast, was governed by a church congregation with official backing from the Connecticut colonial government. The distinction between public and private institutions as well as the legal authority of governments in the operation of academic institutions had yet to be established. By the middle of the 1700s the role of the church in governing the colleges waned and the purpose of a college education expanded somewhat beyond preparation for the ministry. The role of government in the management of colleges remained ambiguous (Geiger, 2005; Thelin, 2004).

According to Geiger (2005), in 1746 the College of New Jersey became the first hybrid model with the control of the college shared by the ministry and the colonial government; the governor sat on the board of trustees. A few other colleges started at this time, Dartmouth College and the College of Philadelphia (now the University of Pennsylvania) most prominent among them. By 1775 there were only 750 students attending college in America. All were male. Harvard College had a total of three professors prior to the late 1700s.

Following the revolution in 1776, the Constitution designated the state governments as having authority for all forms of education, including higher education. The nature of the relationship between states and colleges or universities remained vague. Emboldened by the new Constitution, in the late 1700s several states opened their first public institutions. None of these lasted at first because of a lack of resources (Geiger, 2005). In other cases state governments granted charters to existing institutions, such as Harvard College, to authorize the college to offer academic degrees. The most important unanswered questions about American higher education prior to 1819 were: "Who owns the colleges and what is the role of the state in that ownership?" The Dartmouth College decision in 1819 by the U.S. Supreme Court clarified the question of ownership. The Court found that the charter from the state government authorized institutions to act independently from the legislature. The board of trustees or its equivalent became the legal authority for running institutions of higher education, even those affiliated directly with state governments. This decision permitted both the growth of a private sector in American higher education, one where the state authorized or chartered the college but otherwise had no operational role, as well as declaring boards of trustees the legally responsible agents of what would become public institutions (Stites, 1972). This landmark event was a decision by the courts, not a mandate from national or even state governments.

The expansion of the U.S. in the early to mid 1800s led in part to a regional differentiation in the role of higher education. The original states, especially those in the Northeast (e.g., Massachusetts) and Mid-Atlantic (e.g., Pennsylvania), remained strongly committed to what became private higher education. Even with the expansion of public higher education in those states, the private institutions remain the most prestigious (Thelin, 2004). In contrast newer territories became the bedrock of an emerging public sector of higher education. These states also led the way in establishing small, independent liberal arts colleges which prior to the 1850s became a major source for providing access to higher education. Consider the State of Ohio, one of the newer states in the mid 1800s. Today Ohio higher education is best known both for its dominant public research university, the Ohio State University, with about 50,000 students, *and* for its large collection (46) of private liberal arts colleges with enrollments typically less than 2,000 students.

The period immediately following 1850 greatly influenced what was to become contemporary American higher education. The Morrill Land Grant Act of 1862 (a second Morrill Act in 1890 followed) was the first major federal commitment to higher education. The federal government promised to give each state land for a college as long as that institution focused on science and agricultural or mechanical arts. In addition to creating colleges that evolved over time into major universities such as Michigan State University and Penn State University, the federal initiative established a precedent for federal involvement in higher education (even if indirect) as well as stimulating the movements to incorporate professional education in college and university curricula and to include public service as an accepted role for American higher education. During this era women participated in large numbers for the first time. The Morrill Act enabled students from lower economic means to enroll in higher education. The first institutions for African Americans were built. The adoption by the University of Michigan and Johns Hopkins University of the Humboldtian model incorporating graduate education and research along with liberal education into a single institution led to what has become the modern American research university (Geiger, 1986, 2005). Along with this development came the growth of a full-time professoriate, the differentiation of academic institutions into more specialized departments, and the emergence of the powerful presidents required to manage these more complex institutions.

During the early 1900s standardized curricula and a shared credit system were in place. Most colleges adopted a common degree model with four years designated for undergraduate degrees. Many colleges and universities combined to form national associations (e.g., the American Association of Universities) to promote communication between academic institutions and to lobby Congress on their behalf. All of these developments emerged from the "marketplace" of higher education albeit with important incentives from the federal government.

The U.S. started moving toward what Trow (2001) calls universal higher education (more than 50% participating in some form of higher education) between the two world wars, reaching that level after World War II. Community colleges were developed to assist in the movement toward mass higher education. The great expansion of American higher education occurred after World War II. In particular the GI Bill, which paid the cost of going to college for returning servicemen, greatly expanded both overall participation in colleges and universities and opened access to people who otherwise would not have considered going to college (Thelin, 2004). During this period Michigan State University, as one of many examples, grew from 4,000 students (as Michigan Agricultural College) to 42,000 (as Michigan State University). Following the launch of Sputnik by the Soviet Union, the federal government set up the National Science Foundation and invested millions of dollars in university-based research as well as subsidizing the graduate training of many future scientists and engineers. Academic institutions competed for these funds and were free to accept or reject the money.

The growth and competition for resources encouraged the enlargement and professionalization of academic administration as well as the pursuit of prestige and status among academic peers (Jencks and Riesman, 1968). During this period many institutions, not just research universities, began to view research and scholarship as the primary function of professors

(Fairweather, 1993). Over time the service mission expanded to include the role of higher education in economic development (Fairweather, 1988).

This brief history shows the complex relationship between federal and state governments and American colleges and universities. It demonstrates the importance of key events and individuals in the evolution of a market-based system, one that differs dramatically from Ministry-based models. Most importantly, it demonstrates that the modern American university "system" had modest origins, succeeded in large part because of its diversity, and continuously adapted to changing societal needs because of its emphasis on responding to the needs of its various constituents.

The Structure and Governance of U.S. Higher Education

Types of Institutions and Enrollment Patterns

According to the most recent statistics from the U.S. Department of Education and the Carnegie Foundation for the Advancement of Teaching, in 2004 the U.S. had 4,392 degree-accredited institutions of higher education enrolling 17,571,104 students (Carnegie Foundation for the Advancement of Teaching, 2007).[1] In addition there are an estimated 5,000 (or more) non-accredited proprietary institutions, many offering certificates or specialized training but not degrees (National Center for Education Statistics, 2000). Overall about 66% of American citizens participate in some form of higher education during their lives (American Council on Education, 2001). The latest Carnegie classification scheme assigns colleges and universities to the following types (in abridged form):

- *Associate's Colleges* including all two-year institutions and a small number of four-year institutions where 90% of the degrees awarded are two-year. These institutions most typically are called community colleges.
- *Baccalaureate Colleges* including institutions where bachelor's degrees represent the majority of degrees awarded and the number of master's and doctoral degrees awarded are very small. The majority of these colleges, many of them liberal arts colleges, are private.
- *Master's Colleges and Universities* including institutions awarding bachelor's degrees, at least 50 master's degrees annually, and fewer than 20 doctoral degrees per year. Formerly Carnegie called this category "comprehensive universities."
- *Doctoral-granting Universities* including institutions awarding a minimum of 20 doctoral degrees per year. This category includes what Carnegie formerly called research universities.
- *Specialized Institutions* including separate engineering, business, health-related, and other professional schools as well as tribal colleges.

As shown in Table 2.1, 1,815 institutions are Associate's Colleges; these institutions enroll about 38.9% of all students. Another 766 are Bachelor's Colleges enrolling 7.9% of all students. Master's Colleges and Universities comprise 665 and 22.2% of all students. The 282 institutions that are designated doctoral-granting institutions enroll 27.9% of all students. The 838 specialized institutions enroll 3.2% of all students. Another 26 institutions enrolling less than 0.1% have no designation.

Table 2.1 also shows the distribution of institutions by source of control. Public institutions are related in some way to a state government. Public institutions range from small community colleges (two-year degree programs) to large research universities. Private, not-for-profit institutions are the formal designation for what we typically call "private higher education" in the U.S. These institutions range from very small bachelor's institutions to major research universities. Private, for-profit institutions are an emerging sector. The latter differs from private, not-for-profits in that they are not required by law to invest most of their profits back into the operation of the institution. The University of Phoenix is one example.

Private colleges and universities tend to rely more on tuition as a revenue source than public institutions, charge higher tuition and fees than public colleges and universities, and respond more to the pressures of stakeholders (alumni, key donors, and the like) than public institutions; the latter respond more to public policy and pressure than do the privates (Levy, 1992). Private institutions are often less influenced by court decisions than public institutions. For example, the primary political battleground about affirmative action, or racial preference programs to remediate past discrimination, has focused on elite public research universities such as the University of California–Davis, the University of Texas–Austin and the University of Michigan–Ann Arbor. Private universities have been free to set their own policies on affirmative action within the context of legislation and court decisions (Bowen and Bok, 1998). One key to success among private institutions lies in their distinctiveness or the ability to portray their unique attributes to potential students and funding agencies (Clark, 1970).

In general, private institutions offer fewer programs and services. Public institutions are more likely to add programs and increase enrollment to meet demand (Levy, 1992). Although today the public sector in American higher education enrolls the majority of students, before the great public expansion in the 1950s and 1960s private institutions provided a way for many people to gain access to higher education. Importantly, state governments authorize *both* public and private not-for-profit institutions to grant degrees even though the state may not be directly involved in managing the institutions.

The Carnegie categories mask substantial variation among institutions within a category. Bachelor's institutions, as one example, range in size from an enrollment of 96 to an enrollment of 13,260. Associate's degree institutions

Table 2.1 The Universe of American Colleges and Universities

Type of Institution	Public #	Private, not-for-profit #	Private, for profit #	Total #	% of enroll.
Associate's Colleges	1,078	134	603	1,815	38.9
Baccalaureate Colleges	152	541	73	766	7.9
Master's Colleges and Universities	268	353	44	665	22.2
Doctoral-granting Universities	166	108	8	282	27.9
Specialized Institutions	68	603	167	838	3.2
Other	5	7	14	26	0.1
Total	1,737	1,746	909	4,392	100.2

Source: Carnegie Foundation for the Advancement of Teaching, 2007.

range in size from less than 200 students to more than 25,000 students (Carnegie Foundation for the Advancement of Teaching, 2007).

Neither source of control – public or private – nor institutional type necessarily conveys status in the U.S. Many private research universities, such as Harvard University and Stanford University, are among the elite. So too, though, are public universities such as the University of California–Berkeley, the University of Michigan–Ann Arbor, and the University of Texas–Austin. Moreover, many small, selective liberal arts colleges offering primarily bachelor's degrees, such as Williams College and Oberlin College, have an elite standing in the academic world (for undergraduate education) equal to the elite research universities. The top liberal arts colleges have the highest ratio of bachelor's recipients going to graduate school and disproportionately produce future faculty members (Fuller, 1986).

Elite academic institutions play a distinct role in American higher education. Research universities, the elite among graduate-oriented institutions, comprise only 6.4% of all accredited institutions but enroll 27.9% of American college students. The majority of faculty members in *all* colleges and universities received their Ph.D. or other advanced degrees from research universities. The research university is a model to which most other four-year institutions with the exception of elite liberal arts colleges aspire; they set the standard for quality of graduate education. Finally, research universities are the stalwarts of American research much of which ultimately enhances standards of living and economic development.

Consider the doctoral-granting category, more specifically the subdivision known as "research universities." These institutions contain public and private institutions. They range in full-time equivalent enrollment from 1,480 students to more than 47,000. Their instructional expenditures range from $35 million to $407 million (National Center for Education Statistics, 2004). Some research universities have generated substantial research for more than 100 years; others have only recently achieved this stature (Feller and Geiger, 1995). A study of three public research universities found substantial evidence of this variation within the purportedly homogeneous category of public research universities. The University of Tennessee–Knoxville is strongly committed to undergraduate education, a latecomer to high levels of research productivity, and disproportionately dependent on a few academic disciplines (e.g., physics) for much of its research productivity. The Ohio State University (OSU) has a more even distribution of research productivity across departments. Despite its long-term commitment to research, OSU has made an institutional commitment to undergraduate teaching as evidenced by a financial incentive award program for departments demonstrating instructional effectiveness. The University of Texas–Austin is the most committed to research of the three with high research expectations embedded throughout the institution. Unlike the other two universities, there is less visible commitment to enhancing the value of undergraduate teaching in faculty work[2] and fewer incentives to encourage such a commitment (Fairweather and Beach, 2002).

The Federal Role

About 15% of all expenditures on higher education in the U.S. come from the federal government (American Council on Education, 2001). The U.S. Department of Education does not develop a national plan for higher education nor does it attempt to coordinate higher education policy within or across states. The federal government provides direct support for a very small number of institutions, primarily those with special, historic functions (e.g., Howard University, the only historically Black research university, and Gallaudet University, the major university for deaf and hard-of-hearing students).

The most prominent federal role in higher education lies in providing various forms of subsidy to help students go to college. The GI Bill after World War II provided federal subsidies to assist returning veterans go to college. Between 1963 and 1993 the National Defense Student Loan (NDSL) Program provided grants or loans to encourage enrollment in science and engineering. Today, the majority of federal funds for students fall into two categories: Pell Grants to assist low-income students in going to college and subsidized loan programs. Over time the federal government has shifted its focus of support away from grants, which students do not need to pay back, toward loans, which students must pay back (Heller, 1999). Most student financial aid today goes to undergraduate students. The federal commitment to subsidizing graduate students in the sciences and engineering has waned. The predominant form of financial support for graduate students today comes from graduate assistantships and teaching assistantships typically provided by the institution, not the federal government (Fairweather, 2006).

In the U.S., federal financial aid, whether in the form of a grant or a loan, goes directly to the student who in turn pays the university. For both public and private institutions, the board of trustees of the institution (or sometimes the board of multi-campus systems) sets tuition and fees, not the federal or state government. This approach is consistent with a market-oriented student choice model. Federal financial aid can be used for any accredited college or university; the monies are not restricted to public institutions or to any particular type of institution. In 2001 6.8 million students received grants from federal government, 7.8 million received loans. 53% of all student aid recipients now obtain loans, reflecting a shift in the burden of paying for college toward the student and parents. In 1999–2000 64% of all graduating students borrowed money from at least one federal program. The average student debt grew from $9,188 in 1992–1993 to $16,928 in 2002–2003 (Fairweather, 2006). One consequence of this trend toward higher student debt is concern about the effect of costs on access to higher education, which I explore in a later section.

The federal government also provides about 60% of all university-based research and development (R&D) (Gladieux et al., 1994). These funds come from a variety of federal agencies, including the National Institute for Health, the National Science Foundation, and the various federal departments. Although the top research universities receive most of this money, the distribution has broadened over time; the top ten universities dropped in their overall percentage of the federal R&D monies from 43 to 21% between 1950 and 2000 (Feller and Geiger, 1995). About two-thirds of federal R&D dollars is spent by universities for basic research. Universities and their faculties must compete for the majority of federal R&D monies.

At different points in American history, the federal government intervened in higher education to promote the national interest. Such interventions typically have been indirect; none involve interfering with the daily operations of institutions. Among the key historical interventions are the Morrill Land Grant Act of 1862, the GI Bill, the development of the National Science Foundation to fund university research, providing subsidies for several predominantly minority institutions, and the Fulbright Scholars program.

Less visible but often influential are federal tax policies and benefits (Wolanin, 2003). The federally approved not-for-profit status granted to accredited American colleges and universities is crucial to the effective operation of these institutions, especially those with limited financial resources. Allowing donors to deduct gifts to universities from their taxes has been central to the ability of American institutions of higher education to raise money from their alumni and other constituencies. Student scholarships and fellowships are often non-taxable, which makes it easier for their recipients to attend college. Families saving for their child's college education can do so through tax-deferred accounts.

Federal legislation also can affect the operation of American colleges and universities. Academic institutions must be in compliance with anti-discrimination legislation such as the Civil Rights Act of 1964, the Americans with Disabilities Act, and Title IX (barring sex discrimination) (Wolanin, 2003). The Dole-Bayh Act of 1981 encouraged technology transfer by giving universities control of the patents produced through research on their campuses even if the research was funded by the federal government (Fairweather, 1988).

The federal government provides resources for national data collection about higher education. The National Center for Education Statistics in the U.S. Department of Education is authorized by Congress to collect national data on all aspects of American education.

Finally, decisions made by the U.S. Supreme Court have helped shape American higher education. As mentioned previously, the Dartmouth case led to the development of the private sector of higher education as well as to the designation of independent boards of trustees as the legal entity responsible for all types of institutions. The Yeshiva case defined faculty members in private institutions as managers and ergo not qualified to form collective bargaining units, whereas faculty members in public institutions were designated employees and able to unionize. The Baake, Hopwood, and University of Michigan cases all helped shape affirmative action admissions policies in public colleges and universities.

The State Role

State governments provide the majority of public funds for American public higher education. State governments led the way during the expansion of higher education in the 1950s and 1960s, an era during which the public institutional share of total enrollment in higher education increased from 60% to 80%. Similarly, the public percentage of all American institutions of higher education increased from 35% to 55% between 1950 and 1980 (McGuinness, 1999). Concern about the relative decline in state funding for higher education is a major policy issue, which I discuss in a later section.

State governments often lead reform efforts in higher education. State governments led the accountability movement in American higher education. Innovations such as the Western Governors' University, a technology-based distance delivery institution using an innovative competencies-based curriculum, have often been led by state governmental leaders (McGuinness, 1999).

States vary substantially in their politics, size, culture, and economies. These differences are reflected in how they organize, coordinate, and govern their systems of higher education. *Coordinating boards* are agencies states use for various monitoring functions. These functions include statewide coordination planning, policy analysis and problem resolution, mission definition, academic program review, budget development/funding formulas/resource allocation, program administration information/assessment/accountability systems, and institutional licensure and authorization. *Governing boards* refer to legal entities responsible for institutions in a state even though the operational details are usually left to individual campuses. The variation between states in their use of coordinating and governing boards is as great as the variation between different national systems of higher education.

I have selected five out of 50 states to demonstrate the wide variation between the ways that the 50 states organize higher education.[3] *California* has a coordinating board called the California Postsecondary Education Commission. This board focuses on public higher education. The Commission advises the legislature, governor, and academic institutions on major policies. It develops and maintains a statewide database. The Commission reviews budgets, advises on need for new campuses to meet demand, and reviews proposals for new academic programs in the public sector. The Commission has no governing authority over public institutions in the state. The state has three governing boards: The Board of Regents for the University of California System (ten universities and three research labs); Board of Trustees for California State University (23 public colleges and universities); and a Community College Board (72 community colleges). These boards determine tuition policy, faculty and administrative pay structures, and so on. In addition, each community college has a local governing board. Each system has a president (e.g., the President of the University of California System). Each branch of the University of California and California State University has its own chancellor.

Maryland has a coordinating board called the Maryland Higher Education Commission. The Commission coordinates six segments of higher education, public *and* private. These include the University System of Maryland, Morgan State University, St. Mary's College of Maryland, community colleges, independent or private institutions, and private career or vocational schools. Unlike the California coordinating board, the Maryland Commission is responsible for approving campus mission statements, reviewing campus performance, administering student financial aid, preparing two-year master plans, reviewing institutional and sector operating budgets, reviewing capital expenditure requests, prescribing degree requirements, and administering state funds to private institutions. In addition, the Maryland Board of Regents, a governing board, is the legal entity responsible for the public colleges and universities. Community colleges and private institutions have individual governing boards.

Michigan has no statewide coordinating board or planning commission. Each public university has its own governing board (board of trustees). For newer public four-year institutions, boards are appointed by the governor. For the three oldest public institutions, the boards of trustees are elected in statewide contests. Community college governing boards are elected in local or regional elections.

The University of the State of *New York* is responsible for *all* levels of education as well as libraries and museums in the state. It is chartered to license and inspect institutions, certify professionals, and apportion financial aid. The Board of Regents of the State of New York, established in 1784, is responsible for setting policy and supervising all educational activities in NY. It is not, however, a true governing board. The State University of New York, with 32 two-year and 32 four-year institutions is governed by its own Board of Trustees. The City University of New York with six two-year and 13 four-year institutions also has its own Board of Trustees.

Finally, the Board of Regents of the University of *Wisconsin* is a state-wide governing authority and a coordinating board wrapped into one. It is responsible for 13 public four-year institutions and 13 two-year schools. The Wisconsin Technical College System Board manages the vocational-technical sector separately, which is more or less the community college sector in Wisconsin.

The External Environment

In the U.S. private philanthropic foundations, institutionally based voluntary associations, and regional consortia play important roles in higher education. *Private philanthropic foundations* such as the Carnegie Foundation, Rockefeller Foundation, and Ford Foundation have provided millions of dollars to colleges and universities over the years. Most focus on institutional development; only a few support research. *Institutionally based voluntary associations* include such organizations as the American Council of Education, which gathers national information on American higher education and often acts as its advocate with Congress. Other examples are based on type of institution (e.g., the Association of American Universities for top research universities, the American Association of Community Colleges), professional associations (American Society for Engineering Education as one example), and specialized associations such as the College Entrance Examination Board which supervises the national SAT examination for aspiring college entrants. These voluntary associations form powerful lobby groups and promote communication between member institutions. Finally, *regional consortia* permit states in distinct regions to share information and coordinate student exchanges and similar programs. They are not accreditation agencies and are not responsible for ensuring the quality of academic programs. The regional consortia in the U.S. include the Southern Regional Education Board, Western Interstate Consortium on Higher Education (WICHE), New England Board of Higher Education, and Midwestern Higher Education Commission (Hacleroad, 1994).

Accreditation, Quality, and Standards

Ensuring academic quality in American higher education is a function of voluntary cooperation between authorized accreditation agencies with academic institutions and, in some cases, academic programs. Quality assurance is not a governmental function (Gates et al., 2002). Academic institutions have an incentive to seek accredited status, however, in part because it is a requirement for their students to receive federal financial aid.

Eight regional accreditation agencies are responsible for accrediting academic institutions. The first of these was established in 1885. These institutional-level accrediting agencies are supplemented by various professional accrediting bodies, which focus on programs such as engineering, business, art, dance, journalism, law, and medicine. All accreditation agencies are authorized to operate by the U.S. Department of Education, which otherwise does not participate in the process. Accreditation groups are represented nationally by an umbrella organization, the Council for Higher Education Accreditation. This self-regulatory process evolved in large part because the size of American higher education would make any centralized process onerous and probably unsustainable.

Accreditation is the voluntary, nongovernmental, self-regulatory structures and processes to assure that an institution has the financial and academic resources to operate effectively and to maintain academic standards. Accreditation for some academic programs (e.g., engineering, medicine) also exists. The focus of program-level accreditation varies by the accreditation agency.

Accreditation involves self-study, peer review by teams via a site visit, action by the accreditation agency, and follow-up monitoring and oversight. The academic program or institution prepares an in-depth self-study and sends it to the accreditation agency. The agencies select site visit teams comprised of distinguished faculty members and administrators to visit the program or institution; agency staff members are not directly involved in the assessment process. The site visit is meant to gather and validate information. The team then prepares a report and makes a recommendation for accreditation status, which can range from accredited, to probation (pending improvements), to not accredited. Accreditation generally is granted for a period of five years at the institutional level (Gates et al., 2002).

Financing U.S. Higher Education

The increasing cost of attending higher education to students, their parents, and state governments as well as the effects of cost on access and questions about the long-term value of an increasingly expensive education are among the top policy concerns confronting American higher education today. The fundamental questions are where the money for higher education comes from and how colleges and universities spend it. Keep in mind that whatever the tuition and other costs to students for attending a college or university, the cost to an academic institution of educating that student *always* exceeds the revenue generated by tuition and fees even in the most expensive private universities. The cost of educating a student at all types of institutions has increased at least as quickly as the increase in tuition during the past decade (Fairweather, 2006).

Where the Money Comes From

Table 2.2 shows the revenue sources for public and private American academic institutions. At almost 40%, tuition and fees account for the largest source of revenue for private institutions. Sales and services as well as endowment income are second and third in importance, respectively. State governments provide the highest percentage of revenue for public institutions although tuition is also among the top categories of revenue. This average masks substantial variation of state support for public institutions. State support ranges from as little as about 6% of the operating budget for Penn State University, a state-related institution, to more than 90% at some

Table 2.2 Percentage Distribution of Revenue for U.S. Universities, 2000–2001

Revenue Category	Public Two-Year	Public Four-Year	Private Four-Year
Tuition and Fees	19.5	17.8	39.6
Federal Government	5.5	12.4	17.6
State Government	44.5	33.7	1.5
Local Government	19.5	0.6	0.6
Private Gifts	1.2	5.9	18.3
Endowment Income	0.1	0.9	−7.8*
Sales and Other Services	6.1	25.0	24.6
Other	3.6	3.7	5.7

Source: National Center for Education Statistics, 2004.

Note
*Endowment income varies by year. In 2000–2001 endowment income decreased along with the drastic decline in the stock market. More typically the percentage of revenue accounted for by endowment income is (positive) 5 to 10%.

community colleges. The federal government accounts for about 17% and 12%, respectively, of the revenue of private and public four-year institutions (Fairweather, 2006). The relatively high contribution of the federal government to private institutions reflects the large number of federally subsidized student loans and federal research dollars. Over time the relative contribution of state governments to public institutions has decreased while the relative contribution of student tuition as a source of revenue has increased (Fairweather, 2006).

Where the Money Goes

Table 2.3 shows that instructional costs are the largest category of expenditure at all academic institutions. This trend holds true even at research universities (National Center for Education Statistics, 2004). As expected research expenditures comprise important expenditure categories for public and private four-year institutions, not for public two-year institutions although such expenditures account for only about one-third as much as expenses for instruction. Expenditures on public service are the province of public institutions.

Policy Challenges

American higher education is confronted with three major external policy challenges: increasing costs and how to pay for them, changes in the makeup of college students, and globalization and economic development.

Cost, Affordability, and Access

The dominant political issue in American higher education today is the increasing cost to students and their parents of attending college, the resulting

Table 2.3 Percentage Distribution of Expenditures in U.S. Universities, 2000–2001

Type of Expenditure	Public Two-Year	Public Four-Year	Private Four-Year
Instruction	43.3	27.7	32.2
Research	0.1	12.8	11.0
Public Service	2.4	4.6	1.8
Academic Support (Libraries etc.)	8.5	7.7	8.5
Student Services	10.1	3.8	7.1
Institutional Support	15.2	7.7	13.0
Scholarships and Fellowships	4.0	4.7	1.3
All Other Categories	16.4	31.0	25.1

Source: National Center for Education Statistics, 2004.

decline in affordability, and the potential negative consequences for access (National Center for Public Policy and Higher Education, 2006). During the past ten years tuition at public institutions has increased 51% adjusted for inflation; the comparable percentage increase at private institutions is 35% (Fairweather, 2006). This year alone the University of California (UC) system, which historically has charged among the lowest fees of any public system in the U.S., raised its fees by more than one-third. Although the UC system remains below the national average for public research universities in its costs for students, the high percentage increase resulted in significant negative public perception of the university.

For public higher education increased costs for students are in part a result of declining public investment in real terms since 1980 (Zumeta, 2006). Increased costs to students are also a function of the competitive pursuit by academic institutions of prestige, which has resulted in adding expensive new degree programs, building and maintaining the latest in laboratories, and improving technological infrastructure. Understanding the costs of higher education and estimating trends is complex because several relevant measures of cost differ in the trends they show. *Student price*, the cost to students of attending college, can be estimated by the *sticker price* or the *net price*. Further, these prices may or may not be adjusted for inflation. Trends in the *sticker price*, defined here as tuition plus room and board, unadjusted for inflation show a percentage increase during the past five years of 31% in private four-year universities and 44% in public four-year institutions. Adjusted for inflation, the increase drops to 17% and 28%, respectively. The *net price*, or the price the student actually pays after subtracting tax breaks, fellowships, and other forms of assistance that the student need not pay back from the sticker price, shows much smaller rates of increase.

Affordability is the ratio of either sticker price or net price to the median income. Using sticker price, the affordability of college for students has declined for all types of institutions between 1995–1996 and 2003–2004, although based on net prices it has not changed much between 1995–1996 and 2003–2004 (Fairweather, 2006). Even so, students from an average family can expect to pay up to 40% of their family's income to attend private universities and about 16% of their income to attend public four-year institutions. Community colleges are much less expensive (Fairweather, 2006).

The relatively high (and increasing) cost of attending college comes at a time when attaining a college degree is more important than ever. Not only does attaining a degree increase career earnings (College Board, 2004), today participation in the global, information-based economy has made a college degree mandatory for most Americans. One consequence is that American college students are more in debt when they graduate than ever before (Fairweather, 2006). Another consequence is that American colleges and universities today spend great effort on raising revenue from alumni, inventions developed by their faculties, and other non-traditional sources. Ironically some of the money they raise is used to provide fellowships to students, particularly those who otherwise could not afford to attend. Not surprisingly in this environment, legislatures and the general public now commonly call for increased scrutiny and more accountability.

Efforts by colleges and universities to control costs also have internal consequences. Many universities have turned to part-time professors for some undergraduate teaching responsibilities, which may adversely affect the quality of education (Baldwin and Chronister, 2001). Technology-based degree programs are in vogue in part (purportedly) to increase instructional efficiency. The movement to increase the quality of undergraduate instruction initiated in part by Ernest Boyer's seminal *Scholarship Reconsidered* (1990) conflicts with the pressures on faculty members to conduct more research and obtain external funds (Fairweather, 1996).

Student Diversity and Changing Demographics

The image of the typical undergraduate student as between 18 and 22 years of age and living in a residence hall, and the average graduate student being 25 years old having started the graduate program shortly after receiving the baccalaureate degree, no longer applies in American higher education. Almost one-half of all undergraduate students today are aged 24 or older. More than 10% are over 40 years of age. Only one-fifth of undergraduate students do not work; 41% work part-time and 39% work full-time. Across all types of institutions, 52% of undergraduates attend full-time, 48% attend part-time (National Center for Education Statistics, 2004).

Racial/ethnic minorities make up the fastest growing segment of the general population but trail in their participation in higher education (National Center for Education Statistics, 2004). Successful preparation of and inclusion in higher education is fundamental to the long-term economic future of the U.S.

International students comprise the majority of graduate enrollments in engineering, sciences, and mathematics (Oliver, 2007). Resolving immigration issues, such as visa policies, is crucial to maintaining a strong presence of these international students in American academic institutions. Continued leadership in the sciences likely depends on it.

Finally, demand for technology-based instruction has been fueled by working adults and to a lesser degree by international students. It is likely that the proportion of all instruction delivered through technological means will increase over time.

Globalization and Economic Transformation

Higher education contributes to economic development through human capital, whether by educating students or professional development, basic and especially applied research, and technology transfer (Fairweather, 1988). Colleges and universities also directly affect local and regional economies by generating jobs and tax revenues (Fairweather, 2006) Every dollar invested in Michigan public universities, as an example, results in about an additional $6 in state economic benefits (Carr and Roessner, 2002).

The policy focus today, however, is not on traditional economic benefits but on the contribution higher education might make to economic development and revitalization. The globalization of the economy and the concomitant displacement of jobs and industries make clear that citizens no longer can expect to make a decent living without some form of higher education. Equally important, most states now view higher education as the key to economic transformation, assisting state economies to move from traditional manufacturing toward knowledge-based economies (Fairweather, 2006).

Conclusion: The Adaptable System

Although these challenges are significant and may result in major shakeups along the way, American higher education has faced many such transformational periods in its history. It has survived, even thrived, in spite of or perhaps because of these challenges. The diverse, pluralistic model of American higher education, mixing public and private sectors, various types of institutions with distinct missions, and multiple entry points to students, forms its own type of adaptive system, one capable of adjusting to substantial changes in the external environment. The adaptability can be seen in the development of new types of institutions to meet growing demand, such as community colleges and, more recently, virtual universities. It can be seen in the development of new internal structures, such as organized research units to complement traditional disciplinary research, and new personnel arrangements such as the use of non-traditional faculty positions to complement tenure-track staff. Adaptability is evident even in formal state structures such as the expansion of the California State University mandate to permit offering doctoral degrees because the capacity of the University of California does not meet the demand. There is every reason to believe that this highly adaptive "system" is up to yet another significant challenge.

Notes

1. The Carnegie Foundation for the Advancement of Teaching no longer prints updates versions of its classification system. The data are available online. For the last version in print see McCormick (2000).
2. The University of Texas–Austin has a fine Center for Teaching Excellence yet teaching as an activity in faculty rewards remains under-valued.
3. This section draws upon data issued by the Education Commission of the States (2007).

References

American Council on Education. *A Brief Guide to U.S. Higher Education.* Washington, DC: American Council on Higher Education, 2001.

Baldwin, Roger, and Jay Chronister. *Teaching Without Tenure: Policies and Practices for a New Era.* Baltimore, Maryland: Johns Hopkins University Press, 2001.

Bowen, William, and Derek Bok. *The Shape of the River: Long-term Consequences for Considering Race in College and University Admissions.* Princeton, New Jersey: University of Princeton Press, 1998.

Boyer, Ernest. *Scholarship Reconsidered: Priorities of the Professoriate.* Princeton, New Jersey: Carnegie Foundation for the Advancement of Teaching, 1990.

Carnegie Foundation for the Advancement of Teaching. *The Carnegie Classification of Institutions of Higher Education, 2005 Edition.* http://www.carnegiefoundation.org/classifications/index.asp?key=799 (accessed November 15, 2007).

Carr, Robert, and David Roessner. *The Economic Impact of Michigan's Public Universities.* Washington, D.C.: SRI International, 2002.

Clark, Burton. *The Distinctive College: Antioch, Reed, and Swarthmore.* Chicago: Aldine, 1970.

College Board. *Education Pays 2004: The Benefits of Higher Education for Individuals and Society.* New York: College Board, 2004.

Education Commission of the States. http://www.ecs.org (accessed November 30, 2007).

Fairweather, James. *Entrepreneurship and Higher Education: Lessons for Colleges, Universities, and Industry.* ASHE-ERIC Higher Education Research Report No. 6. Washington, DC: Association for the Study of Higher Education, 1988.

Fairweather, James. "Faculty Reward Structures: Toward Institutional and Professional Homogenization." *Research in Higher Education* 34 (1993): 603–624.

Fairweather, James. "Myths and Realities of Academic Labor Markets." *Economics of Education Review* 17 (1995): 179–192.

Fairweather, James. *Faculty Work and Public Trust: Restoring the Value of Teaching and Public Service in American Academic Life.* Boston: Allyn and Bacon, 1996.

Fairweather, James. *Higher Education and the New Economy.* East Lansing, Michigan: Educational Policy Center at Michigan State University, 2006.

Fairweather, James, and Andrea Beach. "Variation in Faculty Work at Research Universities: Implications for State and Institutional Policy." *Review of Higher Education* 26 (2002): 97–115.

Feller, Irwin, and Roger Geiger. "The Dispersion of Academic Research in the 1980s." *Journal of Higher Education* 66 (1995): 336–360.

Fuller, Carol. *An Analysis of Leading Undergraduate Sources of Ph.D.s, Adjusted for Institutional Size.* Ann Arbor, Michigan: Great Lakes Colleges Association, 1986.

Gates, Susan et al. *Ensuring Quality and Productivity in Higher Education.* ASHE-ERIC Higher Education Research Report 1. Washington, DC: Wiley, 2002.

Geiger, Roger. *To Advance Knowledge: The Growth of American Research Universities, 1900–1940.* New York: Oxford University Press, 1986.

Geiger, Roger. "The Ten Generations of American Higher Education." In *American Higher*

Education in the Twenty-first Century, 2nd edition. Edited by Philip Altbach, Robert Berdahl, and Patricia Gumport, 38–70. Baltimore, Maryland: Johns Hopkins University Press, 2005.

Gladieux, Lawrence, Arthur Hauptman, and Laura Knapp. "The Federal Government and Higher Education." In *Higher Education in American Society.* Edited by Philip Altbach, Robert Berdahl, and Patricia Gumport, 125–154. Amherst, New York: Prometheus Books, 1994.

Hacleroad, Fred. "Other External Constituencies and their Impact on Higher Education." In *Higher Education in American Society.* Edited by Philip Altbach, Robert Berdahl, and Patricia Gumport, 199–224. Amherst, New York: Prometheus, 1994.

Heller, Donald. "The Effects of Tuition and State Financial Aid on Public College Enrollment." *Review of Higher Education* 23 (1999): 65–89.

Jencks, Christopher and David Riesman. *The Academic Revolution.* Garden City, New Jersey: Doubleday, 1968.

Johnstone, D. Bruce. "Patterns of Finance: Revolution, Evolution, or More of the Same?" *Review of Higher Education* 21 (1998): 245–255.

Levy, Daniel. "Private Institutions of Higher Education." In *The Encyclopedia of Higher Education, Volume 2.* Edited by Burton Clark and Guy Neave, 1183–1195. Oxford: Pergamon Press, 1992.

McCormick, Andrew. *The Carnegie Classification of Institutions of Higher Education, 2000 Edition.* Menlo Park, California: Carnegie Foundation for the Advancement of Teaching, 2000.

McGuinness, Aims. "The States and Higher Education." In *American Higher Education in the Twenty-first Century.* Edited by Philip Altbach, Robert Berdahl, and Patricia Gumport, 183–215. Baltimore, Maryland: Johns Hopkins University Press, 1999.

National Center for Education Statistics. *Students at Private, For-Profit Institutions* (NCES 2000–175). Washington, DC: US Government Printing Office, 2000.

National Center for Education Statistics. *Digest of Education Statistics 2004.* Washington, DC: US Department of Education, 2004.

National Center for Public Policy and Higher Education. *Measuring Up 2006: The National Report Card on Higher Education.* San Jose, California: National Center for Public Policy and Higher Education, 2006.

Oliver, Julia. *Graduate Students and Postdoctorates in Science and Engineering: 2005.* Washington, DC: National Science Foundation, 2007.

Slaughter, Sheila and Larry Leslie. *Academic Capitalism: Policies, Politics, and the Entrepreneurial University.* Baltimore, Maryland: Johns Hopkins University Press, 1997.

Stites, Francis. *Private Interest and Public Gain: The Dartmouth College Case, 1819.* Amherst, Massachusetts: University of Massachusetts Press, 1972.

Thelin, John. *The History of American Higher Education.* Baltimore, Maryland: Johns Hopkins University Press, 2004.

Trow, Martin. "American Higher Education: Past, Present, and Future." *Educational Researcher* 17 (1988): 13–23.

Trow, Martin. "From Mass Higher Education to Universal Access: The American Advantage." In *In Defense of American Higher Education.* Edited by Philip Altbach, Patricia Gumport, and D. Bruce Johnstone, 110–143. Baltimore, Maryland: Johns Hopkins University Press, 2001.

Wolanin, Thomas. "The Federal Role in Higher Education." In *The NEA Almanac of Higher Education.* Edited by Harold Wechsler, 39–51. Washington, DC: National Education Association, 2003.

Zumeta, William. "The New Finance of Public Higher Education." In *NEA 2006 Almanac of Higher Education.* Edited by Harold Wechsler, 37–48. Washington, DC: National Education Association, 2006.

3

Structural Changes in Higher Education
The Case of the United Kingdom

Peter Scott

Introduction

The development of mass higher education, often glossed as 'massification', has sometimes, instinctively and thoughtlessly perhaps, been regarded as an essentially endogenous phenomenon, an expression of the internal dynamics of the evolution of higher education systems as much as (or more than) simply one element, and perhaps a subordinate and secondary element, in the wider development of contemporary society with its own multiple glosses – 'knowledge society', 'risk society', 'audit society' and the rest (Beck 1992, Castells 1996–1998, Power 1997, Scott 1995). Too often massification has been viewed from the inside-out – for example, in terms of its impact on the rest of the education system or on the labor market – rather than from the outside-in – for example, the ways in which political change (notably the growth of democracy and a mass-media culture), shifts in economic and occupational structures, and social and cultural transformations have themselves shaped the development of higher education.

As a result structural changes in higher education have often been seen in isolation, as self-willed reforms, rather than as responses to the wider currents of individualization (and other forms of identity formation based on gender, ethno-religious affiliation or simply consumerist life-style), new patterns of production and consumption (for example, 'vital' capitalism) and new knowledge structures (which embrace both techno-science and the resistances to it, and the much wider social distribution of knowledge production on which both depend). Perhaps in our reluctance to see these far-reaching changes in universities and colleges as effectively being determined, in quasi-Marxist fashion, by deeper changes in socio-economic structures, we may sometimes have swung to the opposite extreme, by insisting that massification is a largely autonomous – or, at any rate, self-referential – phenomenon and also by denying, or at any rate down-playing, the multiple reflexities that bind contemporary higher education systems to their host societies.

This inwardness perhaps has been more pronounced in the United Kingdom where memories of a more elite, and certainly a more intimate, style of higher education are more recent and, as a result, there has been a greater reluctance to embrace massification than elsewhere. This reluctance has had two effects. The first, of course, has been a failure to situate the development of higher education in the United Kingdom since 1945 (or, better perhaps, the 1960s when the first decisive break was made with an essentially elitist conception of higher education) in the context of the very substantial changes that took place in British society in the second half of the twentieth century: in the political world the rise (and supposed decline) of the welfare state, the dramatic irruption of Thatcherism and its feeble, at best, reversal by New Labour; in the economic sphere the decline of old industrial Britain and the triumph of a 'new economy' of hyper-consumerism, financial services and the 'virtual worlds' of IT, design and lifestyle; in the social world the decline of hierarchy and deference but also the erosion of class-based solidarities and the rise of more individualized (and contrived?) biographies; and in the cultural domain the creativity of popular culture (and its subsequent 'capture' and commodification by the media industry). At an empirical level few, if any, connections have been made between these dramatic changes and the radical extension of the higher education 'franchise'. As a result the intriguing question – what difference has this seven-fold expansion of higher education between 1963 and 2007, this mass production of a graduate population, made both to the structure and the tone of British society? – has gone largely unanswered in sociological terms. The second effect has been the yawning gap between the remarkable flourishing of social theory offering fascinating (and often compelling) meta-interpretations of social, economic, political and cultural change and the largely atheoretical, even banal, accounts of the growth of mass higher education systems.

This chapter attempts to remedy some of these deficiencies by weaving together the development of higher education and these wider trends. It does so under three overall headings: first, the expansion of higher education (from the inside-out, i.e. the growth of student numbers and the increase in the number, and type, of institutions; and from the outside-in, i.e. the implications of the increasing size of the graduate workforce and the emergence of a 'graduate culture'); second, changes in the mission and goals of higher education (in terms both of teaching and of research, although both categories have become more diverse and diffuse, and increasingly overlapping); and finally, globalization (not simply in a direct sense, i.e. the expansion of international students and growth of other forms of international collaboration, but also in an indirect sense, i.e. the impact of a global – and necessarily free-market? – economy trading increasingly in 'virtual' products, and in which knowledge has become a valuable commodity, on the organization, governance, funding and ethos of higher education).

The Expansion of Higher Education

The expansion of higher education – from fewer than 250,000 students in the mid-1960s to more than two million today – has itself been the most dramatic structural change in higher education in the United Kingdom, a change moreover that has triggered a large number of other structural changes (National Statistics 2006). However, expansion has produced normative as well as structural change. In the 1960s higher education in England and Wales (and, to a more limited extent, Scotland) remained an exceptional system, still relatively immune from the democratizing currents that had transformed higher education in the United States since 1945 and also insulated from the 'entitlement' regimes that prevailed in most of the rest of (western and southern) Europe whereby all those who had passed the *baccalaureate, abitur* or their equivalents were entitled to university places. Across the Atlantic and across the Channel mass higher education systems were already emerging strongly, but imperceptibly so in England and Wales. As a result levels of participation still lagged behind, as did the production of graduates despite lower wastage rates.

The academic culture also continued to be shaped by this (comparative) under-development, the persistence of an essentially elitist system of universities (although the other elements within higher education, so-called 'advanced further education' and teacher training, offered greater – and wider – opportunities). The structure of disciplines, styles of pedagogy and the tight association of teaching and research – all reflected this distinctive academic culture, which in turn reflected low levels of participation in higher education. It is even possible to argue that the stubborn persistence of a scholarly culture and reluctance to embrace a wider intellectual culture, in England and Wales if not Scotland, can also be attributed to the exceptional nature of its higher education system well into the second half of the twentieth century. However, in the first decade of the twenty-first century this under-development has been overcome. Levels of participation match, and by some measures, exceed those in the United States and the rest of Europe. Overall the system recruits rather than selects its students. The UK has become the largest producer of graduates in Europe with 1.8 million students and low wastage (graduation rates of 80 percent of those initially enrolled). Although it has sometimes been said that the UK acquired a mass system of higher education in a typical fit of absentmindedness, there can be no doubt that no other label can be used to describe the present system. As a result many of the exceptional characteristics of UK higher education have been dissolved:

- The curriculum is no longer determined by traditional academic taxonomies: multi- and inter-disciplinary programs have become increasingly common (encouraged by the combination of instrumentalism and consumerism which has come to dominate higher education since the Thatcher period);
- A pedagogic revolution is in full swing – fuelled partly by this loosening of these traditional taxonomies, partly by advances in learning

8

technologies and partly by changes in the abilities, expectations and aspirations of students themselves;

- The tight links between research and teaching, so typical of the old scholarly (and scientific) culture, have also been weakened as both have developed their own distinctive economies in terms of personnel, careers and organizational structures (even though, in intellectual terms, the two have become less distinctive domains).

Some of the exceptional characteristics of UK higher education, of course, have persisted – such as a dwindling degree of intimacy (despite worsening staff/student ratios) and a horror of 'wastage' (when students drop/stop out, even for good reasons). But the extent to which these characteristics are really relic-mentalities from the lost age of elite higher education or evidence of new imperatives – the rise of a student 'market' in the case of academic/pastoral intimacy or of the so-called 'new public management' in the case of wastage – remains unclear. The safest conclusion is that, although important differences persist between UK higher education and other systems, the former is an unambiguously mass system (Clark 2006, Ramsden 2007).

However, the impact of both expansion in a quantitative sense and of massification in a qualitative sense on the structure of UK higher education needs to be carefully disaggregated. The expansion of student numbers has been largely accommodated by increasing the size of institutions rather than increasing their number (in Scotland, although the bulk of expansion took place in the higher education sector without any increase in the number of institutions, a slightly different pattern of growth prevailed with most higher diploma, i.e. sub-Bachelors, courses being offered in further education colleges). With a few exceptions the pattern of universities and other higher education institutions in 2008 is essentially the pattern determined in the 1960s. In the intervening four decades there has been nothing to compare with the wave of (enforced) mergers of colleges of technology, art and (a little later) education which created the English and Welsh polytechnics (since 1992 the so-called 'new', or 'post-92', universities). The change of institutional labels – from colleges of advanced technology, and later polytechnics, to universities – has disguised this remarkable fact, that the massification of UK higher education took place within a relatively fixed institutional framework. This meant that the impact of massification has been felt by all institutions because all institutions, with very few exceptions (Oxford and Cambridge, and some specialist institutions), have increased in size, in most cases willingly although funding incentives and 'efficiency' squeezes have helped to persuade them to expand.

Arguably many of the important changes in organizational cultures which have taken place in the past three decades, the decline-and-fall of 'collegiality' and the rise of much criticized 'managerialism', have been an inexorable (and largely mechanistic?) response to this substantial increase in the average size of institutions rather than being a deliberately planned ideological project, although this assessment would be challenged as too benign by some commentators (Ferlie et al. 1996, Tapper 2007). But this effect may not simply have been confined to the governance and management of institutions; their academic character may also have been modified as larger institutions inevitably took on more pluralistic and heterogeneous missions. Of course, an alternative path was possible – to preserve the special character of elite universities by shielding them from these expansionary effects and accommodating expansion by creating more institutions. But that path was not followed in the UK, with the inevitable but probably unforeseen consequence that the sharp binary distinction between universities and polytechnics (although never as sharp as in other binary systems) became fuzzier and fuzzier and eventually had to be abandoned (although, as explained below, the trigger for abandoning the binary system was political, the twin erosions of the independence of local government and the autonomy of the traditional universities).

The impact of expansion on higher education's social base also needs to be carefully disaggregated. Although massification has promoted the democratization of higher education in the long run, it does not follow that mass higher education systems are necessarily better at promoting social mobility than elite systems in the short term. Access to the UK's more restricted higher education system of the 1960s and 1970s was no less biased in favour of students from privileged social backgrounds than the apparently more open US and other European systems which existed at the same time (or than the more extensive system which now exists in the UK?). There was always a route open to 'scholarship boys' in post-war Britain (less so for 'scholarship girls', for reasons which will be discussed below). Openness in the context of access to higher education is a complex concept; openness in aggregate terms, for a whole society, is not necessarily the same as openness for individuals. Also wider access is only variable; its positive effect can easily be cancelled out by others such as a widening income gap, the decay of class solidarities or significant changes in occupational structures (which have all been characteristic of Thatcher-Blair Britain).

This may help to explain the uneven impact of the expansion of higher education on the life-chances of different groups, apparent both in terms of input, i.e. opportunities to enter higher education in the first place, and of outputs, i.e. graduate salaries and career prospects. In 'input' terms women (without qualification) and ethnic minorities (in a more qualified sense because they still tend to be concentrated in less prestigious institutions and the fortunes of different ethnic minorities vary substantially) have benefited; working-class students, especially males, have seen little improvement in their relative chance of going to university (although in absolute terms much larger numbers of working-class students are now enrolled) and adults, despite the beacon-like success of the Open University and the popular political discourse of 'lifelong learning', have only registered small (and precarious?) gains (Kelly and Cook 2007). In 'output' terms similarly differential patterns can be observed. Non-graduates from the most socially advantaged groups, admittedly a small number because of near-universal participation rates, are still likely to earn more than graduates from working-class homes. The differential between male and female earnings is as great among graduates as in the general population. Both facts illustrate how little mass higher education systems can counteract deeper social inequalities.

Indeed mass higher education systems, which because of their scale and social penetration are more deeply embedded in their societies than elite systems, may actually have a reduced capacity to produce social change. This may be apparent in three different ways:

- First, the existence of a mass graduate workforce (and, of course, the accelerating obsolescence of technical – and other forms of expert – knowledge) has generated an increasing demand for various forms of up-skilling and re-skilling. As a result the number of postgraduate students has increased even more rapidly than the number of undergraduate students, an inevitable characteristic of all mass higher education systems. But, because those selected for postgraduate study tend to be the more successful (and the more socially selected students), this not only directly confers on them additional advantages but also indirectly reduces the value of undergraduate qualifications;
- Second, in a similar effect, the expansion of higher education has intensified the exclusion of the decreasing (but still substantial) number of young people (and adults) who do not participate. In elite higher education systems enrolling less than 10 percent of the relevant age group the penalties for non-participation were much less severe than they are in a mass system enrolling upwards of 40 percent of the age group. In this way massification may have contributed to marginalization;
- Third, massification has stimulated the emergence of a distinctively 'graduate culture', a bundle of career opportunities, social habits and cultural mentalities enjoyed by those who have experienced higher education. To a significant extent this new 'graduate culture' has substituted for traditional middle-class, or bourgeois, culture – because 'graduateness' has now become an indispensable component of that traditional culture which it is increasingly difficult for non-graduates, however socially privileged, to access; but also because this new culture appears at any rate to be less class-bound and less hide-bound. Some of the reluctance of young working-class males to participate in higher education may arise from their antipathy to

what they perceive as merely a new form of bourgeois culture; to go to university may have come to be stigmatized, however inchoately, as a form of class treason, a more explicit rejection of one's cultural roots than was ever required of working-class 'scholarship boys' who 'bettered themselves'. This new 'graduate culture' also has intriguing affinities with the growth of creative entrepreneurialism (Florida 2005) which may attract those with high ambitions and aspirations while discouraging the more marginal and excluded.

The way in which the expansion of student numbers has been implemented since the mid-1960s also illustrates, as well as reinforcing, the ambiguities of the impact of massification on the structure of the UK higher education. This expansion was not a steady process; instead there were two bursts of rapid growth – in the 1960s and early 1970s; and then the late 1980s and early 1990s – interspersed by periods of, if not steady-state at any rate much slower growth – the years between 1974 and 1987; and the years after 1994 (although growth rates picked up again with the election of New Labour in 1997; the past decade has been a period of intermediate expansion). Several explanations for this uneven pattern of growth are available. One is that it reflected the wider pattern of economic growth – true in the decade following the oil-price shock of the mid-1970s; but not true of the years since 1992 when the economy has grown at almost unprecedented rates. Another, related, explanation is that the expansion of higher education has closely mirrored increases, or reductions, in public expenditure – in one sense a tautology because higher education in the UK remains a largely publicly funded sector and, although public funding has apparently declined as a proportion of total income, it remains the dominant driver. Public expenditure on higher education has increased by more than the average for all public spending. It is probably more accurate to say that public funding for higher education now flows through multiple channels – funding council grants, home students' fees which are funded up-front by the State, research council grants and so on. In another sense. this explanation is less true because the second period of rapid growth was accompanied (indeed, achieved) by substantial reductions in the unit-of-resource (in other words expansion was funded as much through improved productivity as by increased resources).

A third explanation of uneven growth is that it was determined by funding mechanisms, some intentional but others unintended. Higher education institutions decided to grow, or not, depending on the incentives provided by these funding mechanisms. These incentives might be positive, as they have been during the past decade when the Higher Education Funding Council for England (HEFCE) allocated funded additional student numbers (ASNs). But they might also be negative, as they were during the second burst of rapid growth because this seemed to be the only way institutions could remain financially viable even though they recognized that expansion was eroding unit costs. The existence of the binary system until the early 1990s, with its separate and not always well coordinated funding bodies and allocation systems, was a further complication. Any attempt to ration growth in the traditional universities to protect the unit-of-resource, the traditional policy of the former University Grants Committee, simply increased the expansionary pressures in the polytechnics and colleges.

A fourth possible explanation of stop-start growth is that it mirrored wider demographic patterns, especially among young adults (which, for all the talk of lifelong learning, remain the key constituency for UK higher education) – true enough in the first burst of rapid growth when the number of 18-year-olds was building towards a post-war peak (and the Robbins committee even talked of a 'crisis' of under-supply in terms that echoed housing shortages); but the opposite is true in the second burst when the size of the 18-year-old population was declining (and the Treasury, and the then Department for Education and Science, seriously considered the possibility of deliberately not meeting current demand in full; 'tunnelling through the hump' was the favoured phrase to describe this policy). A fifth explanation is that throughout the past half century demand for higher education was determined not by crude demography but by the number of qualified entrants, which in turn was predetermined by changes in secondary education. This is perhaps the most convincing explanation because the first burst of growth followed quickly on from the large-scale establishment of comprehensive schools (which substantially enlarged the pool of potential entrants beyond that produced by grammar schools); and the second burst followed on from the replacement of GCE O-levels by the General Certificate of Secondary Education (GCSE), which had a similar effect. This suggests that prospects for further expansion depend more on what happens in secondary schools than on any direct action taken by higher education. However, there is a sixth explanation of this uneven pattern expansion, which grows out of this fifth explanation. This emphasizes the impact of wider social and cultural change, which is expressed through reforms in secondary education. The introduction of comprehensive schools was one element within a much bigger cultural 'moment' in post-war Britain. Arguably the introduction of GCSEs reflected the further erosion of class differences, combined with the emergence of much tougher (anti-liberal?) public attitudes, which together constituted Thatcherism. If this broader explanation is accepted, it underlines the need for an outside-in analysis of the development of higher education in the UK (Scott 2007).

Diversity and Heterogeneity

The second major influence on the changing shape of higher education in the UK has been the diversification of missions among universities and colleges. However, as with the expansion of higher education, this diversification needs to be carefully disaggregated – in two senses. The first is the contrast, and interplay, between direct restructuring – in other words, the deliberate creation of institutions with distinctive (and divergent?) missions; and also the development of legal instruments, management structures and funding incentives designed to sustain this differentiation – and the indirect influence of other trends which tend to promote diversification of missions – notably, of course, the expansion of the system which has broadened the social base of higher education but also wider socio-economic change and cultural shifts. The second sense is that a distinction must also be drawn between the factors promoting diversification: those which are distinctive to UK higher education (and are more likely to be political in origin); and those which apply more generally to all modern higher education systems (and reflect more fundamental changes in the configuration of teaching and research.

The major structural reform designed to promote diversification of institutional missions in UK higher education was the development of the so-called binary system by Anthony Crosland, the Secretary of State for Education and Science, in the mid-1960s. This was probably the highest-profile initiative in Europe to articulate a system which differentiated between traditional universities and other institutions of higher education (Pratt and Burgess 1974, Robinson 1968). So the abandonment of the binary system at the beginning of the 1990s had a special resonance. However, the binary system in England and Wales actually represented a weaker form of institutional differentiation than prevailed in the rest of Europe (including Scotland) and in most of the rest of the world – in two important respects.

First, it can be argued that the creation of the polytechnics by means of (sometimes forced) mergers between colleges of technology, art and (later) education was as much a process of convergence as of differentiation. The polytechnics were unambiguously higher education institutions which their predecessor institutions had not been (as the labels used to describe them, such as 'advanced further education', suggested). It is often argued that Crosland's binary policy was a 'rejection' of the recommendations made in the Robbins report of 1963. But it was the Robbins report which first used the label 'higher education' to embrace three previously uncoordinated sectors – the traditional universities, advanced further education and teacher training (Robbins 1963). So it is just as plausible to argue that Robbins prepared the way for Crosland, in terms of concepts if not detailed policy.

Second, universities and other higher education institutions were more weakly differentiated in the UK than in many other countries. There was no restriction on the levels of courses that the polytechnics could offer – as, for example, there was (and is) in many American state systems where doctoral (and sometimes masters) programs are reserved to top-tier institutions, i.e. traditional research universities. Long before the polytechnics were even established PhD programs had been offered in the non-university sector. Nor were differences of educational philosophy clear cut. Although the polytechnics offered more vocational and professional courses and universities more (to borrow wider European labels) 'academic' or 'scientific' courses, there were many exceptions – both ways. The major elements of differentiation were not educational (some of the universities were actually substantially more vocational in their focus than the polytechnics – for example, the former colleges of advanced technology which were re-designated as universities in 1965) but administrative and legal. Until the 1980s polytechnics were not able to award their own degrees – de jure; de facto they had done so almost from their establishment. Also until 1988 they were not independent corporations, like the traditional universities, but were subject to the control of local education authorities. This emphasis on legal and administrative rather than educational differentiation was reflected in the use of the label, the 'autonomous sector', to describe the universities and the 'public sector' to describe the polytechnics.

In the circumstances – fuzzy educational differentiation (at best) and clear-cut legal and administrative differentiation between universities and polytechnics – the evolution of the binary system towards the present unified (but, of course, differentiated) system of higher education in the UK was perhaps inevitable. Essentially this was a political phenomenon, as much explained by the waning power of local government and its progressive subordination to Whitehall/Westminster in Margaret Thatcher's Britain as by the development of the polytechnics themselves (whether described in terms of their growing institutional maturity or of so-called 'academic drift' as they attempted to emulate the universities). It is revealing that the formal abandonment of the binary system in 1991, as a mechanism for encouraging the differentiation of educational missions, followed quickly on from its actual abandonment as a system of legal and administrative differentiation in the terms of the Education Reform Act of 1988 when polytechnics were established as free-standing corporations independent of local authorities, thus nullifying the former distinction between the 'autonomous sector' and the 'public sector' (both universities and polytechnics now being both 'autonomous' and 'public'; the detailed differences between the two sectors in terms of governance were merely technical). It may also be revealing that in Scotland, where the dynamic between local and central government was different, the binary distinction between traditional universities and central institutions (CIs), the equivalent of the polytechnics in England and Wales, was less 'political' – not because the educational differences were less (in fact there was probably a clearer division of labor between universities and CIs) but because it was less embroiled in a struggle between local and central government. To the extent that the abandonment of the binary system represented an explicitly educational policy it was as much to do with the subordination of the tradi-

tional universities to public control as it was about the elevation of the polytechnics to (approximate) equality.

Since the creation of a formally unified system in the early 1990s differentiation of missions has not been promoted by establishing different categories
of institution; in fact, the opposite has happened as the Government has
relaxed the rules for institutions acquiring university status. (In 2006 a further
category of 'new-new-new' universities was established, for example, Canter-
bury Christchurch, Worcester and Winchester, following the 'new-new' universities of the 1990s, the former polytechnics, and the 'new' universities of
the 1960s, the green-fields campus universities such as Sussex, Warwick and
York.) Instead differentiation has been pursued through funding mechanisms, targeted initiatives and (to a limited extent) 'strategic development', i.e.
partnerships, alliances and (in a very small number of cases) institutional
mergers. However, none of these has been straightforward.

Funding Mechanisms

The ability to use funding mechanisms to promote differentiation of institutional missions has been limited for a number of reasons. First, the Higher
Education Funding Council for England (HEFCE) has been committed to the
principle of (broadly) like funding for (broadly) like activities, a principle
which to a considerable extent flows from its status as a funding rather than a
planning body. As a result funding for teaching is distributed formulaically;
the main driver is 'price group' of which there are four (A – clinical subjects;
B – science and engineering; C – other laboratory or studio based subjects,
e.g. fine art; and D – arts and social sciences). So Cambridge or Imperial
College is funded, for teaching, at the same rate as Bolton or Bedfordshire. A
review of the 'T' funding method is currently underway, but there has been no
suggestion that the principle of like-for-like funding should be abandoned.
Where premiums exist – for example, for part-time students or students on
two-year vocationally oriented Foundation Degrees – they apply to all institutions; they are designed to compensate institutions for the additional cost of
such provision and no deliberate 'policy steer' is intended. Funding for
research is distributed selectively, following the results of successive Research
Assessment Exercises (from 1986 to 2008). However, whatever other successes
the RAE may have enjoyed (for example, in improving research strategy and
management within institutions), it has not succeeded in concentrating
research funding. In fact, the degree of concentration has, marginally,
declined between the early 1990s and the present – which is unsurprising
because the former polytechnics have invested heavily in building their
research capacity. The number of top-rated units, and of institutions with at
least one top-rated unit, has increased with successive RAEs – which, of
course, is why HEFCE (although not its Scottish and Welsh counterparts) has
had to restrict the units which now receive R funding to try to maintain the

same degree of selectivity. Nor have there been substantial movements of funding between institutions as a result of successive RAEs, with the exception of some smaller specialist, generally non-university, institutions which have registered big funding gains or losses (often producing financial turbulence which HEFCE has been forced to 'mitigate').

Targeted Initiatives

Alongside T and R funding, which accounts for more than 90 percent of the HEFCE grant to institutions (and the grant of the Scottish and Welsh funding bodies), there are some targeted funding streams. Some are also distributed formulaically; in England the largest is for widening participation which, in theory, is available to all institutions but, in practice, mainly benefits the so-called post-1992 universities (the former polytechnics) which recruit many more disadvantaged students than the traditional, or pre-1992, universities (although, once again, it is important to note that the widening participation premium is designed to reflect the assumed higher cost of teaching these students rather than a reward for 'politically correct' behaviour, despite the suspicions and complaints in universities with student intakes especially skewed to the socially privileged). Other targeted funding streams are distributed following competitive bids made by institutions – the best example in England is the Centres of Excellence for Teaching and Learning (CETLs), which were launched following the 2002 White Paper on higher education and are designed to promote good practice in teaching (to balance the allegedly overweening preoccupation with research?). However, the overall impact of these targeted initiatives has been muted. The main reason is that in the case of larger multi-faculty universities, which recruit the bulk of the UK's students, the gains and losses have a tendency to balance each other out, leaving their financial position essentially unchanged. Their major impact has probably been felt not at system level, where their record of promoting restructuring has been disappointing, but within institutions by providing 'external' support and legitimation for activities which might otherwise have been in danger of being labelled as marginal, rather as the major impact of the RAE has been to improve institutional research strategies and management. However, this has been at the expense of increasing the accountability burden on institutions (and, perhaps, encouraging a cynical 'compliance' culture?).

Strategic Development

The third means by which differentiation of missions has been promoted is through strategic interventions, in England by using HEFCE's strategic development fund (SDF) and in other parts of the UK through similar mechanisms. But success has been limited – for two main reasons. The first is that the funding bodies do not have an explicitly planning role and lack powers of direction, while institutions have closely guarded their autonomy. So it has been impossible to secure significant change without the consent of institutions. The nature of governance in UK higher education has been a further obstacle; university councils (with majorities of lay members), when faced with the prospect of mergers, have typically seen it as their responsibility to defend the integrity of their institutions. The second reason is that the funding available to HEFCE and the other funding bodies to promote strategic change has been limited. In neither of the two major mergers in the past decade has HEFCE been a prime mover – in the case of the merger between the University of Manchester and the University of Manchester Institute of Science and Technology (perhaps better described as a re-amalgamation), the most powerful sponsor was the Regional Development Agency, and other regional and civic organizations; and in the case of the merger between the University of North London and London Guildhall University to form London Metropolitan University the drive came from within the two institutions (and especially the former). Most strategic interventions by funding bodies have contributed to 'tidying-up' the system – for example, by facilitating the merger of small, and perhaps unsustainable, colleges into larger universities. In a few cases these interventions have acted as catalysts for significant restructuring, but only when it has been judged to be sensible in pragmatic terms; a good example is the physics consortium among several Scottish universities brokered by the Scottish Funding Council (and now extended to other subjects). In no case has a funding council been able to use its capacity for strategic intervention to enforce differentiation of mission on unwilling institutions.

At first sight the comparative failure of policy instruments to promote significant differentiation of institutional missions in the post-binary era is puzzling. There are perhaps two broad explanations. The first is that the terms-of-engagement have changed – from differentiation in terms of educational orientation, which broadly prevailed between the mid-1960s and the late-1980s as long as the formal distinction between universities with their, supposedly, more academic focus and the polytechnics with their, again supposedly, more vocational orientation was maintained; to differentiation in terms of research mission, qualitatively as measured by the RAE and quantitatively by measuring research intensity. Of course, the two different processes of differentiation overlapped and intertwined. As the academic–vocational distinction faded during the 1980s, new bases for differentiation were suggested; a good example was the proposal to impose an R-X-T categorization of institutions (R – research-oriented; T – teaching-oriented; and X – mixed) which was never implemented and was eventually superseded by the RAE. More recently an attempt has been made to resurrect this proposal by suggesting a two-fold categorization of universities into 'research-intensive' and 'business-facing' (a proposal which unfortunately relegates the majority to the uncomfortable intermediate category of the 'squeezed middle'!). One reason for this attempt may be recognition that the RAE itself has failed to produce the degree of differentiation that had been anticipated by some policy makers and institutional leaders – perhaps wrongly because this was not the primary objective of the RAE which was (and is) to fund high-quality research wherever it is undertaken. In any case it does not seem that such a crude attempt to differentiate between institutional missions will be any more likely to succeed than earlier attempts – partly because the policy instruments to implement it are too feeble; but mainly because a neo-binary model has no future in UK higher education.

The growing intrusion of the market is also a complicating factor. In the first decade of the twenty-first century the emphasis has shifted once again, from functional differentiation (whether in terms of educational orientation, as in the binary period, or in terms of research mission, as in the immediate post-binary period) to reputational differentiation (as expressed through Teaching Quality Assessment, and then National Student Survey, 'scores' and through newspaper league tables). As with the earlier shift there is some overlap and even correlation. After all functional differentiation was not without implications for institutional reputation; some functions were, and are, regarded as nobler than others. Moreover, some of the 'scores' which are included in league tables are derived from RAE outcomes and similar measures. However, there is a crucial difference. Functional differentiation, as determined by policy instruments, is compatible with the establishment of a stable hierarchy of institutions. Reputational differentiation, as determined by the market, is not. Even if the overall pattern of institutions remains broadly unchanged, the position of individual institutions can change substantially – and unpredictably because reputational criteria are both discretionary and subjective and consequently outcomes are more volatile. In short the market, however imperfect, has a systematic tendency to undermine carefully organized institutional categorization; in that sense it is the enemy of differentiation. In another sense, of course, the market promotes other (perhaps more superficial?) forms of differentiation as institutions seek to secure competitive advantage by occupying the most attractive market niches (and, if some niches are firmly occupied, they must try to occupy others).

However, the second explanation for the puzzling failure of policy interventions to promote differentiation is that the post-binary UK higher education system was becoming more not less differentiated – but as a result of its interior dynamics rather than because of external policy interventions. In other words, there was no 'problem' which policy interventions were required to 'solve'. The major drivers of differentiation have come from within what the late Martin Trow termed the 'private life' of higher education (Trow 1973). Already broad churches, 'teaching' and 'research' have become broader still – as a result of the internal dynamics of disciplines, changes in technology which have opened up new learning possibilities, the opening-up and diversi-fication of higher education's social base, new social and political imperatives with regard to research priorities, the wider social distribution of 'knowledge production', and so on. In the case of 'teaching' the development of new dis-ciplines, and the renewal of established disciplines, have accelerated. The interplay between academicism and vocationalism has become more complex (and more 'fuzzy'). The same has happened to the interplay between (to adopt the labels current in UK higher education) 'widening participation' and 'employer engagement'. In both these examples concepts and practices which once seemed opposed have co-mingled. In the case of 'research' far-reaching changes have taken place in both its epistemologies and social practices and in how knowledge is produced, validated and disseminated – changes which have been summed up under the label of 'Mode 2' knowledge (Gibbons et al. 1994, Nowotny, Scott and Gibbons 2001). Once again the interplay between these more open patterns of knowledge production on the one hand and on the other the imperatives of so-called 'world-class research' which so preoc-cupy university and national leaders is highly complex – and ambiguous; as with 'teaching' these concepts and practices co-mingle rather than confront each other.

Perhaps the most accurate way to summarize the structural changes that have taken place in UK higher education in the decade and a half since the abandonment of the binary system is to conclude there has been a drift away from systemic differentiation towards institutional diversification. For a number of reasons – the weakening of the traditional bases of differentiation, the shift of focus from educational orientation to research engagement, the drift from functional differentiation (top-down, policy-driven and poten-tially stable) to reputational differentiation (bottom-up, market-driven and volatile) – it has become progressively more difficult to distinguish between different categories of higher education institution. But at the same time (almost) all institutions, regardless of their origins or labels, have been subject to the same complexities as concepts and practices in 'teaching' and 'research' have rapidly evolved – and to similar social, economic, political and cultural demands. As a result most institutions have undergone a process of internal diversification, as they have taken on new roles and as functions once regarded as peripheral have moved closer to the core. A good example is that bundle of activities such as technology transfer and community engagement which are often described as 'enterprise'. Perhaps the best illustration of this shift from systemic differentiation to institutional diversification is provided by the declining popularity of terms such as 'aca-demic drift' (which suggests an essentially linear process whereby less noble institutions attempt to emulate more noble institutions) and their replace-ment by terms such as 'mission stretch' (which suggests a multi-dimensional/directional accumulation of functions). The latter certainly offers a better description of UK higher education, and of its component institutions.

Globalization

The third major influence on the evolving pattern and structure of UK higher education has been globalization – which, of course, is itself a complex (even contradictory) evolving phenomenon (Featherstone et al. 1995). It is in this third area that there is perhaps the most prominent gap between the wider debates about globalization, which have produced a remarkable range of new theoretical insights and intriguing meta-narratives, and the narrower discussions about its impact on higher education, where the often banal debate has taken place largely within the more limited (and anachronistic?) context of internationalization. As a result attention has sometimes been concentrated on secondary effects – for example, the increasing flows of international students and the establishment of global alliances between universities – rather than primary impacts – for example, on higher education's engagement (entanglement?) with the so-called knowledge society and on its 'public' character (including its governance, funding and institutional cultures). Both secondary effects and primary impacts, of course, are important. But the former cannot properly be understood without reference to the latter (Scott 2005).

It is routinely assumed that UK higher education has become more international over the past four decades – and that this must be due, although in unexamined ways, to the impact of globalization. But both parts of this assumption must be critically examined. First, is it true that UK higher education has become more international? It certainly appears to be true in the context of the 'public life' of higher education, the world of institutional managers and policy makers. Ministers have placed increasing emphasis on the need for the UK to defend, and increase, its 'market share' of international students. Internationalization strategies have proliferated in universities (but, then, so have many other kinds of strategy). Institutions have invested major resources in recruiting international students who, since fees for international students were, in effect, de-regulated in the 1960s, have become a key funding stream for many UK colleges and universities; and, more recently, institutions have begun to develop international alliances and partnerships on a significant scale, partly to guarantee a continuing flow of international recruits and partly to strengthen their reputational 'brand'.

However, this apparently inexorably intensifying activity must be seen in a wider context. First, although the number of international students in UK higher education has increased at a spectacular rate, the total number of students has increased even more rapidly (although the figures are complicated by the key distinction between international and non-UK European Union students, and also by the progressive enlargement of the EU). So it is not necessarily true that, in quantitative terms, UK higher education has become more international than other systems (Comparative figures on international students are notoriously difficult to obtain; for example, the UK and Germany count international students in quite different ways). Secondly, the discourse of internationalism is balanced by an equally powerful discourse of localism – for example, the drives towards 'widening participation' and 'employer engagement' which have already been discussed. So neither is it necessarily true that, in qualitative terms, UK higher education has become more international. The contribution of the new universities, the former polytechnics, has been ambiguous in this respect. On the one hand they include some of the most active international recruiters with some of the highest proportions of international students; on the other hand they tend also to be regional recruiters, enrolling more local students than the traditional universities.

The second part of the assumption can also be questioned. In UK higher education the major incentive to recruit international students (and to establish international partnerships, which are typically designed to strengthen these recruitment efforts) has been to increase revenue. This has represented one of the few areas in which institutions have been free to recruit as many students as they liked, because the number of UK students has always been capped (although the precise mechanism has varied); and also one of the few areas in which institutions have been free to set their own fees without the intervention of the State. The next most important incentive, particularly influential among politicians, has been the desire to exploit the UK's imperial past (and post-colonial connections) and its present status as the second largest Anglophone country to secure diplomatic, commercial and cultural advantages. This has been apparent in successive iterations of the so-called Prime Minister's Initiative on international education – and the synchronization of political and academic targets (notably China) (British Council 2006). Both these incentives are essentially domestic in their origins – or, at any rate, UK-centric. The drive to make UK institutions more international, not only by increasing the diversity of the student (and staff) population through international recruitment but also by deliberately internationalizing the university curriculum and the (UK) student experience, although not absent, has typically come in third place.

The question of whether UK higher education has become more international is also difficult to answer if the focus is on its 'private life', its academic evolution whether expressed in terms of teaching or of research.

Part of the answer has already been briefly mentioned; both the curriculum and the student experience have become more international in content (many more courses with 'international' in their titles) and orientation (although in seeking to account for the multiculturalism of the modern British university it is sometimes difficult to disentangle the indirect effects of the increasing ethnic diversity of the UK population from the direct effects produced by the presence of more international students). But, just as the drive to internationalization has generally been subordinate to the desire of institutions to increase their revenue from international students and the desire of Governments to maximize the influence of the UK, so these effects may need to be regarded as essentially secondary phenomenon. The comparative lack of interest in the Bologna process, and the wider processes of Europeanization, may illustrate the natural level of their enthusiasm for introducing non-UK elements into the university curriculum and the student experience, in the absence of the two other more powerful drivers.

However, the internationalization of research appears to be an unambiguous phenomenon. The data on citations, joint-authorship and the like suggests that research in the natural and applied sciences, (with more qualifications) the social sciences, and (with more still) scholarship in the humanities have become more international over the last half-century. But even so three considerations (caveats?) must also be mentioned. First, research has always been an international endeavour. Secondly, it has become more international partly as a result of logistical and technological factors such as cheap air travel, email and the Internet. Thirdly, research in the natural sciences is now disseminated almost entirely through the medium of English (and research in the social sciences largely so). While this has certainly promoted the integration of the research enterprise and increased the velocity with which its findings are circulated (= more international?), it may have been at the expense of pluralism (= less international?). The equation of 'world-class' research with research published in English is deeply problematical in some disciplines.

Even if it is conceded that UK higher education, by and large, has become more international, it remains unclear to what extent this can be attributed to the impact of globalization. The answer depends on which of several types of globalization is being considered. Although the dominant type remains that of cultural pluralism and political liberalism combined with (subordinated to?) socio-economic neo-liberalism – in effect, democratic capitalism projected onto the global plane, other types exist – for example, global 'resistances' to democratic capitalism, whether left-libertarian or authoritarian-fundamentalist. By interpreting the engagement of higher education with globalization as being almost exclusively with this single, currently dominant, type there is a risk that any subsequent debate about the future of world-wide higher education will succumb to hubris – and suffer the same fate as triumphalist accounts of the 'End of History' in the early 1990s. The banal and atheoretical quality of the debate within the UK about the impact of globalization on higher education increases this danger.

This is best illustrated perhaps in the context of two dominant strands of ideological assertion:

1. The first is that globalization in the form of democratic capitalism inevitably undermines the basis of the post-war welfare state because the ultra-mobility of financial, economic and human resources inexorably erodes the tax base on which the welfare state depends – a dubious assertion in terms of empirical evidence but a persuasive ideological discourse nevertheless. Applied to higher education this discourse calls into question the 'public' character of most higher education systems, including the UK system. The 'privatization' of higher education becomes inevitable, whether in terms of higher tuition fees (because, as the welfare state declines, the tax base shrinks and public expenditure can no longer meet the funding requirements of universities). This process of 'privatization', of course, is a threat not only to publicly funded universities but also to not-for-profit private universities, which also serve public purposes, because it is driven by a commercial, even capitalist, dynamic.

2. The second strand intersects with this first strand. It is that globalization is one aspect of the so-called knowledge society, an economic formation in which virtual goods simultaneously tradable around the world have become the most dynamic form of wealth – and, among virtual goods, knowledge is the most important of all (and, of course, financial and cognitive resources are combined to produce some of the knowledge society's most powerful instruments, such as cutting-edge financial products). If this is accepted, and if it is further accepted that universities play a central role in the production of tradable knowledge (both research and graduates), their organizational culture must be transformed. It is not simply their funding base (doomed to decline along with the welfare state) that must be reformed, but also their governance (more managerial and less collegial) and even their core values (tradable knowledge not 'open' science, workforce development rather than socio-cultural critique).

However, the longer-term impact of globalization on the structure and pattern of UK higher education is likely to be more nuanced, even if short-term effects are assumed to be to emphasize the struggle to recruit more international students, to establish more international partnerships and to erode the 'public' character of the system. Other types of globalization are likely to resonate, and engage, with other aspects of the UK system – for example, its growing cultural pluralism produced by the increasing ethnic diversity of its student population and, perhaps, by a revival of more critical intellectual traditions notably in the social sciences.

Conclusion

Three major influences on the developing structure of UK higher education have been considered in this chapter – the expansion of student numbers and the growth of institutions; the diversification of roles and the differentiation of institutional missions (which are not the same); and finally globalization or, more prosaically, internationalization. These are the three major influences that have reshaped higher education in the UK over the past four decades – from an elite and sharply segregated system in the mid-1960s (but a system which has demonstrated its capacity for radical extension) to a mass and fluidly differentiated system in the first decade of the twenty-first century (but a system which still possesses the powerful folk memory of more traditional, but also utopian, values). In each case the processes by which these influences have shaped the higher education system have been complex and also contradictory, reflexive and also ambiguous. They have produced multiple effects, planned and unintentional. So it has not been a simple story – but a grand social and cultural narrative nevertheless.

The detailed debates which preoccupy UK higher education – or, at any rate, its leadership class – need to be seen in the context of this grand narrative, the system's *longue durée* (to borrow Fernand Braudel's compelling phrase). The controversy about whether the current cap on the level of fees which institutions can charge UK (and other EU) students is one example. At one level it is simply a pragmatic question – institutions are under-funded; the state is unable to provide sufficient funding; so alternative income sources must be explored, the most substantial and reliable of which is to charge students higher fees. At another level it is an ideological question – it is seen as positively desirable that the 'users' of higher education should be expected to make a more significant contribution to its cost (because, in a fundamental sense, the market is virtuous while the state is pernicious, or because it ensures the relevance and currency of the courses institutions offer). But at a third level the issue of 'raising the cap' can be related to the wider and deeper evolution of the UK higher education system (and all mass systems in the developed world?) – for example, the extent and the inevitability of privatization within a global context and the possibility of new forms of public academic enterprise emerging.

The controversy about the future of the RAE and, in particular, the replacement of a peer-review based system with a metrics system in the form of the proposed Research Excellence Framework can be considered in similar ways – pragmatically as a mechanism for reducing bureaucracy (and increasing the accuracy and consistency of research ratings); ideologically as a method for redirecting research investment from pure or 'blue skies' research to more applied or translational forms of research; or more fundamentally in the context of the evolution of new forms of knowledge production. In both cases the, no doubt temporary, resolution of these controversies is likely to be more heavily influenced by the former, pragmatic considerations – a deal to raise the fees cap to, say, £5,000 or to remove it but to limit the amount of the state-provided loan available to students; and a modified Research Excellence Framework which retains more substantial elements of peer review. But this review of the evolution of UK higher education over the past half century suggests that the longer-term resolution of these, and other policy issues, will be more heavily influenced by the deeper structures of the system, the emergence of new social, economic and cultural forms and the expression of both in fundamental changes in the interior life of teaching and research. In short the *longue durée*, not the quick fix.

References

Beck, Ulrich (1992) *Risk Society: Towards a New Modernity*, London/Newbury Park, CA: Sage.

British Council (2006) *Prime Minister's Initiative for International Education (PMI2)*, London: British Council. [http://www.britishcouncil.org/eumd-pmi-about.htm/]

Castells, Manuel (1996, 1997 and 1998) *The Information Age: Economy, Society and Culture* (Vol. 1: *The Rise of Network Society* [1996], Vol. 2: *The Power of Identity* [1997], Vol. 3: *End of Millennium* [1999]), Oxford: Blackwell.

Clark, Tony (2006) *OECD Thematic Review of Tertiary Education – Country Report: United Kingdom*, Department for Education and Skills: Research Report: RR767. [http://www.dfes.gov.uk/rsgateway/]

Featherstone, Mike, Scott Lash and Robert Robertson (1995) *Global Modernities*, London: Sage.

Ferlie, Ewan et al. (1996) *The New Public Management in Action*, Oxford: Oxford University Press.

Florida, Richard L. (2005) *Cities and the Creative Class*, Abingdon, Oxon: Routledge.

Gibbons, Michael, Camille Limoges, Helga Nowotny, Simon Schwartzman, Peter Scott and Martin Trow (1994) *The New Production of Knowledge: The Dynamics of Science and Research in Contemporary Societies*, London/Newbury Park, CA: Sage.

Kelly, Kathryn and Stephen Cook (2007) *Full-time Young Participation by Socio-Economic Class: A New Widening Participation Measure in Higher Education*, Department for Education and Skills: Research Report RR806. [http://www.dfes.gov.uk/rsgateway/]

National Statistics (2006) *Education and Training Statistics for the United Kingdom: 2006 Edition* (Internet only), Issue No. Vweb 03/2006. [http://www.statistics.gov.uk/default.asp/]

Nowotny, Helga, Peter Scott and Michael Gibbons (2001) *Re-Thinking Science: Knowledge and the Public in an Age of Uncertainty*, Cambridge: Polity Press.

Pratt, John and Tyrrell Burgess (1974) *Polytechnics: a report*, London: Pitman.

Power, Michael (1997) *The Audit Society: Rituals of Verification*, Oxford: Oxford University Press.

Ramsden, Brian (2007) *Patterns of Higher Education Institutions in the United Kingdom: Seventh Report*, London: Universities UK/Guild HE.

Robbins Report (1963) *Higher Education* (Report of the Committee on Higher Education, chaired by Lord Robbins), London: Her Majesty's Stationery Office.

Robinson, Eric (1968) *The New Polytechnics*, Harmondsworth: Penguin.

Scott, Peter (1995) *The Meanings of Mass Higher Education*, Buckingham: Open University Press.

Scott, Peter (2005) 'The Opportunities and the Threats of Globalization', in Glen A. Jones, Patricia L. McCarney and Michael L. Skolnik (eds), *Creating Knowledge, Strengthening Nations: The Changing Role of Higher Education*, Toronto: University of Toronto Press.

Scott, Peter (2007) *Demographics and Higher Education in Europe: United Kingdom*, Bucharest: UNESCO/CEPES.

Tapper, Ted (2007) *The Governance of British Higher Education: the struggle for policy control*, Dordrecht: Kluwer.

Trow, Martin (1973) *Problems in the Transition from Elite to Mass Higher Education*, Berkeley, CA: Carnegie Commission on the Future of Higher Education.

4

Nordic Higher Education in Transition

Agnete Vabø and Per Olaf Aamodt

Introduction: Setting the Scene

The central theme of the volume is to analyse how national/regional systems of higher education are adjusting structurally to the current pressures for change. How are they responding to the challenges presented by expansion, globalization, in some cases by radical political and economic development, and everywhere by the rising expectation that higher education needs to contribute more to the welfare of the wider society? This chapter analyses the changing higher education systems of the Nordic countries (Denmark, Finland, Norway and Sweden) with the major emphasis on the Norwegian system. The focus will be on the broad pattern of development over the past fifty years, and placed in the context of the evolving character of the Nordic welfare state. Developments in higher education are part of a wider picture, which reflects new thinking about the scope of the state's social responsibilities and how those responsibilities should be delivered.

Following World War II, and under the leadership of social-democratic governments, the Nordic educational systems – including higher education – played a central role in shaping and cementing the development of national values. The 1960s and 1970s were particularly important periods in this process, which – especially in Norway – was marked by the strength of the egalitarian values underlying the expansion and diversification of the higher education system.

Even though public sector institutions, including universities, were subjected from the late 1980s (as has occurred in most European welfare states) to the introduction of 'New Public Management' principles, the way of organizing and steering higher education remained fairly stable (Bleiklie, Høstaker and Vabø, 2000). In the last few years, however, the Nordic higher education systems have experienced a range of radical reforms. These aim to transform the sector in terms of:

1. Establishing new principles of institutional organization and system steering. This includes changes in the formal relationship between higher education institutions and the state as well as in the structure

of institutional governance (placing external representatives on university boards and limiting the number of representatives elected by academics);

2. Introducing a new funding system linking grants to the production of student credits and the number of research publications;

3. Introducing new degree structures;

4. Exposing higher education in the Nordic countries to the pressures of internationalization.

And very recently higher education policy in all the Nordic countries has shown a marked sympathy towards the development of elitist institutions.

The Nordic Higher Education Systems: The Post-1945 Pattern of Change

Traditional Cultural Values

Given the significant differences between the higher education systems and social structures of the Nordic countries, it is somewhat problematic to treat them as similar systems. Nonetheless, they do have several features in common that help to explain the emergence of a Nordic response to the pressures for transformation.

The higher education systems of the Nordic countries build on a strong relationship between higher education and the state. Universities and colleges are essentially state owned and funded by the state. Their academic employees are civil servants. In the post-war period, egalitarian ideas of higher education as a public good have had a major impact on the policies of the various governments (Välimaa 2005). In contrast to liberal (USA, Canada, Australia) or corporatist welfare state models (France, Germany), the social democratic welfare state model of the Scandinavian countries to a larger extent builds on the universal welfare rights of citizens independent of their economic and occupational status (Korsnes, Andersen and Brante 1997). According to Esping-Andersen (1990) the liberal welfare state model is characterized by targeted distribution to the poorest citizens. The corporatist model relies less on market mechanisms than does the liberal model, but it has a weak discriminatory element in its distribution policies and is strongly family-centered. The third model, typical of the Nordic countries, is related to social democratic policy (in a wide sense) and incorporates the elements of redistribution and universal contributions. Access to and the funding of higher education may also be seen in this context. Higher education institutions were assigned an important role in effecting the central policy goals of the welfare state. However, the egalitarian values mainly concerned access to higher education with the pursuit of research underwritten by more elitist values designed to sustain the principles of scientific quality.

The Pattern of Expansion

In all Nordic countries, higher education has undergone a rapid expansion, starting around 1960 (Aamodt & Kyvik 2005, Kim 2002). In Norway, the number of students increased from about 50,000 in 1971 to more than 200,000 in 2000, but since then, enrollment has been fairly stable (Figure 4.1).

Aamodt & Kyvik (2005) discuss some of the main reasons for this expansion, of which a key factor is the technological development and related changes in the organization of labor, which increases the demand for a higher qualified workforce.

The development of the welfare state does not only constitute the political context for higher education, it has also an independent effect on the demand for more highly educated manpower. For many jobs in the public sector, especially in healthcare, social services and education, formal educational entrance requirements are a necessity. The growth of the welfare state and expansion of public employment has been closely connected to an increasing number of professional workers. This also represents changes in the role of the state: a bureaucratic state becomes a welfare state, and moves towards the construction of a rational and scientifically based system of governance. While the classical professions like law, theology and medicine were connected to the 'old' state, the 'new' state, or more widely the 'new' public sector, has led to an expansion of what may be characterized as 'welfare state workers' (teachers, nurses, other health-related professions, social workers, and all kinds of social scientists) (Eriksen, 2001; Torgersen, 1994).

Thus there has been the growth of a new middle class labelled 'The Professional-Managerial Class' or the 'service class' (Goldthorpe 1982, 2000). This service class consists of both private and public employees and its growth is closely connected to the expansion of higher education. While the

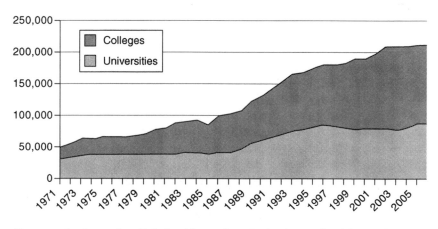

Figure 4.1 Students Enrolled in Norwegian Institutions of Higher Education, 1971–2006.

expansion in higher education has been strong in all European welfare states since the mid-1950s, there have been variations in the rate of expansion, which has certainly not been linear. With a specific focus on the Nordic countries, Aamodt and Kyvik (2005) identified a first wave of expansion from the 1950s to the early 1970s, a stagnation period until the late 1980s, and then a second wave of expansion in the early 1990s. Since then a certain degree of stabilization has been established. The Norwegian trend (Figure 4.1) illustrates the pattern.

The policy solutions and the re-structuring of the higher education system to cope with massification have varied over time and between countries. A general trend, discussed by Martin Trow as early as the 1970s (Trow 1974), is that massification is impossible without increasing the diversity of higher education in response to both a larger student population with an increasing variety of abilities and interests as well as the wide-ranging needs of the labor market. The most common feature in many countries has been the establishment of a sector of institutions as an alternative to the universities.

During the early years expansion took place within the university sector, leading to growth in existing institutions as well as the establishment of new universities. Many universities more than doubled their enrollment in a decade. But very little actually happened to the internal structures: degree programs were mainly unchanged, as were the modes of teaching. Traditionally students combined attendance at lectures (a few hours each week) with self-study, followed by examinations at the end of the year or sometimes even later. This teaching mode was flexible enough to cater for a rapidly growing number of students, but at the same time investments in buildings, administrative infrastructure and the expansion of faculty were sufficient to make this possible. This 'more of the same' mode of growth met with little resistance and, moreover, the creation of new universities was often opposed by the existing universities.

The second stage in the massification process was the establishing of alternative institutions, characterized by more vocationally oriented studies, with smaller research resources than universities and often, but not always, shorter study programs. For example, in Norway, the first new regional colleges were established around 1970, and a number of professional schools (teaching, engineering and later nursing) were upgraded and awarded higher education status. This led to a fragmented structure with a large number of small institutions, and in 1994, about 98 colleges were merged into 26 regionally organized state colleges.

In Finland, an alternative sector, the polytechnics, came into existence 20 years ago but has since grown rapidly. Denmark established a divide between long, medium-long and short study programs rather than creating a distinctive institutional sector, and these alternatives also developed in Sweden under the 'Högskolan' umbrella, either within specific institutions or within the traditional universities. However, if we compare the academic orientation of the various sectors, e.g. the Finnish polytechnics and the Norwegian university colleges, their profiles may vary considerably. For example, the Norwegian university college sector is dominated by the welfare state professions, while the Finnish AMKs (polytechnics) are more oriented towards technology.

With the presence of the 'alternative' sector, different institutional landscapes became visible: binary, unitary or hierarchical. Perhaps more important is how this sector contributed to a broader diversity of study programs. Whether to create a balance between keeping the whole sector together or to create different sectors has, therefore, been a main policy dilemma.

The Bologna Declaration and the Structure of Degree Programs

The third stage has been the reform of degree programs, reforms primarily aimed at changing the university sector, and leading to shorter programs and more efficient progression through those study programs. Two-tier structures came into existence with the option of leaving university and entering the labor market after the completion of the first tier degree, a measure that also went hand in hand with attempts to make this first degree more professional. Although such developments had been going on for many years, these changes were reinforced by the international reform process that was encouraged by the Bologna Declaration. In line with the Bologna Declaration of 1999, the Bachelor/Master degree structure (3+2 years) was implemented at all levels in the Norwegian universities, scientific colleges and state colleges in the autumn of 2003.[1]

Since the 1980s, the duration of studies and the quality of teaching and learning in Norway has been of considerable concern due to the increased number of students at all levels of the higher education system and the corresponding increase in the percentage of those failing exams (Vabø 2000). For the educational authorities, the Bologna process represented a legitimate opportunity to abolish the old study structure and replace it with a degree system more efficient at dealing with the needs of a mass system of higher education. The wish to participate in European student exchange programs had also created a need for more internationally standardized degree programs.

Other factors, such as the need for adjusting studies to the (perceived) needs of society, were also relevant. Norwegian higher education institutions have had a permanent role as social and economic contributors in terms of supplying the market with an appropriate academic labor force. Today, however, this role has intensified, in the process weakening the autonomy of the academic profession. We can now observe more differentiated and shifting conceptions in the public policy debate of the relevance of the academic enterprise. There is a growing concern about the role of research and the part the academic profession should play in helping to sustain economic development. In contrast to its neighbouring countries – Denmark, Finland and Sweden – Norway is still highly dependent upon a raw material based economy (oil, gas and fish). The concern with the future role of higher education in Norway has to be understood against this backdrop; the natural resources are expected to come to an end within the next two generations and it is therefore crucial to remodel the business structure accordingly. A national infrastructure for the support of innovations and entrepreneurship is being developed – including the creation of Technology Transfer Offices ('TTOs') at the universities. Higher education institutions are now expected to take more responsibility for initiating collaboration with the business community. They are also being encouraged to demonstrate the commercial applicability of scientific methods and results (Vabø 2007).

Although all the Nordic countries have adapted their degree structures in line with the recommendations of the Bologna Declaration, we will briefly review the various national responses to show how the actual changes vary greatly from country to country, and are indeed in some cases no more than cosmetic in character. Both in Denmark and Finland there has been a 3+2 structure since the 1990s, which is still in place. Finnish universities nevertheless consider the five-year master's degree as the normal course. The Finnish polytechnics (AMK) offer shorter and more vocationally oriented degrees, and in Denmark the bachelor's degree rarely serves as a final vocational degree. The Finnish implementation, however, also focuses on the quality of the education, with increased emphasis on student guidance and follow-up.

One aspect of the development of the modern mass education systems has been the attempts to eradicate dead ends and to create flexible transitions for students without too much loss of time. In this respect Finland and Norway may be said in a Nordic context to represent opposite extremes. In Finland, the fairly restrictive routines for transition between AMKs and universities have been subject to intense discussion. The structure functions to maintain the differences, but also results in a rigid system. Thus in the Finnish model the university and university college sectors function as two separate qualification pillars, with colleges offering vocationally oriented study programs of short duration whereas the universities offer academically oriented studies of a longer duration. By way of contrast, the developments in Norway in the 1980s gradually went in the direction of a more liberal and flexible regime with rules permitting a greater mix of programs on the basis of a 'time-for-time' principle (Vabø 2002: 151).

Moreover, in Norway, the introduction of the new degree system is part of a larger reform process called 'The Higher Education Quality Reform'. This reform represents an attempt to achieve a higher degree of efficiency through the devolution of authority to the higher education institutions, the provision of stronger leadership, increased emphasis on internationalization, the formation of an autonomous central organization for quality assurance and accreditation as well as the development of criteria for institutional audit, new pedagogical designs along with a new funding model that is supposed to provide stronger incentives for institutions to make improvements.

While certain of the European higher education systems, for example the British models, have had to make few adjustments to the Bologna initiative, since it was actually in line with their structures and practices (Teichler 2005: 104–107), it represented a radical break with many of the traditions in Norwegian higher education. In the political reaction to Bologna, the university boards typically supported the new structure, while claiming that fresh resources were needed in order to implement best practice, such as improving the quality of teaching. Typical opposing arguments are that the assumed higher level of concern with student progress (the new system promises a tighter coupling between student feedback, administrative reaction and course improvement) means less time to do research, with the likelihood of a long-term negative impact upon the teaching and learning process in higher education. The module structure means less (disciplinary) control, both with respect to the content of programs (the syllabus) and the socialization of the students. Modularization and the more frequent evaluation of students are seen as conflicting with the belief that students need time to develop a deeper and more general understanding of the knowledge base of disciplines. The belief, reflected in certain quarters in most of the countries subject to the Bologna process, is that the quality of higher education has become shallower.

The Pressures of Internationalization

From being a highly privatized affair organized nationally, and even locally, the internationalization of higher education has become a major political issue (particularly in Norway) during the last two decades, which has ramifications at both the national and institutional levels. In contrast to the old internationalization, typically initiated and managed by academic staff on an individual basis, the new internationalization has a more formal, institutional and collective character (Trondal et al. 2001). It affects most aspects of higher education: students through their participation in 'study abroad' programs, decisions as where best to undertake research training, its impact upon the criteria for recruitment to academic positions, and its influence upon the content and conduct of academic work – both with respect to teaching and research (Vabø, 2007a,b).

The intention was that the 3+2 Bachelor and Master programs should lead to an increase in international student mobility, with students working for the first degree (the bachelor's degree) having the right to spend a semester abroad during their study period. The Bologna process aimed *inter alia* to develop comparable degree programs, to establish a system of credit transfer (ECST system), to facilitate student and academic staff mobility, and to enhance European cooperation in quality assurance. An increasing number of formal agreements on staff and student mobility have been made with overseas higher education institutions, and a range of study programs now use English in constructing the syllabus and as the teaching language.

Nevertheless, it is important to note that the progress of the internationalization of higher education is far from smooth. The 'new' internationalization activities within higher education are affected by many challenges and obstacles, and it often takes considerable resources to construct something as seemingly straightforward as effective student mobility programs. A recent survey even concluded that academic staff did not consider student mobility as an important ingredient in encouraging quality enhancement in higher education. There is also an important debate about the use of the English language in Nordic higher education. Some argue in favor of the need to sustain a Nordic scientific language from both a democratic perspective as well as a means of securing common access to scientific knowledge. However, for the Nordic and similar countries characterized by fairly small academic bases, it is generally considered to be very important to engage in broad-based movements that encourage academic cooperation.

A Modified Model of Nordic Higher Education?

In spite of the impossibility of shielding the Nordic systems of higher education from the pressures of internationalization, some of the main developments taking place suggest to many that the traditional academic and cultural motives are being supplanted by economic and more market-based interests. Undoubtedly there is, in the Norwegian as well as the wider Nordic context, competition between different discourses on how to internationalize higher education and research with respect to a range of variables: what language should be used, the rationale for cooperation, and to what extent it should be directed towards aiding and showing solidarity with more underdeveloped regions rather than co-operating with nations and their higher education systems that are essentially in 'the Western Bloc'.

It would be dangerous, however, to see the Nordic systems as simply responding to regional political pressures (the Bologna process) and global economic forces. The Bologna process presented a historical opportunity for both universities and colleges to develop and establish many new study programs, both at the bachelor's and master's level. These new programs are thematically very diverse: cultural studies, innovation/entrepreneurialism, health studies, education/learning, management, ICT, new technology, ecological concerns, development studies, area studies (for example, African studies) and even courses that focus on the concerns of particular social groups (feminism and labor history). Thus reformers within the Nordic countries were presented with an opportunity to introduce new curricula and pedagogical methods, an opportunity which they seized.

Furthermore, many of the new programs, often with a science base and inter-disciplinary structure, are seen as necessary to the education of a new professional class. They are perceived as central to the needs of the expanding knowledge society in which there is closer collaboration between higher education and industry. Moreover they often have an international focus both in terms of content (dealing with, for example, global issues such as Maritime Law, Gender and Development, or Peace and Conflict Studies). Invariably they are taught in English and often designed in co-operation with foreign higher education institutions involving the exchange of both staff and students (Vabø 2007).

This development in Nordic higher education is often interpreted as demonstrating the emergence of a new pattern of stratification in higher education, in broad terms distinguishing between academic and vocationally oriented studies. However, a closer investigation of the profile of the new study programs developed recently in Norway calls for a more differentiated theoretical understanding. There are numerous examples of new programs that are not directed towards specific occupational training. The role of higher education is not only to fit people into the vertical occupational structures and systems of social stratification but also to educate them to become effective citizens in various arenas – the political, the economic, the social and the personal. In fact the new programs suggest that higher education has become an instrument of social management. From this perspective higher education is integrated into a globalized mass culture rather than serving local needs and interests (McEneaney and Meyer 2000). It is responding to the emergence of a socially more complex student mass, as well as playing a socializing role with respect to the individual's need for purpose and development. This is expressed through the numerous new areas of study being offered. Typically the new management studies are characterized by curricula designed to suit the interests of the individual student with the intention of securing their engagement, whereas technical knowledge is reduced in favour of more general knowledge presumed to be relevant to a wider range of occupations (transferable skills as opposed to disciplinary knowledge).

This may be interpreted as higher education defining itself more flexibly (it becomes more problematic) as it responds to the demands of students, employers and the public sector for more distinct connections between education and careers (La Pidus 2001: 273–274). In this model of higher education it becomes a continuous lifelong process in which employers are given greater responsibility, and which can best be interpreted as the start of a flexible, if specialized, process of personal development rather than the specialization of the field of study into which the individual is socialized, as being a worthwhile goal in its own right.

We see, therefore, clear examples of universities and colleges responding to the demand for qualifications in new and expanding fields of employment (e.g. in technical subjects which in return may make valuable contributions to local industries). Like Calhoun (2006), one could evaluate positively the new lines of study based on their applicability and alternative modes of assessment: Do the new study programs represent specialist knowledge or knowledge relevant to the wider population? Do they represent traditional authoritative knowledge or knowledge that may contribute to greater social justice and broaden social access to higher education?

The Nordic Higher Education Systems: A New Elitist Model?

The Nordic countries, especially Norway and Sweden, as part of the wider reforms in higher education, upgraded several colleges into universities, and many new master's programs have been developed in the university college sector. There is now (not the least from the political center) a growing concern that this may lead to reduced quality in higher education. Resources are spread out thinly over many small specialist fields, accompanied in some cases by the absence of a research tradition, and the presumption that higher degree programs can tap into resources meant for the undergraduate studies. In line with developments in other European countries, not the least the UK, this has led to an increased focus on developing strategies to improve the concentration of resources, for example by proposing to merge institutions, developing formal networks and encouraging other forms of cooperation. But, as we will see, these developments are tied up with the ambition to have more outstanding research universities that can compete on the international stage.

Since the 1980s, the concern that the Nordic higher education systems need to compete effectively in terms of the global competition that has increasingly enveloped higher education has led to major reforms. The changes taking place in Nordic higher education today incorporate market-oriented modes of governance, performance-based funding, more variety in funding sources, and public–private partnerships within research and researcher training. These are all developments that relate to the same global processes, which are characterized by the gradual de-coupling of the state as guarantor of academic quality, giving governing bodies greater autonomy, viewing higher education as a productive process, and with more power ceded to external stakeholders and administrators as planners and organizers of the academic community (Høstaker and Vabø 2008).

The new lateral forms of management (systems of quality assurance and accreditation and funding based on results) force the higher education institutions to become more pro-active in terms of responding positively to such demands while ensuring their ability to sustain and strengthen their existing research capacity. The need to redefine and reorganize institutions of higher education should be understood against this backdrop. Thus new structures emerge, designed to assess institutional performance, which result in the ranking and differential funding of institutions of higher education.

Although the egalitarian aspects of the Norwegian higher education system could be illustrated by the similar financial and legal conditions that govern the relationship between the state and the institutions, as a social system, higher education will always be characterized by informal hierarchies, given the differences in social and academic status between various disciplinary fields (Bourdieu 1988). Therefore, despite its egalitarian traditions, the academic fields of the Nordic countries are highly asymmetric regarding the distribution of scientific capital and academic reputation (Broady 1991). But the situation has been intensified by the new patterns of institutional stratification, as well as new modes of organizing knowledge production, that follow from the elitist values which now, to a larger extent, make up the framework within which public policy for higher education and research in the Nordic countries is formulated. The establishment, for example, of national elite universities, centers of excellence, PhD schools, the transformation of faculties and basic academic units into 'schools', and the mergers of university departments are invariably justified by the apparent need to create more research-intensive universities. New forms of management, incentive-based funding systems as well as attempts to make a clearer distinction between research and teaching functions are also important aspects of this new framework.

The most distinctive measures so far are the proposals from the Danish and Finnish governments to create new national elite universities. In Finland, a recent proposal from an official working group suggested the merging of the Helsinki University of Technology, the Helsinki School of Economics, and the University of Art and Design of Helsinki. It is argued that this would create a university of international standing as well as benefit the universities themselves and improve Finland's competitive edge in the global economy.

In the spring of 2007, Denmark implemented rather radical mergers within the whole sector of R&D – reducing the number of national research institutes from 25 to 15, and the number of universities from 12 to 5. The University of Copenhagen, Aarhus University and the Technical University of Denmark are supposed to form the center of gravity of the new elite institutions. The radicalism of the reforms is reinforced by the fact that certain former independent research institutes were merged with the universities. Typically, the mergers occurred before any decisions are made about the reorganization of the internal structures of administration and governance. The newly merged higher education institutions are currently working actively to develop new internal structures that hopefully will make the merged institutions a success – the building of new physical facilities, the creation of new research groups, graduate schools, and departments, the development of study programs and the implementation of appropriate incentive structures (Vabø 2007a).

The Norwegian Quality Reform opened up the opportunity for state colleges and specialized universities to get university status based on an accreditation process. The most important criteria for university status are at least five study programs at master's level and four doctoral degrees. Before the reform, Norway had four universities, six specialized university institutions, two colleges for arts, 26 state colleges and 17 private institutions. During the last two years, two state colleges (Agder and Stavanger) and the specialized university institution for agriculture have been granted university status based on these criteria. Furthermore, many other colleges are currently in the process of qualifying for university status, and according to a recent report from a National Commission (NOU 2008), this may lead to a situation where Norway has 12 universities.

The overall diagnosis of the commission report is that Norwegian higher education is fragmented, with many small institutions and units. There is also a strong growth in the number of master's degrees, sometimes with a rather narrow focus, with few students, and weak scientific qualifications of the staff. In the commissioners' opinion, Norway is moving in the opposite direction to most other countries. One of the main proposals from the commission is to create new multi-campus universities in all regions of Norway by merging existing institutions. Some of these new universities will be based on a merger of state colleges, while others will be combinations of both present universities and state colleges.

It is too early to judge the outcome of the policy process and the decisions concerning the future structure of Norwegian higher education. The proposals from the commission have so far been met with rather strong resistance, and it is improbable that this model will be the prevailing one as a whole, but it is possible that some networks of state colleges will emerge to establish new universities.

Unsurprisingly, given the egalitarian culture of Norway, the debate about elite universities has been fierce, and it is the oldest universities that have been the first to adopt a strategy to become more elitist and international in focus. They are introducing more demanding entry requirements for students, by reducing the total number of students and by implementing measures that would enable them to compete for inclusion in the international rankings. Larger university colleges aspire to full university status by recruiting more students at bachelor's level in order to develop and finance the master's and doctoral programs. Small colleges are aiming to specialize in particular niche areas at the undergraduate level (Stensaker and Østergren 2007). Such developments are very likely to result in the creation of a more sharply defined university hierarchy. However, the funding structure set limits on the university strategy of reducing first degree students, since a considerable proportion of their funding come from the credits 'produced' by these students.

It is reasonable to expect that the current prestigious universities will benefit the most from the new policies designed to create a more elitist and sharply differentiated system of higher education (more research-intensive institutions with a selective allocation of resources to support top quality research, attract the most talented researchers and students, and to promote the idea of excellence). In that sense, the elitist turn may also be interpreted as the creation of a legitimate space for universities to reconstitute their relative positions in the national systems of higher education. Also, given the supra-national influence of bodies such as the EU and the Nordic Council of Minis-ters, these processes of change are critical to placing the challenge to Nordic higher education in a comparative perspective.

Such developments are also indicative of how the Nordic model of higher education is part of the wider transition from the welfare state to the welfare society, in which the state expects that higher education institutions will to a much greater extent operate as entrepreneurs in a (global) market. The intro-duction of tuition fees, the establishment of elite institutions, and a stricter selection of students are preparations for such challenges. However, the outcome of these changes remains ambiguous. For instance, given that social inequality rather than the welfare state is seen as a serious threat to economic growth, there is now considerable international interest in the traditional social engineering practices of the Nordic welfare states. For example, their success at combining high birth rates with a significant proportion of women both in higher education and in the labor force has been highlighted. The past, therefore, may still have a great deal to teach the present.

Conclusion

Regarding the expansion process in higher education during the last 50 years, it is our observation that this development in many countries, but not all, has undergone three different stages. The first is the growth of the traditional uni-versities, both within existing institutions and the establishment of new ones. The second stage is the establishment of a new sector of alternative institu-tions, leading to a number of models (e.g. binary or hierarchical). The third stage is related to a series of reforms in the degree structure as well as reforms in teaching, closely linked to the Bologna process. These three stages are clearly visible in all Nordic countries, but not appearing simultaneously and taking different forms.

It is reasonable to conclude that Norway is the Nordic country having under-gone the most radical changes under the umbrella of the Bologna process. From having been characterized as a reluctant reformer, the Norwegian higher educa-tion system has in recent years been subject to radical waves of change. The reforms implemented in 2003 were ambitious in scope, establishing new princi-ples of organizing institutions and steering them politically, a new funding system, new degree structures, new modes of teaching and evaluation, and incorporating various aspects of internationalization as important ingredients.

At present, several developments are taking place. The higher education systems are adjusting both in terms of their structures and academic missions in response to the new demands stimulated by the processes of expansion and globalization. A large number of formal agreements on international staff and student mobility have been made. Many new academic programs have been developed. For instance, cultural studies, studies in entrepreneurship and innovation, and development studies are illustrative of the more universal character of higher education. Some of these changes may also be related to demand for a stronger link between higher education and the labor market, with an increased emphasis on the 'employability' of graduates. The traditionally strong organizational coupling of teaching and research is being loosened, and a stronger divide between lower and higher levels within the systems is developing, for example with the attempts to establish self-contained graduate schools. New forms of stratification emerge, both vertically and horizontally, exemplified most strikingly by developments to establish elite universities and centers of excellence.

The traditional equal status of university institutions once found in the Nordic countries, and also to some extent in Continental Europe, is under pressure. In line with ongoing developments in other Nordic states, a recent white paper on the priorities of Norwegian higher education for the next two decades suggests that in order to enhance quality, there needs to be a continuing merger of colleges and universities accompanied by the further development of centers of excellence and researcher training schools.

From a Nordic perspective, the Norwegian higher education system is fairly young and marked by egalitarian values and a lack of formal institutional hierarchy. Historically, the role of higher education has been central to the implementation of the central policy goals of the welfare state. But, influenced in part by recent international developments in higher education, the debate on the role of higher education and research in society has shown a marked elitist turn, and some interested parties have suggested that the University of Oslo should be granted the status of an elite university. While this development seems less of a problem in Denmark and Finland, such proposals have been met with great resistance in Norway.

In fact, the recent white paper on the future of Norwegian higher education actually rejected the idea of creating a national elite university. But such debates are indicative of the fact that the cultural values are in transition, of a shift from the welfare state to the welfare society, and with the state steadily converted to the idea that higher education institutions should operate as entrepreneurs in a (global) market.

Note

1. Following proposals in a report to the Storting (the Norwegian parliament) on higher education submitted by the Government in March 2001 (report No. 27 to the Storting, 2000–2001).

References

Aamodt, Per Olaf and Svein Kyvik. 'Access to higher education in the Nordic countries.' In *Understanding Mass Higher Education. Comparative perspectives on access*, edited by Ted Tapper and David Palfreyman. London/New York: RoutledgeFalmer, 2005.

Bleiklie, Ivar A., Roar Høstaker and Agnete Vabø. *Policy and Practice in Higher Education.* London: Jessica Kingsley, 2000.

Bourdieu, Pierre. *Homo Academicus.* Stanford: Stanford University Press, 1988.

Broady, Donald. *Sociologi och epistemologi: Om Pierre Bourdieus författarskap och den historiska epistemologin.* Stockholm: HLS förlag, 1991.

Calhoun, Craig. 'The University and the Public Good.' *Thesis Eleven* 84 (1) (2006): 7–43.

Eriksen, Erik O. *Demokratiets sorte hull.* Oslo: Abstrakt forlag, 2001.

Esping-Andersen, Gøsta. *The Three Worlds of Welfare Capitalism.* Cambridge: Policy Press, 1990.

Goldthorpe, John H. 'On the Service class, its formation and future.' In *Social class and the division of labour. Essays in honour of Ilya Neustadt*, edited by Anthony Giddens and Gavin Mackenzie. Cambridge: Cambridge University Press, 1982.

Goldthorpe, John, H. *On Sociology. Numbers, Narratives, and the Integration of Research and Theory.* Oxford: Oxford University Press, 2000.

Høstaker, Roar and Agnete Vabø. 'Knowledge, society, higher education and the society of control.' *Learning and Teaching* 1 (1) (2008): 122–154.

Kim, L. *Lika olika.* Stockholm: Högskoleverket Report, 2002.

Korsnes, Olav, Heine Andersen and Thomas Brante (eds). *Sosiologisk leksikon.* Oslo: Universitetsforlaget, 1997.

LaPidus, Jules B. 'Graduate Education and Research.' In *In Defense of American Higher Education*, edited by Philip G. Altbach, Patricia J. Gumport and D. Bruce Johnstone. Baltimore: The John Hopkins University Press, 2001.

McEneaney, Elizabeth H. and John W. Meyer. 'The Content of the Curriculum. An Institutionalist Perspective.' In *Handbook of the Sociology of Education*, edited by Maureen T. Hallinan. New York: Kluwer Academic/Plenum Publishers, 2000.

NOU. *Sett under ett: ny struktur i høyere utdanning.* National Commission report. Oslo, Ministry of Education and Research, 2008.

Stensaker, Inger and Katarina Østergren. 'Strategic responses to the Quality Reform. A comparative study of changes in Norwegian Higher Education.' Manuscript prepared for the biannual conference, Bergen 2007. Bergen: Norges Handelshøyskole, 2007.

Teichler, Ulrich. 'New Patterns of Diversity in Higher Education: Towards a Convergent Knowledge.' In *Governing Knowledge: A Study of Continuity in Higher Education*, edited by Ivar Bleiklie and Mary Henkel. Dordrecht: Springer, 2005.

Torgersen, Ulf. *Profesjoner og offentlig sektor.* Oslo: Tano, 1994.

Trondal, Jarle et al. *Internasjonalisering av høyere utdanning. Trender og utfordringer.* Oslo: NIFU skriftserie 28, 2001.

Trow, Martin. 'Problems in the Transition from Elite to Mass Higher Education.' In *Policies for Higher Education, from General Report on Future Structures of Post-Secondary Education.* Paris: OECD, 1974.

Vabø, Agnete. *Mytedannelser i endringsprosesser i akademiske institusjoner.* Rapport 1/2002. Bergen: Stein Rokkan senter for flerfaglig samfunnsforskning, 2002.

Vabø, Agnete. 'Globalisering av høyere utdanning – utdanningssosiologiske perspektiver og utfordringer.' In *Arbeid, kunnskap og sosial ulikhet*, edited by Johs Hjellbrekke, Ole Johnny Olsen and Rune Sakslind. Oslo: Unipub, 2007a.

Vabø, Agnete 'Research intensive universities: On limits and possibilities.' Paper presented at the CHER conference. Dublin, 2007b.

Välimaa, Jussi. 'Globalization in the concept of Nordic higher education.' In *Globalization and Higher Education*, edited by Akira Arimoto, Futao Huang, and Keiko Yokoyama. International Publication Series No. 9. Hiroshima: Research Institute for Higher Education (RIHE), 2005.

Wendt, Kaja (ed.). *Det norske forsknings- og innovasjonssystemet – statistikk og indikatorer 2007* [*The Norwegian research and innovation system – statistics and indicators 2007*]. Oslo: The Research Council of Norway, 2007.

5

Latin American Higher Education
Hope in the Struggle?

Alma Maldonado-Maldonado

Setting the Scene

The Socio-Economic and Political Context

Democratic systems in Latin America are still recent. In Peru, only in 1980 did the military government give way to civil government. In Argentina, the first free elections took place only in 1983 after a period of military rule. Brazil finally had a civil president in 1985, after a long period of political instability. In Uruguay, the military regime ended in 1985, while in Chile the Pinochet government ended as recently as 1989. After 75 years of same-party rule in Mexico, a different political party finally won the presidency in 2000. The social, political and electoral institutions are still young and in many cases weak and unstable. Another absurd situation is the extreme, and in some cases, absolute power elites can hold in Latin America.

Indeed, although some countries (e.g., Costa Rica) have had more political stability than others, on average Latin American democratic regimes are still in a process of consolidation. Several crises and social conflicts, including civil wars, have accompanied the evolution of the political systems in the region. Understanding the political context in Latin America and the importance of political power is crucial to analyzing the situation of higher education institutions, and the role that they have played in the region.

In addition to the political situation, the economic context in the continent is markedly unstable with perhaps the greatest inequalities in the distribution of wealth and income in the world. High inflation and devaluation are two constants in the economic history of Latin America and, even considering all the range of differences amongst the Latin American countries, the whole region of Latin America could be defined by its socio-economic imbalances, inequalities and contradictions.

The Latin American countries are located at the high to medium levels of human development, and no individual Latin American country is located at the lowest level (United Nations Development Program, 2006). However, based on the Human Development Indicators, Latin America seems to be the most unequal region in the world – even more so than Africa, which is in

73

general a poorer continent but with fewer contrasts among its population. On the Gini index, which measures the income inequalities in a country, in a ranking of 124 countries 11 Latin American countries rank between 100 and 124 where the country located first indicates the least inequality and the last the highest inequality. Obviously, national socio-economic disparities are also reflected in the educational systems, including the higher education systems.

According to the World Bank, from 1990 to 2004 the number of poor people did not decline in Latin America. Moreover, from 1995 to 2005 there has been a slight decline in Latin America's employment-to-population ratio, indicating that although "there has been job creation, it has been insufficient to absorb the growing labor force" (International Labor Organization, 2005: 33).

A recent special issue of *The McKinsey Quarterly* identifies one of the three major challenges in Latin America as "insufficient education." The other two are "economic disparity" and "a business environment that drives entrepreneurs into the informal economy" (*The McKinsey Quarterly*, 2007). The Economic Commission for Latin America and the Caribbean (ECLAC) provides another depressing social indicator, claiming that "on average, close to 37% of Latin American adolescents between 15 to 19 years of age drop out of school at some point in the school cycle" (ECLAC, 2002: 103). Actually, following estimates by the International Labor Organization (2005) and the UNESCO's Latin American Higher Education Institute (IESALC, 2006) (IESALC being its Spanish acronym), in 2003 approximately 42,865,000 young people in Latin America were neither studying nor working. If almost 43 million young people do not work or study in Latin America, what do they do? This chapter explores the role higher education has played in this difficult context and what the sector's challenges are in response to this situation.

Between Tradition and Reform

Edmundo O'Gorman (1984) points out that more than being discovered, the Americas were invented. He was referring to the ideals, desires and ventures projected onto the new continent from the old world. He discusses the main differences between Anglo-Saxon culture compared to the cultures of the Spanish and Portuguese in terms of their processes of colonization. Although it is impossible to generalize about Latin American colonization, *mestizaje* (racial and cultural mixing) and *isolation* are the two main keys to understanding the patterns of colonization, since they represent the extremes of how the colonizers related to the indigenous population: either they mixed with the indigenous peoples, exterminated them or simply kept their societies separate.

History always provides elements to interpret the present. In this case the colonization processes of the Americas shaped in many ways the development of the socio-political cultures and created their most significant institutions.

Unsurprisingly, the history of universities in the region shares this colonial heritage. Unlike the Portuguese, English or Dutch, the Spaniards decided to establish universities on the continent. They established the first universities in Santo Domingo (1538), Lima (1551), and Mexico City (1551) (Perkin, 1991; Tünnermann, 1991). By way of comparison, the important US universities were created much later (e.g., Harvard in 1636 and Yale in 1701). Spaniards used the Universities of Salamanca and Alcalá as models for founding universities in the new territories (Figueiredo-Cowen, 2002; Perkin, 1991). By the time North America was discovered, Spain had the largest empire in the world. The Spanish idea of colonizing the new world was to extend Spain's dominance in all possible dimensions (religion, culture, language). One way to pursue this colonization was to pay considerable attention to the training and education of the Spanish descendents (called *criollos*) who were born in the new world. This was achieved by establishing different types of educational institutions, which included pontifical universities. Approximately "25 universities were created in Hispanic America by the Catholic Church and the Crown in colonial times" (Bernasconi, 2007b: 27).

However, it is only in the historic national universities (e.g. in Argentina, Mexico, Peru, Venezuela, the Dominican Republic, Guatemala, or Paraguay) that it is possible to distinguish some remnants of the tradition of the pontifical universities, and then mainly at the symbolic level. After the countries' independence (mostly between the years 1810 to 1820), the new model adapted to reopen universities was brought from post-revolutionary France, which is the reason for describing them as Napoleonic (with an emphasis on professional higher education, and with a division between teaching faculties and research centers) (Figueiredo-Cowen, 2002). To discuss the historical development of the university model in Latin America would be a major undertaking. However, most of the main consequences of the later stages of this development are analyzed in this chapter.

Certainly, Latin American higher education institutions have played a major role in the development of the nation states by shaping the systems of national and local government, educating the elites, and nurturing the national cultures and consciousnesses (Rodríguez and Casanova, 1994; Torres, 1994). Ordorika and Pusser (2007) have used the concept of the "nation-building university" to describe the role these institutions have had on the public. Today, Latin American higher education represents a diversified system that is continually growing (IESLAC, 2006). It is composed of numerous institutional varieties of higher education (for example, universities, technological and professional centers, and higher education institutes among others). Options have expanded with increasing enrollment, the variety both responding to and helping to create demand.

Some studies have analyzed the evolution of Latin American higher education by attempting to characterize stages in the evolution of the systems.

According to Rama (2006) the first reform stage related to university autonomy and the links to the state; the second reform stage was about increasing market pressures and the establishment of a dual system of public and private institutions; and the third stage focused on the development of quality assurance strategies and the internationalization of higher education.

Other authors have classified the systems according to various defining characteristics: size, type of institution, financing or missions. For example, García Guadilla suggests categorizing institutions by the size of enrollment. Using this criteria, the mega systems (over one million students) are Brazil, Argentina and Mexico; the large systems (from 500,000 to one million students) include Colombia, Peru and Venezuela; the medium-sized systems (from 150,000 to 500,000 students) are Bolivia, Chile, Ecuador and Cuba; finally, the small systems (under 150,000 students) are Costa Rica, El Salvador, Guatemala, Honduras, Nicaragua, Panama, Paraguay, the Dominican Republic and Uruguay (García Guadilla, 2000). Again, rather than exploring the typology or classification of Latin American higher education institutions, this chapter discusses its internal tensions, challenges and transformation.

Not surprisingly, therefore, the development of higher education in Latin America has not been exempt from the crises and tensions endemic to its diverse colonial history, turbulent political development and challenging economic context. However, rather than focusing on the development of Latin American higher education systems, this chapter discusses the main challenges for higher education institutions in this region. Latin American higher education systems have been struggling with massive demographic pressures and the high expectation that expansion will bring tangible benefits. Because of the particular colonial heritage, the economic constraints, the instability of political regimes and the fragility of social institutions, the responses from the institutions of higher education to the challenges they face have so far been limited. The topics of access, finance, state co-ordination, national developments in research, and the pressures of globalization are essential to understanding the current crisis in Latin American higher education. These will be the main themes covered in this chapter. It is within the context created by these pressures that the systems of higher education in Latin America are evolving and will continue to develop; they set the framework for structural change.

Responding to Access Demands

Brunner points out that higher education in Latin American was massified in spite of the market. For example, in 1950, adult illiteracy rates for the region were almost 50%. A major literacy effort took place over the following 20 years; this effort coincided with the expansion of higher education, and by 1970 the illiteracy rate had fallen to 18% (Brunner, 1987: 29). And according to Mollis:

In 1950, there were approximately 1.5 million students in higher education; in 1995 more than eight million ... In 1950, there were 105 universities in Latin America, and by the 1990s there were over 700, among more than 2,500 institutions of higher learning, including teacher colleges, technical institutes and junior colleges.

(2006: 504)

More recently, Latin American enrollment in higher education has increased from 7.5 million in 1994 to 13.8 million in 2003 (IESALC, 2006). According to the Task Force on Higher Education and Society, "in 1995 more than 47 million students were enrolled in higher education in [the] developing world, up from nearly 28 million in 1980" (2000: 27). Thus higher education enrollment in Latin America represents about 27% of enrollment in the developing world (García Guadilla, 2006). Naturally, it is necessary to make distinctions among both countries and institutions. Mexico, Brazil and Argentina are the countries with the largest number of students, while the countries with fewest students are the Central American nations (6% of the total), and the Latin American Caribbean (with less than 1%).

The decision to expand access to higher education institutions in Latin America has to be understood as the response by government and society to the growing demand for education. Given the population growth, the demand for higher education has increased in recent decades. Since Latin American governments have been unable to open more institutions, the responses to this demand have been met by opening more private higher education institutions, establishing more non-university institutions and, more recently, allowing international providers to offer higher education programs by directly buying institutions or establishing joint degree programs between local institutions and international partners.

During the 1980s, a period characterized by economic crises in Latin America, international organizations were particularly active in the region. The International Monetary Fund (IMF), the World Bank, the Inter-American Development Bank (IDB), the Economic Commission for Latin America (ECLAC) were suggesting, and in some cases imposing, the application of structural adjustment plans, the main goal of which was the reduction of public funding at all levels within the educational systems. In higher education this meant, besides a reduction in state financial support for public institutions, drastic changes in the way these institutions were financed, the imposition of more accountability mechanisms, and the redirection of public funds from public universities to vocational schools (Winkler, 1994; World Bank, 1994).

Table 5.1 shows the increase of the enrollment at non-university higher education institutions. A clear example of this particular shift is Mexico. In a period of 14 years only three new public universities were founded, while 45 technological institutions or centers and 35 private higher education

Table 5.1 Enrollments at Non-University Institutions of Higher Education

Country	1994	1999	2003	
			Enrollment	As % of Total Higher Education Enrollment
Argentina	395,000	395,000	530,000	26
Bolivia	20,000	21,000	23,000	8
Chile	120,000	122,000	160,000	29
Colombia	121,000	150,000	190,000	18
Mexico	120,000	240,000	235,000	11
Paraguay	10,000	20,000	30,000	29
Peru	310,000	360,000	390,000	45
Uruguay	7,000	9,000	11,000	15
Venezuela	220,000	260,000	395,000	40
Total	1,323,000	1,577,000	1,964,000	23.4

Note
Constructed by author from González, 2006: 187.

institutions (university and non-university) were established in the same period (Organization for Economic Co-operation and Development – OECD, 2004).

Defining private institutions in Latin America is less problematic than in other regions around the world since most private higher education institutions do not receive direct public financing (Maldonado et al., 2004). However, the situation is changing, because there are currently more private institutions receiving public subsidies or indirect public funds through the competition for particular projects. According to García Guadilla,

> the private sector in the region has grown very significantly during the last three decades, increasing from 31% of the establishments in 1960 to 54% in 1995. In turn, enrollments more than doubled over that period, increasing from 15% to 38%.
>
> (2006: 25)

Besides the different characteristics of the public and private systems, there has also been a historical tension between the two sectors, for example in the competition for prestige or for student enrollment. According to García Guadilla (2006: 251) between the period 2000 and 2002 most countries showed enrollments in private institutions of 40% and beyond. Countries included within this group are: Brazil, Chile, Colombia, El Salvador, Costa Rica, Paraguay, the Dominican Republic, Venezuela, Nicaragua and Peru. Only Cuba reports less than 10% of their enrollment in the private higher education sector.

One of the main concerns regarding the expansion of the private higher education sector in Latin America has to do with the quality of education. Most of the private institutions are considered to be of low-quality, "garage institutions" or "unsupervised institutions" (Mollis, 2006)

An important element in any discussion of higher education access in Latin America is the impact of unemployment. The rates of unemployment in the region are disturbing. According to Hopenhayn, "young people [aged 19 to 24] account for about 50% of all unemployed workers in nearly every country in the region." Indeed, in the region "the youth unemployment rate is twice the overall unemployment rate and three times the rate for adults; in some countries it is as high as five times the rate for adults over age 45" (Hopenhayn, 2002: 1). So a major problem in the region is not only what to do with the young people who are unable to access higher education and are unemployed, but also, what are the chances of higher education graduates finding a job once they finish their studies? Thus Castro and Levy's (2000) examination of the need for professional education to train people for specific occupations; although they emphasize the current disconnection between the education provided and the labor markets.

A major question is who are the individuals who can access higher education in Latin America. In this regard, it is evident that income and cultural capital impact upon the stratification of access and employability. For instance, according to Hopenhayn,

in Honduras in 1997, the unemployment rate for the first income quartile was 13.1 times higher than the rate for the fourth quartile (the highest income level) [...] In Brazil, circa 1997, youth unemployment was 10.1% in the fourth quartile, compared to 22.7% in the first quartile.

(2002: 3)

The fact that there has been a recent reduction in birth rates across the region does not mean the pressures for access to higher education and employment in Latin America will not continue to intensify given the current age distribution of the population (Villa & Rivadeneira, 2001).

One of the challenges regarding higher education access is how to plan and sustain the enrollment of students in systems with limited resources inside, and by no means certain employment opportunities for their graduates outside. The debate between satisfying the demand for traditional professions in Latin America (lawyers or administrators) versus the need to respond to the demands of the local labor markets generates a permanent tension in most Latin American countries. This discussion includes economic, political, social, and also moral dilemmas. In most Latin American countries, a non-university career has less prestige than a university career (which does not necessarily translate into worse employment opportunities). Those with low income and less cultural capital have less freedom to pursue a university degree or follow a professional career. Consequently, the destiny of the large majority of the population living in poor conditions is already set.

Nonetheless, an important consideration to take into account is the role of Latin American universities in enhancing the social mobility of their graduates, especially the first generation students. In most Latin American countries, higher education represents a big chance, sometimes the only chance, for social mobility, even more so in the context where the economies are increasingly driven by knowledge production (Slaughter and Rhoades, 2004).

Mexico provides some important examples of the issue of social mobility. For instance, in 1996, 72% of the parents of incoming college students at the Universidad Nacional Autónoma de Mexico (UNAM) were reported as either retired, unemployed, farmers, low skilled workers or housekeepers (UNAM, 1996). In a more recent report, de Garay (2006) points out that after having studied 80 higher education institutions in Mexico, that while 85% of incoming students at public universities are first generation, about 87% of those attending the prestigious private universities are second generation students. Naturally every Latin American case is different. Stratification is presented in varying ways depending on the socio-economic context and the public/private distribution of the enrollment.

The responses from governments to inequalities have been also different. One strategy has been the establishment of affirmative action policies for the admission processes. For instance, Brazil has started such policies based on race or low-income student quotas (Schwartzman, 2004, 2007). Venezuela is also applying parallel strategies such as the program "Higher Education for All" (Muhr and Verger, 2006)

However, these initiatives have resulted from the political will of key actors and the particular historical juncture of these nations. Such efforts are needed in more spaces and for longer time periods in all the regions, otherwise they will remain no more than anecdotes.

The Tension between Funding and Equity

Economic constraints have been a constant feature of the Latin American higher education system. The key issues associated with the financing of higher education in Latin America are:

1. Achievement of more equal access in the context of the scarcity of resources;
2. Privatization of the system;
3. The political use of financing;
4. Efficient and transparent institutional management of resources.

An examination in 2002 of the financing of higher education as a percentage of the country's GDP reveals that Venezuela and Cuba have the highest relative expenditures (over 2%), while the Dominican Republic (.27), Guatemala (.28), Uruguay (.40) and Colombia (.71) have the lowest. In general most countries, except Argentina, Costa Rica and Panama, have increased their expenditure percentages since 1990. However, the overall average of higher education expenditure is still well below other OECD countries (García Guadilla, 2006; UNESCO, 2006).

Public financing covers the largest percentage of higher education financing, and it seems unlikely that this will change in the short term. According to Rodríguez, the largest percentage of higher education financing in Latin America comes from the state. In the cases of Panama, Costa Rica, Uruguay, and the Dominican Republic higher education institutions receive more than 80% of their funding from the public purse. However, for Argentina, Bolivia and Colombia the figure goes from 79% to 70%, with additional funding coming mainly from resources generated by the institutions themselves (Rodríguez, 2006: 75). It seems unlikely that this regional dependence primarily on public financing will change in the short term.

Discussing public expenditure per higher education student, García Guadilla affirms that the regional average in 2002 was US$2,381. Expenditure per student ranges from below US$700 (the Dominican Republic, Guatemala and Bolivia) to over US$3,000 (Brazil, Mexico, Cuba and Venezuela) (García Guadilla, 2006: 254). These numbers reflect both the economic differences between countries and the disparities in the priority given to higher education expenditure. In 2004 the average expenditure per student for OECD countries was about US$14,000. The OECD also reports that in public institutions the average estimate for the same year was US$11,500 compared to Brazil US$9,000, Chile US$6,500 and Mexico US$5,900 (OECD, 2007). It is very important to mention that the great contrast in terms of expenditure reflects the differences between research and teaching higher education institutions. While the second average reported by OECD in 2007 shows the expenditures only in public institutions (most of them being research universities), the first numbers, reported by García Guadilla, present the expenditure per student in all types of higher education institutions in a country (most of them being teaching institutions). In other words, the expenditure per student in a research university is almost double (or more) the expenditure per student in a teaching institution in the region.

Given that higher education access in Latin America is insufficient to meet the needs of the region, the input of additional resources has often functioned as a control mechanism designed to transform the higher education institutions in the region. For example, privatization is directly related to the financing of higher education. In Latin America privatization can be understood as two different things: the growth of private higher education institutions or the increase of private and market mechanisms to finance higher education institutions, including public institutions (Altbach, 1999). There are several examples of both in Latin America. In some countries private institutions have started to receive public funds, either directly (e.g., Chile) or indirectly (e.g., Mexico). On the other hand, all higher education institutions have increased the implementation of market practices and the commercialization of services, such as expanding the number of *diplomados* and professional training programs, charging for the use of laboratories and the renting of university premises.

In a context where the most important universities, socio-politically and historically speaking, are public institutions there is a critical debate about the public benefits of private institutions. In this respect each Latin American country deserves its own particular analysis given their unique traditions and local characteristics. For instance, some nations such as Brazil and Colombia, have a long tradition of private higher education, while in others, such as Uruguay, this is a new development. However, there is a clear increase in low-quality private institutions, which most of the students of low-socio-economic status attend. Since, as stated earlier, economic circumstances and cultural capital influence access to higher education, these students have difficulty accessing the most privileged institutions (private and public).

In various ways privatization is compatible with the agendas of international organizations. The strategies have followed the same pattern: first, show the failure of the public management of state-owned companies, such as financial irresponsibility, large bureaucracies and corruption. Then, given these failures, privatization of these companies is justified as the only survival mechanism. This formula has been applied in many sectors, particularly those related to the regional energy and the oil industries. In higher education, it is implemented by the incorporation of more managerial instruments, whose origins are to be found in the private sector.

There is one interpretation of the changes that helps us to understand the wider implications of the movement towards privatization in higher education that is, the idea of academic capitalism as developed by Slaughter and Rhoades (2004). It defines the knowledge/learning regime where colleges and universities have become more entrepreneurial within the development of the post-industrial economy. Within academic capitalism, knowledge is viewed less as a public good and more as a commodity to be capitalized on in profit-oriented activities. This theory has been mainly applied to high-income economies, where knowledge plays a more important role. Yet, the phenomenon is also visible in some Latin American countries where due to insufficient public resources universities have been moving towards profit-oriented activities. In Latin American this expression is still limited but, nonetheless, the region in general has adopted more market-oriented policies than in the past.

Some of the problems regarding the financing of higher education have to

do with the <u>management of resources</u>. <u>Excessive centralization and corrup-</u>
<u>tion</u> are two of the main problems widely shared by Latin American higher
education institutions. There has been a general lack of transparency, which
has led to the implementation of mechanisms designed to establish greater
accountability (Mollis, 2006). Because research public universities in Latin
America are still regarded as an engine for national development and a
mechanism for social mobility, it is an enormous challenge for them to
demonstrate the improvement of their efficiency and their ability to achieve
their goals. Besides conducting research and teaching, universities in Latin
America have incorporated, at least since Latin American countries became
independent nations, "dissemination" as one of their missions. Originally
"dissemination" meant promoting literacy programs in rural and poor
communities, sending groups of students and teachers to teach citizens how
to read and write. Since then, dissemination has meant spreading the scientific knowledge they produce to the wider society, and also spreading high
culture to the population at large by making it accessible to all societal groups.
Given this legacy, it is critical for higher education institutions to demonstrate
their financial probity and good management.

State Co-ordination: Evaluation and Accreditation

Since the 1980s the implementation of evaluation policies (which are invariably attached to additional economic resources) has become a key control
mechanism in Latin American higher education systems. Evaluation has functioned as the engine to transform both the systems and the institutions, but it
has not been without negative consequences. The policies are not always co-
coordinated and sometimes are even contradictory to other programs.
Mexico, for example, provides an excellent example of the creation of ineffec-
tive evaluation programs at all levels and sectors within the educational
system (Casanova, 2006; Ibarra Colado, 1993).

Neave affirms that the impulse for the creation of the evaluative state "had
its immediate origins in the general public expenditure crisis" (1998: 273).
One of the features of the "evaluative state" is the creation of many intermediate bodies between the state and the higher education institutions. They
have different structures, organizations and purposes, but share the common
goal of taking responsibility for quality assurance procedures relating to the
teaching and learning process. Some evaluative bodies share nomenclature as
well as general purposes. Most Latin American countries have established
intermediate bodies in order to develop, promote, and achieve evaluation
mechanisms. Some of these bodies are specialized in modes of accreditation,
while others are dedicated to evaluating specific populations, such as faculty
or students (Fernández Lamarra, 2006).

Where the emphasis has been upon following quantitative indicators, as is
generally the case, other important aspects of higher education – the nature of

the teaching and learning process including the individual contact with students, and the actual content and relevance of published research – may be overlooked. For example, several studies in Mexico have shown that there is a tendency to ignore how the essential aspects of academia, like educating students and producing knowledge, actually impacts upon the social realities of Latin American countries (Díaz Barriga, 1993; 1995).

Because of their complex political situations Latin American universities have fought to preserve the idea of autonomy as a necessary characteristic of their identity. This began with the Reforma Movement in 1918 in Cordoba, Argentina, subsequently spreading to Peru, Chile, Cuba, Colombia, Guatemala and Uruguay (Arocena & Sutz, 2005). A second wave of reforms involved universities from Brazil, Paraguay, Bolivia, Ecuador, Venezuela and Mexico (Marsiske, 1999). It is only since the implementation of evaluation policies in the 1980s that the state has started to exercise more direct policy control over higher education than at any time in the past (Mendoza Rojas, 2002). Latin American governments have learnt that through evaluative mechanisms they have been able to reduce institutional decision-making spaces. Under the umbrella of the evaluation discourse and in the pursuit of quality, governments have been able to promote the idea that higher education institutions should be accountable and adapt their practices to incorporate the evaluation culture. In many ways evaluation has been the ideal mechanism for exercising control because of its connection with public financing: if institutions, groups or individuals want additional resources they need to participate in the evaluation programs.

The idea of establishing a new means of coordination through linking financial resources to evaluation results may require a new social contract, one that redefines the relationships among state, government and society. Increasing accountability in institutions may be positive as long as it comes together with a real drive to improve the higher education systems. Indeed, more public resources are required but the problem goes beyond making additional resources available. It requires a discussion of the merits of different national higher education projects, the incorporation of institutional quality procedures and an analysis of how higher education institutions can best accomplish their missions.

Research and Nation Building in Latin America

There are two main issues that are relevant to the role of research and technology in national development in Latin America: the marginal role of science and research within the higher education systems, and a lack of effective organization of scientific research. There are very few resources, problems in the organizational infrastructure, insufficient governmental interest in investing in these areas, and – not surprisingly – few returns (Cetto and Vessuri, 1998).

Assuming knowledge production is a key element in the economic growth of developing countries, especially middle-income economies (UNESCO, 1992), Latin America lags behind other regions, as measured by indicators such as the number of patents registered, the development of graduate programs, and the training of researchers. In 1995, there were 185,393 graduate students in Latin America, about 75.6% of them in public institutions. In the period 2000–2002 there were 535,198 graduate students, 68.4% in public institutions (García Guadilla, 2006: 253). This represents an important increase, but the growth has been faster in the private sector. This could be of problematic benefit considering that most of the private graduate programs concentrate on social and administrative areas and less on scientific ones. If Latin American countries need to produce more applied scientific research, this requires the training of more scientists. In this case, therefore, the growth of graduate education in the private sector may not have been entirely useful.

In terms of postgraduate enrollment, as a percentage of total enrollment, there are considerable variations, ranging from Cuba with 7.7% to El Salvador with only 1.1%. For Venezuela, Mexico and Colombia the figure ranges from 7% to 5%, with 4% for Panama and 3.3% for the Dominican Republic. The rest of the countries have less than 3%: Brazil (2.8%), Chile (2.6%), Honduras (2.5%), Guatemala (1.5%), and Bolivia (1.4%). However, it is very important to consider the overall dimensions of the differing systems, including their quality and areas of specialization. For example, 2.8% of total enrollment in Brazil, with approximately 107,400 graduate students, is very different from the 4% figure in Panama, with about 5,340 graduate students (Rama, 2006: 76).

Another indicator of a country's research capacity is the number of researchers in the general population. Cuba is by far the top country in Latin America with 2,633 researchers per million inhabitants. The figure for Argentina is 539, Chile 459, Brazil 221, and Mexico 212, with Ecuador and Panama having the lowest figures, 42 and 31, respectively (Cetto & Vessuri, 1998). In comparison, the USA has 3,694 scientists per million inhabitants while Canada has 2,241. Again the numbers reflect the disparities among Latin American countries, and the inequalities between them and developed countries. It is also important to note that, as is the case with other Latin American data, there are discrepancies between different sources.

Most countries invest less than 0.4% of their GDP in R&D. For comparison, the US invested 2.26% (OECD, 2005). The contribution to R&D from government funding ranges from 90% in Ecuador to 13% in Colombia. In Bolivia, Colombia, and Uruguay private industry is the main source of funds, while Panama is a peculiar case as most of its R&D funding comes from abroad (UNESCO, 2006).

Finally, the number of patents and publications reported at the Science Citation Index (SCI) and the Social Science Citation Index (SSCI) show the marginal position worldwide of most Latin American higher education institutions – with perhaps the exception of Brazil (Bernasconi, 2007a; Steiner, 2007). Regarding patents registered in the US, for the period from 1977–2004, El Salvador, Guatemala and Honduras registered the lowest numbers: 17, 38 and 19 patents respectively. Argentina, Mexico and Brazil registered the highest numbers: 881, 1,561 and 1,713 respectively. Taking an international comparison, during the same period China registered 2,593, India 1,921 and the US 1,725,549.

A possible solution to addressing the shortage of scientific infrastructure in Latin America is to make strategic decisions as to which areas should be supported. Thus a major challenge is how to take advantage of areas that are already well developed, and how to reduce the gap in knowledge production between developed and developing countries. However, this is an important debate, and there is no clear agreement about the role of research universities in developing countries as well as what their wider role in these societies should be (Altbach, 2007). For Latin American universities, as the dissemination of knowledge and culture is part of their traditional missions, it may make more sense to consider this dimension in any discussion of the future role of higher education institutions in the promotion of research and technology in the region.

Globalization and Local Necessities

In an era where regions such as Europe are transforming their higher education systems in response to the pressures of the knowledge economy and globalization (Ginés Mora, 2007), the question of how Latin America is reacting to these new challenges is important. Responding to both local necessities and globalization is a major challenge for higher education in this region.

Following Knight's definition (2006), there are essentially two interconnected types of cross-border education: the movement of people (e.g. students or faculty) and the movement of instruction (e.g. programs or institutions). Both types exist in Latin America, but yet again there are important variations, depending on the country and local context.

The intrusion of the international providers of higher education parallels the expansion of the private higher education sector in the region. Clearly, the state's responsibility for ensuring access to higher education is in decline for both privileged and low-income populations. Besides the direct participation of foreign universities, several collaborative agreements have been signed between Latin American universities and international partners.

According to Didou (2005), the total number of relationships reported between Latin American countries and foreign higher education institutions – other Latin American nations included – is almost 1,100. The four modes of operation are: distance education, franchises along with the setting up of campuses, alliances, and agreements. European providers are the majority within the mode of distance education (approximately 54), presumably with the majority from Spain. In the case of franchises and setting up campuses the US has 28 institutions operating in Latin America, while the second place is for other Latin American institutions working in the region (13). There are only nine European providers in this mode. Alliances and agreements are clearly the largest forms of co-operation with about 125 alliances and approximately 816 agreements. The reason for such large numbers in these categories is because their nature is more diverse and they are less demanding forms of commitment.

Cross-border education also impacts upon emigration issues and transnational activities with both negative and positive consequences. Of the Latin American students studying abroad, 61% go to other countries in the Americas, 36% to Europe, and only 2% to Oceania and 1% to Asia. The main destinations in the Americas for Latin American students are the US (about 80%) and Cuba 11%. The leading countries in Europe where Latin Americans study are Spain (32%), France (19%), and the UK (14%) (Didou, 2006: 25). The imbalances amongst the Latin American countries in terms of the number of international students hosted are illustrated in Table 5.2.

One of the most important risks in relying on international institutions to provide higher education is the possibility of encouraging a "brain drain." Latin American countries are losing highly skilled professionals, a problem that has been largely ignored. An example is Mexico with 8% of all Mexican scientists working in the United States, which outnumbers Canada's loss of 6% (OECD, 2005). As Mexico has almost 2,000 fewer researchers per million inhabitants than Canada, this represents a serious drain of resources. Another example is Brazil: in 1999–2000 there were 1,273 Brazilian scientists working in the US; in contrast Spain, with a larger base of researchers, had 1,729 (OECD, 2005).

The pressures of globalization upon higher education in Latin America have to be placed in the context of broader initiatives to develop the region, such as the so-called "Washington Consensus" (introduced by the World Bank in 1989 – see Williamson, 2000) and the creation of the Free Trade Area of the Americas (FTAA). However, the Washington Consensus failed in part, according to the former chief economist of the World Bank, Joseph Stiglitz, because it never was a "consensus," but an imposition (Gorostiaga, 2000: 25). The FTAA was created in 1994 when the heads of state of 34 democracies in the region agreed to build a continental free trade area (FTAA, 2006). Initially, they agreed to complete negotiations by 2005, but several political and economic crises in the region along with the September 11th attacks have stalled the initiative.

Though higher education was affected indirectly by the Washington Consensus (reducing public financing in general), or within the discussions of the FTAA, there are other initiatives that have a more direct higher education

Table 5.2 International Students Received and Sent by Country

International Students Received		Students Sent	
Country	No. of Students Received	Main Destinations	No. of Students Sent
Cuba	17,500		
Chile	5,000	United States	1,612
		Argentina	745
		Germany	624
		France	512
		Spain	427
		ALL COUNTRIES	5,670
Argentina	3,500	United States	3,644
		France	838
		Spain	802
		Germany	519
		United Kingdom	434
		ALL COUNTRIES	8,107
Uruguay	2,000		
Mexico	1,900	United States	13,329
		United Kingdom	1,973
		France	1,452
		Germany	977
		Spain	937
		ALL COUNTRIES	22,368
Bolivia	600		
Trinidad and Tobago	500		
Costa Rica	500		

Note
Constructed by author from Didou, 2006 and Institute of International Education (IIE) *Atlas*, 2007.

focus. For instance, in the context of the World Trade Organization (WTO) and General Agreement on Trade in Services, higher education is seen as another service to be regulated (Bassett, 2006; OECD, 2002). Within the region, there is also the role played by MERCOSUR (The Southern Common Market), created in 1991. This international organization has attempted to have more impact at the higher education level than other organizations like NAFTA, although its results to date have not been very effective (Fernández Lamarra, 2003; Mecham, 2003).

The problem for Latin America in all the various international forums is its inability to construct an overall regional perspective, and that most of the individual countries have to negotiate from a position of relative weakness, both economically and politically. Although there have been interesting cooperative initiatives in Latin American higher education, such as the network of Macro-Universities, to date these have been insufficient to be really effective (Red de Macro Universidades de América Latina y el Caribe, 2007). In order to promote effective initiatives, they must include genuine exchanges of academic ideas, communicate the shared experiences (good and bad practices) of higher education, and increase co-operative development projects.

Another tension between the global and local is reflected in the recent fever of global rankings. The two most popular rankings, one published by the Institute of Higher Education at the Shanghai Jiao Tong University and the other by *The Times Higher Education Supplement* in the UK, have been broadly questioned in their methodologies (Marginson, 2007; Salmi and Saroyan, 2007). In the first, the top Latin American universities are the University of São Paolo (Brazil) between 102–150, and UNAM (Mexico) and UBA (Argentina) between 151–202. There are only other three universities in the top 500, another from Brazil (University of Campinas) and two Chilean universities (University of Chile and Pontific Catholic University of Chile). In the *Times Supplement* ranking the situation is broadly similar; in the top 200 there are only three Latin American institutions: São Paolo and Campinas (from Brazil), at 175 and 177, and UNAM at 192. If global rankings are used to evaluate international university prestige, Latin American institutions are placed in a difficult position. The important discussion is what it takes to place a research university in the top echelon of "world class universities" in terms of resources, time and the relationship to other higher institutions within a system. In other words, would this be a strategic use of resources in the Latin American context?

In sum, the international rankings are a good example of the pressures and challenges Latin America receives from the global forces. However, learning from history, it appears that only by considering local needs and reaching regional alliances will the higher education institutions be able to develop creative and effective solutions for the continent's problems.

Conclusion

This chapter has presented an overview of the main challenges Latin American higher education systems have faced since their expansion in the 1960s. There are many tensions between the present socio-economic needs of Latin American countries and the development of their higher education systems. On the one hand, higher education institutions need to respond to the pressures of globalization and the challenges of an emerging knowledge economy, but on the other hand they need to respond to the local problems of poverty and endemic socio-political tensions. But the responses have not been very effective: most countries have not planned their higher education growth very wisely, public resources have been used to control institutions but not necessarily to improve them, the universities are far from building a solid research and scientific infrastructure, and pressures for concrete responses to local necessities have increased not declined. And interestingly, considering the diversity of countries forming Latin America, these have tended to be homogenized developments rather than tailored to different national circumstances.

Many actors can be considered to be responsible for the present situation but without educational plans that are integrated into the needs of the economic and social sectors and adapted to the particular national contexts, the prospects for these countries seem at best uncertain.

There are few optimistic signs to observe; especially if it is considered that the region has become very politically active (for example, in 2006 nine presidential elections occurred) with the emergence of a number of more left-wing governments. However, it is not clear how these electoral results would translate into policy implementation and more important in reforming the higher education systems in the region (Maldonado, 2002).

Indeed, there is a long-standing debate as to the most desirable allocation of public resources between those supporting "basic" education versus higher education. There are always questions about the social benefits of higher education, particularly where resources are limited (Lewis, 2003). However, if the goal is about reducing the economic gap between developing and developed countries, then most international organizations, governments and higher education stakeholders agree that knowledge production is an important part of this purpose. If Latin American higher education can increase access, especially for low-income groups and first-generation college students, their higher education systems will become stronger social engines and more vital players in national development.

Finally, in a region such as Latin America, it would be dangerous to think of higher education only as part of the problem. If we are not to lose all hope for the region's future, it has to become part of the solution.

References

Altbach, Philip. "Comparative perspectives on private higher education." In *Private Prometheus. Private higher education end development in the 21st Century,* edited by P. G. Altbach. Westport, CT: Greenwood, 1999.

Altbach, Philip. "Empires of knowledge and development." In *World Class Worldwide. Transforming research universities in Asia and Latin America,* edited by P. G. Altbach and J. Balán. Baltimore: The Johns Hopkins University Press, 2007.

Arocena, Rodrigo and Sutz, Judith. "Latin American universities: From an original revolution to an uncertain transition." *Higher Education* 50(4), 2005: 573–592.

Bassett, Roberta. *The WTO and the university: Globalization, GATS, and American higher education.* London/New York: Routledge, 2006.

Bernasconi, Andrés. "Are there research universities in Chile?" In *World Class Worldwide. Transforming research universities in Asia and Latin America,* edited by P. G. Altbach and J. Balán. Baltimore: The Johns Hopkins University Press, 2007a.

Bernasconi, Andrés. "Is there a Latin American model of the university?" *Comparative Education Review* 52(1), 2007b: 27–52.

Brunner, José Joaquín. *Universidad y sociedad en América Latina*. Mexico: Universidad Autónoma Metropolitana-Azcapotzalco-Secretaría de Educación Pública, 1987.

Casanova, Hugo. "Mexico." In *International Handbook of Higher Education*, edited by Forest James and Philip Altbach. Dordrecht: Springer, 2006.

Castro, Claudio de Moura and Levy, Daniel. *Myth, reality and Reform: higher education policy in Latin America*. Washington, DC: Inter-American Development Bank, 2000.

Cetto, Ana María and Vessuri, Hebe. "Latin America and the Caribbean." In *World Science Report*, UNESCO. Paris: UNESCO, 1998.

Díaz Barriga, Ángel. "La evaluación universitaria en el contexto del pensamiento neoliberal." *Revista de la Educación Superior 88*, 1993: http://www.anuies.mx/servicios/p-anuies/index2.php?clave=publicaciones (accessed January 20, 2008).

Díaz Barriga, Ángel. *Universitarios: institucionalización académica y evaluación*. Mexico: CESU-UNAM, 1995.

Didou, Sylvie. *Internacionalización y nuevos proveedores externos de educación superior en América Latina y el Caribe*. México-Caribe: ANUIES-IESALC, 2005.

Didou, Sylvie. "Internacionalización de la educación superior y provisión transnacional de servicios educativos en América Latina: Del voluntarismo a las elecciones estratégicas." In *Informe sobre la educación superior en América Latina y el Caribe 2000–2005*, edited by IESALC. Caracas: IESALC-UNESCO, 2006.

Economic Commission for Latin American and the Caribbean (ECLAC). *Social Panorama of Latin America 2001–2002*. Washington, DC: ECLAC, 2002.

Fernández Lamarra, Norberto. "Higher education, quality evaluation and accreditation in Latin America and MERCOSUR." *European Journal of Education* 38(3), 2003: 2.

Fernández Lamarra, Norberto. "La evaluación y la acreditación de la calidad: Situación, tendencias, y perspectivas." In *Informe sobre la educación superior en América Latina y el Caribe 2000–2005*, edited by IESALC. Caracas: IESALC-UNESCO, 2006.

Figueiredo-Cowen, María. "Latin American universities, academic freedom and autonomy: A long term myth?" *Comparative Education* 38(4), 2002: 471–484.

Free Trade Area of the Americas. Official Website, 2006. http://www.ftaa-alca.org/View_e.asp (accessed November 2, 2007).

Garay, Adrián de. 2006. "Los contextos de aprendizaje de los jóvenes universitarios mexicanos." http://66.102.1.104/scholar?hl=en&lr=&q=cache:zfQi9lWJ48AJ:eprints.upc.es/cidui_2006/pujades/comunicaciones_completas/doc251.doc+related:znuHoBQL30kJ:scholar.google.com/ (accessed January 20, 2008).

García Guadilla, Carmen. *Comparative higher education in Latin America. Quantitative aspects*. Caracas: IESALC-UNESCO, 2000.

García Guadilla, Carmen. "Higher education financing in Latin America." In *Higher education in the world 2006. The financing of universities*, edited by Global University Network Innovation (GUNI). New York: Palgrave-Macmillan, 2006.

Ginés Mora, José. "The Bologna Process in European Higher Education: Issues, Trends and Implications for US Universities." Conference presentation, University of Arizona, Tucson (January 14, 2007).

Gónzalez, Humberto. "Instituciones de educación superior no universitaria." In *Informe sobre la educación superior en América Latina y el Caribe 2000–2005*, edited by IESALC. Caracas: IESALC-UNESCO, 2006.

Gorostiaga, Xavier. "In search of the missing link between education and development." In *Private Prometheus: Private higher education and development in the 21st century*, edited by Philip G. Altbach. Westport, CT: Greenwood Press, 2000.

Hopenhayn, Martin. "Youth and employment in Latin America and the Caribbean: Problems, prospects and options." Conference proceeding. *Youth Employment Summit*. Alexandria, Egypt. September 7–11, 2002. http://www.yesweb.org/gkr/res/bg.eclac.reg.doc (accessed November 2, 2007).

Ibarra Colado, Eduardo (coord.) *La Universidad ante el espejo de la excelencia*. México: UAM-Iztapalapa, 1993.

Institute of International Education. *Atlas of the student mobility*. The official website of Project Atlas. http://atlas.iienetwork.org/ (accessed November 2, 2007).

Instituto Internacional de la UNESCO para la Educación Superior en América Latina y el Caribe (IESALC). *Informe sobre la educación superior en América Latina y el Caribe. 2000–2005* Caracas: IESALC-UNESCO, 2006.

International Labour Organization. "Global trends in employment, productivity and poverty." International Labour Organization official website, 2005. http://www.ilo.org/global/lang–en/index.htm (accessed November 2, 2007).

Knight, Jane. "Commercial crossborder education: implications for financing higher education." In *Higher education in the world 2006. The financing of universities,* edited by Global University Network Innovation (GUNI). New York: GUNI-Palgrave-Macmillan, 2006.

Lewis, William. "Educating global workers." *The McKinsey Quarterly,* December, 2003: http://www.mckinseyquarterly.com/public_sector/educating_global_workers (accessed December 10, 2007).

Maldonado-Maldonado, Alma. "Higher education research in Latin America." *International Higher Education* 28, 2002: 23–25.

Maldonado-Maldonado, Alma, et al., *Private higher education: An international bibliography.* Greenwich, CT: Information Age Publishing, 2004.

Marginson, Simon. "Global position and position taking: The case of Australia." *Journal of Studies in International Education* 11(1), 2007: 5–32.

Marsiske, Renate. *Movimientos estudiantiles en la historia de América Latina.* Mexico: CESU-UNAM-Plaza y Valdés, 1999.

Mecham, Michael. "Mercosur: A failing development project?" *International Affairs* 79(2), 2003: 369–387.

Mendoza Rojas, Javier. *Transición de la educación superior contemporánea en México: De la planeación al Estado evaluador.* Mexico: CESU-UNAM, 2002.

Mollis, M. "Latin American University Transformation of the 1990s: Altered identities?" In *International Handbook of Higher Education,* edited by Forest James and Philip Altbach. Dordrecht: Springer, 2006.

Muhr, Thomas and Verger, Antoni. "Venezuela: Higher Education for All." *Journal for Critical Education Policy Studies* 4(1), 2006: http://www.jceps.com/index.php?page10=article&article=63 (accessed January 20, 2008).

Neave, G. "The evaluative state reconsidered." *European Journal of Education* 33(3), 1998: 265–284.

Organisation of Economic Co-operation and Development (OECD). *GATS: The case for open services markets.* Paris: OECD, 2002.

Organisation of Economic Co-operation and Development (OECD). *Revisión nacional de investigación y desarrollo educativo. Reporte de los examinadores sobre México.* Paris/Mexico: OECD, 2004.

Organisation of Economic Co-operation and Development (OECD). *Science and Technology Statistical Compendium.* Paris: OECD, 2005.

Organisation of Economic Co-operation and Development (OECD). *Education at a Glance, 2007. OECD indicators.* Paris: OECD, 2007.

O'Gorman, Edmundo. *La invención de América.* Mexico: Secretaría de Educación Pública (Lecturas Mexicanas, Volume 63), 1984.

Ordorika, Imanol and Pusser, Brian. "La máxima casa de estudios. The Universidad Nacional Autónoma de México as a State-Building University." In *World Class Worldwide. Transforming research universities in Asia and Latin America,* edited by P. G. Altbach and J. Balán. Baltimore: The Johns Hopkins University Press, 2007.

Perkin, Harold. "History of universities." In *International Higher Education: An Encyclopedia,* edited by P.G. Altbach. New York: Garland, 1991.

Rama, Claudio. "La tercera reforma de la educación superior en América Latina y el Caribe: Masificación, regulación e internacionalización." In *Informe sobre la educación superior en América Latina y el Caribe 2000–2005,* edited by IESALC. Caracas: IESALC-UNESCO, 2006.

Rama, Claudio. "Los postgrados en América Latina en la sociedad del saber." In *Informe sobre la educación superior en América Latina y el Caribe 2000–2005,* edited by IESALC. Caracas: IESALC-UNESCO, 2006.

Red de Macro Universidades de América Latina y el Caribe. Official Website. http://redmacro.unam.mx/ (accessed November 2, 2007).

Rodríguez, Francisco. "El financiamiento de la educación superior en América Latina: Una visión panorámica." In *Informe sobre la educación superior en América Latina y el Caribe 2000–2005*, edited by IESALC. Caracas: IESALC-UNESCO, 2006.

Rodríguez, Roberto and Casanova, Hugo. *Universidad contemporánea. Racionalidad política y vinculación social*. Mexico: CESU-UNAM, 1994.

Salmi, Jamil and Saroyan, A. "League tables as policy instruments: The political economy of accountability in tertiary education." In *Higher Education in the World 2007*, edited by GUNI. New York: Palgrave-GUNI, 2007.

Schwartzman, Simon. "Equity, quality, and relevance in higher education in Brazil." *Anais da Academia Brasileira de Ciências*, 76–1, 2004: 173–188.

Schwartzman, Simon. "Brazil's leading university. Original ideals and contemporary goals." In *World class worldwide. Transforming research universities in Asia and Latin America*, edited by Philip Altbach and Jorge Balán. Baltimore: The Johns Hopkins University Press, 2007.

Slaughter, Sheila and Rhoades, Gary. *Academic capitalism in the new economy*. Baltimore: Johns Hopkins University Press, 2004.

Steiner, João. "Brazilian research universities." In *World Class Worldwide. Transforming research universities in Asia and Latin America*, edited by P. G. Altbach and J. Balán. Baltimore: The Johns Hopkins University Press, 2007.

Task Force on Higher Education and Society. *Higher education in developing countries: Peril and promise*. Washington, DC: The World Bank, 2000.

The McKinsey Quarterly, "Editorial," March, 2007. http://www.mckinseyquarterly.com/Public_Sector/Economic_Policy/The_Latin_American_opportunity_1964 (accessed December 10, 2007).

Torres, Alberto. *Currículum universitario siglo XXI*. Buenos Aires: Facultad de Ciencias de Educación-Universidad Nacional de Entre Ríos, 1994.

Tünnermann Bernheim, Carlos. *Historia de la universidad en América Latina: de la Epoca Colonial a la Reforma de Córdoba*. San José, Costa Rica: Editorial Universitaria Centroamericana, 1991.

UNAM. *Perfil de solicitantes y asignados al bachillerato y Licenciatura*. Mexico: UNAM-Dirección de planeación, 1996.

UNESCO. *Science and technology in developing countries: Strategies for the 1990s*. Paris: UNESCO, 1992.

UNESCO. "Institute for statistics." *UNESCO official web page*. www.uis.unesco.org/profiles (accessed May 12, 2006).

United Nations Development Programme. *United Nations Development Programme*. Official website. http://www.undp.org/ (accessed May 12, 2006).

U.S. Patent and Trademark Office. "Patents count by country/state and year. All patents all types." *A patent technology monitoring division report*. Alexandria, VA: U.S. Patent and Trademark Office, 2005.

Villa, Miguel and Rivadeneira, Luis. "El proceso de envejecimiento de la población de América Latina y el Caribe: Una expresión de la transición demográfica." *Bahia Analise* 10(4), 2001: 6–35.

Williamson, John. "What should the World Bank think about the Washington Consensus?" *World Bank Research Observer* 15, 2000: 251–264.

Winkler, Donald. *La educación superior en América Latina. Cuestiones sobre eficiencia y equidad*. Washington: Banco Mundial, 1994.

World Bank. *Higher education: The lessons of experience*. Washington: World Bank, 1994.

6

Higher Education in India
The Challenge of Change

N. Jayaram

> There is ... a quiet crisis in higher education in India that runs deep. It is not yet discernible simply because there are pockets of excellence, an enormous reservoir of talented young people and an intense competition in the admissions process.
>
> **National Knowledge Commission (2007, p. 48)**

India was one of the earliest among the developing countries to have established universities and colleges, and it now has the third largest academic system in the world (behind China and the United States of America). After a long period of protected expansion with state patronage until the mid-1980s, this system is now experiencing unprecedented change. The adoption by the Government of India in 1990 of structural adjustment reforms has meant the gradual withdrawal of state patronage for higher education and a coterminous privatization of that sphere. However, with the government dithering about the long-term policy to be adopted in this regard, higher education in India is now passing through a period of stunted growth and uncertain future. Based on an analysis of the development of India's higher education and its contemporary realities, this essay[1] examines the metamorphosis of a system that was not long ago dubbed as "an immobile colossus" (Dube, 1988, p. 46).

The Colonial Background and the Post-Colonial Expansion

The foundation for India's present system of higher education[2] was laid by the British colonial regime in the mid-nineteenth century (Ashby & Anderson, 1966, pp. 54–146), and the first three universities were established at Bombay (now Mumbai), Calcutta (now Kolkata) and Madras (now Chennai) in 1857. Modeled after the University of London (established in 1836), these pioneer universities were largely affiliating and examining bodies with very little intellectual life of their own. All the universities that were subsequently established developed in an isomorphic fashion set on the pattern of the original universities. The British educational implantation in India was conceived to serve the economic, political and administrative interests of the British, and in particular, to consolidate and maintain their dominance in the country. It emphasized English, which not only was taught as a language, but was also made the exclusive medium of instruction in higher education. The content was biased in favor of languages and the humanities, and against science and technology.

It is not as if the British rulers did not realize the problems associated with such an educational implantation or its adverse consequences for the colonized society. Yet, it was only during the early years of the twentieth century – thanks to the initiative of Lord Curzon, the then Viceroy of India (1898–1905) – that efforts were made to "rescue the original concept of the university from its corrosive narrowness." Several inquiries were instituted during the last three decades of the colonial rule, but "hardly any of their major recommendations were translated into university policy or practice" (Tickoo, 1980, p. 34).

Thus, the legacy of higher education inherited by India at the time of her independence in 1947 was already crisis-ridden. As an integral element of colonial underdevelopment, higher education was "anemic, distorted and dysfunctional." Low levels of enrollment, the "liberal" nature of education, "enclavization" of the institutes of higher learning, and spurious modernization were its festering features (Raza et al., 1985, pp. 100–109). While the obsolescence of the inherited system of higher education, by and large, persisted, the system itself underwent a phenomenal expansion, never seen previously.

In 1947, India had 20 universities and 496 colleges catering to 241,369 students. During the next 55 years she built up a massive system of higher education:[3] in 2001–2002, there were 323 university-status institutions (178 state and 18 central universities, 18 medical and 40 agricultural universities, 52 institutions "deemed-to-be universities," 12 institutes of national importance, and five institutions established under State Legislature Acts), 13,150 colleges, and about 900 polytechnics. The system now employs about 411,600 teachers and caters to about 8.4 million students.

The Institutional Structure of Higher Education

The largest number of Indian universities belongs to the *affiliating* type. They have a central campus housing departments or schools of study that offer instruction at the postgraduate level and undertake research. In addition, a large number of colleges generally offering first degree-level education are affiliated with them. A major task of such universities is to determine and oversee the academic standards of these affiliated colleges and conduct centralized examinations for the candidates enrolled in them. These affiliated colleges may be dispersed geographically, but are under the jurisdiction of a university as determined by law.

The _unitary type of university, on the other hand, is self-contained,_ and has no colleges. Most of them offer both undergraduate and postgraduate courses and undertake research. A few universities are in some sense a mixture of these two types. The territorial jurisdiction of the _mixed_ type of university is usually confined to the city in which it is located. Besides affiliated colleges, this type of university manages its own colleges.

Of the 277 university-level institutions for which data are available, 171 are conventional _multi-disciplinary_ universities; 96 are _professional/technical_ institutions oriented to studies in a few related disciplines like agriculture (including forestry, dairy, fisheries, and veterinary science) (37), health sciences (16), engineering and technology (38), law (4) and journalism (1); and 10 are open universities (Association of Indian Universities [AIU], 2004, p. xi).

The Government of India has conferred upon some university-level institutions the status of "institutions of national importance." These include the first five Indian Institutes of Technology (IIT), three institutions specializing in medical sciences, and one each specializing in statistical techniques and the Hindi language. These institutions are empowered to award degrees which, according to the University Grants Commission (UGC) Act of 1956, can be granted only by a university. The Indian Institutes of Management (IIM), which are also national-level institutions, are not vested with the power to award degrees, though their "fellowships" are treated on a par with university doctorate degrees.

By 2001–2002, the central government had recognized 52 institutions as "institutions deemed-to-be universities" under the UGC Act. These institutions either focus on specialized areas of knowledge (like social work, indigenous medicine, etc.) or are heirs to a tradition (for example, an institution which has been devoted to the spread of Hindi). They are not expected to grow into multidisciplinary universities of the general type.

Outside the university orbit are research institutes funded by the Indian Council for Social Science Research and research laboratories established under the auspices of the Council of Scientific and Industrial Research or maintained by the Ministries of the Government of India. These institutions are not oriented toward the granting of degrees, though they are recognized as centers for doctoral research work, and many scholars working in them are recognized as supervisors of doctoral students registered with universities.

The concept of an "open university" to impart "distance education" is yet another landmark in higher education in India. Open universities seek to cater to the educational needs of those who for whatever reasons cannot enroll in traditional forms of higher education or those who want to pursue their studies at their own pace and time. Introduced in 1962, this channel of higher learning was initially under the control of the conventional universities. In addition to ten open universities, there are 104 institutes of correspondence courses or directorates of distance education functioning under conventional universities, and these cater to about 820,000 students, accounting for 13 percent of the total enrollment in universities and colleges.

Enrollment Rates and Background

The bulk of the expansion in enrollments at the postsecondary level took place during the 1950s and the 1960s, when the rate of expansion was as high as 13–14 percent per annum. During the past few decades, the rate of expansion has come down markedly. It was 6.1 percent in 1982–1983, peaked at 7.4 percent in 1989–1990, and has declined to a stable 4 to 5 percent since then. While this rate of expansion is apparently of a managable magnitude, the university system has never been tuned to the effects of the earlier expansion of enrollment. The shortages in the infrastructure then have only become magnified now.

Despite the massive growth in higher education, barely 7 percent of the 18- to 24-year-old age group is currently enrolled in higher education institutions, "which is only one-half of the average for Asia" (National Knowledge Commission [NKC], 2007, p. 48). Unrealistically though, the National Knowledge Commission hopes to raise this percentage to 15 by 2015 (p. 48). Analysis of the data for 2001–2002 (Kaur, 2003, p. 366) reveals that those enrolled in arts (46.1%), science (19.9%) and commerce/management (17.9%) together accounted for nearly 84 percent of the students in higher education. Among the rest, 6.9 percent were enrolled in engineering and technology, 3.2 percent in law, 3.1 percent in veterinary science, and 1.3 percent in education.

As for gender, women's representation is higher in education (51.2%) and medicine (44%) than arts (38%), science (38%), and commerce (35.6%), and is least in engineering/technology (21.5%) and agriculture (17.4%). Women's representation in higher education has improved over the decades, and they now form about 40 percent of the total enrollment. They are better represented in higher education in the states of Kerala (60%), Goa (58.6%), Punjab (52.9%) and Pondicherry (52.6%), and the union territories of Andaman and Nicobar Islands (57.8%) and Chandigarh (55.5%). In 15 other states/union territories their proportions are between 40 percent and 50 percent. However, their representation is very low in Rajasthan (32.6%), Arunachal Pradesh (29.7%) and Bihar (23%).

A substantial number of places in institutions of higher education are by law reserved for the Scheduled Castes, Scheduled Tribes and Other Disadvantaged Classes – the traditionally indigent and socially excluded sections of society. The latter is a flexible category, and in many states quite a large number of people are covered under it. The number of students belonging to these groups has increased over the years, and in 2002–2003, they constituted about 10 percent of the enrollment. However, their participation in some faculties (like medicine and engineering) is insignificant. While the policy of protective discrimination in favor of these caste groups has created some academic problems, it has without doubt substantially helped these traditionally disadvantaged sections of the population.

India's present system of education can be considered top heavy – that is, secondary and tertiary sectors appropriate about 60 percent of educational expenditures. As for socioeconomic class, the main beneficiaries of this system belong to the top 30 percent of the income groups, who occupy about 70–80 percent of the places at the secondary and university levels. Moreover, there is a pronounced urban bias in higher education; about 60–75 percent of the students in different courses hail from urban areas. In sum, there is an enormously unequal distribution of opportunity and benefits throughout India's higher education system – an issue with significant political, social and economic ramifications.

The Quality Question

As is to be expected, rapid expansion of higher education has been at the cost of its quality.[4] The quality of education offered is, no doubt, highly varied. Some institutions, despite the general deterioration of quality, have maintained very high standards, including the Indian Institutes of Technology (IITs) at Chennai, Kanpur, Karaghpur, Mumbai, and New Delhi; the Indian Institutes of Management (IIMs) at Ahmedabad, Bangalore, and Kolkata; the Indian Institute of Science (Bangalore); the Tata Institute of Fundamental Research (Mumbai); the National Law School of India University (Bangalore); and a few exceptional departments in some universities. Some affiliated colleges also have maintained high standards.

The deterioration in quality is most glaring in the state universities in general, and at the undergraduate level in affiliated colleges in particular. This crisis now also encompasses the conventional postgraduate (MA, MSc and MCom) courses offered in the university departments. These courses are now performing an extended "baby-sitting" function. This is understandable considering the relatively low unit-cost of running these courses, and that the students entering this stream pay absurdly little toward their education – far less than paid by students in the private-sector primary schools. The unregulated expansion of this sector of education has been invariably identified as the main cause of its crisis of quality.

What goes on in the name of higher education in many a state university and college is pathetic: In many institutions, the physical facilities are so deplorable and the library and laboratory facilities are so woefully inadequate that they have earned the sobriquet "academic slums" (Jayaram, 1999, p. 112). While lack of resources – a general refrain heard in this context – is primarily responsible, we cannot blame it alone. What is serious is that even the prescriptions governing the minimum qualifications for the appointment and promotion of academic staff are violated; the minimum number of working days is not met; the calendar of academic activities exists only on paper if at all,, and the administration has virtually collapsed. All this has adversely affected the quality of education imparted in India's colleges and universities.

Not surprisingly, not even one Indian university or institute found a place in a 2004 academic ranking of top 100 universities and institutions of higher education in the world, and only two institutes and one university were ranked, below 500: IISc (Bangalore) (ranked in the bracket 202–301), IIT (Kharagpur) and University of Calcutta (Kolkata) (both ranked in the bracket 404–502) were the top three Indian institutions of higher education in that order.[5]

The undue emphasis on certification rather than on the teaching-learning process has distorted the orientation of university education. Practically everything that takes place in the university system is geared to examination. Not surprisingly, it is in matters relating to examination and certification that we find a host of problems and scandals. Obviously, many innovations undertaken in the university system relate to examinations – e.g., weighting for internal and external evaluations, grading system, continuous evaluation, etc. – and the prevention of tampering or faking marks–cards and certificates – e.g., the computerization of examination records, insertion of holograms on marks-cards, lamination of degree certificates, etc.

Appreciating the need for a centralized authority vested with the power to provide funds and to set and coordinate standards of higher education, within a decade of India's achieving independence the University Grants Commission (UGC) was established by an Act of Parliament in 1956. Though modeled after the British UGC (established after World War I), the UGC in India is endowed with the responsibility of regulating academic standards. It receives money from the central government and is accountable to Parliament.

On its part, the UGC has been undertaking several schemes to provide substantial support to universities and colleges to strengthen their teaching and research activities. Among other schemes supported by the UGC, the Committee for Strengthening Infrastructure in Science and Technology, the College Science Improvement Program, the College Humanities and Social Science Improvement Program, the Faculty Improvement Program, and the Special Assistance Program deserve special mention. Financial assistance is extended to teachers to do research and to attend seminars, symposia and workshops. Promising young teachers with an interest in research are offered funds under the Career Award Scheme, and the renowned among senior teachers are given National Associateships. These schemes have, no doubt, injected a degree of vitality in the system, but the trend toward their ritualization is too apparent to be ignored.

Though the UGC is expected to play a lead role in higher education, it is endowed with very little power. Considering the inordinate number of universities and colleges it is required to oversee, the UGC has been reduced virtually to a fund-disbursing agency, incapable of enforcing its own recommendations. Also, given the diarchy in higher education – with the UGC expected to oversee it and the state governments regulating it in practice – higher education has remained a virtually unbridled horse (Pinto, 1984, pp. 63–107). The National Knowledge Commission (NKC), therefore, considers it necessary and desirable to establish an Independent Regulatory Authority for Higher Education (NKC, 2007, pp. 53–55).

The standards of academic performance in professional education are coordinated and regulated by statutory bodies such as the Indian Medical Council, the All India Council of Technical Education, the Bar Council of India, the Dental Council of India, the Pharmacy Council of India, and the Nursing Council of India. The Indian Council of Agricultural Research looks after agricultural education, and the Central Advisory Board of Education is the national level coordinating body for making general policies on education.

In 1994, as a belated step in the direction of quality control in higher education, following the National Policy of Education (Ministry of Human Resource Development [MHRD], 1986), the UGC set up an autonomous body called the National Assessment and Accreditation Council (NAAC). Initially the scheme of assessment and accreditation was voluntary, but the idea of an external institution doing this was not well-received by universities and colleges. By January 2008, the NAAC had assessed and accredited only 140 universities and 3,644 colleges; it had completed re-accreditation of 125 institutions – 11 universities and 114 colleges – that had been assessed first in 1998–1999 (*NAAC News*, January 2008, p. 14). The scheme is now mandatory, and the universities and colleges failing to get themselves assessed and accredited will be deprived of developmental grants. How far this will improve the state of affairs in higher education, even if indirectly, remains to be seen.

Weak Research Orientation

Paradoxically, the large and experienced system of higher education in India is hardly known for its excellence in research. The number of "Indians" among Nobel laureates in science is negligible – only three, to be specific, namely, C.V. Raman, H. Khurana and S. Chandrashekar – and in economics, only Amartya Sen. The number of renowned scientists can be counted on the fingers of one hand. Only 46 Indians – three engineers and 43 scientists – have become Fellows of the Royal Society. The reputed scientists of the contemporary generation are mostly working outside India. The scientific journals published from India are not generally of international quality. Research publications by Indians in reputable international journals are few and far between.[6]

Not surprisingly, Indian scientists have a poor citation index. The former Director General of Council of Scientific and Industrial Research (CSIR), R.A. Mashelkar cites a report which records India's decline in the number of scientific papers cited in the International Science Citation Index from 15,000 to 12,000 during 1980–2000: whereas India slipped from eighth in the world in 1980 to fifteenth in 2000, China improved its position from fifteenth to ninth! In absolute terms, there was, no doubt, an increase in the number of citations of Indian scientific papers – from 56,464 in 1981–1985 to 90,162 in 1993–1997 (that is, by 59.68 percent). But this increase appears to be infinitesimal compared to the stupendous increase in the number of citations of Chinese scientific papers for the corresponding period – from 8,517 to 77,841 (that is, by 813.95%) (R.A. Mashelkar, cited in *The Navhind Times*, Panjim, 2 November 2002, p. 11). Quoting a CSIR Report, B. Vijayakumar notes that "In the entire history of CSIR of India, only three out of over 20,000 papers published by the scientists have been cited 100 times against a world average of one in every 250." He further adds that a paper with "thousand citation counts" (that is, a paper that has been cited 1,000 times) is either nil or extremely rare (Vijayakumar, 2003, pp. 4–5). No wonder there has been a growing disquiet over the declining quality of science education and research in the country.

More importantly, whatever little significant research that is credited to Indian scientists has been conducted in institutes – like the Indian Institute of Science (IISc) (Bangalore), Tata Institute of Fundamental Research (TIFR) (Mumbai) and the Indian Institutes of Technology (IITs) (Chennai, Delhi, Kanpur, Kharagpur and Mumbai) – and the laboratories under the umbrella of the Council of Scientific and Industrial Research (CSIR), rather than in the universities.[7] Thus, there has been a peculiar disjunction in Indian higher education: the concentration by the expanding university system on "retailing knowledge," rather than on creating and refining knowledge, with that function assigned to specialist institutes and laboratories outside the university system (see Jayaram, 2007).[8] This disjunction is clearly a reflection of the persistence of the colonial legacy of universities as retailers of knowledge.

Appreciating that teaching without research is sterile, on its own initiative and in accordance with the changing educational policies, the UGC has been undertaking several schemes to provide substantial support to universities and colleges to strengthen their teaching and research activities (Jayaram, 2007, pp. 83–85). Perhaps the most significant effort of UGC in the direction of research-oriented universities is its heavily funded scheme of "Universities with Potential for Excellence" (UGC, 2002–2003, pp. 127–128). Under this scheme, five universities – Jadavpur University, Jawaharlal Nehru University (New Delhi), University of Hyderabad, University of Madras (Chennai), and University of Pune – have each been given each a generous development grant of Rs. 300 million[9] for five years. While three of them have definite specialized concerns, two have a general spread. The UGC further proposes to select 100 colleges with potential for excellence and give them each a development grant of Rs.10 million.

Market Economy and the Changing Demand for Courses

Structural adjustment reforms adopted since the early 1990s have had a significant impact on the demand structure of higher education. At last the expansion of traditional programs of study seems to have outstripped the demand for them by students. While generally the more gifted students have always avoided these programs, even the less gifted now appear to be turning their backs on them, invariably opting for professional programs such as medicine, computer science, information technology, and business management. If they cannot gain access to such programs, they would rather try their hand at courses with narrow but specialized job prospects, such as packaging, plastic technology, fabric designing, air conditioning and refrigeration, etc. The fact that good students are no longer taking up basic science courses[10] has seriously affected the academic programs of reputed science institutions such as the Indian Institute of Science (Bangalore), which has now come out with incentive schemes to urge meritorious students to take basic sciences at the graduate level.

The lack of a link between conventional courses and the job market seems to have become too apparent for students and their parents.[11] At best, the employers – not only in the private sector, but also in the government – use the conventional degrees as sieves for filtering the large number of applicants for the limited number of jobs. The unemployment situation, particularly among conventional degree holders, has worsened over the decades, with the government no longer able to absorb them in public employment. Aggravating the situation is the economic liberalization program, which demands knowledge and skills generally not possessed by conventional degree holders. It is only natural that those who have been using conventional courses as waiting rooms are either seeking early entry into the job market at lower levels, with the option of obtaining formal university qualifications later, or entering courses that carry better job prospects. Those who still seek conventional graduate courses are generally the weakest students, or the first-generation students from rural and indigent backgrounds (the Scheduled Castes and Scheduled Tribes), especially those who are supported by financial assistance from the government.

While the demand for conventional courses has tapered off, the demand for professional and other allied courses has been increasing incessantly, in spite of escalating unemployment even among the professional degree holders. Many educational entrepreneurs are unduly eager to offer such "moneymaking" courses in medicine, dentistry, nursing, engineering and technology, business management, computer science, and education. The latest scandal in the universities concerns the granting of permission to colleges to start these courses. Many of these institutions are inadequately equipped to offer any education, let alone professional education. The gross and brazen violation of the norms stipulated by such bodies as the Medical Council of India, the All India Council for Technical Education, etc., is a matter of serious concern.

To enhance their marketability and employment prospects, students taking professional courses try to specialize in a given field or obtain qualifications and skills in some sophisticated courses not generally offered by the universities. A glance at Indian newspapers reveals the number and variety of courses currently offered by various institutions outside the sphere of the university system. These institutions, and the academic entrepreneurs who run them, seem to be extraordinarily sensitive to the variety of knowledge and skills demanded by the changing market economy. They are also extremely flexible, both in what they have to offer and how they go about offering it. While the demand for skills and knowledge is their *raison d'etre*, the maintenance of quality is their badge of success. As in any commodity market, one has to pay more for better-quality education.

It is important to note that in spite of (or essentially because of) the fact they are outside the orbit of the university system, such institutions of higher learning have not only survived but even thrived. Some of them have earned a niche for themselves in higher education, and even recognition from academia and employers abroad. As statutorily established academic entities, the Indian universities have sadly lacked competition, and they brook no competition either. With the liberalization of the economy and the state gradually shedding its responsibility for higher education – and with the UGC being no more than a mute witness to the gradual decaying of the university as a public institution – the Indian university system is progressively becoming little more than a convenient label and in the process increasingly marginalized. Irrespective of one's ideological predilections, it is now conceded that the future of higher education in India will be determined by the market economy and the private sector.

Decline of State Patronage

While public expenditure on education in India has always been inadequate for meeting the needs of "education for all,"[12] throughout its history the state has highly subsidized higher education (Tilak, 2004a). Structural adjustment has meant a drastic cut in public expenditure on higher education: between 1980–1990 and 1994–1995, the share of higher education in development (plan) expenditure decreased from 12.6 percent to 6 percent, whereas the same in maintenance (non-plan) expenditure declined from 14.2 percent to 11 percent (Tilak, 1996). Overall, the allocation for higher education, which had peaked at 28 percent in the Fifth Five-Year Plan (1974–1997), has steadily declined in the successive Plans to just 8 percent in the Tenth Five-Year Plan

(2002–2007), which is the same as the allocation in the First Five-Year Plan (1951–1956).

The annual growth rate of public expenditure on university and higher education, which was 13.1 percent between 1980–1981 and 1985–1986, had fallen to 7.8 percent between 1980–1981 and 1995–1996 (Shariff & Ghosh, 2000, p. 1400). As a proportion of total government expenditure, the share of higher education declined from 1.57 percent in 1990–1991 to 1.33 percent in 2001–2002. Considering the trends in per student expenditure – from Rs 7,676 in 1990–1991 to Rs 5,873 in 2001–2002 (in 1993–1994 prices) – the decline in public expenditure on higher education would appear even more drastic (Tilak, 2004b, p. 2160).[13] The National Knowledge Commission's hope that "government support for higher education should be at least 1.5 percent, if not 2 percent of GDP, from a total of 6 percent of GDP for education" (NKC, 2007, p. 55) would remain just that.

Thus, the state, which had hitherto been the dominant partner in funding higher education, is finding it harder even to maintain the same level of funding for higher education. Financial constraint, however, does not affect all sectors of higher education equally: invariably, non-professional courses are more adversely affected than their professional counterparts. Furthermore, the efforts to privatize higher education by encouraging private agencies to establish institutions of higher learning have enjoyed only limited success in general education and non-professional courses. Thus, state universities and their affiliated colleges are the ones in the financial doldrums.

The gradual decline in state patronage of higher education has been accompanied by its inability to address the need for reforms within conventional higher education. The National Policy on Education (Ministry of Education [ME], 1985), its Program of Action (MHRD, 1986), and their review by the Acharya Ramamurti Committee (MHRD, 1991) were all pre-structural adjustment reform initiatives. Neither the phenomenal fall in the demand for conventional courses in the BA and BSc streams, nor the remarkable spurt in the demand for courses in such areas as computer science and information technology, biotechnology, and management studies, was anticipated.

Private Initiatives in Higher Education

The void created by the waning state patronage for higher education is now being filled by private entrepreneurial initiatives. Two types of private initiatives in Indian higher education can be identified. First, there are private colleges and institutes that are formally affiliated with a university. They offer courses approved by a university, and their students write examinations conducted by that university; the successful among them are given degree certificates by the university. While the institutions belonging to the minority communities enjoy certain administrative privileges granted by the Constitution of India, in all academic matters the private colleges and institutes are governed by the university.

Many of these private colleges receive financial assistance to the tune of 80–85 percent of their expenditure; in addition, they are permitted to collect a small fee from the students to make up the balance. As such, these colleges must observe the grant-in-aid code formulated by the government. At the other end of the spectrum are the unaided private colleges that have to generate their own financial resources. They have considerable leeway concerning administration and the collection of fees from the students.

The concept of a purely private university (of the American type) is new in India. The bill to provide for the establishment of private universities, introduced in Rajya Sabha (the upper house of Parliament) is still pending. While the government is keen on privatization, the private sector is unhappy with some clauses of the bill, such as those concerning the formation of a permanent endowment fund of Rs.100 million, the provision of full scholarships to 30 percent of the students, and the government monitoring and regulation of the system (Tilak, 2002, p. 12).

Meanwhile, invoking the existing legal provisions (e.g., the UGC Act), several private institutions of higher education have been given the "deemed-to-be university" status. Also, considering that higher education is a concurrent subject under the Constitution (that is the responsibilities are shared between central and state governments), some states (like the newly formed Chattisgarh) have enacted private university acts of their own, and private universities have begun to mushroom in these states. This has, no doubt, attracted the adverse attention of the UGC, which, however, feels helpless to intervene. Following a public interest litigation suit challenging the constitutional validity of the Chattisgarh legislation allowing registration of private universities without providing for even basic educational facilities, the Supreme Court of India has quashed that legislation.[14]

In contrast are the privately owned and managed colleges, institutes and academies conducting courses outside the purview of the universities. Typically, they offer courses in such areas as packaging, corporate secretaryship, marketing management, financial management, hotel management and catering technology, tourism administration, software marketing, computer applications, fashion design, etc. Unlike the diploma courses offered by the polytechnics, some of these courses offered by well-known institutes are accredited with professional bodies in the area, often even outside the country.

Another educational innovation that has come from private initiatives is the concept of the "twinning program." This program involves collaboration between two educational systems, with both systems taking responsibility for teaching and training of students and one of them holding the right to award educational credentials. The program may involve collaboration between an Indian institution and a system abroad (international educational collaboration), or between two systems of education within the country (intranational educational collaboration).

International educational collaboration is slowly gathering momentum. In India, it was originally devised as a way out of the governmental stranglehold on private institutions of higher learning and the enervating rigidity of the university system. Such international educational collaboration is not, however, confined to professional education. To meet the demand for high quality first-degree education, especially in areas such as computer science, some private colleges have entered into twinning programs with universities abroad.

Such international educational collaboration involving twinning programs is significantly different from the more direct marketing endeavors of foreign educational establishments. Several universities – not necessarily famous ones – in Anglophone countries such as Australia, Canada, New Zealand, the United Kingdom, and the United States of America are enrolling Indian students for their educational programs. Often there is a distance education component, but most of them have arrangements with reputable institutes in the country for offering contact programs for students taking these foreign university examinations. Some of these universities even hold educational fairs in Indian cities to familiarize those interested in pursuing their educational programs.[15]

All this necessarily implies opening the sphere of Indian higher education to foreign educational establishments. For more than a century, the well-to-do in India have been sending their wards abroad for higher education, with the most talented students obtaining fellowships from the Government of India or foreign foundations. Given the globalization of higher education, such facilities are now being brought into the country. This is akin, no doubt, to the operation of multinational companies in industry and business and as such, it cannot be expected to be free of socioeconomic costs.

It is well known that such high-quality education involving multinational arrangements, often involving job placements, is expensive, especially as compared to the absurdly low-cost education offered by Indian colleges and universities. Moreover, the concept of twinning programs is now taking root intranationally as well. Such programs have effectively combined the advantages of regular and distance modes of higher education. It is also significant that the educational institutions involved are putting their physical, material and human resources to optimum use.

Considering this, it is ironic that the concept of autonomous colleges has not been given the effort that it richly deserves. In light of the current crisis confronting the university system, the need for liberating the best affiliated colleges from their bondage to the university can hardly be exaggerated. The National Policy on Education (1985–1986) recommended the granting of autonomy to select colleges and the UGC endorsed this recommendation. By 1990, 500 colleges were envisaged to be given an autonomous status; yet by 2003, only 135 colleges had been granted this status (AIU, 2004, p. xii).

Vested interests of the university managers and the political bureaucracy of the state governments have ensured that this innovation remains virtually grounded.

The Uncertain Future

The structural adjustment reforms adopted by the Government of India since 1990 have necessitated a policy of disinvestment of the public sector and opened up privatization in various spheres of the economy. For higher education, however, the government is hesitant to pursue this policy vigorously. Rather, a different strategy is in operation: there is now a moratorium on the establishment of new educational institutions (especially of the conventional type) under the public sector and an imposition of ceilings on student strength in the existing institutions. The academic profession is being downsized through a freeze on recruitment, reduction in the number of teachers, and rationalization of teachers' work. There is a proposal to introduce the contract system for hiring teachers in the future. At the same time, self-financing colleges (especially in areas of professional education) are encouraged, and the proposal to raise fees in the public higher education institutions is on the anvil. On the one hand, these measures, it is feared, will raise the cost of higher education and make it less accessible to the masses, but on the other hand they may – given the government's inability to regulate the private educational institutions – adversely affect the quality of education (Kumar & Sharma, 2003).

Closely related to the foregoing trends is the internationalization of higher education referred to earlier. This is in conformity with the policy of liberalization of education as a service sector under the General Agreement on Trade in Services (Bhushan, 2004). While the requisite legislative provisions are not yet in place, the education sector "opened-up" in April 2004, and foreign universities and educational institutions (especially from the Anglophone countries) have begun to offer competition to the existing educational institutions in the country. As observed earlier, there is a fear that this might result in draining resources from India, as well as introducing strong foreign cultural and political influences (Kumar & Sharma, 2003, p. 607).

The lack of a coherent long-term policy perspective is characteristic of higher education in India today. While the Government of India – irrespective of the ideological predilections of the party combinations in power – is committed to structural adjustment reforms and liberalization, which necessarily implies gradual withdrawal of state patronage for higher education and the privatization and internationalization of this sector, it appears to be dithering on the issue. Coalition politics, which is the political reality in India today, implies no party can introduce bold policy initiatives. _Ad hoc_ policies and the multiplicity of actors – the central and state governments, the UGC, the All India Council for Technical Education, the universities and colleges, and the emergent private sector – each dealing with the unfolding exigencies in higher education in their own way portend a period of stunted growth and uncertain future.

Conclusion: The Challenge in Higher Education

The conventional university system in India, confronting as it is a systemic crisis, has been incapable of introducing any significant educational innovation or effectively implementing any educational reform. Given the mounting pressure for increasing accessibility and the constraints of democratic politics, the trend in the universities is toward reducing everything to the lowest common denominator or leveling down quality, rather than raising it. The Indian university system is extraordinarily rigid and pronouncedly resistant to change: The impetus to change does not come from within the system. When experiments or innovations are introduced from outside, they are resisted; if enforced, they are ritualized. The fate of such innovations as the merit promotion scheme, faculty-improvement program, vocationalization of courses, semesterization of courses, a curriculum-development center, an annual report, a college-development council, an academic-staff college and refresher and orientation courses are too well known to warrant elaboration (see Jayaram, 2003). It is indeed ironic that higher education, which is expected to function as an agency of change, should itself be resistant to it.

The void created by the paralysis and drift of the conventional university system is being filled by private entrepreneurial initiatives. Thus, significant educational innovations and experiments are currently taking place in institutions outside the university orbit and in the private sector. In view of the rapid expansion of (and increasing variety in) knowledge and skills, there is enormous scope for educational innovations and initiatives. The private institutions have been more responsive to the demands of the economy and industry and the changing employment scenario. They have also shown their ability to match relevance with flexibility both in costs and regulation. This does not, however, mean that all private institutions are necessarily good. Some of them are brazenly commercial establishments out to swindle gullible people looking for better-quality education at affordable prices.

Privatization of higher education is apparently a fledgling but welcome trend: higher education requires it to maintain creativity, adaptability and quality, while the economic trail of liberalization and globalization demands it. Considering the chronic paucity of resources, gradually unburdening itself of the additional responsibility for higher education may be advisable for the government. Instead, it could better utilize the scarce resources for realizing the goal of universal access to elementary education and for improving the quality of school education.

Privatization of higher education, however, is not without social costs. In a polity such as India's, where structured inequalities have been entrenched, privatization is sure to reinforce existing inequalities and to foster inegalitarian tendencies. This necessitates the social supervision of the private sector and effective measures for redressing imbalances resulting from unequal economic capacities and opportunities within the population. How to advance equality without sacrificing quality? How to control the private sector without curbing its creativity and initiative? Here lies the challenge for higher education in contemporary India.

Notes

1. In writing this essay I have drawn on some of my earlier work on higher education in India (see Jayaram, 2003, 2004, 2006 and 2007).

2. Broadly defined, the label "higher education" in India includes the entire spectrum of education beyond 12 years of formal schooling (including the three-year polytechnic programs leading to a diploma which one can pursue immediately after successfully completing ten years of schooling). It is offered in colleges and/or university departments. Based on the nature of their management, we can broadly identify four types of collegiate-level educational institutions: (i) private unaided institutions, (ii) private grant-in-aid institutions, (iii) institutions managed by the state government, and (iv) institutions managed by the universities. While there are internal variations in the principles and practices of management among these institutions, as far as their academic organization is concerned they are all regulated by the university to which they are affiliated or part of. These institutions offer a variety of courses. If the level of instruction imparted depends on the structural type of institution (i.e., junior college, polytechnic, college, or a university department), the quality of teaching often varies with the basic facilities available in a given institution. This again is determined both by the extent and nature of the resources the administrators can mobilize and their motivation to do so.

3. It is important to note that the rapid expansion of higher education in India has taken place in a socioeconomic context in which a substantial percentage of the population is illiterate (34.62% of those who are 7+ according to the 2001 Census), and despite the low rating of education *per se* in the order of national priorities (the educational expenditure as percentage of the Gross Domestic Product rose only marginally, from 2.80 in 1980–1981 to 3.93 in 2000–2001).

4. Lacking any objective measurement of higher-education standards over a period, it is, no doubt, difficult to determine precisely the nature and extent of deterioration. Nevertheless, there is no denying that India's standards compare unfavorably with the average standards in educationally advanced countries. The Education Commission had drawn attention to this as early as the mid-1960s (see Ministry of Education [ME], 1971, p. 66). No wonder, then, that degrees awarded by Indian universities are not regarded by many foreign universities as equivalent to their degrees. In fact, employers in India, including the government agencies, are wary of these degrees.

5. This ranking was based on a study of 2,000 universities and institutions of higher education across the world undertaken by the Institute of Higher Education, Shanghai Jiao Tong University, Shanghai, China. On the methodology of ranking adopted by this study, see http://ed.sjtu.edu.cn/rank/2004/top500list.htm. There is currently no official ranking of institutions of higher education in India. Some news magazines have attempted such a rank of colleges, but their rankings are populist and lack methodological rigor.

6. According to the report of The World Bank's Task Force on Higher Education and Society, the number of papers in sciences and social sciences from India increased only marginally from 13,623 in 1981 to 14,883 in 1995 (that is, by 9.25 percent in 15 years). This is negligible compared to the phenomenal 784.38 percent (from a meager 1,293 to 11,435) increase registered by China during the same period (2000, pp. 124–125).

7. Recently, the UGC has conferred the "deemed-university" status on CSIR (*The Times of India*, Mumbai, May 27 2005, p. 7). However, how this umbrella organization will function as a "university" is not clear.

8. What is said about the disjunction between universities (teaching) and institutes (research) with reference to science would hold good for social sciences, too. This is confirmed by a report on the social science research capacity in South Asia commissioned by the Social Science Research Council, New York in 2001 (see Chatterjee, 2002).

9. In February 2008, Rs.1 = US$0.026 and US$1 = Rs.39.00.

10. According to a report submitted to the Central Cabinet's Scientific Advisory Committee in July 2004, the percentage of students opting for science after Class 12 dropped from 31 percent in the 1950s to 20 percent in the 1990s. Also, those who opted for science courses in the 1950s were the top students, whereas those who opt for these courses today are from the lower-middle academic bracket (*The Indian Express*, Mumbai, 31 March 2005, p. 7).

11. Being aware of the disorientation of the conventional courses, the UGC had recommended the introduction of job-oriented courses at the first degree level. Many universities have introduced a job-orientation component in their undergraduate curriculum mainly because of the funds provided by the UGC for the purpose.

12. An international comparison revealed that in a list of 86 countries, India (with an expenditure of 3.8 percent of the Gross National Product (GNP) on education) ranked only thirty-second in terms of public expenditure on education as a proportion of GNP (quoted in Shariff & Ghosh, 2000, p. 1396).

13. It is significant to note that the Government of India's discussion paper on "Government Subsidies in India" (1997) classified elementary education as a "merit good" and higher education as a "non-merit good" warranting a drastic reduction of government subsidies. The Ministry of Finance has since reclassified higher education into a category called "merit 2 goods" which need not be subsidized at the same level as merit goods (Tilak, 2002, p. 12).

14. Supreme Court Judgment on Private Universities in Chattisgarh, http://www.ugc.ac.in/inside/supremecourt.html (downloaded on February 13, 2008).

15. In its vision document for internationalization of Indian higher education, the UGC's standing committee for the Promotion of Higher Education Abroad recommended holding Indian International Education Fairs in the Gulf countries, Africa and Southeast Asia, and encouraged Study India Programs and partnership with foreign universities.

References

Ashby, E., & Anderson, M. (1966). *Universities: British, Indian, and African*. London: Weidenfeld and Nicholson.

Association of Indian Universities (AIU). (2004). *Universities handbook*. New Delhi: Association of Indian Universities.

Bhushan, S. (2004). Trade in education services under GATS: Implications for higher education in India. *Economic and Political Weekly*, 39, 2395–2402.

Chatterjee, P. et al. (2002). *Social Science Research Capacity in South Asia: A Report* (Volume 6, Social Science Research Council Working Paper Series). New York: SSRC.

Dube, S.C. (1988). Higher education and social change. In A. Singh & G.D. Sharma (eds), *Higher education in India: The social context* (pp. 46–53). Delhi: Konark.

Jayaram, N. (1999). Reorientation of higher education in India: A prognostic essay. In S. Aroni & J. Hawkins (eds), *Partnerships in development: Technology and social sciences, universities, industry and government* (Proceedings of the Sixth INRUDA International Symposium on the Role of Universities in Developing Areas, Paris, 8–11 June 1999) (pp. 111–118). Paris: Ecole Spéciale des Travaux Publics.

Jayaram, N. (2003). The fall of the guru: The decline of the academic profession in India. In P.G. Altbach (ed.), *The decline of the guru: The academic profession in developing and middle-income countries* (pp. 199–230). New York and Basingstoke: Palgrave Macmillan.

Jayaram, N. (2004). Higher education in India: Massification and Change. In P.G. Altbach & T. Umakoshi (eds), *Asian universities: Historical perspectives and contemporary challenges* (pp. 85–112). Baltimore, Maryland: The Johns Hopkins University Press.

Jayaram, N. (2006). India. In James J.F. Forest & Philip G. Altbach (eds), *International handbook of higher education (Part two: Regions and countries)* (pp. 747–767). Dordrecht, The Netherlands: Springer.

Jayaram, N. (2007). Beyond retailing knowledge: Prospects of research-oriented universities in India. In Philip G. Altbach & Jorge Balán (eds), *World class worldwide: Transforming research universities in Asia and Latin America* (70–94). Baltimore, Maryland: The Johns Hopkins University Press.

Kaur, K. (2003). *Higher education in India (1781–2003).* New Delhi: University Grants Commission.

Kumar, T. R. & Sharma, V. (2003). Downsizing higher education: An emergent crisis. *Economic and Political Weekly,* 38 (7), 603–607.

Ministry of Education (ME), Government of India. (1971). *Education and national development (Report of the education commission, 1964–66).* New Delhi: National Council of Educational Research and Training (Reprint Edition).

Ministry of Education (ME), Government of India. (1985). *Challenge of education: A policy perspective.* Delhi: The Controller of Publications.

Ministry of Human Resource Development (MHRD), Government of India. (1986). *Program of action: National policy on education.* New Delhi: The Controller of Publications.

Ministry of Human Resource Development (MHRD), Government of India. (1991). *Towards an enlightened and humane society: Report of the committee for review of national policy on education 1986.* New Delhi: The Controller of Publications.

National Knowledge Commission (NKC). (2007). *Report to the nation – 2006.* New Delhi: National Knowledge Commission, Government of India.

Pinto, M. (1984). *Federalism and higher education: The Indian experience.* Bombay: Orient Longman.

Raza, M. et al. (1985). Higher education in India: An assessment. In J.V. Raghavan (ed.), *Higher education in the eighties* (pp. 95–173). New Delhi: Lancer International.

Shariff, A. & Ghosh, P.K. (2000). Indian education scene and the public gap. *Economic and Political Weekly,* 35, 1396–1406.

The Task Force on Higher Education and Society. (2000). *Higher education in developing countries: Peril and promise.* Washington, DC: The World Bank.

Tickoo, C. (1980). *Indian universities.* Madras: Orient Longman.

Tilak, J.B.G. (1996). Higher education under structural adjustment. *Journal of Indian School of Political Economy,* 8, 266–293.

Tilak, J.B.G. (2002). Privatization of higher education in India. *International Higher Education,* 29, 11–13.

Tilak, J.B.G. (2004a). Public subsidies in education in India. *Economic and Political Weekly,* 39, 343–359.

Tilak, J.B.G. (2004b). Absence of policy and perspective in higher education. *Economic and Political Weekly,* 39, 2159–2164.

University Grants Committee (2002–2003). *Universities with Potential for Excellence.* New Delhi: UGC.

Vijayakumar, B. (2003). Regeneration of quality research in higher education: Ways ahead. *University News,* 41 (41), 3–7.

7

The German "Excellence Initiative" and Its Role in Restructuring the National Higher Education Landscape

Barbara M. Kehm and Peer Pasternack

Introduction: The Breaking of a Taboo

In January 2004, the then Minister for Education and Research of the Federal German Government, the Social Democrat Edelgard Bulmahn, went public with the idea of organizing a nationwide competition among existing universities for considerable extra funding in order to identify a number of German universities which promised to have the potential to become world class universities, able to compete on a global scale. Bulmahn's initiative was based on a decision of the executive committee of the Social Democratic Party taken a few days before which promoted guidelines for the reform of the German higher education system and supported the idea of identifying top level higher education institutions. Bulmahn was not part of that decision-making group within her party but by going public with the idea managed to acquire the responsibility of her Ministry for implementing the decision. As the main reason for this initiative Bulmahn identified the challenges which the German higher education system was confronting and/or would be confronted with in the near future, namely:

- cutting edge research to secure Germany's economic future;
- demographic change requiring the mobilization of all available talents;
- the role of education and qualifications in the knowledge society;
- internationalization, globalization and the European Higher Education Area (EHEA);
- the increasing interdisciplinarity of research and innovation;
- the increasing demands for top research and highly qualified personnel.

The goals of the initiative were (a) to strengthen university research in the face of an observed trend towards its migration to (public) research institutes outside the university sector (e.g. Max-Planck Institutes or Helmholtz

Centers); (b) to strengthen the overall role of universities in Germany; and (c) to strengthen the international visibility of German universities.

The media picked up this proposal immediately and termed it the "search for Germany's elite universities," something that was unheard of in Germany due to the dominating concept of the legal homogeneity of universities (Neave 1996). The initiative caused an outcry among most of the relevant stakeholders in the German higher education landscape and broke a long-standing policy of the Social Democratic Party itself. Even before World War II the Social Democratic approach to education had been one of open access, equal opportunities; education as a public rather than a private good, hence no tuition fees; and the equal treatment of all higher education institutions of the same type. Although these principles do not necessarily contradict the creation of elite institutions, it was argued that the money given to the few would downgrade the others and take much-needed funding away from them. The only stakeholder group supporting, even applauding, the initiative were the employers, who argued that German higher education institutions were good on average but that there was a lack of "lighthouses."

The ministers responsible for higher education and research of the 16 German states remonstrated immediately. On the one hand they were interested in getting money from the federal government for higher education, on the other hand they immensely disliked what they interpreted as another attempt of the federal government to meddle with an area which they considered to be their own responsibility (Kehm 2006). Basic funding of higher education institutions in Germany is the responsibility of the German States. The Federal Government is only directly involved financially in sharing the costs for buildings and funding research in the form of projects. Therefore the Initiative for Excellence was declared as a specific form of project funding by the Federal Government. But it also triggered the beginning of a shift from the legal homogeneity of the German universities (Neave 1996) to a negotiated coordination of diversity, a shift most stakeholders and policy makers were well aware of and which constituted the breaking of a longstanding taboo. The States insisted on negotiations which were started immediately.

History of the Initiative for Excellence

The Compromise

In March 2004, the Federal Government and state governments agreed on a compromise, which consisted of a competitive concept, although the funding issues were still under negotiation. Basically universities had the opportunity to compete in three categories for extra support by submitting respective proposals: (a) graduate schools, (b) centers or clusters of excellence with international reputations, and (c) whole institutions aiming to become "elite" universities (institutional strategies). In order to be eligible for the award in the third category, an individual institution had to be successful in winning funding for at least one graduate school and one center of excellence. In addition, the institution had to submit a coherent and convincing development plan. The German Research Association (*Deutsche Forschungsgemeinschaft* (DFG), which provides funding for basic research on a competitive (peer reviewed) basis and encompasses all disciplines and the German Science Council (*Wissenschaftsrat* (WR) one of the most influential buffer bodies making policy recommendations in the field of higher education, were supposed to organize the application and selection process supported by Commissions (see below, "Shaping the Process") and international panels of peers to review the applications. The DFG was mainly responsible for organizing the selection and review process of the applications for graduate schools and clusters of excellence. The WR was responsible for organizing the selection and review process in the third category of institutional strategic development concepts. As eligibility for the third category was dependent on having won support for at least one graduate school and one cluster of excellence, both bodies had to cooperate to arrive at final recommendations. Representatives of the Federal Government and the States were only supposed to come in to accept the final recommendations or discuss those cases in which no final recommendation was made.

This configuration of the selection and decision-making process was the result of a conflict about the question whether the main influence on the final decisions should be given to the politicians or to the representatives of the academic community. In June 2004 the funding issue was finally agreed. Until 2010 the Federal Government and the state governments planned to invest 1.9 billion euros altogether into this initiative for excellence. From 2006 until 2010 the Federal Government would contribute 250 million euros annually to the project, and the German states 130 million euros.

But the states, especially those governed by the Christian Democratic Party, remonstrated again. In particular the prime minister of the State of Hesse vetoed the agreement to resurrect once again the long-term conflict between the Federal Government Ministry for Education and Research and the states about the issue of what types of initiatives the Federal Ministry could start in the field of higher education, which was the responsibility of the states. Thus, it took another year and some changes in wording until a consensus was finally achieved, in June 2005. The invitation for tenders in each of the three categories was published six weeks later (Bulmahn 2007).

The three categories for which extra funding for a maximum of five years was provided were defined as follows:

- the funding of about 40 graduate schools to promote the education and training of junior research staff, each school receiving approximately one million euros annually;

- the funding of about 30 centers or clusters of excellence to promote cutting-edge research, each center of excellence receiving approximately eight million euros annually;
- the funding of ten top universities (the so-called "elite universities") on the basis of their profiles and research strengths in order to promote the further structural development of higher education institutions in Germany, each university receiving about 25 million euros additional funding per year.

Due to the loss in time because of the lengthy negotiations between the Federal Government and the States, and the complexity of the application and selection process it was decided to have two rounds of selection, the first in 2006 and the second in 2007. There was also some discussion as to whether there should be such a competition every five years.

Shaping the Process

A joint commission was formed composed of the members of the expert commission of the German Research Association and the strategic commission of the Science Council. The task of the commission was to formulate guidelines for the submission of proposals in the three categories, determine criteria for selection, and to organize the selection process. It was decided to organize this process in two steps. For the first step German universities were asked to submit short proposals in any of the three categories (graduate schools, clusters of excellence and/or institutional development concepts). Only after a first round of reviews those universities which were put on a shortlist were asked to submit fully detailed proposals. Then a second round of reviews, including site visits to the most promising candidates, took place before the final decision was made public. The actual number of awards in each of the three categories was to be taken exclusively on the basis of academic excellence (Fallon 2007), however, political decision-makers also participated at a late stage of the selection and decision-making process.

The German Research Association took over the management of the selection of graduate schools and excellence clusters while the Science Council was responsible for the process of selecting institutional strategies and development concepts. An expert commission composed of 14 renowned scholars from Germany and abroad supported by additional external reviewers made recommendations for the awards in the categories "graduate schools" and "clusters of excellence." A strategy commission composed of 12 renowned scholars from Germany and abroad made the recommendations for the awards in the category "institutional development concepts". Both commissions together formed a joint commission which negotiated and arrived at final recommendations for all three categories (Fallon 2007).

This was the point in the selection process at which the political decision makers were supposed to come in. On the basis of the recommendations of the joint commission, the joint commission and representatives from the Federal Government Ministry and from the higher education ministries of all 16 German States formed a Grants Committee that was supposed to arrive at a final decision, whereby the academic members of the Grants Committee had a guaranteed majority of votes over the politicians. This happened indeed in the second round of selections, which took place in 2007, but not in the first round, which took place in 2006. In the first round the joint commission took a final decision and confronted the political decision makers with it when they entered the process. This might have been due to existing time constraints but it very nearly led to a further rejection of the initiative by the representatives of the German States. Only because the reputation of the national and international scholars who took the decision was beyond any doubt did they grudgingly accept it (Zürn 2007).[1]

However, it is also necessary to emphasize at this point that the irritation might have had other reasons as well. Information is currently still hard to come by because all actors involved in the selection of applications and final decisions about the awards in the three categories have been sworn to silence. Neither applications nor reviews have been published as yet. Rumour has it that some of the selection decisions were not sufficiently transparent and based on additional criteria. Eventually there will be more detailed information available but for the time being the issue remains open to speculation.

Results of the First and Second Round of Selection

On January 20 2006 the commission announced the final results of the first round of decisions. For those universities who had submitted an institutional development concept, thus aiming for the "elite" status, this was a day of hope and fear because it had already been made public that not all of the proposals would be accepted. Rejections were expected to backfire on the reputation of the whole university. The mass media had been speculating for weeks about those universities that might be among the chosen ten to officially become the first German elite universities.

Table 7.1 provides an overview of the outcomes of the first round, with the winners announced in October 2006.

The ten universities which made it onto the shortlist in the category "institutional development concepts" were: Technical University Aachen, Free University Berlin, University of Bremen, University of Freiburg, University of Heidelberg, Technical University Karlsruhe, University of Munich, Technical University of Munich, University of Tübingen, and University of Würzburg. What is remarkable about this list is the fact that the majority of institutions are located in the southern states of Germany and that there is no institution from any of the East German states. In the end only three were selected as winners: the University of Munich, the Technical University of Munich, and

Table 7.1 Outcomes of Round 1, German Excellence Initiative (2006)

	Graduate Schools	Excellence Clusters	Institutional Development Concepts
Number to be Selected	About 20 (out of 40)	About 15 (out of 30)	About 5 (out of 10)
First Proposals Received	135	157	27
Selected for Short-list (Full Proposal)	39	39	10
Winners	18	18	3

Source: Fallon (2007: 12), adapted by authors.

the Technical University of Karlsruhe. Of these winners of elite status two universities are located in Bavaria and one in Baden-Württemberg. Both states are located in the southwest of Germany.

Concerning the winners in the two other categories, the distribution is interesting from a geographical as well as subject- or discipline-related perspective. There were 18 winners in the category "graduate schools" from eight different states, the majority again located in southern Germany and only one in East Germany. The subject distribution shows a considerable majority in engineering and life sciences (nine), while there were four each in mathematics and physics, and social sciences and humanities. One graduate school could not be specified according to subject groupings. In the category "graduate schools" it is notable that many of the proposals had a strong interdisciplinary orientation, with the others showing approximately an equal distribution across disciplines.

The 18 winners of excellence clusters are distributed over seven states, the majority again in the southwest and only one in East Germany. Similar to the category "graduate schools" the majority of the winners come from engineering, informatics, and life sciences, three clusters are in mathematics and physics, and only one at the interface of social sciences and humanities.

The results showed such a clear bias towards the natural and applied sciences so that criticism was voiced concerning the criteria for selection, which seemed to favour these subjects and subject groups, while being less compatible with the humanities and social sciences (cf. DFG/WR 2006).

The outcomes of the second round, decided in October 2007, are shown in Table 7.2.

The winners of the second round of selections in the category of institutional development concepts were: the Technical University of Aachen (Northrhine Westfalia), the Free University of Berlin (Berlin), and the Universities of Freiburg (Baden-Württemberg), Göttingen (Lower Saxony), Heidelberg (Baden-Württemberg), and Konstanz (Baden-Württemberg). Four of these six universities (Aachen, Berlin, Heidelberg, Göttingen) had already

Table 7.2 Outcomes of Round 2, German Excellence Initiative (2007)

	Graduate Schools	Excellence Clusters	Institutional Development Concepts
Number to be Selected	About 22	About 12	About 7
New First Proposals Received	118	123	20
Round 1 proposals Carried Forward	21	22	7
Selected for Short-list (Full Proposal)	44	40	8
Winners	21	20	6

Source: Fallon (2007: 13), adapted by authors.

applied in the category "institutional development concepts" in the first round but had been rejected in the end. The two universities which were rejected in this category in the second round were the Humboldt University in Berlin and Bochum University (Northrhine Westfalia). Although the distribution is more varied than in the first round, we find again a clear over-representation of institutions located in southern Germany.

Taking both selection rounds together we have four universities with elite status located in Baden-Württemberg and two located in Bavaria, meaning that two-thirds of the total number of universities with this status are located in the south of Germany. Among the winners in the category of graduate schools the picture is more varied in the results of the second round. Berlin is strongly represented with four institutions, but also once again Baden-Württemberg with five. However, in this round two of the winners were located in East German states. Concerning the subject distribution we find a stronger representation of humanities (three) as well as social sciences (three). With eight graduate schools in the life sciences and biology and four in engineering and computer sciences, these two subject groups are well represented again while the hard pure sciences (mathematics and physics) won three graduate schools.

The winners of the second selection round in the category "excellence clusters" are distributed over ten of the German States, although no institution located in East Germany is among them. Strongly represented are Northrhine Westfalia (four clusters), Berlin (four clusters), and Baden-Württemberg again (four clusters). The subject distribution looks as follows: seven clusters are in the fields of life sciences, biology, engineering and computer sciences, five clusters are in the humanities, and one cluster is in physics (DFG-Pressemitteilung 65/2007).

Two trends which had already became visible in the first round of selections were confirmed in the second round, namely that there were an increasing number of interdisciplinary approaches among the winning graduate schools and excellence clusters and that there were a sizable number of cooperative projects, either in the form of a university cooperating with an extra-university research institute (as is the case for the Karlsruhe institutional development concept formalizing cooperation with a Fraunhofer Institute which won elite status in the first round), or in the form of two universities cooperating within the framework of a graduate school or excellence cluster. The excellence clusters also frequently include the integration of private sector companies. These features were strongly supported in the guidelines and criteria for selection.

Although plans exist to repeat the competition in all three categories in five years' time, no definite decision has been taken yet.

Restructuring the German Higher Education Landscape

Although the Initiative for Excellence is not officially regarded as a move to introduce ranking into the German higher education system, it is an attempt to differentiate the institutional landscape according to a stronger vertical differentiation. Interestingly the direction of this type of differentiation tends to create a tension with the development of convergence triggered by the Bologna reform process, i.e. the introduction of a tiered system of study programs and degrees according to three cycles: Bachelor's, Master's and Ph.D. programs and degrees in the current 45 Bologna signatory countries. In Germany as well as in other European higher education systems that can be characterized as being essentially binary systems consisting of universities and *Fachhochschulen* (universities of applied sciences) or their equivalents, the Bologna reforms have led to a blurring of boundaries between the two institutional types. Although the award of doctoral degrees continues to remain the sole privilege of universities, both types of institutions can now offer Bachelor's as well as Master's programs and the distinction between professional and research Master's programs is not always clear. This has introduced a certain amount of competition at the level of Master's programs.

The initiative for excellence is, however, only targeted towards universities. *Fachhochschulen* can not apply. Experts of the German higher education system basically agree that the initiative will eventually lead to a more vertical form of differentiation. There will be a small group of top universities forming the "elite cluster." There will be a clearly larger group consisting mostly of universities in a middle-level stratum, which will view themselves as solid research universities but will have few opportunities to move into the top group. Finally there will be another large group mainly of *Fachhochschulen*, but also a number of universities, which will be competing against each other mainly for Bachelor's students. These institutions might offer some Master's programs as well but there will be little research, and activities will concentrate mainly on teaching. The interesting areas in this form of institutional differentiation will be at the margins where movement from the top group to the middle group and vice versa as well as movement from the middle group to the lower group and vice versa will take place. This does not necessarily entail a pre-determined place for each individual institution in a given ranking list but rather a grouping or clustering of institutions with the possibility of internal movement.

Following on from this, a tension emerges with regard to mutual recognition and mobility between institutions, which are two other Bologna reform goals. The Excellence Initiative subtly strengthens the view that only institutions which deem themselves to be on the same level of excellence and reputation will cooperate with each other, exchange students among each other, and recognize their respective qualifications. This implies distinctive groupings or clustering with the movement of individuals between them becoming more difficult. For the German higher education landscape this creates the inherent danger that a student moving from a university not involved in the Excellence Initiative to a new university which is involved in it might have problems in securing recognition of previous achievements or even in being accepted at all.

What can be observed already is that the Excellence Initiative did indeed trigger more competition among German universities than ever before. Whether it will also turn out to be the first step in establishing a ranking of German universities remains to be seen. Among those universities which did not participate in the competition as well as those who lost in it there is widespread fear that the additional funding the winners will receive over the next five years will give them such a headstart in developing excellence that the differentiation will be ossified, i.e. the winners now will also be the winners in future competitions.

As Teichler (2006) has pointed out, there are a number of historical phases in German as well as in European debates on the role of diversification and differentiation of higher education systems. In the phase of higher education expansion in the 1960s and 1970s diversification was achieved through creating different institutional types (e.g. polytechnics) and internal (i.e. intra-institutional) differentiation through program diversity. This horizontal differentiation has gradually been replaced in recent years by vertical differentiation due to increased international competition and supported by the growing popularity, in particular among institutional leaders and policy makers, of global and national rankings. To have "elite institutions" or "world-class universities" in one's own national system has almost become an imperative. This development has supported the emergence of the view that generally national higher education systems should be more vertically stratified than before, that success at the top of the system is important, and that the "top" no longer plays in the national league but in a (global) champions league (Teichler 2006). The three elements of this view played a major role in the decision to start the "Excellence Initiative" in German higher education.

But what about the majority of universities (and other higher education institutions) which are not among the top group? The "shock" function of the first two selection rounds in the framework of the German Excellence Initiative has triggered feelings of being a "loser," in particular among those universities which participated in the competition but lost. The other German universities, which did not participate because they knew they would not stand a chance, also feel as if they have been relegated to "the second league" but try to counter this by emphasizing their difference in function and mission. In the face of mass and even universal higher education no national system can afford to cater exclusively for the "top league" of institutions. That would trigger a form of mimetic isomorphism to the detriment of the national higher education system as a whole. In the face of this inherent danger, Marginson and Rhoades (2002) have developed their argument about the increasingly closer relationship between global, national and regional higher education activities in the face of globalization, which they describe as a "glonacal" process.

Rarely discussed is the question raised by Teichler (2007) as to how the emergence of a top stratum of elite institutions will influence the rest of the system. We have mentioned the danger of mimetic isomorphism. But there is legitimate doubt whether the political decision-makers who established the Excellence Initiative really took the decision on the basis of a clear understanding of the need for a new structure of the system as a whole. They wanted "Harvards" in Germany as a matter of prestige without being able and willing to provide funding at a level which would at least come close to what Harvard actually has (cf. Hinderer 2007; Zechlin 2006), but the issue of a new configuration of the system never really came up in the public debates.

Overall, the question of whether steep stratification will be the dominating concept for restructuring national higher education systems in the future, or whether new and different systems logics will emerge, cannot as yet be answered. Certainly the Bologna reform process will act as an intervening variable. In addition, those higher education institutions ranked in the middle and lower strata of a vertically stratified system will have to reorient their functions and missions as well as improve the marketing and visibility of those elements at which they are good or even excellent. Political decision-makers as well as the public will need to take account of this development. After all, the German Excellence Initiative is focused predominantly on research and not at all on excellence in teaching and the provision of other services.

Excellence in the Making and Its Side-Effects

Besides the impact of the Excellence Initiative on the national system, some critical issues have been generated by the selection process, which will now be analysed.

A first point of criticism casts some doubt on the legitimacy of the procedure itself. It is connected to the question of what is rated in the selection procedure: Is it the quality and style of the application or is it proven excellence? The question is whether the winners have been selected on the basis of their performance promises or their past achievements. Indeed, only those universities selected for the shortlist of overall institutional excellence were actually visited by the reviewers. The divide between "excellence achieved" and "excellence in the making" is all the more difficult to determine when it comes to drawing the line between which institution is awarded the final winning place in any of the categories and the very next institution, or even the one equal to it but not selected (Pasternack 2008; Zürn 2007).

A second point of criticism is the inconsistency between the first two categories (graduate schools and excellence clusters) and the third one (institutional development concepts). While the first two categories are clearly based on an evaluation of research output in the past and convincing evidence-based strategies designed to increase and improve this output, the third category actually awards institutional management concepts. These might have merited their own excellence initiative – just like teaching excellence as well – however, the relationship of excellent management strategies to excellence in research is not a given. Instead, the promoters and organizers of the Excellence Initiative made eligibility for awards in the third category dependent on winning at least one graduate school and one cluster of excellence, thus excluding universities that could have provided evidence of overall management excellence but did not score in the other two categories. Although one might argue that it is the combination of excellent research and excellent management which promises to fulfil the expectation to be able eventually – and of course with considerable extra funding – to achieve world-class status, the criticism reported here points to the fact that the first two categories of awards (graduate schools and excellence clusters) are of a different order than the third (institutional development concepts).

The questions here are (a) whether it would not be more logical to talk of various types of excellence, or (b) whether there is a "unifying element" of excellence. Since the Excellence Initiative was explicitly targeted at research it is possible to identify a variety of unifying elements. It could be the individual researcher, a research group, a network, an institute, department, or faculty, and finally – and this is what was awarded in the third category – the university as a whole. We know, however, from widespread criticism of both national and global rankings that no institution is excellent across the board. In addition, the bigger the institution the more heterogeneous it is likely to be. So the question is whether the awards in the third category, which are supposed to have identified potential "elite" institutions, are not rather the result of a compromise, because there was no trust in permitting the dominance of the forms of excellence evaluated in the other two categories (Teichler 2006).

A third issue is the unintended side effects of the Excellence Initiative on the configuration of the system as a whole. It is not yet possible to answer the question as to which way the "elite" institutions will influence the "rest" and, vice versa, which way the "rest" will influence the elite institutions. Furthermore, it remains unclear whether the competition for excellence status will lead to increased resource concentration among and within institutions (i.e. the status of excellence becomes a self-fulfilling prophecy) or whether there will be a more effective use of the overall pool of talents (on the principle that the broader the basis the steeper the top) (Teichler 2007).

Finally, there is currently great concern about the status and reputation of those universities which lost out in the competition or did not participate in it. They feel like members of the second league, and second rate. This is reinforced by the large amount of attention being paid to the winners. Not only did they gain additional resources but there are other effects, namely that they have become more attractive partners for top level institutions abroad, and that they are now actively and successfully recruiting highly reputed academic staff from other universities. That means that those universities which have not won extra funding in any of the categories of the Excellence Initiative lose out twice which makes their effective participation in the next round all the more difficult. There may be a trend towards a new stratification of the German higher education system but it also poses the question as to whether the system will also develop more heterogeneous purposes or whether there will be more homogeneity as all institutions try to achieve the same officially valued goals (Teichler 2007).

Critical Discussion and Conclusions

In summarizing it can be said that the Excellence Initiative was based on a political prognosis of the (global) competitiveness of the German higher education, research and innovation system which identified a number of problems. While the solution for the problems in teaching and learning is seen in the implementation of the Bologna reforms, the solution for the problems in research was seen in a steeper stratification of the system by identifying top research universities and providing them with considerable extra funding. The process which was established to achieve this goal was academic selection based on peer review to provide legitimacy. Due to time constraints and some inconsistencies in the selection procedures, in particular when the first and the second round of selections are compared with each other, some criticism has been voiced that the procedures lacked sufficient legitimacy (Zürn 2007). To improve the situation a number of suggestions have been made:

- to repeat the competition for excellence in research every five or six years;
- to improve the selection procedures;
- to clarify the relationship of the selection criteria to each other;
- to focus on an assessment of the ability to perform.

As Pasternack (2008) recently pointed out in an analysis of the Excellence Initiative as a political program, the Initiative has landed on a different spot than the one from which it took off. Formally it was established as a dominantly government funded higher education support program. Seen from a content perspective it turned out to be an open acknowledgement of existing differences among universities within the German higher education system and forced the system as a whole to focus more on research. With regard to terminology it introduced a particular concept of "excellence" into the public discourse and established the term as the code for "the highest quality," however, without clearly defining which functions are central to the definition of "excellence," In terms of political and public discourse it made tacit knowledge about differences among higher education institutions visible and offered opportunities for the winners to gain more attention. In the context of higher education policy it was a termination of the longstanding fiction of a qualitatively homogeneous higher education system supported by de facto legal homogeneity.

But does it mean that the Excellence Initiative is just a new regular modus of competitive funding or does it imply a paradigm shift for German higher education?

According to Pasternack it is possible to conceptualize the Initiative in three different ways: (a) as a catalytic funding program, i.e. to achieve critical mass for later unassisted development; (b) as a compact funding program, i.e. long-term additional funding for the winners under conditions of suspended competition for them; or (c) as permanent competition for funding, i.e. a succession of calls for tenders in the most important category, the institutional development concepts, possibly with slightly changing focuses.

In the current stage of development, in particular when we also look at developments in other (European) countries, Pasternack concludes that the Excellence Initiative cannot (yet) be cast as a paradigm shift but must be regarded rather as a component of an increasingly competitive culture in the field of higher education. Therefore, the Initiative has a potential catalytic function for the German higher education system. But much will depend on further decisions. Will it be a one-off event or repeated every five years? What will its effects be on the overall German system of research funding? Will it not only entail decisions about the concept and configuration of the system as a whole but also about its overall forms of funding, and the relationship between organization and innovation within universities. As it is almost certain that the Initiative will be an important factor in the establishment of new hierarchies at the national level, within the individual States, within institutions among the subjects and departments or faculties, and finally within departments or faculties (for example, between those being involved in a graduate school or excellence cluster with funding from the Initiative and those not funded), it is most certainly worthwhile not only to analyse the effects of the Excellence Initiative on the overall system's configuration but also to see how the system as a whole actually performs (Teichler 2007).

But there are further conclusions which can be drawn already at this moment in time. First, there is a general trend to integrate research funding within the framework of programs and projects. The Excellence Initiative is part of this development. In this respect it can be said that Germany is a latecomer again as this form of (competitive) research funding has been introduced some time ago in several other European countries. There is, secondly, a trend towards increased competition for funding. Many academics currently have to engage in some form of competitive bidding for even minimal resources. This requirement not only pertains to third party research funding but also to a variety of funding possibilities within their institutions, e.g. tutors and research assistants, seed money, contracts for doctoral students, funding for participation in conferences etc. A growing amount of time is spent on writing applications, submitting reports and the possibility of exposure to further evaluation requirements. In addition, institutional management also expects that academics be involved more than ever before in such competitions, which diminishes the time actually spent on research.

Finally, looking at the use of the term "excellence" in public and political discourse we can note the highly inflationary character it has acquired. Its newly acquired character is also infiltrating widely into the language of calls for proposals, tenders, and applications. Everything has to be "excellent" in order to justify funding. This brings to the fore a tension between performance and status in which it becomes difficult to distinguish between reputation on the one hand and performance on the other. The social construct of excellence based on reputation and the assessment of objective performance become intertwined and raise questions about the validity of peer review. If we cast the Excellence Initiative as a process of differentiation and distribution of reputation, "objective" measuring and assessment are hardly possible any longer, at least not within the classical forms of peer review led by scholarly and scientific criteria (Hornbostel 2007). Time will tell whether in the future a legitimate balance can be found between "attributed" status and reputation and "objective" performance and achievement.

Note

1. For readers not familiar with the intricacies of educational policy making and funding in the Federal Republic of Germany it should be noted that any kind of joint funding by the German states normally follows two annually fixed criteria to determine the proportion of funding each individual state has to contribute for joint projects or initiatives. The criteria are (a) the level of taxes the individual state is able to raise and (b) the size of the population in the individual state. According to these criteria the state of Northrhine Westfalia had to contribute 21.6% to any kind of joint funding for (higher) education in 2007, the State of Bavaria had to contribute 14.9%, and the state of Baden-Württemberg had to contribute 12.7%. All other German states had to contribute less than 10 percent. Thus the states, other than Baden-Württemberg and Bavaria, were unhappy to see a very uneven

outcome to the Excellence Initiative's selection process because it meant that the majority of the German states would indirectly provide funding for universities in these two states, which are already considered to be rich.

References

Bulmahn, Edelgard (2007): "Die Exzellenzinitiative: Genese einer bildungspolitischen Idee." Paper presented at the Conference, "Making Excellence. Grundlagen, Praxis und Konsequenzen der 'Exzellenzinitiative'," November 23–24, Institute of Higher Education Research Halle-Wittenberg (HoF Wittenberg).

DFG-Pressemitteilung (65/2007): "Zweite Runde in der Exzellenzinitiative entschieden." URL: http://www.dfg.de/aktuelles_presse/pressemitteilungen2007/presse_2007_65.html (accessed: December 3, 2007).

DFG/WR (2006): "Gemeinsame Pressemitteilung von DFG und WR 'Erste Runde in der Exzellenzinitiative entschieden'." URL: http://idw-online/pages/de/news179792 (accessed: December 3, 2007).

Fallon, Daniel (2007): "Germany and the United States, Then and Now: Seeking Eminence in the Research University." Paper presented at a Symposium organized by the Center for Studies in Higher Education, University of California at Berkeley, March 26–27.

Hinderer, Walter (2007): *Die deutsche Exzellenzinitiative und die amerikanische Eliteuniversität.* Berlin: Liberal Verlag.

Hornbostel, Stefan (2007): "Evaluation der Exzellenzinitiative. Gibt es objektive Kriterien für Exzellenz?" Paper presented at the Conference "Making Excellence. Grundlagen, Praxis und Konsequenzen der 'Exzellenzinitiative'," November 23–24, Institute of Higher Education Research Halle-Wittenberg (HoF Wittenberg).

Kehm, Barbara M. (2006): "The German 'Initiative for Excellence' and Rankings." *International Higher Education,* 44, Summer, pp. 20–22.

Marginson, Simon and Rhoades, Gary (2002): "Beyond National States, Markets and Systems of Higher Education: A Glonacal Agency Heuristic." *Higher Education,* 43, 3, pp. 281–309.

Neave, Guy (1996): "Homogenization, Integration, and Convergence: The Cheshire Cats of Higher Education Analysis." In: Meek, V. Lynn et al. (eds): *The Mockers and the Mocked: Comparative Perspectives on Differentiation, Convergence, and Diversity in Higher Education.* Oxford: Pergamon, pp. 26–41.

Pasternack, Peer (2008): "Die Exzellenzinitiative als politisches Programm. Fortsetzung der normalen Forschungsförderung oder Paradigmenwechsel." *Die hochschule,* 17, 1 (forthcoming).

Teichler, Ulrich (2006): "The Creative Variety of Higher Education between Over-Diversification and Over-Homogenization: Five Decades of Public Debates and Research Discourse in Europe." Paper presented at the 19th Annual CHER Conference, September, Kassel (Germany).

Teichler, Ulrich (2007): "Exzellenz und Differenzierung: Auf der Suche nach einer neuen Systemlogik." Paper presented at the Conference "Exzellente Wissenschaft im 21. Jahrhundert oder Harvard weltweit in fünf Jahren?," December, Berlin (Germany).

Zechlin, Lothar (2006): "Im Zeitalter des Wettbewerbs angekommen." *Forschung & Lehre,* 8, pp. 446–448.

Zürn, Michael (2007): "Legitimität, Transparenz, Partizipation. Zur Praxis des Begutachtens." Paper presented at the Conference "Making Excellence. Grundlagen, Praxis und Konsequenzen der 'Exzellenzinitiative'," November 23–24, Institute of Higher Education Research Halle-Wittenberg (HoF Wittenberg).

8

South Africa's Elite Universities in the Post-Apartheid Era, 1994–2007

Andre Kraak

Introduction

South African higher education, at the advent of democracy in 1994, was one of the most fragmented, incoherent and iniquitous higher education systems in the world. Such an unjust system had evolved for nearly two centuries, with Apartheid policies after 1948 only accentuating the racial stratification, which had already shaped South African social life. This chapter will examine some of these early influences, but the primary focus will be on the post-Apartheid era.

The post-Apartheid policy period began in earnest after 1990 with the unbanning of restricted black political movements. This final act of reform by the dying Apartheid regime ushered in a vibrant process of policy debate between various anti-Apartheid forces about the characteristics of a future South African democracy. These policy ideas were then consolidated in the period after the democratic elections of 1994. Policy papers became official Parliamentary Green and White Papers before being enacted as official legislation. The main thrust of this new legislation in the higher education realm has been to attempt to unravel the complex determinants of an iniquitous system, and to build a new, unified and more effectively coordinated system to the benefit of all South Africa's citizens.

However, the pursuit of such a single or unified system has not been an easy task. Nor has the impact of the reforms been uniformly felt across the system. There have been some very visible gains, including a dramatic deracialization of institutions that previously enrolled few African students. But, many of the inequities which characterized the past have persisted into the present, irrespective of the good policy intentions. The chapter tries to explain why this has been the case.

A key factor has been the relative failure of the new institutional landscape created in 2004–2005 to reduce the gross inequalities between institutions created by Apartheid. A second and related factor has been the ambivalence displayed by government towards its own policy of building a new unified system. Rather than reducing the institutional differences and inequalities between universities and technikons (polytechnics) as implied by a unified approach, government has acted to perpetuate the old, highly stratified binary model of the past. A third contribution to the persistence of a highly stratified system has been the continued dominance of the national research and development (R&D) system by a small minority of 'elite' institutions. Their dominance today is largely defined by their research excellence and by their success in recruiting the greatest number of high achievers – both academics and students, black and white.

The chapter concludes by suggesting that, whilst the 'old boys club' elitism established in the advantaged white English-language universities still offers its beneficiaries powerful advantages in the labor market, it is slowly being challenged by a new, more instrumental and utilitarian value system amongst a new grouping of African learners. These African students, who constitute the majority population in higher education today, value career-oriented education and access to employment through the former technikon (polytechnic) system more highly than gaining a slice of the upper-class elitism which the former white advantaged institutions used to offer to the children of the colonial, industrial and former state elites.

Early Colonial Influences (1829–1948)

The acute social differentiation of South Africa's higher education institutions has been shaped by three powerful historical determinants. In the first instance, the factors that led to the inception of higher education institutions have played a powerful determining role in their subsequent trajectory. The first higher education institutions were initiated either by private citizens or by the Anglican and Dutch Reformed Churches. These initiatives were focused on the formation of private schools that offered matriculation and preparation for study in European universities for the children of the colonial elite. For example, the South African College, founded in Cape Town in 1829, was at first a private institution but became a publicly funded institution in 1873 when it became known as the University of the Cape of Good Hope. In 1918 it was transformed yet again and renamed the University of Cape Town. Natal and Rhodes Universities had similar trajectories (Mabizela, 2002).

A parallel development occurred within the white Afrikaans community and was driven by their Dutch Reformed faith. Two theological schools were started in Burgersdorp and Stellenbosch in 1863 and 1869 respectively. These early religious initiatives ultimately led to the formation of the University of Stellenbosch in 1916 and the University of Potchefstroom for Christian Higher Education in 1951.

These differing trajectories – one Dutch and Calvinist, the other English and Anglican – also led to the creation of two socio-economic camps within white society, each with their own 'language-religious-cultural' attributes and economic aspirations. These societal divisions were reflected within the university system itself – one sub-system for English-speaking whites, another for Afrikaans-speaking whites.

The pursuit of economic interests consolidated these initial processes. The discovery of gold on the Witwatersrand in the 1880s led to the formation of the Transvaal Technical Institute in 1904. This college ultimately split, with its two satellite campuses becoming what are today known as the Universities of Witwatersrand and Pretoria in 1921 and 1930 respectively (Mabizela, 2002).

The Imposition of a Racially Segregated System (1948–1982)

A second and perhaps most influential determinant in the evolution of South Africa's system of higher education was the Apartheid regime itself, which came into power in 1948. This regime set about the creation of a racially seg-regated system of education as one of its highest priorities. In 1959, the Extension of University Education Act was passed, allowing for the creation of nine separate university colleges for Africans, Coloureds and Indians. Enrollment of blacks was severely circumscribed at universities designated for whites only. These institutions were given very restricted functions and had few resources at their disposal. Research activity was highly circumscribed and the range of academic fields on offer was limited.

The Rise of a Rigid Binary System (1979–1994)

The third determinant in the creation of a highly differentiated and unequal higher education system in South Africa was the emergence of a rigid binary system. Calls for such a system arose because of the rapid economic growth experienced by South Africa in the period 1960–1976. As was the case elsewhere in the world, the demands of a modernizing economy, particularly a growing manufacturing sector, required the production of larger numbers of intermediate and highly skilled workers which – so it was argued – only a binary system of higher education would be able to meet. In 1979, six technikons were instituted. They were for the benefit of whites only.

The new binary system distinguished between two types of higher education provision: (i) academic education provided through universities and (ii) career-oriented education and training provided through technikons (polytechnics). Only universities were allowed to offer undergraduate and post-graduate degree programs and to undertake research. In contrast, technikons offered only national certificate and diploma courses in career-oriented fields, producing graduates directed at intermediate skilled occupations in the South African labor market.

The rigidity of the system had to do with the terminal nature of many courses in the technikon sector. Most courses did not allow for progression into university programs. In addition, the pedagogic model of the technikons was restricted to teaching (of diploma and certificate courses) and placement (of students in workplaces for the purposes of gaining practical experience).

Research activities were not part of their institutional mandate, nor were there any research and development (R&D) linkages with industry. Such a restricted historical trajectory now poses several problems for these institutions in the post-Apartheid era where progression opportunities, applied research activity and links with industry have become the necessary prerequisites of the new universities of technology (Kraak, 2006).

African students were not part of this career-education track until the 1970s and 1980s when racially segregated institutions were built for them in the Bantustans and homelands.[1] A total of nine technikons were built in this period, one each for Coloured and Indian students, and a further seven for Africans. All of the institutions for Africans were located in the homelands and Bantustans, areas characterized by impoverishment and a severe lack of resources. By the early 1990s, 15 Technikons had been established – six for whites, nine for blacks (Winberg, 2005).

A Highly Differentiated System

The interaction and intersection of these three determinants over several decades of institutional evolution has led to a highly differentiated and unequal system. A social hierarchy of distinct institutional categories had emerged – with the elite institutions at the top of the league and the weakest at the bottom. This hierarchy is presented in Table 8.1.

Key Indicators of Hierarchy

The next section provides a brief overview of a few education indicators for the period 1993–1994 which highlight the extent of inequality in the higher education sector prior to the advent of democracy in South Africa. Achievement scores for students enrolled for the final-year Grade 12 Senior Certificate Examination (SCE), for example, were highly uneven with pass rates determined by administrative location – that is, according to the 14 racially defined Departments of Education which administered the Grade 12 examination. The poorest regions, socio-economically, achieved the lowest matriculation scores: KwaNdebele, Lebowa, Qwa-Qwa and KaNgwane. They achieved pass rates in the range of 25–34 percent (Perry and Arends, 2003). These impoverished areas served as feeder communities for neighboring disadvantaged higher education institutions, and as a consequence, they all recruited economically poor students with weak academic backgrounds. In contrast, the elite white institutions recruited students from economically well off communities with pass rates of 94.5 percent in 1994. Participation rates in higher education for whites in the age group 18–24 years was 69.7 percent in 1994. Over two-thirds of white youth leaving school in 1994 acquired a place in higher education, whereas this applied to only 12 percent of African youth, 13 percent for Coloureds, and 40 percent of Indian school-leaving youth (National Commission on Higher Education (NCHE), 1996: 33).

Table 8.1 A Social Hierarchy of Higher Education Institutions, South Africa, 1994

Category	Number of Institutions	Main Institutional Characteristics
1. Historically advantaged, English-language universities	4	Developed several international networks, although restricted by the academic boycott of South Africa Built prestigious research niche areas Strong links with industry Recruited English-speaking white students with good grades Enrollment of black students was restricted by Apartheid laws in 1959, but black enrollments began to increase slowly in the Apartheid reform era of the 1980s
2. Historically advantaged, Afrikaans-language universities	6	Isolated from global academic networks Strong research niche areas Strong links with the Apartheid government, Afrikaans business interests, and the military-industrial complex Recruited Afrikaans-speaking white students with good grades Almost no recruitment of black students even in the Apartheid reform era of 1980–1994
3. Historically advantaged technikons	7	Successful in the production of intermediate level skilled personnel, for example, technicians and technologists, needed by industry. Recruited mainly white students who were academically excluded from access to the universities
4. Historically disadvantaged universities	10	Most of these institutions were started after 1959 to serve the racial segregation imperatives of Aparthe:d. They were often located in the rural areas, reserved for specific ethnic groups, with poorly skilled staff The poorest of students, both academically and economically, enrolled at these institutions
4. Historically disadvantaged technikons	7	Most of these institutions were started in the 1980s to serve the racial segregation imperatives of Aparthe:d. They were often located in the rural areas, reserved for specific ethnic groups, with poorly skilled staff The poorest of students, both academically and economically, enrolled at these institutions
5. Correspondence university and correspondence technikon	2	Unisa was the largest South African higher education institution, providing distance education through correspondence methods of questionable quality. Working adults, blacks who could not enroll at any other institution, and most famously, the entire community of political prisoners imprisoned in Southern Africa between 1948 and 1994, studied here. Technikon SA was started in the 1980s with a mandate to provide career-oriented diplomas through distance education means. Concerns about poor quality provision were also articulated about this institution.
Total	36 institutions of higher education	

Source: Author's own table.

Similarly, funding allocations were highly unequal. Expenditure levels on white higher education was on average 54 percent higher than that allocated to blacks in 1993. Personnel expenditure per full-time equivalent (FTE) enrolled student was R7,600 for historically disadvantaged universities, whereas it was R12,200 for historically advantaged universities. Fixed asset expenditure per FTE enrolled student was R1,300 for historically disadvantaged universities in 1993, whereas it was R2,000 for historically advantaged universities (NCHE, 1996: 45).

The significance of the two indicators highlighted above – school achievement and funding – is that they are key inputs into the higher education process. The inequities which they reflect will impact throughout the system. Unsurprisingly, throughput and graduation rates in higher education reflect precisely the same inequities. Black throughput is far lower than that for white students at all levels of qualification, falling well below international norms. (NCHE, 1996: 35). Similarly, the number of graduates emerging from the historically black universities in 1993 was a mere 43 percent of the levels achieved by the historically advantaged universities. The inequalities are particularly acute higher up the qualification ladder. For example, only 33 black graduates attained doctorates in the higher education system in 1993 as compared with 543 whites (NCHE, 1996: 35).

The Post-Apartheid Period

Government in the post-Apartheid period has consciously sought to undo much of the inequities imposed on higher education by the Apartheid regime. There have been some early successes, the most significant of which has been the deracialization of all institutions of higher education and the dramatic increase in black participation within the system.

To understand the deracialization process adequately, it is first necessary to look at the overall growth trends in higher education during this period, and then to disaggregate the data by race.

Deracialization

There has been tremendous growth in enrollments throughout the 1990s. For example, Subotzky shows that between the years 1988 and 2002, the highest growth rates in enrollment in this period were experienced by:

- historically disadvantaged technikons at 328 percent growth;
- the correspondence technikon, Technikon South Africa, at 314 percent growth;
- historically advantaged technikons, at 201 percent growth; and finally
- historically advantaged Afrikaans language universities, at 167 percent growth.

(Subotzky, 2003a)

These growth rates far exceed those of the historically advantaged English language institutions (at only 51 percent growth) and the historically disadvantaged universities (at a much slower pace of 24 percent). These new patterns of student enrollment are very significant, as firstly, they flag a huge surge in the choice of technikon (of all types – advantaged, disadvantaged and correspondence) over university study, and secondly, the choice of Afrikaans speaking universities over the English speaking universities.

The rapid growth in enrollments was due primarily to the opening up of access for Africans in all of the formerly advantaged institutions. This was most dramatically the case in the former Afrikaans-language universities and the former advantaged technikons, which up until 1990 were all compliant implementers of Apartheid's education policies. Table 8.2 shows the dramatic enrollment increases for African students in all of those institutions that previously did not enroll high numbers of Africans. The increase of African students in the former Afrikaans language universities and the former advantaged technikons is truly massive – from 1 to 52 percent and from 2 to 68 percent of all students respectively in the period 1988 to 2002.

Another interesting trend observable in Table 8.2 has been the dramatic increase in African students at the institutions formerly reserved for Coloured and Indian students (the universities of the Western Cape and Durban-Westville, and the Peninsula and ML Sultan technikons) – from 17 to 50 percent for the universities and from 10 to 65 percent for the technikons. The same trend is visible for the correspondence technikon. In a short period of time, all of these enrollment surges have destroyed a key pillar of Apartheid education – that of racially 'pure' institutions.

One of the implications of these changes has been the tapering off of white enrollments in public higher education. Fewer whites are gaining access to public higher education. There has been an important substitution effect as a small number of white students now enroll at private higher education institutions, while others study at overseas institutions. But for an increasing number of white youth today, access to public higher education has become far more restricted. Participation rates for the 18–24 year old cohort amongst whites has dropped from 69.7 percent in 1993 to 47.7 percent in 2002 (NCHE, 1996: 33; Breier and Mabizela, 2008: 283).

The New Institutional Landscape of Higher Education

Mergers and Incorporations

Another decisive break with Apartheid's past has been achieved by the process of institutional merger and incorporation which saw the number of higher education institutions contract from 36 to 22.

These institutional mergers and incorporations were a central component of the *National Plan on Higher Education* published by the Department of

Table 8.2 Enrollment Shifts by Race and Institutional Hierarchy, 1998–2002

Institution sub-type	Year	African		White	
		Total Number of African Students	African Students as a % of Total Student Population (%)	Total Number of White Students	White Students as a % of Total Student Population (%)
Historically Advantaged, English-Language Universities	1988	4,759	10	36,655	77
	1993	10,231	20	32,363	63
	1996	16,067	30	25,406	48
	2000	24,549	38	24,793	39
	2002	28,840	40	26,332	36
Historically Advantaged, Afrikaans-Language Universities	1988	673	1	65,844	97
	1993	4,538	6	65,436	90
	1996	20,842	24	59,898	70
	2000	73,407	49	63,120	42
	2002	94,219	52	72,417	40
University of the Western Cape and the University of Durban-Westville	1988	2,951	17	403	2
	1993	8,985	40	562	2
	1996	12,691	53	486	2
	2000	9,944	56	362	2
	2002	10,642	50	445	2
Historically Advantaged Technikons	1988	818	2	32,886	94
	1993	10,163	17	43,840	75
	1996	31,424	44	33,000	46
	2000	65,410	68	22,251	23
	2002	71,651	68	21,655	21
ML Sultan and Peninsula Technikons	1988	889	10	319	4
	1993	4,116	31	690	5
	1996	7,791	51	406	3
	2000	11,993	66	336	2
	2002	11,756	65	330	2
Technikon SA	1988	2,097	20	7,334	69
	1993	18,099	36	25,560	51
	1996	48,972	59	25,376	30
	2000	42,712	71	11,053	18
	2002	30,068	69	7,809	18

Source: Adapted by author from Subotzky (2003a).

Education in 2001 (DoE, 2001). They were viewed as mechanisms to create a more efficient system based on fewer institutions enrolling larger numbers of learners thereby allowing for the acquisition of considerable economies of scale and scope.

The National Plan also proposed an entirely new institutional landscape comprising three differing types: universities, technikons and comprehensives. Comprehensives were to be created out of the merger of a university and technikon. The main contribution of this new entity was that they would provide both academic and career-oriented higher education in parallel tracks. Subsequently, through a process of political lobbying (which will be discussed further in a later section of this chapter), technikons were renamed universities of technology in October 2003.

Most of the institutional mergers and incorporations took place during the 2004–2005 period. By January 2006 South Africa had an entirely new institutional landscape in higher education, comprising 22 institutions across the three new institutional categories as is shown in Table 8.3.

The full impact of the mergers and incorporations can be disaggregated into five distinct institutional effects, each representing differing degrees of severity in terms of structural change:

- institutions experiencing new opportunities through merger (eight of the new institutions);
- institutions experiencing minimal change through incorporations (four);
- institutions which experienced some or no loss (four);
- institutions which experienced limited gains (two);
- institutions facing ongoing disadvantage (four).

New Opportunities Through Merger

One of the policy intentions of the merger process was to use the authority of the state to force through a structural break with the discriminatory categories of the past – the former historically advantaged and disadvantaged institutions. This was to be achieved by creating new institutional identities through the merger and incorporation process on the assumption that by joining former advantaged and disadvantaged institutions together, new nonracial identities would emerge over time. These merged institutions would benefit from the more equitable share of the physical educational infrastructure that was previously distributed on the basis of race. The institutions most affected by these dramatic changes were:

- Tshwane University of Technology, which after the mergers had a total headcount of 60,407 students, of whom 86 percent were black;
- the University of Johannesburg, which after the mergers had a total headcount of 45,544 students, of whom 70 percent were black;

Table 8.3 Student Enrollment According to the New HE Institutional Landscape, Contact Students Only, 2005

	Institutions	Form of Institutional Change	Severity of Change	Details of Mergers	Total Head-count	Black Students as % of Total Head-count
ELEVEN UNIVERSITIES						
Historically Advantaged English-Language Universities	University of Cape Town	No change	No change	n/a	21,764	49
	University of the Witwatersrand	No change	No change	n/a	23,626	64
	Rhodes University	Limited institutional loss	Minimal loss	Lost its East London campus	6,322	52
	University of KwaZulu-Natal	Full merger	New opportunities	Merger of the University of Durban-Westville with the University of Natal	40,704	83
Historically Advantaged Afrikaans-Language Universities	University of Pretoria	Incorporation	Minimal change	Acquired the Mamelodi campus of the former Vista University	46,351	40
	University of Stellenbosch	Limited institutional loss	Minimal loss	Lost its Dental School	21,702	27
	University of the Free State	Incorporation	Minimal change	Acquired the Bloemfontein and Qwa-Qwa campuses of the former Vista University	24,659	65
	North-West University	Full merger	New opportunities	Merger of the Potchefstroom University of Christian HE, the University of the North-West, and the Sebokeng campus of the former Vista University	38,596	52

Historically Disadvantaged Universities	University of the Western Cape	Limited institutional gain	Limited gain	Acquired the University of Stellenbosch Dental School	14,580	94
	University of Fort Hare	Limited institutional gain	Limited gain	Acquired the East London campus of Rhodes University	8,790	92
	University of Limpopo	Full merger	Ongoing disadvantage	Merger of the University of the North and the Medical University of South Africa	17,579	99
FIVE UNIVERSITIES OF TECHNOLOGY						
Mergers of the Formerly Advantaged and Disadvantaged Technikons to Create the New 'Universities of Technology'	Central University of Technology	Incorporation	Minimal change	Technikon Free State acquired the Welkom campus of the former Vista University	10,320	82
	Vaal University of Technology	Incorporation	Minimal change	Vaal Triangle Technikon acquired the infrastructure and facilities of the Sebokeng campus of the former Vista University	17,408	94
	Cape Peninsula University of Technology	Full merger	New opportunities	Merger between the Cape Technikon and the Peninsula Technikon	28,961	78
	Tshwane University of Technology	Full merger	New opportunities	Merger between Technikon Pretoria, Technikon Northern Gauteng and Technikon North-West.	60,407	86
	Durban University of Technology (DUT)	Full merger	No change: Mangosuthu Technikon (MT) has not as yet merged with the other two former technikons	Merger of the Natal, ML Sultan and Mangosuthu Technikons plus infrastructure and facilities of the Umlazi campus of the University of Zululand	(DUT) 22,779	93
					(MT) 9,901	100

Table 8.3 continued

	Institutions	Form of Institutional Change	Severity of Change	Details of Mergers	Total Head-count	Black Students as % of Total Head-count
SIX COMPREHENSIVE UNIVERSITIES						
Regionally Defined Mergers of Formerly Advantaged and Disadvantaged Technikons and Universities to Create the New 'Comprehensive Universities'.	University of Johannesburg	Full merger	New opportunities	Merger of the Rand Afrikaans University, Technikon Witwatersrand, and the East Rand and Soweto campuses of the former Vista University	45,544	70
	University of Venda for Science and Technology	No change	Ongoing disadvantage	Converted to a Comprehensive University	10,497	100
	University of Zululand	No change	Ongoing disadvantage	Converted to a Comprehensive University	10,398	99
	Nelson Mandela Metropolitan University	Full merger	New opportunities	Merger of the University of Port Elizabeth, Port Elizabeth Technikon and the Port Elizabeth campus of the former Vista University	24,157	69
	University of South Africa	Full merger	New opportunities	Merger of three distance institutions – UNISA, Technikon South Africa, and the Distance Education Centre (VUDEC) of the former Vista University	207,931	63
	Walter Sisulu University of Technology and Science	Full merger	Ongoing disadvantage	Merger of the University of Transkei, Border Technikon and Eastern Cape Technikon.	24,496	100
TOTAL ENROLLMENTS					737,472	74

Source: Department of Education (DoE), 2006: 29.

- the University of KwaZulu-Natal which in 2005 had 40,704 students, 83 percent black;
- the University of the North West, which in 2005 had 38,596 students, 52 percent black;
- the Cape Peninsula University of Technology, which in 2005 had 28,961 students, 52 percent black;
- Nelson Mandela Metropolitan University, which in 2005 had 24,157 students, 69 percent black.

At the heart of these new institutions listed above is a former advantaged institution paired off with a historically disadvantaged institution (in some cases, pairing comprised the incorporation of two or even three additional sites from previously disadvantaged institutions), with each of the old entities formally dissolving into a new legal entity with newly appointed management and a new governing Council. It has been left to each new institution to define its own approach to further institutional integration. In many cases, there has been considerable duplication of both academic programs and administrative structures. A key outcome of this process, however, has been the creation of six very large entities which are well positioned to benefit from substantial economies of scale and scope. Student demographics have been dramatically deracialized, and the racial composition of staff better reflects the national demographics (although there is still significant room for improvement). It is too early to provide a comprehensive account of whether these instances of social engineering have improved educational conditions for the better. Nonetheless, they signify the most dramatic structural changes so far in the higher education realm.

A seventh case which can be added to this category is the merger of the old correspondence University of South Africa with the correspondence Technikon South Africa to create the 'new' University of South Africa, a mega distance education facility, which after the mergers had a total of 207,931 students, of whom 63 percent were black. It is different, though, to the above-listed cases, which were all contact institutions.

An eighth case refers to the single instance of restructuring, which had not been completed by January 2006. This was the case of the Durban University of Technology, where attempts to persuade the Mangosuthu Technikon to merge with the other two former technikons in the greater Durban area – ML Sultan and Natal Technikons – had failed. This was a delay rather than a setback, and on completion it would constitute the final case of institutional merger between two previously disadvantaged technikons and one advantaged technikon.

Minimal Change Through Incorporations

Several institutions have undergone minimal transformation, experiencing incorporations rather than full-blown mergers which, at most, required the incorporation of a neighbouring site. However, the institutional structures, policies and management teams of the lead institution remained intact. These institutions included the Pretoria University, the University of the Free State, the Central University of Technology and Vaal University of Technology. Most of these incorporations entailed the inclusion of sites which previously belonged to Vista University – a distance institution created by Apartheid for urban black learners who resided permanently in the former 'white' South Africa and not in their so-called designated 'homeland' or 'Bantustan'. Vista University, in fact, constitutes the only case of outright closure through the process of incorporating its multiple campuses into other higher education institutions.

Institutions Which Experienced Little or No Loss

There is a third category of institutional restructuring which for some institutions entailed no change at all. This applies to the Universities of Cape Town and Witwatersrand. In the cases of the Universities of Stellenbosch and Rhodes, they lost minor assets, a dental faculty in the case of the former, an East London campus in the case of the latter. In the main, these four institutions did not undergo major change in their primary institutional identities.

Institutions Which Experienced Limited Gains

Two institutions gained from the losses of Stellenbosch and Rhodes Universities. In the first case, the University of the Western Cape (UWC), a formerly disadvantaged institution, acquired the physical and human resources of Stellenbosch University's dental faculty, which, on amalgamation with the UWC Dental Faculty, created a single mega-training facility for the Western Cape. Similarly, the University of Fort Hare, also a formerly disadvantaged institution, acquired the East London campus previously belonging to Rhodes University. This gave Fort Hare an important presence in an urban location with a campus better integrated into the infrastructure of city life. In contrast, Fort Hare's main campus is located in the highly impoverished hinterland of the rural Eastern Cape, one of the poorest regions in South Africa.

Institutions Facing Ongoing Disadvantage

Finally, it can be argued that in four instances, the disadvantage experienced by black higher education institutions has not been reduced by the mergers and incorporations, but rather, has worsened through the merger of two disadvantaged institutions, leaving behind a larger and therefore more burdened disadvantaged institution. This situation applies in the case of Limpopo University, which was a merger of two previously disadvantaged universities, and Walter Sisulu University of Technology, which was a merger of three previously disadvantaged technikons. In additional cases, two previously disadvantaged institutions have been left unchanged in terms of resources and infrastructure. These are the Universities of Zululand and Venda. The main change impacting on them is a redesignation of purpose to that of 'comprehensive university', but without additional financial, human and infrastructural resources on a large scale, these restructured institutions are unlikely to overcome the burdens of their past.

It is clear that there is significant policy incoherence across these five categories of institutional change. Many of the elite institutions have come out of the restructuring process relatively unaffected. Others have gained valuable additional assets. But a significant number of institutions remain as under-resourced and disadvantaged as they were under Apartheid. The uneven hand of the policy implementation process has been accentuated by a further dynamic of incoherence in the policy formulation process – that is the perpetuation of an outdated form of binary divide, which will be examined in the next section.

Policy Ambiguity and Contradiction

The policy process in South African higher education over the past decade has never had a high degree of certainty regarding its central policy propositions. Policy uncertainty relates, in the first instance, to the high degree of ambiguity shown by key sectors of the higher education community towards the dominant policy approach which emerged in the period 1990–1997 (when the new Higher Education Act was passed), and in the second instance, it relates to the contradictory implementation of this official policy framework in the period 1997–2007. Whereas official policy supported the idea of a more unified, single system of higher education, key stakeholders – including the state bureaucrats in charge of the implementation of higher education policy – gave support to the continuation of an unchanged binary model. This continuity of structural and institutional elements from the past has meant the perpetuation of the social hierarchies and inequalities inherent in South Africa's rigid binary model.

The Case for a Unified System

The National Commission on Higher Education (NCHE) launched in 1995 was the first major policy initiative in higher education post-1994. The main problem it identified in its key findings submitted to government was the absence of any sense of 'system'. This led the NCHE to propose a new regulatory framework that would co-ordinate the higher education band as a single coherent whole, applying uniform norms and procedures with sufficient flexibility to allow for diversity in addressing the multiple needs of highly differentiated learner constituencies and a modernizing economy. The new higher education policy framework called for a more open and unified system based on centrally driven planning and coordination.

At the heart of the notion of a single nationally coordinated system was a strong emphasis on state co-ordination which would strategically 'steer' the higher education system via a regulatory framework based on financial incentives, reporting and monitoring requirements (particularly with regard to key performance indicators) and a system of program approval. The shift in policy framework was dramatic, from a classic binary model to a single system with differentiation derived not from some historically acquired institutional role but via programs which would be identified through systematic planning and coordination so as to steer the entire national system in directions consonant with national socio-economic priorities.

The NCHE was influenced by the world-wide shifts toward more open, massified and inclusive systems of higher education (Scott, 1995). The determinants for mass higher education world-wide had been the widening of access to formerly excluded learner constituencies, particularly women, blacks and working-class students. These developments over the past two decades, globally, have led to an impressive growth in higher educational programs, going far beyond the provision of discipline-based degree qualifications. Much of this expansion has occurred in the fields of recurrent, continuing and professional education and training – the key access points to higher education for the working class and other previously marginalized constituencies.

These developments have had the effect of moving national systems of higher education away from binary or divided systems towards more unified single systems with common features and a homogenizing mission. However, the erosion of functional differences between previously distinct types at each end of the binary divide does not suggest the rise of uniform missions for all institutions in unified systems of higher education. Indeed, system-wide dichotomy has given way to institutional-level pluralism and diversity (Scott, 1995: 169). Differentiated roles were now determined not by rigid divisions within the system, but by the niche areas of provision individual institutions chose for themselves as key areas of specialization and expertise – a process the state could influence through various forms of incentives and constraints.

The Continuation of a Binary Divide

The formal adoption of this new approach – the emphasis on a single, nationally coordinated system of higher education – did not bring with it policy certainty and consensus in the wider South African education community. There was considerable opposition to the idea of a unified system, which arose from two sources: from the technikons themselves, and from the leadership of the historically disadvantaged institutions who believed the new approach would put them yet again at a disadvantage because of their lack of capacity to respond creatively to new program offerings. However, a compromise position soon emerged, which was premised on a middle-ground formulation that supported 'functional differentiation' (a continuation of the binary divide) in the short to medium term, a position that was not principally opposed to a transition to 'flexible differentiation' (meaning a unified system with internal differentiation) in the longer term.

An even stronger position on the continuation of the binary divide was articulated by the *National Plan in Higher Education* in 2001. This report was concerned that the program distinctions between technikons and universities had been dramatically eroded. Technikons had gradually increased their degree offerings both at undergraduate and postgraduate levels (DoE, 2001: 57). The tendency towards uniformity of provision, according to the Plan, 'was worrying'. There had been little evidence of attempts by institutions, it argued, to identify unique institutional strengths and niche areas, either existing or potential, that would differentiate between institutions.

The Ministry's response to these developments was to attempt to halt this erosion by retaining the binary divide between technikons and universities for at least a further five years as 'two types of institutions offering different kinds of higher education programs' (DoE, 2001: 57). This view was ratified a year later by government's finalization of the policy formulation process on institutional restructuring (DoE, 2002).

Technikon Lobbying

At this stage in the evolution of higher education policy (June 2002) there had been little mention or debate in the policy environment about universities of technology, nor of converting technikons into such institutions. This shift came about through political lobbying rather than through a deliberative process of policy evolution.

The Committee of Technikon Principals (CTP) argued that even though the status of the technikons was protected in the National Working Group (NWG) recommendations, their absolute numbers had declined from 15 to 5. This was because of the formation of comprehensive universities, merging technikons with traditional universities, and the amalgamation of several technikons into one institution.

Given their reduced institutional clout, the technikon leaders now began to argue, in direct contravention of their previous policy positions, that 'the name technikon had become a stumbling block' (CTP, 2004: 7). Amongst the problems listed were that technikons were seen as inferior to universities, technikon graduates were not recognized by professional associations, and that technikons were seen as a second or third choice after universities. Membership of international university associations were denied as technikons were not known as degree-awarding institutions of higher education (CTP, 2004: 7).

Against this background of change, institutional drift and declining status, the CTP worked relentlessly at persuading the Minister to reinstate the former pre-eminence of the five remaining technikons through a name change to that of 'university of technology'. The Minister finally relented and gave his approval to the name change in October 2003.

The South African higher education system now has three institutional types – all supposedly universities, but still governed by the logic of the old two-institutional binary divide. There are two substantive problems with this transition. Firstly, two of the new institutions – universities of technology and comprehensive universities – fall far short of being proper universities. Widely accepted criteria for university education would be that such institutions should have: a large cohort of academic staff with doctorates; high research output; staff able to teach on degree programs including doctoral programs; and significant expenditure on research and development (R&D) activity. This is not the case at all with the two new institutional types.

The second problem is that these two new institutional types have come into existence with very few, if any, official state policy documents having been drawn up prior to their enactment as institutions. The institutions have come first and it is assumed that their distinctive missions will evolve later. This has created an environment of policy incoherence and confusion.

Ongoing Advantage and Disadvantage in the Traditional University Sector

Unevenness also characterizes the change process within the traditional university sector. Of the 11 universities in the new system, three remain disadvantaged. These are the Universities of Fort Hare, Western Cape, and Limpopo. The case of the former two institutions is interesting, because they rallied formidable political opposition to a suggestion early on in the policy process to merge with neighbouring institutions. They won this political contest. Both the Universities of Fort Hare and Western Cape escaped a merger, and in fact have benefited from the incorporation of two useful assets – a dental faculty in the case of the Western Cape, and the East London campus of Rhodes University in the case of Fort Hare. However, the burden of improvement now lies firmly with these two institutions themselves, to justify their exclusions from the merger process, and to demonstrate competence at being 'universities' in the universally accepted sense.

The case of Limpopo University is very different, as it is a merger of two disadvantaged institutions separated by several hundreds of kilometers. Unless the state invests heavily in its renewal over the next decade, it will remain a weak and disadvantaged institution.

In sharp contrast, of the remaining eight universities, only two suffered dramatic change during the merger process – the Universities of KwaZulu-Natal and North-West. The other six escaped relatively unscathed. And of these eight, five dominate the research environment in terms of doctoral production, journal output, and R&D expenditure. Yet the policy process never entertained the idea that recognition should be given to an elite group of 'research universities'. Nonetheless, they are indeed, de facto, research universities.

Research and the Dominance of the Elite Institutions

The dominance of the research and development (R&D) environment by a small number of institutions, and the low levels attained by the universities of technology and most of the comprehensives is very evident in Table 8.4, which highlights the dominance of just five elite institutions across all four key indicators of R&D activity. The universities of technology, in contrast, perform very poorly against all of the four indicators.

Conclusion

Radical changes have occurred in higher education in South Africa. Some have been positive, such as the dramatic deracialization of enrollments. In addition, some of the more imaginative mergers have offered new opportunities for the formerly disadvantaged institutions that are now part of larger merged entities. These new institutions provide a solid reservoir of human capital and infrastructural resources for all their constituent parts.

But the benefits are not widespread across higher education. The sector is still torn apart by accusations of ongoing disadvantage in many of the former black institutions. Key indicators on higher education today confirm the continuity of Apartheid-era inequalities in many former black institutions. This chapter has tried to explain why this has been the case. The analysis has provided three reasons. Firstly, the primary policy tool since 1994 has been that of 'mergers' and not that of 'inequality' per se. Mergers were aimed at achieving system-wide administrative and financial efficiencies as well as economies of scale and scope in enrollments and curriculum offerings. The actual reduction of individual institutional inequalities was a secondary concern. The final decisions made in 2002 and 2003 on which institutions would be merged, incorporated or left unaffected were influenced in part by the ability of institutions to resist merger plans or not. The new institutional arrangements which emerged, therefore, were based on essentially political lobbying and not on some egalitarian policy framework dedicated to the reduction of institutional inequalities.

Secondly, a crude form of the binary divide was retained leaving in place the institutional stratification which this had given rise to over the past 30 years. And lastly, in the context of the emergence of a highly globalized knowledge economy, those institutions that have been able to master the acquisition, management and delivery of large-scale research activity across multiple fields are now the leaders in higher education worldwide. In South Africa, five elite institutions have acquired this research reputation.

However, it would not be accurate to suggest that these five institutions set a 'gold standard' to which the entire South African population aspires. Indeed, the rapid enrollment in the former technikon sector as indicated earlier suggests a new emerging set of values in higher education. At the core

Table 8.4 Research and Development Achievements by Institution, in Descending Order based on R&D Expenditure

Institution	R&D Expenditure in R '000s (2004/2005)	Total Research outputs, 2005	Number of A- and B-rated Scientists, 2006	Doctoral Degree Enrollments, 2005
University of the Witwatersrand	394,527	761	69	697
University of Cape Town	343,119	893	108	970
University of KwaZulu-Natal	343,115	949	48	1,081
University of Pretoria	310,000	1,101	59	1,546
University of Stellenbosch	283,402	826	61	804
University of the Free State	117,037	411	11	544
North-West University	103,447	326	10	670
University of South Africa	102,040	520	13	994
University of Johannesburg	95,060	326	13	583
Rhodes University	78,821	253	14	217
University of the Western Cape	73,354	166	11	321
Nelson Mandela Metropolitan University	46,115	209	5	259
Tshwane University of Technology	45,257	88	2	117
University of Limpopo	33,216	106	0	167
Durban University of Technology	32,117	27	0	42
Cape Peninsula University of Technology	28,564	69	1	67
Vaal University of Technology	21,753	17	0	28
University of Fort Hare	21,369	53	1	84
Walter Sisulu University of Technology and Science	15,824	33	0	1
Central University of Technology	15,764	27	0	79
University of Zululand	12,189	44	0	143
University of Venda for Science and Technology	7,400	27	0	40
	2,533,971	7,230	426	9,454

Source: DoE, 2006; Department of Science and Technology (DST), 2006; National Research Foundation (NRF), 2007.

of this new set of educational aspirations is a more utilitarian and instrumental view of higher education – now viewed as a societal resource that holds out the promise of a job. In the new nonracial South Africa, the cultural symbols represented by the old elite institutions – both English- and Afrikaans-speaking – hold far less appeal to the majority student population than was the case in the Apartheid past.

In the new nonracial South Africa, the upper-class symbols of 'refinement' and 'high culture' which the white elite English language universities sought to cultivate, and the strong sense of dedication to service in the interests of the state and community, which the elite Afrikaans language institutions sought to perpetuate, have now given way to a much more inclusive and pluralistic set of values.

The universities of technology route with its associated career-oriented education, is now considered a far more valuable track to pursue than was the case three decades ago. This observation was confirmed by Cosser and du Toit who undertook a large-scale survey of 12,000 Grade 11 (aged 16) students in 2001. The key question put to these students, the majority of whom were African, concerned the choices that they would make in terms of their future 'hoped-for' learning trajectories. Although A-grade students continued to choose universities as their first choice of higher learning, a high proportion of learners amongst the B- and C-graded learners chose the technikon route even though they would have qualified academically for access to university education. Cosser and du Toit show that it was largely African students who chose technikons as their most favored destination after school, whereas significant numbers of white learners first chose private institutions and then only the traditional elite institutions.

Enrollments at private higher institutions do not constitute a large percentage of total higher education enrollments, peaking at about 30,000 students in 2001 before restrictive government regulations in 2001 saw the number of local and foreign private institutions decline. Subotzky (2003b: 426) reports that whereas only 33 percent of enrollments at South African owned private higher institutions were white, in transnational private higher institutions, white enrollments rose to 54 percent. Although a very small trend at this stage, enrollments in these institutions for white South Africans appears to serve as an alternative to accessing public higher education, particularly for those who can afford to pay the higher private tuition fees.

In contrast to the higher education choices made by economically well-off white students, African learners from socio-economically advantaged backgrounds still chose technikons by a large margin (Cosser and du Toit, 2002). These choices are shaped by the easier access routes into universities of technology, and by perceptions of less strenuous academic demands. But the choices are also political. Strong resentment towards the elite English institutions continues amongst black learners and black academics who view these institutions as places where racial stereotypes and racial categorization continue to this day.

What all of the above suggests is a higher education system socially stratified in less predictable ways than in the past, with technikon (now university of technology) and private provision competing with the elite institutions for the B- and C-grade African learners. All of this suggests a more pluralistic higher education environment that offers the potential for overcoming the acute institutional inequities still present in the system.

However, for this to occur, two pre-conditions will need to be met. Firstly, quality of provision has to dramatically improve in the universities of technology, the comprehensive and the private institutions benefiting from this new instrumental market for higher learning. In the case of the universities of technology, for example, their technological focus, applied research outputs and linkages to both private industry and government's varied interventions in the economy will need to be dramatically strengthened. They will also need to employ more staff with doctorates and to offer master's and doctoral programs in cutting-edge technology fields.

The second condition is that the universities of technology will need to offer better chances of acquiring worthwhile employment than is currently the case. With a burgeoning economy that has reached a 5 percent growth rate for the first time in three decades, this realignment of institutional role with the employment aspirations of South Africa's total population is a realistic possibility and it may create a less socially stratified higher education system over the next 10 to 20 years. But this turnaround is not guaranteed and it will require significant resources, commitment and effort on the part of all stakeholders in South African higher education.

Note

1. A 'homeland' was an Apartheid-inspired area designated as a self-governing territory for differing categories of Africans, defined largely by tribal groupings. Some of these territories were later decreed as so-called 'independendent' states or 'Bantustans'. These included the former Transkei, Bophuthatswana, Venda and Ciskei.

References

Breier, Mignonne, and Mahlubi Mabizela. 'Higher Education.' In *Human Resources Development Review 2008: Education, employment, and skills in South Africa*, edited by A.H. Kraak and K. Press. Cape Town: HSRC Press, 2008.

Committee of Technikon Principals [CTP]. *Position, Role and Function of Universities of Technology in South Africa*. Pretoria: Committee of Technikon Principals, 2004.

Cosser, Michael and Jacques du Toit. *From School to Higher Education? Factors affecting the choices of Grade 12 learners*. HSRC Publishers: Cape Town, 2002.

Department of Education [DoE]. *National Plan for Higher Education*. Pretoria: Government Printers, 2001.

Department of Education [DoE]. *The Transformation and Reconstruction of the Higher Education System*. Pretoria: Government Printers, 2002.

Department of Education [DoE]. *Education Statistics in South Africa at a Glance in 2005*. Pretoria: Government Printers, 2006.

Department of Science and Technology [DST]. *Research and Development Survey, 2004/5.* Pretoria: Government Printers, 2006.

Kraak, Andre. 'Academic drift in South African Technikons: beneficial or detrimental?.' *Perspectives in Education.* 24 (3) 2006: 135–152.

Mabizela, Mahlubi. 'The evolution of private provision of higher education in South Africa.' *Perspectives in Education.* 20 (4) 2002: 41–52.

National Commission on Higher Education [NCHE]. *Discussion Document: A Framework for Transformation.* Pretoria: Government Printers, 1996.

National Research Foundation [NRF]. *Facts and Figures 2007.* Pretoria: National Research Foundation, 2007.

Perry, Helen, and Fabian Arends. 'Public schooling.' In *Human Resources Development Review 2003: Education, employment, and skills South Africa.* Cape Town: HSRC Press; East Lansing: Michigan State University Press, 2003.

Scott, Peter. *The Meanings of Mass Higher Education.* Buckingham: Open University Press, 1995.

Subotzky, George. 'Public Higher Education.' In *Human Resources Development Review 2003: Education, employment, and skills in South Africa.* Cape Town: HSRC Press; East Lansing: Michigan State University Press, 2003a.

Subotzky, George. 'Private Higher Education and Training.' In *Human Resources Development Review 2003: Education, employment, and skills in South Africa.* Cape Town: HSRC Press;, East Lansing: Michigan State University Press, 2003b.

Winberg, Chris. 'Continuities and discontinuities in the journey from technikon to university of technology.' *South African Journal of Higher Education.* 19 (2) 2005: 189–200.

9

The Legacy of Planning
Higher Education Development in China

Kai-Ming Cheng, Yan Wang and Su-Yan Pan

Preamble

China's rapid growth in its economic power is paralleled by its development in higher education. One dimension of the development is the spectacular expansion in the scale of the higher education system. The other dimension is the emergence of elite universities, which are competitive in the international arena.

Since 1999, in strong contrast to an earlier policy of conservatism, China has launched a dramatic expansion of its higher education system. By the end of 2007, the total student population in China's higher education system was 25 million (Ministry of Education, 2007), which is by far the largest in the world.[1] Meanwhile, in the same period of time, China started building 'a few first-rate world-class universities'. The net result of the campaign is the emergence of elite universities, Peking University and Tsinghua University in particular, which are highly positioned in the international ranking of universities.

Incidentally, both dimensions of development loom high on national policy agendas around the world. Therefore, China's higher education development has attracted much attention in the international community.

This chapter observes that the development of China's higher education in the past decade represents a deviation from the socialist manpower-planning ideology and its associated principles of resource allocation. However, it also argues that we can still find in the higher education system some influence of the manpower-planning legacy.

The Expansion

China started expanding its higher education system in 1999. It started after the enactment of the Law of Higher Education in 1998, and the now well-known speech made by the then President Jiang Zhemin in May at Peking University's Centenary Celebration (known as the 985 Speech).

Before the summer of 1999, the Ministry of Education announced that admissions in the following academic years should be increased by 50%, and that applied to all institutions across the entire nation. The target was

Table 9.1 New Entrants in Regular Higher Education Institutions (1998–2005)

Year	Undergraduate Entrants	Annual Increase of Undergraduate Entrants (%)
1998	1,083,600	8.32
1999	1,596,800	47.40
2000	2,206,100	38.16
2001	2,682,800	21.61
2002	3,205,000	19.46
2003	3,821,701	19.24
2004	4,473,400	17.05
2005	5,044,600	12.77
2006	5,460,500	8.24

Note
Constructed from *Statistical Bulletin on Education*, MOE, 1998–2005. Also from J. Li (2002) *High Rate Expansion of China's Higher Education: Issues, Problems and Response.* http://www.unescobkk.org/fileadmin/user_upload/apeid/Conference/11thConference/ppt/5B_jin g.pdf.

basically reached. The following year, similar expansion was commanded at 25%, but the actual growth in intake almost reached 40%. In 2001, while the Ministry was not keen on promoting further expansion, the actual intake still increased by 22%. Thereafter, the intake saw an annual growth of around 20% until 2004. Meanwhile there has been a spectacular mushrooming of private institutions, which has further boosted the capacity of the higher education system. One may say that expansion never comes to a halt, although the official policy of expansion was limited to the first three years after 1999.

By the end of 2007, the higher education student population grew to 25 million. This accounts for a gross enrollment ratio of 22% (Ministry of Education, 2007). It is noticeable, though, that these figures also include students in full-time institutions, which could otherwise be classified under the non-formal education category. Nonetheless, even if we count only formal and regular full-time higher education, the total student population is 17.4 million, still the largest in the world on all counts.

The Manpower-Planning Legacy

Nonetheless, the dramatic and bold expansion of higher education represents a discontinuity in the trend of higher education development in China. Ironically, although the emphasis on education has always been central to the Chinese culture, there had been only very conservative growth in the scale of higher education before this recent expansion. This is a conspicuous exception among the family of so-called 'Confucian cultures', or 'chopstick cultures' such as Japan, Korea and Taiwan, all of which have seen oversupply of higher education in recent years.[2] The following analysis presents the context in which this conservative development of higher education development took place.

The People's Republic of China was established in 1949. Until the beginning of the open economic policies in the late 1970s, China adopted manpower planning in the strict sense of the term. In a comprehensive framework of a socialist planned economy, the education system and its student intake every year were planned strictly according to requirements indicated by manpower-planning forecasts. Hence, the design of the particular programs and the student intake in each program echoed the projected manpower demand in the year after these students graduated. Such manpower demands in turn were derived, in the final analysis, from the Five-Year Plans for national economic development. As such, and with the industrial manufacturing base as the major clientele of highly skilled manpower, university graduates were meant for appointments only at the apex of the pyramidal structure in factories. The net result is that there was only limited demand for higher education.

China also suffered from the almost total destruction of its higher education system during the Cultural Revolution (1969–1976). During the Revolution, universities were targeted as one of the major strongholds that created and spread bourgeois ideology as well as being the breeding ground for petit bourgeois intellectuals. The idea was to totally revamp the cultural values of such institutions and replace them with institutions led by peasants and workers who would then run the place according to proletarian ideologies. By the end of the revolution in 1976, there were over 46,800 institutions (Ministry of Education, 1984: 239) at tertiary level, such as Workers' Colleges, which recruited only those with 'worker' or 'proletariat' status, and taught only Marxist ideology and pragmatic 'production skills'. Universities and other traditional higher education institutions were virtually totally abandoned.

Universities and colleges were revived almost immediately after the ending of the Cultural Revolution, even sooner than the launch of the other early reforms in the economy. The first higher education entrance examination was resumed in 1977. There was a deep thirst for higher education that had been suppressed for a whole decade. There was such a strong demand for higher education that in 1977 there were two admission exercises in the same year. A large number of very fine people who were deprived of the opportunity of higher education during the Cultural Revolution were admitted. Much of the current leadership, including academic leadership, belongs to the group who were students during these early reform years.

However, ever since the late 1980s, there had been a visible reluctance within the Government to expand higher education further. It was kept at a modest annual intake of around three million students, which is a very small number in a nation with a population of 1.3 billion. The overall student population in higher education saw only incremental growth over the ten

Table 9.2 Enrollment In Higher Education (1978–1998) (in thousands)

1978	1980	1985	1990	1991	1992	1993	1994	1995	1996	1997	1998
860	1,140	1,700	2,060	2,040	2,180	2,540	2,800	2,910	3,020	3,170	3,410

Note
Constructed from *Educational Statistics Yearbook*, various years.

years before the expansion of 1999. The annual growth was limited to 7.41%. Even the expansion of the general secondary schools, which prepare candidates for higher education, was capped.

The real reason for such a reservation against expansion is unclear. There were speculations, mostly from the West, that it was the fear of strong student movements that had slowed the expansion of higher education. However, the expansion that started in 1999 seemed to have dispelled that speculation. One rational explanation is that the Government felt the need for more highly trained manpower in order to face the challenge of the knowledge economy. The other explanation, which is widely circulated among intellectuals in China, was that economic studies had concurred that expanding higher education would be the best way to attract investment from private savings, which would otherwise stay idle in the banks. Regardless, the expansion took place with a speed and on a scale that have made it impossible for government policies to steer. It is a clear demonstration that there is both a policy intention as well as a social aspiration for more higher education.

The rapid expansion was apparently achieved without undue practical difficulties. Outsiders would find it difficult to understand how this could be accomplished with no drastic increase in resources. The financing of higher education in China is such that government appropriation plays a less important part, although most of the institutions are public institutions. The institutions have to generate their own incomes through economic activities such as manufacturing or providing services. Since 1997, tuition fees are collected and have become part of the institutional income. There are also private donations, but at the moment they are significant for only the more prominent institutions.

There are indeed criticisms and complaints among Chinese academics that the expansion was not accompanied by comparable increase of resources, and hence there is a perceived decline in the quality of higher education, typically reflected in a significantly less favourable student-teacher ratio (Pan, 2003: 1–5). Indeed, the average teacher-student ratio was 1:11.6 in 1998, but declined to 1:17.9 in 2006 (Ministry of Education, 1999, 2007). However, there is no study that identifies any deterioration of quality in real terms.

There are also significant signs of graduate unemployment in China. There is the worrying phenomenon that in major cities, there are young graduates who have chosen to stay at home and fail to engage in any economic activities. There is also the possibility of hidden unemployment in the strong demand for postgraduate studies, which is sometimes regarded as a way of avoiding unemployment. However, there are also arguments that the apparent 'unemployment' is a consequence of individual inflexibility in the choice of jobs or reluctance to engage in seeking out a job, rather than a failure in matching higher education to the labor market.[3]

What is interesting is that the Government policies in favour of higher education expansion are not swayed by such observations. This is an obvious deviation from the manpower-planning ideology (where matching higher education to assumed manpower needs was the central concern) to a belief in the proactive creation of educated human resources (where human resources development is expected to precede economic development). This is reflected in a major policy research report with the title *From a Population Giant to a Great Nation of Human Resources* (2003),[4] a line which is now written into national policy.[5]

Structural Reform

The deviation from the manpower-planning ideology is also reflected in the pattern of structural reform in the higher education system. There were relatively few institutions of higher education when compared with the population in China. Before the Cultural Revolution, in the early 1960s, there were only around 400 higher education institutions in the whole nation, hosting a total of around 700,000 students (Ministry of Education, 1984, 150).

At the beginning of the economic reform, in the early 1980s, there were around 700 institutions of higher education in China, and a total student population of approximately one million (Ministry of Education, 1984, 50). By convention, they belong to three categories: those under direct control of the Ministry of Education, those financed and administered by the various other Ministries, and those financed and administered by the provincial authorities.

The categories require some explanation. Institutions under the Ministry of Education are usually universities and are given most attention. They receive more resources and hence are usually of a higher quality. They recruit students from all over the nation, and their graduates can find jobs throughout China. The provincial institutions have more limited resources, and their student intake and graduate employment is confined to their respective provinces. They are 'local' universities, although a province in China could have a population of over 100 million people.

The ministerial institutions are a special category perhaps unique to China. They were established under the socialist system where the respective Ministries are self-sufficient and hence self-contained in almost all aspects of their activities. For example, each Ministry trains its own required personnel. The

Table 9.3 Comparison of the Number of Institutions in each of the Categories between 1978 and 2006

	Ministry of Education	Other Ministries	Provincial Authorities	Non-Government
1978	38	217	343	370
1990	36	316	759	
2005	73	40	1,681	547
2006	73	32	2,179	596

Notes

1 Constructed by author from Wang, J. X. & W, G. Z. (2006) Yuan buwei zhishu gaoxiao xueke jianshe tanxi http://library.crtvu.edu.cn/wwwroot/xueke/uploadfilelunwen/2007117161622 155.pdf.

Liu, R. (2007) Zhan quanguo gaoxiao zongshu chaoguo 95% difang gaoxiao gai benxiang hefang? http://www.edu.cn/fa_zhan_364/20070521/t20070521_233604.shtml.

Anonymous. (2006) Jiji tuijin gaodeng jiaoyu tizhi gaige http://www.chinesejy.com/ Article/443/498/2006/2006061679222.html.

Ministry of Education of P. R. China. (2007) 2006 Quanguo jiaoyu shiye fazhan tongji tongbao http://www.moe.gov.cn/edoas/website18/info29052.htm.

Ministry of Education of P. R. China. (2007) 2005 Quanguo jiaoyu shiye fazhan tongji tongbao http://www.moe.gov.cn/edoas/website18/info20464.htm

Ministry of Education of P. R. China. (2006) Quanguo putong gaoxiao mingdan http://www.moe.gov.cn/edoas/website18/info19550.htm.

Ministry of Education of P. R. China. (2007) Minban xuexiao shuji xueshengshu (1994–1998) http://www.edu.cn/20011105/3008194.shtml.

Ministry of Textiles (disbanded in the mid-1990s), for example, used to train its own technical manpower for the textile mills. However, it also trained its own accountants, medical doctors, teachers and other personnel who worked for the Ministry. This is perhaps easier understood when one realizes that the Ministry ran its own banks, hospitals and schools for its members. Hence, the Ministry of Textiles ran its own university in Shanghai (which is now renamed Donghua University). It also had its own teacher training colleges in order to staff its own primary and secondary schools.

The non-government[6] institutions have just appeared on the horizon. Non-government institutions are usually called private institutions in other systems. The term 'private' is perhaps less than accurate in the Chinese context, because the public–private demarcation is sometimes difficult to unravel. A 1999 study revealed that among the non-government institutions, many of them were actually run by NGOs, which sometimes in China are seen as public organizations. There were also some other institutions, which were run by government departments but for a profit.

A major transition in the past two decades has been one of decentralization. First, the Ministries are required to transfer their institutions to provincial authorities, although a few of the stronger institutions have been transferred to the Ministry of Education. Second, even with the institutions non-State run (people-run)

Table 9.4 Types of Sponsors of Non-Governmental Higher Education Institutions (1999)

Nature of Sponsoring Bodies	Different Democratic Parties	Academic, Professional and Research Associations	Enterprises	Government Departments	State Maintained Higher Institutions	Others	Total
Numbers of Minban Higher Institutions	11 (10.7%)	22 (21.4%)	3 (2.9%)	9 (8.7%)	8 (7.8%)	50 (48.5%)	103

Notes
Constructed by author from Cheng, K.M., Cheung, K.W. and Yip, K.Y. 'Marking *minban* education from public education'. Paper presented at the Comparative and International Education Society Annual Meeting, April 14–18, 1999, Toronto.

Table 9.5 Growth of Non-Governmental Higher Education since 2002

Year	No. of institutions	Student population
2003	173	810,000
2004	228	1,397,500
2005	252	1,051,700
2006	278	1,337,900

Source: Ministry of Education, (2003, 2004, 2005, 2006) Educational Development Statistics.
http://www.moe.gov.cn/edoas/website18/info5184.htm;
http://www.moe.gov.cn/edoas/website18/info14794.htm;
http://www.moe.gov.cn/edoas/website18/info20464.htm;
http://www.moe.gov.cn/edoas/website18/info29052.htm

2012 (ACE) + 800 + 4 million

under the control of the Ministry of Education, there is a scheme of 'co-building', in which provincial authorities are expected to participate in financing these institutions, in return for the admission of local students.

The overall trend is (a) to maintain a small number of quality institutions under direct control of the Ministry of Education; (b) to gradually phase out the ministerial institutions; (c) to increase provincial participation and ownership of institutions; and (d) to encourage the establishment of non-government institutions.

Significantly, in 2002 there was an enactment of the Law for the Facilitation of Non-Government Education. The Law, which applies to all levels and sectors of the education system, has sent a strong message encouraging the establishing of non-government institutions. Since then there has been a remarkable growth of the non-government sector in higher education.

The growth of the non-government sector represents the development of the market sector in higher education. The insertion of the word 'facilitation' in the relevant law is an indication of the will of the National People's Congress to express a positive attitude towards the private sector. However, such an expression in turn reflects the variety of opposition expressed at local levels against the private sector. There is a general convention in the Chinese tradition, which believes that education should be 'clean' from profits and that the private ownership of education should be avoided.

The Notion of Vocational Higher Education

Another development is the apparent indulgence of higher vocational education in policy thinking in China. There is therefore policy pressure to encourage the establishment of vocational higher education institutions.

However, this may not be matched by expectations in the labor market. There has been a remarkable change in the workplace where small work units prevail. In 2006, for example, 99.7% of the registered companies in Shanghai were SMEs (Small and Medium Enterprises). They hosted 86.8% of all the employees and commanded 69.2% of the total assets. Such small work units are fluid in their structures, and hence entail great flexibility in their person-nel. If we look at it from an educational point of view, there is a general trend of a mismatch between what people learn before graduation and what they end up doing after graduation. It is no longer easy to channel graduates into targeted pigeonholes in the job-market.

Added to flexibility and mismatch is the trend toward employees changing jobs more frequently. There is no official statistics about the rate of changing jobs in China. The general perception is that lifelong membership of an organization is very unlikely, and even lifelong identification with a single occupation is becoming more blurred. It is anticipated that if the service sector continues to expand, the frequency of changing jobs and changing careers will become more likely. In this context, treating higher education as a kind of vocational training may not be a viable policy option.

Nonetheless, the notion of vocational training is perhaps more than a matter of policies. It is also a matter of assumption and belief in society. Employers in China tend to employ people with matching qualifications. For example, accountancy firms tend to recruit only accountancy graduates, and ICT firms tend to recruit only computer engineers. There is an unchallenged assumption that these are specialist jobs and hence should go to people only with specialist training, hence the need for vocational higher education. However, among the multinationals in China, people are hired with much weaker reference to their training. Skills-training is often seen as something that can be completed relatively quickly, and the personality and potential of the prospective recruits become the focus of attention.

One may argue that the more traditional Chinese practice is due to the residual influence of the manpower-planning years, which emphasized the matching of supply and demand for manpower to the specialist division of labor. This is perhaps understandable since the socialist planned economy, though launched as an antithesis to the capitalist economy, echoed and indeed reinforced the rigid structure of industrial establishments. This belongs to the ideology of the industrial era. When a market economy is introduced, and when the service sector exceeds the growth of the manufac-turing sector, vocational training in general faces serious challenges, let alone the installation of vocational training at the higher education level.

The emphasis on vocational higher education could easily become a mis-conception that would lead to the suppression of generic learning at the higher education level. The notion of vocational higher education also sends a misleading signal to students that higher education is for specialist training, and hence they should aspire to work in a job dictated by what they have learnt before graduation.

In addition to the misconception on vocational specialization is the emphasis on the level of academic degrees. In particular, in the Chinese labor market, students with a Master's degree in general receive higher salaries than those with only a Bachelor's degree, and even higher for someone with a Doctoral degree. Elsewhere, the value of a higher degree is significant only within the academic profession or terms of specific professional training (such as an MBA). In China, the value of higher degrees perhaps reflects the ancient belief that more scholarly study would add to people's capability.

Non-Formal Higher Education

The picture of higher education in China would not be complete if we did not include the non-formal sector. There is a whole spectrum of non-formal learning modes in higher education in China. The most significant are the Television and Broadcasting University and the Self-study Examination System.

The Television and Broadcasting University hosts countless learners, and in most of the provinces there is a major campus of the Television and Broadcasting University. As is indicated by its name, television and radios are the main means of delivery. There has been a national effort to build satellite receivers throughout the nation to make sure that TV signals are received even in remote and mountainous corners of the country. More recently, there is an ongoing endeavor to enrich the system with web-based communications.

The Self-Study Examination is one of the largest distance learning systems in the world. It is held twice every year, with over ten million candidates per year. Closely following the tradition of the Imperial Civil Examinations in ancient China, the system structurally comprises only examinations. People register with the Self-Study Examination, which imposes few requirements. In reality, there are numerous courses run by various institutions preparing candidates for the Examination. Hence, it is safe to say that there is an abundance of opportunities for individuals to pursue learning beyond secondary schooling. The system reflects the national culture in China where people aspire for education as a significant step towards the improvement of one's life.

This is of course a marked deviation from the planned system before the recent reforms. Adult education has always been an important part of the education system even during the times of the planned economy. However, then such study was part of the work assignment. People enrolled in adult education classes upon the recommendation (often a requirement) of his or her superior, who would consider such study as part of the manpower upgrading process. Members who attended these programs were given release from work or even a sabbatical to pursue such study.

The system of self-study examination, along with the other opportunities for learning, have broken through the manpower-planning ideology, which is now much diminished. Nonetheless, there is still a reluctance to officially recognize study in the non-formal mode. With very few exceptions, most of these programs belong to the 'adult education' category and do not award degrees. Nonetheless, increasingly strong market forces have been challenging the rather rigid demarcation between adult education and the formal sector of higher education.

Building World-Class Universities

Philosophically, the building of 'a few world-class universities' is antithetical to the principles that prevailed over China at the height of socialism. During those years the entire nation was a centralized state. Local governments at all levels were no more than executive branches of the Central Government. As such, there was a strict egalitarianism and all higher education institutions received the same resources from the central government. Higher education institutions were no exception.

It was Deng Xiaoping, the late Chinese Communist leader who launched the reform campaign after the Cultural Revolution, who advocated 'allowing a few to become rich first' as a basic philosophy which is the deliberate opposite of what is often known as 'equalized poverty'. The advocacy, one of pure pragmatism, proved an effective break-away from the social egalitarian ideology of that time, and has been seen as underpinning the success of economic reforms that followed. The strategy of 'a-few-to-get-rich-first' was first translated into Project 211 in higher education.

Project 211 is shorthand for 'Building 100 First-Class Universities for the 21st Century'. It is basically a scheme of competitive extra funding. Institutions nominate themselves for the scheme, undertake evaluations and scrutiny, and are given substantial extra funding for academic excellence in specific areas. Project 211 has been through two rounds, and is moving into the third round in 2008. By encouraging competition Project 211 has been a breakthrough from the top-down designation of centers of excellence.

Closely parallel to Project 211 was the movement towards merging institutions. Institutional merger was a separate initiative aiming at economy of scale. It was initiated at a time when many higher education institutions were still very small in size and could not see any hope of substantial advancement without enlargement. Thus Project 211 helped facilitate mergers, and in some provinces, in order to attract additional resources, institutions were merged in order to maximize opportunities of being identified for Project 211 funding. As is to be expected, not all mergers have been successful. However, perhaps the most successful is Zhejiang University, a merger of five institutions, which has successfully rationalized its structure and has risen to between third and fifth in the national ranking of research universities. Another example is Yangzhou University, which is a provincial institution in the province of Jiangsu. It was a merger of seven institutions. However, there are many other mergers that have been less successful.

A more significant project is Project 985. It was initiated by the then President Jiang Zemin in his speech at the Centennial celebration of Peking University, May 1998, hence the name. In his speech, he called for the establishment of 'a few first-rate world-class universities'. This was a message in favour of the further concentration of resources on a selected few universities. In this project, two tiers of universities were selected. On the first tier, Peking University and Tsinghua University were each given a one-off grant of 1.8 billion RMB (local currency, equivalent to 225 million USD). The size of the grant is remarkable, since it represented more than three times the annual expenditure of each of these universities. On the second tier, seven universities were selected, and each given a grant of 1.2 billion RMB (150 million USD).

These colossal grants have posed the universities immense challenges. The size of the grant was beyond their imaginations. Universities now faced the challenge of developing a dream or a vision to match the size of the grant, which was very different from their past experience. In a very short period of time the campuses were almost totally rebuilt. There was a mushrooming of state-of-the-art laboratories and facilities. There was the creation of positions where professors were paid several times the normal salary. In a way, although money is not everything, this seemed to be a good way to mobilize the zest amongst academics for becoming a 'world-class university'. Indeed, the campaign has also stimulated increased collaboration with foreign institutions, further bringing the universities into the international arena.

Tsinghua University, which is seen as the MIT of China, has seen fundamental changes because of the grant from Project 985. Tsinghua was designated to concentrate on only Science and Engineering during the years of strict manpower planning. Since the opening up of the system, Tsinghua has tried to move away from its technical base and build itself into a comprehensive university. This was largely achieved in the early 1990s and the grant from the Project 985 in 1999 has further allowed the university to transform itself into a research-led university. Thanks to the grant, Tsinghua University has been successful in substantially increasing its graduate student intake. It has built infrastructures that have allowed it to secure national funding to build new laboratories and extend its research base into other disciplines. The grant has also made possible the recruitment of star professors from overseas at high salaries. Moreover, the grant has made it possible for Tsinghua to establish its own Medical School, as well as enabled the 'acquisition' of other institutions in sports and art. Tsinghua now has ample resources for internationalization and the facilitation of extensive collaboration, including creating partnerships with overseas institutions (Pan, 2003, 2006). English has also started to be used as the medium of instruction in selected programs.

International ranking has reinforced the success of Project 985. Although the Shanghai Jiaotong University ranking, which sets the benchmarks for top-tier research institutes, has disappointed almost all universities in China,[7] *The Times Higher Education Supplement* ranking has included both Peking University and Tsinghua University among its top ranks.[8] In a recent ranking in

Taiwan of Asian universities, which concentrates on academic publications, Peking and Tsinghua Universities are again high on the list.

In any case, the term 'world-class universities' is a notion that is open to different interpretations. It is both an appeal and a campaign for a vision. In lieu of a more comprehensive and legitimate means of identification, the rankings have become the default benchmark for world-class universities. In this context, Peking University and Tsinghua University have already achieved the goal of entering the elite club.

It is interesting to observe the role of these 'world-class universities' in the development of the entire national system. First, while Project 211 entails competition and hence institutions may aspire to be included, Project 985 rests on selection by the central government and there is little room for competition. In other words, a built-in mechanism does not exist for institutions to climb a quality ladder. Therefore, the 'world-class university' notion remains with the selected few, and does not seem to have mobilized the entire system for quality enhancement. In a way, we may say that the Project 985 is one of exclusion, where apart from the exclusive chosen few, the majority of the institutions in the nation do not have an opportunity to enjoy the resources that would enable them to become 'world-class universities'. As such, the selected universities symbolize the first as well as the last of a system that aspires after 'world-class' status.

This model of developing a selected few into 'world-class universities' seems to be attractive to many nations. Many other countries have adopted the same 'exclusion' model and concentrate on a few institutions. For example, Saudi Arabia is planning to develop two 'elite universities'.[10] Pakistan has planned to establish six to eight 'world-class universities' in partnership with developed systems of higher education.[11] Thailand has identified four universities as potential candidate for the world's top 100 and Asia's top 50.[12] Malaysia has also aspired to build a few 'apex universities' with extra resources from the central government.[13] Thus the Chinese model seems to have encouraged some national governments to employ a top-down approach in selecting and building their own elite universities.

There are other examples of building 'world-class universities' that might reflect on the nature of the China model. Germany, originally motivated by the Chinese model, launched a campaign in 2004 to build 'world-class universities' by nomination and competition. The campaign, which yielded its first results in 2006, has created a system-wide aspiration for excellence in higher education (Salmi, 2007). Indonesia, as another example, also launched the idea of the 'world-class university', however, the Minister made it clear that the concept 'should become a "fever" that would provide hope for all institutions'.[14]

The Chinese model does not seem to incorporate the idea of spreading 'excellence' across the system. The net effect is that those institutions that are relatively low in quality remain low, with little incentive and opportunity to climb the ladder. The hierarchy becomes static. In other words, the campaign has brought a few institutions into the higher international ranks, but most of the other institutions remain deprived.

One may see this as part of the 'planning legacy'. The planned economy that prevailed over the entire nation in the first thirty years of the People's Republic was realized not only as a structure, but also as an ideology that underpinned people's thinking across all sectors of society. In other words, it was a pervasive concept that infiltrated all walks of life. The selection of the nine universities in Project 985, for example, was done almost entirely by the central authority. However the selection went through unchallenged. Society at large accepts Beida (shorthand for Peking University) and Tsinghua as *the* legitimate candidates for world-class status. Society at large has apparently endorsed the preferential treatment granted these elite universities.

The ranking of these universities in the international league tables seems to confirm people's belief that the central government has made the right decision, although one could equally argue that this is a circular argument: these universities excel because they have been given privileged resources. The circular argument is further reinforced by the recent institutional evaluation of Peking and Tsinghua universities, in that they have scored A in almost all items in a checklist of 14 items drawn up for a 'research university'. This is a nation-wide institutional evaluation exercise conducted by the Ministry of Education. All public universities have to be evaluated. Panels of experts in different academic disciplines from within and outside China are formed and spend a whole week in the respective institution, visiting all departments and administrative divisions. Moreover, there is random inspection of classes and of examination scripts, in order to achieve a comprehensive assessment of the quality of education in the institution.[15]

Hence, there are indeed transparent measures to monitor the quality of education in the 'elite' institutions. From a macroscopic point of view, it is an interesting integration of direct manipulation from the central with a transparent system of accountability. Likewise, one may also argue that Project 985 and Project 211 are complementary to each other, although the long-term effects of these two projects will only be fully realized in the future.

Concluding Remarks

China's higher education system has grown tremendously in the last decade. Parallel to the spectacular expansion is the emergence of elite universities with 'world-class' status. It has taken China's higher education system a long journey to arrive at the present situation. There remains a basic struggle with the legacy of manpower planning, which believes that higher education can be structured to meet the manpower needs of the labor market. Such a legacy has almost completely ignored the fact that: (a) it is not unusual to see a mismatch between what the students learn and the work they do in society, (b) the contemporary workplace has a much more demanding expectation of university graduates, which concentrates on personalities and attitudes, rather than specialist knowledge, and (c) people change jobs and careers as opposed to pursuing a rigid and stable job structure.

However, one can remain optimistic about the trend of development. The rapid expansion of the non-government or private sector is beginning to challenge the formal government structure in higher education. The decreasing contribution of government appropriations to public institutions is also allowing them to respond directly to changes in the workplace. Meanwhile, the forthcoming reform of the government structure will inevitably further undermine the residual influences of the planning ideology.

Notes

1. The second largest system of higher education is that of the United States, which is around 15 million. This is followed by India with 11 million, which is however still growing
2. Taiwan and Korea reached 'oversupply' of higher education at the turn of the twenty-first century, which means the number of higher education places exceeds the number of high school graduates. Japan has been in this situation since 2006.
3. This is the point made by Professor Weifang Min, a Stanford graduate, Council Chairman of Peking University, in response to a question raised at a World Bank's Regional Bank Conference on Development Economics (RBCDE), Beijing, January 16–17, 2007.
4. This is the report of a major policy research commissioned by the Ministry of Education. It involved almost 100 senior researchers drawn from the whole nation. Its main theme is how to turn the population burden into a huge pool of human resources.
5. In a press conference on March 15, 2008, Zhou Ji, the Minister of Education, noted that the average length of education for a Chinese citizen was 8.5 years, and for the new entrants into the labor market, 10 years. Therefore, 'Our nation is already being transformed from a population giant to a nation of human resources'. Recorded in CCTV.com.
6. The non-government institutions are often known as the *minban* institutions in the literature. 'Minban' literally means 'run by the people' or 'run by the community'.
7. The SHJT ranking uses six indicators, which include Nobel Laureates among the alumni and professors, as well as publications in *Nature* and *Science*. Both Peking and Tsinghua Universities were way outside the top 100.
8. The THES ranking also used six indicators, including international peer review and employer review, as well as numbers of international teachers and students. Peking University was ranked fifteenth in 2006 and Tsinghua twenty-eighth.
9. This is a ranking produced by a semi-official organization in Taiwan.
10. This was launched in December 2006, in a national forum at Riyadh.
11. This was announced on December 3, 2007 in a World Bank conference in Kuala Lumpur.
12. This is the implementation of a plan that was announced in 2006.
13. Announced in December, 2007.
14. Conversation with the Minister of Education, Indonesia, February 12, 2008.
15. The evaluation of Peking University and Tsinghua University were both done in November, 2007.

References

Ministry of Education (1984) *Achievement of Education in China, Statistics 1949-1983*. Beijing: People's Education Press.

Ministry of Education (1999) *1998 Quabguo jiaoyu shiye fazhan tongji gongbao* [*Bulletin on National Statistics for Education Development 1998*]. Beijing: People's Education Press.

Ministry of Education (2007) *2006 Quabguo jiaoyu shiye fazhan tongji gongbao* [*Bulletin on National Statistics for Education Development 2006*]. Beijing: People's Education Press. http://www.moe.gov.cn/edoas/website18/info29052.htm

Pan, M. (2003) 'Higher education in China in the 21st Century: Elite and Mass.' *Proceedings of the International Conference on China's Higher Education: Inheritance and Reform, December 21–23, 2003*. Xiamen: Xiamen University Press, 1–5.

Pan, S.-Y. (2003) *How Higher Educational Institutions Cope with Social Change: The Case of Tsinghua University, China*. Unpublished Ph.D. Thesis, The University of Hong Kong, Hong Kong.

Pan, S.-Y. (2006) 'Economic Globalisation, Politico-cultural Identity, and University Autonomy: The Struggle of Tsinghua University in China.' *Journal of Education Policy*, 21(3), 245–266.

Salmi, J. (2007) 'The Challenge of Establishing World-Class Universities (Box 5).' Paper presented at the Second Conference on World Class Universities, November 1–3, 2007, Shanghai.

10

Excellence in Dutch Higher Education
Handle With Care

Frans Kaiser and Hans Vossensteyn

Introduction

Excellence is a much used word and concept in modern higher education policy. Increasing numbers of governments and higher education institutions strive for excellence in teaching, research and service. This can for example be seen in the increasing role of classifications and rankings in higher education. The rankings produced by the University of Shanghai Jiao Tong, the *Times Higher Education Supplement*, and *US News* and *World Report* are just a few examples. Excellence can be defined in multiple ways, but is generally understood as "top-of-the-bill" among peers. But because only a few can generally be among the best and many want to belong to the best, there has recently been a growing market for all kinds of rankings in higher education. As higher education is a multiple product business, with teaching, research and service functions in many fields and of various forms, many institutions can in certain respects be among the best. That means that many higher education institutions can find their own niche with which they can profile themselves.

In this chapter we explore to what extent excellence and profiling are important in Dutch higher education. Dutch higher education has expanded rapidly over the past 50 years and therefore created a larger diversity in terms of institutions, students, staff and functions. Nevertheless, Dutch higher education has kept its basic characteristic of being a binary system with, on the one hand, the academically oriented universities and on the other hand, the more professionally oriented Universities of Professional Education ("*hogescholen*"). Enrollment in both sectors of the system increased dramatically till the early 1980s and continued to grow steadily afterwards in the professional sector. The role of elite institutions in structuring this expansion is non-existent, simply because there are no elite institutions in the Dutch higher education system and policy actually did not allow this to happen. However, for some time there have been internal and external pressures to change the reluctant Dutch position towards vertical differentiation. In this chapter these pressures and the way the higher education system has responded to them will be discussed.

The Dutch Context

The higher education system is a binary, predominantly public system, by deliberate choice. Although there have been many debates on loosening up or even abolishing the binary divide, the notion of two co-existing "equal but different" sectors has been backed up politically over the last few decades. The _hogescholen_-sector (or the universities of professional education, as they prefer to call themselves) has evolved from a process of upgrading and merging upper secondary vocational schools, that started in the 1950s and "ended" in 1986 when the sector became part of the system of higher education. Hogescholen offer four-year Bachelor's programs and may offer one-year professional Master's programs. Doctoral degrees may be awarded by the universities only. In addition, universities offer three-year Bachelor's programs, one-year Master's programs and two-year research Master's programs. Universities have substantial research portfolios whereas the _hogescholen_ have a (still) limited portfolio that comprises practice- oriented research activities.

During the last two decades, the expansion was mainly in the hogescholen sector. The changing labor market structures and corresponding shifts in demands for higher education, especially for women, may be seen as important factors contributing to this trend (Kaiser and Vossensteyn, 2005: 100).

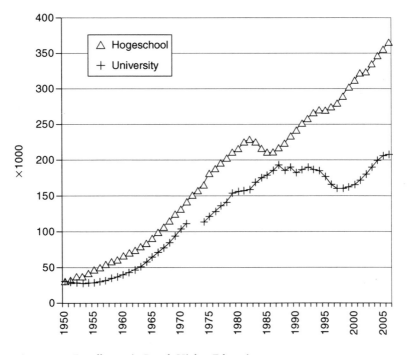

Figure 10.1 Enrollment in Dutch Higher Education.

Dutch higher education can be characterized as an open access system: applicants who hold the required entrance qualifications (for *hogescholen* a five-year secondary diploma, for university a six-year pre-university diploma) are entitled to participate in higher education. Both the political system and society at large consider this openness as a crucial characteristic of the higher education system. It is a cornerstone of the belief that every citizen should have equal opportunities to access higher education and to secure the position in society (s)he wants. This meritocratic character is combined with the deeply ingrained egalitarian, and perhaps conformist, character of Dutch society. "Acting differently to what is regarded as ordinary is simply not done" (*"doe gewoon dan doe je al gek genoeg"*). A well preserved assumption is that all higher education institutions provide high quality programs and that there is no vertical diversity in terms of quality between institutions. Therefore *hogescholen* and universities are regarded as equal in terms of level, but different in orientation. In this setting, the existence of an elite sector, or of elite institutions, does not fit, and is by many regarded as a taboo.

Internal and External Pressures to Differentiate in Quality

Dutch society is small and relatively open to external influences. Its multiculturalism and generally tolerant character are examples of that. But openness also means that many stakeholders can have an influence on the course of events. That means that a mainly public sector like higher education is subject to pressures arising from both the national and international context. The buzzwords of the international context, globalization and internationalization, have created some real pressures on Dutch higher education towards profiling and (more) vertical differentiation in quality of teaching and research (see e.g., Marginson et al., 2007).

Both the Bologna process and the Lisbon strategy of the EU put the competitiveness of higher education high on the agenda. The Bologna process places the international visibility of higher education programs in the context of the increased importance of international mobility of students and staff. The common assumption is that a program or an institution needs to be of outstanding quality in order to be highly visible and to attract large numbers of the best international students. That puts "excellence" in the focus of higher education policy. The Lisbon strategy puts the struggle for excellence in a broader framework. Here the global (economic) competitiveness of a nation is the focus and the role of higher education is to push the competitive edge. The nation needs highly talented and educated people and the higher education system has to identify and provide them. Higher education is regarded as a key factor in innovation and competitive power (Commission of the European Union, 2006: 7). This international focus on competition has lead to an increase in policy rhetoric and policies in which the striving for excellence has a prominent place. The cultural and political unease with elitism and the backing of winners has diminished.

By giving higher education institutions some leeway to differentiate in teaching, the government tried to improve the competitiveness of higher education institutions (Hermans, 2002: 6). The minister used the metaphor of a *high plain with peaks* to illustrate that the overall quality of Dutch higher education should be high for all students but that the talented and gifted elite should be provided with excellent programs that would bring them to a top-quality level.

Competing in the international arenas is not the only driving force that has made the Dutch politics and public more open for vertical differentiation in quality. The traditional resentment of wasting resources (God's creation) has given the Dutch the reputation of being rather frugal. This basic part of the nature of (a large part of) Dutch society applies also to the waste of talent. An incident in 1996, the "case of Meike Vernooij" with the "almost perfect student" being rejected for medical studies, triggered a chain of events that put differentiation in quality and cherishing excellence and talent high on the political agenda for the decade to follow. To understand this incident a short detour to *numerus fixus* programs and selection is needed.

In order to enter a higher education program an applicant has to hold a qualifying secondary education diploma. This guarantees entrance to most programs. For a number of specialized programs, like creative arts and sports, applicants have to show additional special skills or competences. Entrance is furthermore restricted for a number of other programs like medicine, veterinary science, physiotherapy and dentistry, mainly for capacity reasons (*numerus fixus*). The number of places available in each program is set by the government.[1] Applicants for these places were selected through a system of weighted lottery, the weights being determined by the grade point average of the school leaver diploma. In 1996 a secondary school leaver with nearly perfect grades (Meike Vernooij) was denied access to a medicine program, two years in a row. Since individual institutions were not allowed to admit students, bypassing the central admission system, the minister intervened when one university wanted to admit this applicant. Despite her high weight in the lottery (due to her high grades) that particular applicant was rejected for two consecutive years. The student went off to study abroad on a very good scholarship. This received massive media attention. Both the general public and the parliament called for a change in the selection procedures. More than ten years later, this call still echoes through the higher education policy debates.

So altogether, the higher education system and government were challenged to respond to national and international pressures, all within the constraints of social, cultural and legal settings.

System Responses and the Role of Excellence

When looking at the responses to the above mentioned challenges there are two classes of responses, both with a different legal scope (or character). The first class refers to the responses that either remain within existing legal frameworks or seek to change existing legal frameworks. These type of responses or changes refer to the whole higher education system. The second class refers to responses within the restrictive framework of "legal experiments." In this second type of responses one can find initiatives that focus on excellence-oriented initiatives at a limited number of institutions or programs and often for a limited period of time. The legal foundation for these initiatives generally is sanctioned by a special law on experiments and not a change in the regular law(s) that apply to higher education.

Type 1 Responses: Responses within the Regular Legal Framework

SELECTION

Partly due to the media hype following the Meike Vernooij incident, the system to select applicants for *numerus fixus* programs was revised in 1999. Applicants for these programs with a score of eight (out of ten) or higher are now admitted directly. At least half of the remaining places are filled through the central lottery system but higher education institutions are now allowed to select applicants themselves (decentralized selection). They may use their own criteria, like special motivations or talents. In a 2002 review of this decentralized selection mechanism it was found that universities only selected 17% of their new entrants in the *fixus*-programs and *hogescholen* 34% of their entrants.

There are doubts regarding the effectiveness of selection. Students selected by the higher education institution did not perform better than other students and the costs are considerable due to individual assessments and interviews (Commissie Ruim baan voor talent, 2007: 10).

STRUCTURAL CHANGES

In 2002, the structure of higher education programs changed completely. In the framework of the Bologna process the Dutch government decided to replace the existing four- and five-year programs with the bachelor–master structure. According to the Minister, international competitiveness was one of the central drivers for the introduction of the new degree structure (Hermans, 2002: 6). In the turbulent period of the introduction of the bachelor–master structure, there was also a discussion on the introduction of "topmasters." An advisory group made a number of recommendations to the minister to create the opportunity for Master's programs of outstanding quality to apply for the status of "topmaster" (Werkgroep Topmasters, 2002). The recommendation was discussed but there has been no follow up. One of the big obstacles was that "topmasters" should be allowed to charge higher tuition fees to cover the costs of more intense training methods and better teachers. Students and parliament feared that a differentiation in tuition fees could harm access to higher education (see also the later discussion in this chapter). As a result "topmasters" do not exist (as yet) in the Dutch higher education system.

Universities now may offer general (domain) Master's and research Master's programs. Open access to Bachelor's programs did not change, but access to Master's programs may now be restricted by the higher education institution.[2] Most Master's programs now have developed pre-Master's programs or bridging programs to admit students from differently oriented Bachelor's programs. Access to research Master's is relatively selective, which has led many to consider the research Master's programs to be "excellent" Master's programs.

PROGRAMS AND COURSES FOR TALENTED AND AMBITIOUS STUDENTS

Most universities offer special programs or courses for highly gifted, talented and motivated students. In the *hogescholen* such programs have only recently been introduced (since 2005). These special programs or courses flourish under a wide variety of names. Honors programs, honors courses, plus-programs, excellence tracks, specialization options, and master classes are the labels most frequently used. Despite the variety of labels, these programs have a lot in common. They are organized as an add-on to the regular Bachelor's program but taking the special program does require obtaining additional credits. Participants in the programs are selected (on academic or motivational criteria from the students in the regular program) and classes are organized in a small group setting in which interaction between teacher and students is an important element.

Universities have been experimenting with "honors programs" since the early 1990s. Due to the rapid massification of higher education, interaction between teachers and students had diminished and teaching was more focused on providing basic quality for the mass than on providing high quality for the gifted or ambitious. The sense of "academic community" was completely lost. Many academics have struggled with this downside of the massification of higher education. In the years following the introduction of the "peaks and high plains" paradigm, the phenomenon of honors programs gained momentum. Most universities offer such programs not only for promoting excellence, but also for strengthening their institutional profile. A renowned honors program may help to attract more (talented) students and high quality teaching staff (Eijl et al., 2007).

FINANCIAL MEASURES

In the initial plans for the creation of a "high plain with peaks," the restructuring of the funding mechanism was seen as an important pre-condition for bringing about this change. The existing funding mechanism was (and still is) mainly quantity driven. The more graduates a higher education institution produces, the larger its piece of the public funding pie will be. Quality or difference-in-quality were not in the equation. Therefore a new demand-oriented funding mechanism was developed. The introduction of learning entitlements or (vouchers), in combination with differential tuition fees was supposed to create quality-driven competition in the higher education market. Although the mechanism as such found some support, it was not in the end implemented. Expected problems in logistics, the higher level of uncertainty regarding institutional funding, and particularly an expected administrative burden, aroused a lot of discussion. A sudden change of government abruptly resulted in the termination of the project as the Liberal Party was no longer part of the coalition government.

In the latest proposals for restructuring the funding mechanism, there are some quality-driven elements, but the expected effects on quality and excellence are at best indirect. In early 2008, a commission was established to think through a scenario for linking part of the budget to quality, but defining quality and institutional resistance to have winners and losers within the same budgetary constraints appear to make such an attempt very difficult.

To stimulate excellence and foster the talented and ambitious students in a more direct way, government has provided some additional funding, but these funds have been rather limited. In the Strategic Agenda for 2008 to 2010 (Ministerie van Onderwijs Cultuur en Wetenschappen, 2007b) there is a €50m budget for projects to promote excellence in higher education.

In the Strategic Agenda, there is also extra money available for (teaching) staff development. Improving the quality of the teaching staff is regarded as a strong mechanism to improve the quality of teaching and the quality of the graduates (Onderwijsraad, 2007).

Financial support for talented students is almost non-existent. Higher education institutions are not allowed to provide special scholarships to individual students. Since August 1, 2006, there is a national scholarship program (the Huygens scholarship program) to attract excellent foreign students and to send out excellent Dutch students. The budget available (€4m for foreign students and €1m for Dutch students) will be doubled after 2008. In 2006 167 students were selected for such a scholarship.

RECOGNITION OF EXCELLENCE

Since 2002 higher education programs need to be accredited by the Nederlands-Vlaamse Accreditatieorganisatie (NVAO), the Dutch-Flemish accreditation agency. Based on the reports of a visiting organization (VBI) the NVAO decides whether a program meets the basic standards for accreditation. In a first draft of the accreditation system, a "star-system" was proposed to rate the relative quality of programs. Such a system would have created a transparent vertical differentiation in the system, but the proposal was rejected by the higher education institutions (Commissie accreditatie hoger onderwijs, 2001).

Since 2006, to accommodate for some diversity, higher education institutions may apply for a "distinction" when they are accredited. If a higher education institution thinks a program has special characteristics or is of extraordinary quality, it may ask the Visiterende en Beoordelende Instanties (VBI) to examine the program to substantiate such a claim. The VBI then may confirm or reject the claim. The NVAO may acknowledge the assessment of the VBI, which allows the higher education institution to use the NVAO-distinction. Until 2007, only one NVAO acknowledgement of extraordinary quality and seven for special characteristics have been given (Ministerie van onderwijs cultuur en wetenschappen 2007).

Type 2 Responses: Experiments

Any policy that may have an impact on the accessibility of higher education and threatens the equality of chances for citizens is a political hot potato. In such a high sensitivity context, "experiments" are gaining popularity in the development of Dutch higher education policy. To find out whether legal or structural reforms will have the desired effect, "experiments" are allowed that go beyond the current legal and structural frameworks. These experiments are then monitored and evaluated by a public committee. In 2005 the Committee "Ruim baan voor talent" was installed to oversee experiments regarding entrance selection, differentiation of tuition fees, and the creation of honors programs.

ENTRANCE SELECTION

In 2004 there were two positions in the debate on entrance selection. On the one side were the people who thought selection to be a necessary instrument to get the right student in the right place. These proponents for strong selection used the American elite universities as an example of how selection could contribute to excellence. On the other side were those who thought that selection added little value to the selective final exams of secondary education.

During the period of the experiments (2005–2007) the discussion changed. The focus shifted from selection as an instrument to exclude those with less (or different) talents to selection as a way to match students and programs. Selective programs should not pick only the best students but should create a specialized profile that calls for specific talents. Such required talents then would have to be matched to the talents of the applicants through the selection mechanism. Therefore the ten experiments became more focused on matching programs and students rather than on selecting the best students. In the experiments students were selected at the entrance of regular programs (i.e., programs for which the *numerus fixus* does not apply or for which no special skills are required). In most cases, selection leads to a better match between students and programs. The matching programs had a specific profile and a corresponding educational set-up. The full effects of the experiments cannot yet be evaluated, but there are some indications that in some of the experiments the quality of students is higher than average resulting in slightly lower drop-out rates. Whether that is due to selection, the educational set-up or self selection is not (yet) clear.

A SPECIAL CASE OF ENTRANCE SELECTION: HONORS COLLEGES

In 1998 a new response to the excellence challenge emerged. In Utrecht the first *University College* was established. This university college is the "honors college" of the University of Utrecht. With this very selective school at undergraduate level, the university wanted to make a stand against the large scale and anonymous education that (according to its founding fathers) dominated Dutch universities. New entrants (around 200 annually) are selected on motivation, international orientation and intellectual capacity. They work in small groups, tutored by excellent teachers and all live on campus. A few years later a second honors college was established in Middelburg (the Roosevelt Academy), founded jointly by the University of Utrecht and the Hogeschool Zeeland). A third University College was established in Maastricht in 2002. All of these university colleges operate as liberal arts colleges, providing Bachelor's degrees in arts and in science. In 2006 the first honors college in the *hogescholen* sector was established. The Ministry of Education, Culture and Science invested €1.9m in this college of the Hogeschool Windesheim, opening its doors in 2008. The two universities in Amsterdam have also developed plans to start up Amsterdam University College in 2009. This college will have a science focus, in addition to the liberal arts character that it will have in common with the other existing honors colleges.

All honors colleges are residential colleges, which is unique in Dutch higher education. Courses at the Colleges are challenging and demanding. The programs, all taught in English, carry a higher study load than standard undergraduate bachelor programs. Students must be highly motivated and are expected to work hard. So far the honors colleges are considered to be a success story; student demand exceeds the number of places available and the colleges are often referred to as an effective route to excellence.

All honors colleges are schools or departments of existing public higher education institutions. However, their set up (as residential programs, with strict selection, and demanding programs) creates an image of "elite institutions." This "elite" character was strengthened by the finding of the Committee Ruim baan voor talent that students of the three University Colleges have a higher social background status than students in other programs (Commissie Ruim baan voor talent, 2007: 19).

ENTRANCE SELECTION IN MASTER'S PROGRAMS

Since the introduction of the bachelor–master structure (see above) selection at the entrance of Master's programs is allowed. However, higher education institutions are not completely free in how they select their Masters' students: motivation is not allowed as a selection criterion. To gain insight into the use and effects of motivation as a selection criterion, two experiments were started. One of these two was assessed as positive, the other as inconclusive (Commissie Ruim baan voor talent, 2007: 20). This did not lead to any changes in the general policies regarding selection in the Master's programs.

DIFFERENTIAL TUITION FEES

Tuition fees for Bachelor's and Master's programs (at publicly funded higher education institutions) are fixed by the government (in 2007/2008 it was €15,389). Students are eligible for student support (if they meet the conditions regarding study progress and parental income) but higher education institutions are not allowed to offer their students special scholarships.

In the policies regarding vertical differentiation in quality, differentiation of tuition fees is considered to be a central element. More excellence requires more financial resources and students in "excellence" programs need to provide part of these resources through higher fees. In 2002/2003 an Interdepartmental Policy Study was set up to explore the opportunities for differential fees (IBO, 2002/2003). The committee found advantages and disadvantages in tuition fee differentiation. Advantages include a higher level of profiling and more top-quality programs. But problems with access procedures and too high prices to attract talented students (from abroad) were regarded as disadvantages. After heavy social and political debates the idea was dropped.

More recently some higher education institutions have been allowed to experiment with higher tuition fees for specific programs. Of the five experiments, only two raised the tuition fee substantially. Due to the small scale of the experiments, no conclusions could be drawn regarding the effect the higher fees have on accessibility. In the preliminary evaluation of the experiments, the ban on scholarships was considered to be problematic. The Commissie Ruim baan voor talent (2007) advised that the institutions should have the opportunity to provide scholarships, in addition to the existing Huygens scholarship program.

EXPERIMENT IN OPENING THE SYSTEM TO NEW PROVIDERS

The public higher education system is a relatively closed system. Private for-profit organizations cannot enter the system nor are they eligible for public funding. Since 2004, the government has developed plans to open up the system to all providers of higher education services and create a level playing field for all providers. The introduction of such an "open system" is seen as one of the ways to improve the quality, efficiency and accessibility of the higher education system. The plans encountered a lot of skepticism, since little was known of the effectiveness of the instrument and of its possible negative side effects (Burger, et al., 2004; IBO, 2004; Onderwijsraad, 2004). The ministry therefore started an experiment in 2007 in which access to the public system was opened up for a limited number of new providers.[3] Partly because of the ban on differential tuition fees, the expected impact on the quality of higher education programs and vertical differentiation is very limited (Baarsma and Gerritsen, 2006).

Conclusion

At the start of this chapter we stated that there are no elite institutions in the Dutch higher education system and that the role of elite institutions in the process of rapid massification is therefore non-existent. However, if we look at the responses of the higher education system to internal and external pressures towards quality, excellence and diversity, we may have to reassess that statement as gradually more vertical differentiation has been and is still being created in Dutch higher education. First of all there are some "elite institutions" – honors colleges – emerging from the university sector. Although the honors colleges are not real institutions (they are departments of existing universities), their set-up as highly selective residential schools with different and more intense teaching methods creates at least an image of an elite institution. Their number and size is still small but there are plans to establish more of them.

Second, the emergence of numerous honors programs is another indication that the Dutch higher education system is diversifying in a vertical way. The honors programs are far less "elitist" than the honors colleges but they have a clear focus on attracting and challenging talented and ambitious students. The number of honors programs offered in the university sector is far higher than the number of honors colleges, and the fact that these programs are run alongside regular programs gives them a less elitist image. Also the sense of "academic community" is less developed than at the honors colleges. The excellence the honors programs aim to promote is focused more on a *different* quality than on a *higher* quality.

Thirdly, this difference between the two types of quality has been a central element in the debates on the role of excellence in higher education. This was clearly illustrated by the discussion regarding selection at the entrance of bachelor programs. In the early stages of the debate, selection was seen as picking the best students (in terms of highest grades), in line with the practice in Anglo-American systems. Later on, the common view on selection changed. Selection became a tool for matching students and programs in order to improve the optimal use of the talents of all students. Selection became less an instrument to achieve vertical differentiation, but to enhance horizontal differentiation. This change of tone in the debate is an important point in our reassessment of our statement regarding the role of elite education in Dutch higher education, because it represents the voices of those who argue that elite higher education should not emerge in Dutch higher education. It resembles more closely the much older paradigm of "similar quality but different orientation" which is used to show the differences, for example, between university and professional education. Even though there was a moment in the debate where vertical differentiation was stimulated and even though there are some changes in institutional landscapes that may be labeled as vertical differentiation, it is this change of tone that pulls the plug on any substantial move towards a larger role for elite institutions.

A fourth observation may be that the binary divide is becoming more articulated in terms of excellence. Most of the excellence-oriented initiatives can be found in the university sector, and the *hogescholen* continue to grow at a much faster rate than the university sector and is therefore becoming the "mass" sector. However, the size of the universities' excellence initiatives, in terms of student participation, is rather insignificant and *hogescholen* are picking up on excellence initiatives as well.

Finally, talking about excellence and elite institutions in higher education is still a sensitive topic in the Dutch context. The government sees a certain need to improve the quality of higher education and to stimulate the "production" of excellent graduates, but it is reluctant to develop a clear policy to reach those goals. This is probably also an effect of political and student resistance against more diversity, marketization, quality differentiation and competition, which are all believed to hinder access for the poorer students. The solution chosen is typically Dutch: set up some committees and have them oversee and evaluate some experiments. These policy try-outs in a contained environment have to provide the government with more insights into the effects of excellence-oriented initiatives. With this piecemeal and experimental approach, the government tries to maneuver in this sensitive policy field. But the experiments are often of a small scale and surrounded with many limiting conditions. Therefore the results in many cases may be disappointing and not bring the expected benefits. As a result, policy change towards a more market-oriented approach to stimulate diversity and excellence is likely to be slow. Therefore the title of this chapter characterizes very well the way Dutch government and society at large deal with the role of excellence and elite institutions in higher education: handle with care!

Notes

1. The number of places in numerus *fixus programs* was in 2007 around 12.5% of the total number of new entrants. In the university sector this percentage is more than twice as high than in the *hogescholen* sector (21% vs. 9%).
2. A higher education institution has to offer its own Bachelor graduates access without selection to at least one Master's program.
3. In 2006 17 programs were proposed for participation in the experiment, provided by 12 new providers (and 5 providers already in the system).

References

Baarsma, B. and M. Gerritsen (2006). *Het meten van de effecten van een open(er) bestel HO*. Amsterdam, SEO.

Burger, K. et al. (2004). *Een Open Bestel in het middelbaar beroepsonderwijs en het hoger onderwijs*. Den Haag, Centraal Planbureau.

Commissie accreditatie hoger onderwijs (2001). *Prikkelen, presteren, profileren*. Den Haag, Ministerie van Onderwijs, Cultuur en Wetenschappen.

Commissie Ruim baan voor talent (2007). *Wegen voor talent*. Den Haag, Tweede Kamer der Staten Generaal.

Commission of the European Union (2006). *Progress towards the Lisbon objectives in education and training*. Brussels, European Union.

Eijl, P. et al. (2007). *Honours. Tool for promoting excellence*. Utrecht, IVLOS.

Hermans, L. (2002). *Wijziging van onder meer de Wet op het hoger onderwijs en wetenschappelijk onderzoek en de Wet studiefinanciering 2000 in verband met de invoering van de bachelor-masterstructuur in het hoger onderwijs, Memorie van antwoord*. Den Haag, Eerste Kamer der Staten Generaal.

IBO (2002/2003). *Collegegelddifferentiatie in het hoger onderwijs, Eindrapportage van de werkgroep collegegelddifferentiatie*. Den Haag, Ministerie van Onderwijs, Cultuur en Wetenschappen.

IBO (2004). *Open bestel*. Den Haag, Ministerie van Onderwijs, Cultuur en Wetenschappen.

Kaiser, F. and J.J. Vossensteyn (2005) "Access to Dutch Higher Education: Policies and Trends", in T. Tapper and D. Palfreyman (eds) *Understanding Mass Higher Education: Comparative Perspectives on Access* (pp. 92–120). London, RoutledgeFalmer.

Marginso, S. et al. (2007) *Thematic review of tertiary education: the Netherlands*. Paris, OECD.

Ministerie van onderwijs cultuur en wetenschappen (2007a). *Kennis in kaart 2007*. Den Haag, Ministerie van Onderwijs, Cultuur en Wetenschappen.

Ministerie van Onderwijs Cultuur en Wetenschappen (2007b). *Strategische agenda voor het hoger onderwijs-, onderzoek- en wetenschapsbeleid*. Den Haag, Ministerie van Onderwijs, Cultuur en Wetenschappen.

Onderwijsraad (2004). *Ruimte voor nieuwe aanbieders in het hoger onderwijs*. Den Haag, Onderwijsraad.

Onderwijsraad (2007). *Kwaliteit belonen in het hoger onderwijs?* Den Haag, Onderwijsraad.

Statistics Netherlands (2008). Statline, Voorburg/Heerlen, 12 March.

Werkgroep Topmasters (2002). *Over de top, Duidelijkheid door differentiatie*. Enschede, CHEPS.

11

Polish Higher Education in Transition
Between Policy Making and Autonomy

Ireneusz Białecki and Malgorzata Dąbrowa-Szefler

The Development of Higher Education in Poland 1990–2006

Poland's socio-economic and political transformation after 1989 meant that in the field of higher education 1990 also marked the beginning of fundamental changes. The legal basis for those changes was created by a new law on higher education, passed on September 12, 1990 (henceforth referred to as the 1990 Act).

The process of material and structural changes initiated in 1990 did not end with the completion of the process of political transformation, but has continued to this day, driven by a number of factors, including:

- society's growing educational aspirations;
- higher education institutions operating in a free-market environment and adapting to its mechanisms;
- European cooperation, giving the changes a common direction through the implementation of the Lisbon and Bologna Strategies;
- globalization processes, shifting the balance between national and international factors in favor of the latter (new models, competition).

Therefore, in the 1990–2006 period it is possible to discern two periods of change: firstly the adaptation of the system to the conditions and demands of the free-market economy, and secondly a period in which changes are determined chiefly by international factors. It is hard to say when exactly the former was supplanted by the latter, but for the sake of argument we can assume the year to have been either 1996 (Poland's admission to the OECD) or 1999 (the Bologna Strategy).

Characteristics of the Expansion of Poland's Higher Education System in the 1990–1999 Period

The 1990 Act gave higher-education institutions autonomy and self-government and declared respect for the traditional academic values. A number of factors previously subject to government regulations (e.g. number of annual student admissions, division of funds between faculties, election of presidents) now came under the institutions' jurisdiction.

Other important factors playing a role in the transformation of Poland's higher-education system during the period in question included the following:

1. strong growth in student numbers and age-participation rates;
2. privatization – the marketplace's growing impact on both the structure of education and the financing of public higher education institutions;[1]
3. commercialization of studies – the emergence of the sector of non-public higher-education institutions, the introduction of fees for non-regular ('extramural' and 'evening') courses at public institutions;
4. diversification of the educational models and missions of higher education institutions;
5. growing contradictions between the tendency for quantitative growth and the need to maintain quality standards.

The trends observed in Poland are similar to those observed in other EU countries in the 1980s and even earlier (Clark, 1998; Williams, 2003).

Characteristics of the Development of Poland's Higher Education System in the 2000–2006 Period

A major influence in the sector's development in the period in question is the Bologna Strategy, whose provisions are gradually being implemented. The Strategy's objectives include:

- ensuring ever-higher education quality levels through the evaluation of fields of study;
- growth in student mobility;
- comparability of studies and diplomas;
- introduction of a three-tier system of higher education.

It is widely believed that important elements of the system still need to be reformed and overhauled so that Polish higher-education institutions can successfully face the challenges of globalization. This applies to issues such as the financing of higher-education institutions, student co-payment, potential changes in the model of the academic career, the institution management model, and the consolidation and concentration of institutions. All these issues are being discussed in the academic community, the settlement of which will subsequently become the pillars of the higher education system development strategy, which is being drawn up.

Quantitative Development of Poland's Higher Education System

Alongside the growth in student numbers (an almost fivefold increase over the course of fifteen years), participation rates grew: the gross ratio from 12.9 to 48.9 percent, and the net ratio from 9.8 to 38.0 percent.[2] Consequently, more than one in three young people aged 19–24 study at the tertiary level. The number of students per 10,000 inhabitants reached 562 in 2005/2006, a higher number than in France (346), the UK (381), and other EU countries (Central Statistical Office, 2007a).

The dynamic growth in student numbers in 1990–2006 was driven, on the one hand, by the society's growing educational aspirations, and, on the other, by a significant broadening of the tertiary-level education on offer (for instance, the introduction of bachelor-degree studies). One can assume that in part the rise in the supply of student places was an adaptive reaction on the part of higher education institutions to the growing demand for studying.

Demand was so strong that many departments saw several, or even more than ten, candidates per place, but the insufficient number of teachers and infrastructure deficiencies meant that, in the early period at least, not all candidates could be enrolled. An important reason for the gap between the demand for studies and the available number of places was the demographic trend of 19-year-olds, which peaked in Poland in 2002/2003 at 677,400 (Central Statistical Office, 2004a).

The sector of non-public (private) higher-education institutions grew rapidly in the 1990s in response to the society's growing educational aspirations and growing demand for higher studies. However, because of the subsequent gradual decline in the number of young people aged 19–24 (which

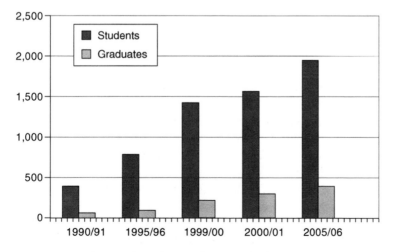

Figure 11.1 Students and Graduates of Higher Education Institutions in Poland in the Academic Years 1990/1991–2005/2006 (in thousands).

will decrease by over 500,000 between 2006–2013) and the competition from foreign schools (as a result of greater student mobility in the context of the Bologna Strategy), the student growth rate has been decelerating, and in 2006/2007, the number of admissions actually fell slightly. Sectors, institutions and departments are therefore competing ever more aggressively to at least maintain their admission levels. The question arises to what degree this competition helps to improve the quality of education, eliminating the weaker institutions and consolidating the position of the better ones.

Third degree (Doctoral) Studies

The 1990–2006 period was also characterized by strong growth in the number of admissions for doctoral and postgraduate studies. Those eligible for doctoral studies in Poland are candidates with a Master's degree or its equivalent (e.g. those qualified as medical doctors). The number of PhD students grew twelve-fold in Poland in the period from 1990/1991 to 2005/2006 (from 2,695 to 32,725).[3] Moreover, higher-education institutions offer postgraduate courses, which are an alternative form of education for holders of Master's titles. Unlike doctoral studies, the purpose of these forms of postgraduate study is to deepen the student's practical knowledge, which can then be utilized directly in his or her professional career. The number of these postgraduate students reached 135,930 in the academic year 2005/2006, about four times as many as in 1990/1991, and has continued to grow.

One can assume that the sharp rise in the number of doctoral and other postgraduate students reflects, on the one hand, the desire to deepen one's knowledge or passion for a subject, but also the pressures of labor-market competition. One can assume that the latter applies in particular to the students in postgraduate courses and less so to doctoral students. While many of the latter are highly talented individuals willing to continue their academic careers, there is also a significant percentage who enroll on doctoral courses without any vision of their future career or simply because they have been unable to find a job (Dąbrowa-Szefler and Sztabiński, 2007).

The Situation of the Academic Staff

The sharp rise in the number of students on all levels of tertiary education created an increased burden for academic teachers. Their number could not rise quickly enough due to the lack of sufficient financing, but also, to some extent, because of the procedures of obtaining academic degrees and titles, which were and are a requirement to teach at higher-education institutions. So while the number of students rose almost fivefold in the period in question, the number of academic staff grew by a mere 40 percent (Dąbrowa-Szefler and Jabłecka, 2007; Dąbrowa-Szefler and Sztabiński, 2006).[4] The insufficient supply of academic staff, in turn, has resulted in a situation where the majority of teachers work at more than one institution.

Changes in the Structure of Higher Education: The Diversification of the Educational Model

Sectors of the Higher Education System

During the communist period higher-education institutions in Poland were almost all part of the public sector. There existed three non-public Church-affiliated institutions with the right to award the master's degree (the Catholic University of Lublin, the Academy of Catholic Theology, and the Christian Academy of Theology). However, since the beginning of the transformation of Poland in 1990, the sector of non-public (private) institutions has been developing rapidly and by 2006/2007 the number had risen to 318, against 130 public institutions. However, the non-public sector is highly fragmented, providing education to 640,300 students (33 percent of the total), against the public sector's 1,301,100 (67 percent). As can be deduced from the above data, growth in the non-public sector after 1990 was stronger than in the public sector. The growth rates in student numbers per sector are shown in the figure below.

Whereas the number of students in the 2006/2007 academic year was down by some 12,000 (0.6 percent) from the previous year, the fall affected chiefly the public sector. The number of freshman students in that sector fell by 7.5 percent, whereas in non-public schools, by only 1.7 percent. In general, the fall in the number of students has been brought about by demographic changes – a sharp fall in the number of young people aged 19–24. It has been offset, however, by a rise in the percentage of young people entering tertiary education. As a result, participation rates have continued growing (see the above discussion), with Poland maintaining its leading position among the EU member states in terms of higher education students per 10,000 inhabi-

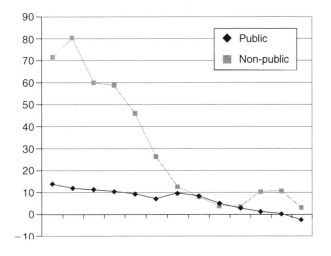

Figure 11.2 Percentage Student Growth Rates by Sector.

tants as well as in absolute numbers.[5] In this context it is not surprisingly to discover that the public and non-public higher education sectors have been on uneasy terms, competing not only for students, but also for staff and for state subsidies.

Types of Institutions and Priority Fields of Study

One factor with important significance for the functioning of higher education institutions is their division into academic and vocational sectors. The basis for this division is not (as the descriptive labels could suggest) the different institutional missions, but rather the quality of the teaching staff and the accompanying degree of autonomy. An academic institution has at least one organizational unit which has the right to award PhD titles, which is dependent on the number of teachers with professorial, doctoral, and post-doctoral (*doktor habilitowany*) degrees employed by that unit. Whereas a vocational institution, according to legislation introduced in 2005, is a higher-education institution without the right to award PhD titles, and therefore one employing fewer senior staff. Vocational institutions offer first- or second-degree courses, either Master's courses, or just first-degree (Bachelor's) courses.

Significant changes took place in 1990–2005 in the structure of education by field of study. In the 1990/1991–2000/2001 decade, the most popular courses among students were business-related majors (such as the MBA), accounting for 27.6 percent of the total number of students, almost double that of the pre-1990 level. They were followed by technical and pedagogical majors, though both saw their share in the total number of students fall: from 16.5 to 9.2 percent for technical majors, and from 14.1 to 11.3 for pedagogical majors. A sharp decline in demand for medical studies also caused their overall share to fall from 10.1 to only 2.4 percent. Though the number of medical students continued to grow in absolute figures, it was at a slower pace than the overall number of students.

Since 2000, trends have been changing, with demand again growing for medical studies (their share up to 5.3 percent in 2006/2007) and IT studies (5.2 percent). Business and administration studies remained the most popular group of majors in 2006/2007 in terms of both students (22.6 percent of the total) and graduates (27.1 percent), though their share has fallen in the last two years (Central Statistical Office, 2007a,b). The growing demand for medical and IT courses seems to be driven, amongst other things, by the availability of jobs in these sectors in the EU.

Financing Public Higher Education Institutions

Public Spending

Spending on higher education represented 0.95 percent of total public expenditure in Poland in 2006. This excludes spending on higher-education institutions' research activity, which is financed from another section of the state budget, and under a separate procedure. The 0.95 percent includes spending on teaching activity, student support, and capital spending. While until recently it has been on a par with the EU average, it is absolutely unsatisfactory in the context of the Bologna Strategy's objectives.

Central government subsidies account for the bulk of public spending on tertiary education, local governments' share being minute. Government subsidies are distributed between higher-education institutions on the basis of a formula, which acts as a policy instrument. The purpose of the formula, introduced in 1993, was to stimulate student enrollment and to motivate young non-PhD teaching staff to enroll for PhD courses. The formula, which remained in place (with some modifications) until 2006, 'awarded the quality of the given institution's teaching staff'. However, a new funding-allocation formula introduced by the recent bill on higher education is based on complex algorithms incorporating several weighted components, including a student to faculty with doctorates component (only regular students) and a research component (including the number of research projects secured). It also takes into account the number of departments that are entitled to grant doctoral and post-doctoral (*doktor habilitowany*) titles, the mobility of students and the staff, as well as the cost-effectiveness of the doctoral programs of different subjects. The algorithm differs depending on the institution's type and mission (the regulations discriminate between academic and vocational, military, medical, art, public-service, naval, and aviation institutions). Two other government subsidies are allocated according to a different algorithm, that is:

1. a student support subsidy;
2. a capital-spending subsidy (for public institutions only).

It needs to be stressed that the right of private HEIs (subject to certain criteria) to apply for government subsidies, as provided for in the 1990 Act, remained until 2004 (when they were ended due to budgetary constraints). However, on the basis of the 2005 Act, and the appropriate secondary provisions, non-public higher-education institutions have been receiving a government subsidy towards the teaching of regular first-degree students, regular doctoral students and the salaries of academic staff, as well as towards the maintenance and upkeep of premises. A tendency has therefore been clearly visible for granting the public and non-public sectors' equal rights with regard to state financing.

Both sectors, in turn, were from as early as 1990 able to use a second source of public expenditure, which is located in the Ministry of Science and appears in the form of full or partial subsidies for research projects of a varying nature. With few exceptions, private institutions did not take advantage of that option, their research staff failing to apply for such subsidies.

Public Institutions' Revenue Sources: The Role of Private Expenditure

The main revenue source for public higher education institutions is government subsidies for teaching activity (from the 'higher education' section in the central budget) and for research activity (from the 'Science' section of the budget). In total, these represented 61 percent of the public institutions' overall revenue in 2005. The remainder came from tuition fees and from commercial research activity. The bulk of the non-subsidy revenue was generated by tuition fees, which in 2006 represented an average 27.5 percent of total operating revenue and 33 percent of tuition revenue (Central Statistical Office, 2007b). The share of tuition fees in the revenue of HEIs has fallen recently (in 2000, it was 36.3 percent), as a result chiefly of a decrease in the number of tuition-paying students at public institutions.[6]

The Issue of Tuition Fees

There exist two groups of students at public institutions: those studying free of charge in regular courses and those studying in fee-paying non-regular courses. This situation – with its inequality – has come about as a compromise between the constitutional guarantee of free education at public institutions (the Constitution of the Republic of Poland, Article 70, paragraph 2), and the growing demand for funding, resulting from a gap between rapidly growing student numbers and inadequate growth in real terms of government spending. The government can subside only some students – those that perform better than others at entrance exams. The number of fee-paying (non-regular) students at a public institution must not be higher than the number of its regular students. The supporters of the proposition that all students, non-regular as well as regular, should pay fees, have been citing the following arguments:

- the need for greater transparency in the financing of higher studies ('equal terms for all');
- the need to limit income redistribution on behalf of regular students, the majority of whom come from higher-income (better educated) families;
- the potential for improving course attendance and timely-completion indicators;
- the potential for improving the quality of education as a result, among other things, of higher expectations from students as recipients of educational services.

The main argument raised against the idea of charging fees for regular courses is that it would restrict access to tertiary education for talented young people from socially and economically impaired groups (those from lower-income families or living far from the university cities).

The OECD Review of Tertiary Education Poland 2007 points to the need for introducing tuition fees for all forms of study at public HEIs with a simultaneous broadening of student support (making it more easily available and offering higher maintenance grants). Due to budget constraints, and thus the likely difficulties in securing higher subsidies for the purpose, this can most easily be done by modifying the structure of current student support, including reducing the share of performance-related grants. The issue is unlikely to be solved in the near future, since it requires working out a consensus between the institutions themselves, student organizations, and policymakers. It would also require amending the appropriate constitutional provisions and designing a financing model that would neither reduce HEIs' revenues nor increase the cost of study for students, as that could hinder demand for tertiary education, including the access to it for talented young people from lower-income families.

HEIs' Autonomy, Expansion and Relationships with their Environment

If we consider what factors brought about such a sharp increase in student numbers in the period in question, we doubtless have to take into account the changes that had taken place in both the secondary- and tertiary-education sectors.

The transition to a free-market economy in the 1990s took a heavy toll on many sectors of the economy. Heavy industry such as mining or steel, and, periodically, the automotive and shipbuilding industries were particularly hard hit. Preparing qualified workers for these industries were vocational schools of either a secondary or semi-secondary (basic) level. In the pre-1990 period, a basic vocational school and then employment in heavy industry were, particularly for boys, an attractive career prospect: a relatively brief period of study followed by relatively high wages in the heavy industry sector. In the 1960s, 1970s and 1980s, upon completing primary school, seven in ten boys and almost five in ten girls went to vocational schools. In the 1990s, however, the media started reporting the growth in unemployment, particularly among vocational school graduates. Unemployment among tertiary school graduates, in turn, was minimal, and a gap was growing between the wages of tertiary-education workers and those with secondary or lower education (Rutkowski, 1996). The signals from the labor market, conveyed and amplified by the media, were creating a growing sense that education, and higher education in particular, made economic sense.

It is worth adding that secondary schools were financed proportionately to their number of students, and that in small and medium-sized towns secondary schools were often clustered into educational units, often located in the same building, combining vocational schools with a grammar school. This made it possible to transform, relatively smoothly and flexibly, depending on the inflow of candidates and their preferences, vocational schools into grammar schools, opening the way to higher studies. As a result of the changes in the secondary-school education structure in the 1990s and early 2000s, almost one in two students studied in grammar schools, the main purpose of which is to prepare students for tertiary education. The percentage of secondary-level students studying in basic vocational schools fell in that period from over 50 percent to 10–15 percent.

Just like secondary schools, public higher education institutions received a government subsidy proportional to their number of regular students. Students of non-regular ('extramural' and 'evening') courses as well as all students of non-public HEIs, in turn, are charged tuition fees. Thus both public and private institutions' revenues depend on the number of their students, both those financed by the state budget and those paying for themselves. By boosting enrollment, the under-funded public HEIs were able to generate a significant extra income, whereas for non-public institutions it was the basis of their existence.

Enrollment Growth and the Labor Market

It seems therefore that the more than fourfold rise in the number of students in the past decade can be attributed to growing aspirations for studying and to an adaptive reaction from the – profiting from it – secondary schools and higher-education institutions. As far as the latter are concerned, the supply of tertiary programs seems to have been a function chiefly of the academic community's capacities and interests and, to some extent, the prospective students' expectations, and the labor market's needs were also identified and considered, but perhaps to a lesser degree. The scale at which the supply of programs grew depended on the type of study in demand.[7] Most new places were created in fee-paying courses (both at public institutions and non-public ones).[8] There was also above-average growth in the places available in the social sciences (especially in economics) and pedagogical courses, both at private and public HEIs, though, in the context of the latter, the teaching profession (of whatever specialty) can hardly be said to be among the most sought after on the market. The sharpest growth, however, in the number of the available places, and that at both public and non-public HEIs, took place in business-related courses. Marketing-and-management became a particularly popular choice, as did, though to a somewhat lesser degree, finances-and-banking. In these two specialties, the supply of places matched demand from would-be students. Both were 'trendy', corresponding with the free-market 'ideology' that was taking its grip on Poland, though one can have certain doubts whether the number of graduates has not already exceeded the labor market's demands. The percentages of students in social science-related courses, such as sociology, psychology or political science, also grew at an above-average pace, while growth was below-average in the number of law and IT students. The number of places in technology-related courses also grew but at a relatively weak pace.

In 2004, business and administration students accounted for 23 percent of the total of students in public and non-public HEIs, while social-science students accounted for 13 percent, pedagogy students for 11.3 percent, and technology-related (engineering, manufacturing, construction) students for 9.2 percent of the total (Central Statistical Office, 2004a, b).

It seems that the growing labor market will manage to absorb the numerous graduates of social science and business-related courses. This is due to Poland's rapidly growing services sector, but also to strong growth in the number of jobs available in central and local public administration, as well as in the corporate sector, all of which in the past were not necessarily filled by graduates and which often do not require specialist marketing or business knowledge. However, what psychology, sociology or economy students learn, besides those with computer and language skills, should prove useful in such positions (Białecki and Domański, 1995; Białecki, 2001).

The strong growth in the number of places available in the social sciences and business-related courses not only reflected young people's aspirations, but was also driven by the relative ease of boosting admission levels at both public and non-public institutions (Sztandar-Sztanderska et al., 2004). Basically, increasing the number of students, especially fee-paying ones, at existing social-science related courses, or creating new places in those courses, took little more effort than improving the utilization of existing lecture rooms and contracting more work time from teachers. This led to the proliferation of non-public institutions where professors of public institutions taught on a second job-basis, often using their parent institutions' libraries and teaching aids.[9]

Though we lack reliable data and estimates, it seems that the number of graduates of pedagogy courses is more than sufficient to fill vacancies and new jobs created as the education services market expands (due, for instance, to growing demand for lifelong learning). However, the growth in the number of pedagogy students can be explained with supply side factors – the ease and relatively low cost of offering such courses, as well as with demand-side ones – the candidates' belief that on the labor market any degree matters as long as it is a degree, and that a degree in pedagogy can be obtained at a relatively low cost and without much effort.

It is worth adding that hiring public-institution professors on a second-job basis for non-public HEIs was, especially in the early period (the 1990s), relatively easy and inexpensive for social science and business-related departments. At first, a professor pursuing a second job at a non-public institution not only had no obligation to secure permission to do so from his or her parent institution, but also did not even have to notify it about the fact. More recently, tighter regulations have been introduced, and acquiring a second teaching job requires notifying the parent institution, whose president can, in certain cases, refuse permission.

The supply of places in IT courses grew at a slower pace than in social science and business-related ones, not only because of the significant cost of the necessary equipment, but also because IT degree-holders had considerably more and better-paid job offers outside the education sector. The same applies to lawyers (where growth in the supply of course places was also below-average and failing to match demand), for whom starting a legal practice, writing legal opinions or offering consulting services was a much more attractive prospect economically than getting a second teaching job.

For public-institutions, growth in the number of regular (non-paying) students meant higher government subsidies, which proved profitable. However, the subsidy is divided between faculties proportionately to their number of students. The extra revenue, in turn, from higher tuition fees for paying students was also retained by the faculty (besides a small overhead charged by the president) and was usually used in large part towards pay rises for the academic faculty. Moreover, enrollment growth at non-public HEIs created extra employment possibilities for the public-institution teaching staff. Thus enrollment growth at public HEIs reflected, in the first place, their faculties' interests, as it boosted their revenues, and was driven by the individual faculties' policies rather than the given institution's overall policy. Public HEIs' enrollment policies were thus an aggregate of the policies of autonomous faculties rather than the result of an independent institution-level strategy. In the non-public sector, on the other hand, enrollment growth stemmed from institution-level strategies rather than being a faculty-driven process.

In all, it seems that strong growth in enrollment levels (over fourfold in the past decade) was fuelled by, above all, rapidly growing supply, reflecting the interests, in the first place, of private institutions, and in the second case of public ones – those of their faculties and staff. This is one of the reasons why the more cost-intensive forms and fields of study have seen weaker enrollment growth. Moreover, the structure of the supply of studying places responded more to would-be students' aspirations rather than to the labor market's needs.[10] It seems that what would be needed in order to better tailor the program and structure of tertiary courses to the economy's needs, besides detailed employment statistics, would be a more active role taken by the state, creating a forum where the interests of higher-education institutions' partners (employers, students, local governments) could be articulated and balanced.

The demographic trend means that for the first time in many years, the supply of places available in tertiary courses has in some cases outstripped demand. This represents a clear danger, above all for the financially weaker and poorer-quality fee-financed private HEIs. However, even renowned public institutions have also been losing students (and fees) in some programs, such as pedagogy, geography, library science or philological studies. In the early 1990s, before HEI quality rankings were popularized, the hierarchy of the forms of study looked like this: most highly valued were non-paying regular courses in trendy and attractive fields of study at several renowned state universities. These were chiefly the Warsaw University and the Jagiellonian University in Cracow, both listed near the bottom of the Shanghai Jiao Tong University ranking. The sought-after programs included, in various configurations, business and management, economics and econometrics, IT, law and certain social science courses, and outside universities: medicine, architecture, electronics, telecommunications. The exact configuration has changed, of course, to the rhythm of the changing trends and various circumstances. During the period of Poland's EU accession, for instance, there was a sharp rise in demand for courses with the word 'European' in their title.

On the second level of attractiveness was roughly the set of programs, at the same institutions, but offered in non-regular paying courses. This was a consequence of the fact that on enrollment, candidates with the best test results were admitted to non-paying regular courses, while those who performed less well were offered places in fee-paying courses. On the third level in the ranking was a similar group of programs, but at private HEIs.

Rankings of higher-education institutions drawn up by the main opinion forming magazines have since modified the hierarchy. The best private HEIs are beginning to successfully compete with the most attractive programs of the public institutions.[11] The rankings are usually drawn up on a peer-review basis, assessing the quality of teaching staff, programs, and conditions of study. Data on graduates' earnings and career paths are not included. Still, one of the rankings' effects is that the higher-ranked programs attract better candidates and have better students, improving the quality of the higher-ranked HEIs and programs. Ranking information is especially important for private HEIs as it helps to steer the choices of candidates. Whilst it may not bring about quality enhancement, it does invite the development of marketing strategies.

Quality assurance and improvement emerges as an important issue during the rapid expansion of higher education. It is easy to argue why quality should decrease in line with increasing enrollment in higher education. Accreditation bodies, both state and private, try to assure the maintenance of minimum formal standards such as the number of teaching hours, or the range of courses in degree programs, or the academic degrees of teaching staff but this still does not enhance quality. Furthermore, ranking and competition by themselves do not lead to quality teaching. The peer review of teaching staff and student evaluation questionnaires are quite common in Polish universities but are perhaps taken less seriously in public institutions, which lack a tradition of peer review. However, internal systems for quality improvement are developing at Polish universities. Currently private schools, especially the leading ones, care more about quality enhancement, while the best state schools usually have more motivated and intellectually challenging students and dedicated teachers and, consequently, are under less pressure.

Rapid age-participation growth and increase in student numbers in the past decade were a favorable result of steadily growing and widespread aspirations for studying. However, the response on the part of higher-education institutions might have been better, including more developed and appropriate links to the labor market's needs. If this did not happen, it was because of missing links between the HEIs and their environment. If we look at the debate in Poland on the higher education system, we will see that the single most quoted barrier to development is insufficient funding. Undoubtedly, this is one of the most important problems, but HEIs' poor relations with their environment are mentioned far less often. Better relations with the local community could also have had a favorable impact on HEIs' finances, for example by a stronger focus on the generation of applied knowledge corresponding to the needs of the region and its economy. There is also a need for closer collaboration with small and large businesses along with local government in drawing up study programs, training courses and designing joint research projects. Such collaboration has so far been largely missing. What is needed are better communication and debate as the basis of HEIs' collaboration with partners potentially interested in their activity.

It seems that the successful development of such a debate and subsequent fruitful collaboration requires a stronger, more pronounced role on the part of both central and local government in creating a policy to harmonize the strategies of the HEIs with their partners' expectations. A limited step in this direction is the central government's national development plans (for example the National Development Plan, 2007–2013). These are drawn up on the basis of sector development programs[12] and regional development strategies. They appear, however, to be a product of the work of experts and bureaucrats rather than a genuine debate-based integration of various interests and expectations resulting in an actual modification of higher-education institutions' plans and strategies.

There are probably other reasons too, but if positive collaboration between HEIs and business has been missing, if HEIs have hardly engaged in offering adult training courses and generating applied knowledge for the economy and the government administration, then one of the most important reasons is the fact that collaborative institutional discussion is missing. What seems to be needed is changing a tradition that combines bad habits from the communist period with certain deep-rooted academic values. On the one hand, the communist period has left a deep aversion to planning, whether central or sectoral plans, and a strong sense that top-down projects hinder rather than aid development. On the other hand, the academic community nurses a strong tradition of rather narrowly construed autonomy and academic liberties, which was reinforced by the battle for independence fought by universities during the communist period.

It seems that the academic community is dominated by the conviction that autonomy, construed as the freedom of research and teaching, is a value unto itself. What is being forgotten is the need to serve society, the third component of the university's mission. The freedom of research boils down to searching for truth. Moreover, the prestige of theory, of knowledge for knowledge's sake, continues to exceed by a wide margin that of applied knowledge (though it also seems that, especially amongst younger staff, performing services for the administration, undertaking consultancy and offering expert advice are slowly gaining in importance).

Autonomy in the Eyes of the Academic Community

Autonomy so construed is perceived as an inseparable attribute of a properly functioning higher education institution and as a necessary condition of a proper academic community. A substantial part, perhaps the majority, of the academic community believes also that the more autonomy for HEIs and their staff, the better. In ideological matters, such as self-identification or definition of the institution's mission, autonomy is construed as delegating all authority to collegial bodies.

A more practical notion of autonomy is less popular in the academic community: the view that autonomy is an instrumental, gradable and functional value. Locating too much authority in the collegial bodies (the senates and the faculty boards) could restrict the autonomy of the institution as a whole. While academic autonomy confers the authority to define institutional missions, it need to recognize its obligations towards society, including an obligation to serve it through mutual collaboration and the generation of applied knowledge.

Moreover, autonomy in the version professed by the Polish academic community is often construed as independence from the expectations and aspirations of the professional communities corresponding to the academic disciplines. The culture of professionalism, so strongly present in the Anglo-Saxon tradition, has hardly taken root in Poland. That is why the mode of practicing science, of creating knowledge and drawing up the curricula (at least in the social sciences and humanities) appears more autonomous in Poland, more academic, and less dependent on the professions and professional culture than in Western Europe or North America.

Though the education standards designed by the Ministry of Science as the basis for drawing up tertiary course curricula include a component called the 'graduate's profile', which defines what the graduate should know and be able to do in order to practice in a given profession, professional associations have little say in how those standards are compiled, and the 'graduate's profile' has little impact on how the – autonomous in this regard – faculties draw up their course curricula. Thus this means of adapting tertiary programs to the labor market's needs also fails. Higher education institutions, especially good public ones, continue to shape the model of the graduate in imitation of the faculty member.

If we consider how the changes transforming the higher-education sector are brought about, we can point to three, partly overlapping, determining pressures. These are: the interests of the academic community and other HEI stakeholders functioning autonomously; the market coordination of these interests and aspirations; and thirdly, the decision-making and policy implementation process itself – at the level of the autonomous faculties, within the different public and non-public HEIs, and by the higher education organized interests along with the central government.

If we interpret the expansion of higher education and the accompanying rapid growth in participation levels in Poland over the last decade and half, in terms of these three forms of pressure we can come up with the following conclusions. The rise in participation rates, in the number of students both fee-paying and non-fee-paying, can be explained in terms of supply (as it was determined by the interests and capacities of the HEI staff) meeting the demand from would-be students. There was an impression that it was a 'seller's market', in which the terms of the exchange were dictated by the providers of educational services. Absent from the equation was a powerful articulation of the needs of the labor market. There continues to be a lack of adequate data on the number of jobs available in the different branches of the economy, and on the skills and competences needed, which could be translated into educational programs. The market mechanism, and the forms of articulation accompanying it, has failed to stimulate the delivery of lifelong learning, the generation of applied knowledge, or efforts towards enhancing educational standards. What is needed here is policy direction from the state, up to now a weak partner in the policy-making process during the period of transformation.

Notes

1. Before the 2005 Act came into force, the official nomenclature was: 'state higher-education institutions' and 'non-state higher-education institutions', today it is 'public' and 'non-public' institutions.
2. Gross ratio: the ratio of tertiary-education students to total of young people aged 19–24. Net ratio: the ratio of students aged 19–24 to total of young people aged 19–24.
3. Doctoral courses can be offered only by organizational units approved by the Central Commission for Academic Degrees and Titles.
4. Due to the data-gathering methods used, the figure is undoubtedly exaggerated.
5. There were 2,146,000 students in Poland in the academic year 2005/2006 (including foreign students), or 562 per 10,000 population (Central Statistical Office, Poland Statistical Yearbook, Warsaw 2007). Excluding foreign students, there were 1,953,800 students in 2005/2006, and 1,914,400 in 2006/2007.
6. As a result of the demographic decline of those aged 19–24.
7. Besides tuition fees, another major cost for out-of-town students is rent. Tuition fees in the student's home town will often be lower than the rent in a big university city where non-fee-paying courses are available. The location of non-public HEIs often took into account the possibilities offered by the given region's commuter transit network.
8. In 2000–2005, about one third of all students were non-fee-paying students and two-thirds were fee-paying students. Among the latter, about a half were students of non-

regular courses at public HEIs, and the rest were students of non-public HEIs paying tuition fees irrespective of the type of course.

9. That was a typical model in the mid-1990s. Today, non-public HEIs rely more and more on their own staff and develop their own curricula.

10. It is worth adding that as the age-participation rate, now at about 50 percent, grew, the distribution of the incentives to study changed. Besides the desire to gain knowledge and skills, to learn and develop, more and more students have been interested in simply obtaining a degree at the lowest possible cost in order to improve their labor market position. Some HEIs and branches have clearly oriented themselves towards this type of student.

11. Public HEIs are usually much larger institutions than non-public ones. The former count their students in the tens of thousands, whereas the latter count them in thousands and are usually geared towards one or more specializations. That is why it is reasonable to compare public HEIs' faculties and branches with whole, usually economics or social science-oriented, non-public HEIs.

12. For example, the Ministry of National Education and Sports, *Education Development Strategy 2007–2013*.

References

I. Białecki and H. Domański, 1995, 'Employment opportunities in Poland's changing economy', *European Journal of Education*, 30(2): 171–185.

I. Białecki, 2001, 'Goals and policies of higher education reform', *Higher Education in Europe*, XXVI(3): 351–366.

Central Statistical Office, 2004a, *Higher Education Institutions and Their Finances in 2003*. Warsaw: Central Statistical Office.

Central Statistical Office, 2004b, *Demographic Forecast for 2005–2007*. Warsaw: Central Statistical Office.

Central Statistical Office (GUS), 2007a, *2007 Statistical Yearbook* (Teaching and Education in the School Year 2006/2007). Warsaw: Central Statistical Office.

Central Statistical Office, 2007b, *Higher Education Institutions and Their Finances in 2006*. Warsaw: Central Statistical Office.

B. Clark, 1998, *Creating Entrepreneurial Universities. Organizational Path of Transformation*. Paris: International Association of Universities.

M. Dąbrowa-Szefler and P. Sztabiński, 2006, *Doktoranci o sobie i swoich studiach doktoranckich. Raport z badania* [PhD Students about Themselves and Their Doctoral Studies. A Study Report], Warsaw University Center for Science Policy and Higher Education.

M. Dąbrowa-Szefler and P. Sztabiński, 2007, *Modele studiów doktoranckich a potrzeby nauki i rynku pracy pozanaukowej. Raport z badań jakościowych* [Models of Doctoral Studies and the Needs of Science and the Non-science Labor Market], Warsaw University Center for Science Policy and Higher Education.

M. Dąbrowa-Szefler and J. Jabłecka, 2007, *Szkolnictwo wyższe w Polsce. Raport dla OECD* [Tertiary Education in Poland. Report for OECD]. Warsaw: Ministry of Science and Higher Education.

Law of 12 September 1990 on Higher Education, *Journal of Laws 1990*, no. 65.

Law of 27 July 2005 on Higher Education, *Journal of Laws 2005*, no. 164.

Law of 24 August 2007 on Amendments to the Law on Higher Education, *Journal of Laws 2007*, no. 176.

Ministry of Science and Higher Education Ordinance dated 2 April 2007 on the Allocation of Government Subsidies for Public and Non-public Higher Education Institutions, *Journal of Laws 2007*, no. 79 pos. 534.

J. Rutkowski, 1996, 'High skills pay off: the changing wage structure during economic transition in Poland', *Economics of Transition*, 4(1): 89–112.

U. Sztandar-Sztanderska, B. Minkiewicz and M. Bąba, 2004, *Oferta szkolnictwa wyższego a wymagania rynku pracy* [The Tertiary Education System's Offer and the Labor Market's Needs]. unpublished report commissioned by the National Economic House, Warsaw.

G. Williams, 2003, *The Enterprising University: Reform, Excellence and Equality*. Buckingham: Open University Press

Part II
Elite Institutions in the Age of Mass Higher Education

12
What is an 'Elite' or 'Leading Global' University?

David Palfreyman and Ted Tapper

When discussing the concept of the 'elite', 'top', 'global', 'global brand', or 'world-class' university the focus is almost inevitably and invariably on the level of the research output of a particular institution, rather than on, say, its teaching quality or the ratio of highly qualified applicants for the limited number of undergraduate places or the socio-economic background of its students. In practice, of course, the 'top' research university will probably also be deemed to have high-quality teaching, and it almost certainly will be occupied by high-scoring school-leaver students carefully selected from among the many well-qualified applicants who come disproportionately from the upper end of the socio-economic scale (as in the case of Oxbridge and the Ivy League). These higher education institutions (HEIs) will also probably be the older/oldest ones in the national system higher education (HE), and will often occupy attractive sites replete with quadrangles as well as possessing imposing ivy-clad stone buildings with towers (Rothblatt (2008); and Berquist and Pawlak (2008: 193–201) on 'The Tangibility of Space and Residency'). Moreover, such HEIs will, usually, be located in economically vibrant, culturally interesting, and socially progressive parts of the relevant country, and often this means the capital – for instance, Tokyo University, Peking University and Tsinghua in Beijing, UCL and Imperial in London (but not Oxford nor Cambridge, although, interestingly, each is only some fifty miles from London and each was connected to London early in the 1960s UK motorway building phase). In the case of the USA, clearly Washington is an exception, but Harvard, MIT, Yale and Princeton cluster around New York–Boston, while Berkeley and Stanford grace San Francisco – see Florida (2005, 2008) for discussion of the geography and sociology of creativity (can a Government 'buy' through extra taxpayer funding such world-class status for one of its HEIs if the HEI is located in a dreary part of the world?!). The research output will usually be extensive and spread across a broad academic range, but an institution can achieve 'top' status on a fairly narrow span of intensive academic research activity (for example, the concentration on science at MIT, CalTech, or Imperial; the focus on the social sciences at LSE; the fact that Princeton has neither medicine nor engineering).

The only exceptions to this profile of a 'top' or 'leading' university in global terms are the French *grandes écoles* and the US prestigious liberal arts colleges such as Williams and Vassar, where the teaching is usually deemed excellent and the students are academically (and socio-economically) elite but the overall research reputation of the institution is not ranked as leading. Moreover, whereas historically there may once have been a time when 'top' universities catered for a socio-economically elite student intake that was not necessarily and automatically also hugely academically distinguished in terms of school-leaver entry scores (nor, indeed, in terms of degree output – the Oxford 'Gentleman's Fourth'!) and when such HEIs were not always 'research-led' in modern terms. It seems that now, in the context of academic meritocracy, no elite HEIs in any national system (still less if such HEIs have pretensions to be 'global players') are simply and merely some kind of socio-cultural finishing-school where admission can be gained on the basis of rather modest academic performance in secondary education: see Tapper and Palfreyman (2000: ch 4), and Soares (1999) on Oxford (and, by implicit extension, Cambridge); along with Keller and Keller (2001) on Harvard, Axtell (2006) on Princeton, and Karabel (2005) on admissions policy at Harvard, Yale and Princeton, plus Soares (2007) on admissions to Yale and other elites; also Golden (2006) on access to US elite HEIs and Duke (1996) on educating 'The Whole Man and the Gentleman Scholar' as US Ivy League HEIs tried to import the Oxbridge residential and tutorial teaching model (Palfreyman, 2001; Tapper & Palfreyman, 2000: chs 3, 5).

So, the elite university is academically elite, at least certainly in terms of the educational qualifications of its undergraduate student intake (and these students are almost certainly from the higher socio-economic groups), and it is very likely indeed that the elite university's teaching will be highly rated along with its research (but research is central to this HE elitism: Lang (2005)). The HEI may well, in addition, be seen as culturally significant and prestigious in terms of its location and buildings, as having historic presence in the wider society in terms of educating political leaders, and as being worthy of much media attention relative to other HEIs – even to the extent of serving as the setting for many novels and their related films: see Dougill (1998) on Oxford specifically; Proctor (1957) on the English university novel generally but especially within that genre on 'The Cult of Oxford' (ch IX); and Carter (1990) and Showalter (2005) on the campus novel. Such novels were once often written by Oxford Dons (notably, as 'the exemplar', J.I.M. Stewart, aka Michael Innes) and focused on how the Oxbridge ivory towers were being besieged by proletarians, women, foreigners, and scientists seeking to gain access to the sacred cloisters and hallowed quadrangles – happily, all have since been welcomed in. Another strand of the genre is the crime novel set in Oxford: Colin Dexter's 'Inspector Morse' novels and spin-off TV series (now followed by 'Lewis') have given Oxford University and its colleges a higher murder rate than New York, Los Angeles or Chicago suffer in their worst years!

Here David Watson (Watson & Maddison, 2005; Watson, 2007) provides an amusing aside: in an email exchange with David Palfreyman he listed the varying HEIs featuring in a collection of UK 'Top Tens' according to a range of wildly differing criteria (inter alia research, number of overseas students, graduate employability, student satisfaction, proportion of students earning a first-class or upper-second degree, and even 'gay friendly' locations!). The Shanghai Jiao Tong University ranking referred to below puts Cambridge first and Oxford second amongst HEIs, then Imperial, UCL, Manchester, Edinburgh, Bristol, Sheffield, Nottingham, KCL. The *Times Higher* list puts Oxford first, then Cambridge, Imperial, LSE, St Andrew's, UCL, Warwick, Bristol, Durham, and KCL. The ten HEIs with the largest number of overseas students include Warwick, Manchester, UCL, Oxford and LSE; the ten HEIs scoring highest in the National Student Survey include only Oxford and St Andrew's from amongst the fourteen mentioned so far; the ones with the highest proportion of 'top' degrees includes Oxford, Cambridge, Bristol and St Andrew's from these fourteen; the Top Ten HEIs with the highest percentage of students from the lowest socio-economic groups includes none of the fourteen; and the ten most 'gay friendly' HEIs includes only Durham and Edinburgh from the fourteen dominating the SJTU, THES and the overseas students rankings. In short, there are many ways of calculating a Top Ten; but rankings based on research (SJTU), on reputation (THES), on popularity with overseas students, and (to a lesser extent) on degree results do seem to have some overlap ... As Watson comments elsewhere (Watson, 2007: 38):

> Institutions need to know if they are entering one competition or several. It is tactically important to know whether there is a single set of rules, or several; and, if the latter, how far we [the HEI] can afford to fall behind in any one of them while 'winning' in others.

He goes on to ask whether HEIs should curb their enthusiasm for this competition, especially if the ranking methodology is 'neither rational nor scholarly' ('an inexact science', 2007: 40).

What academic literature is there on the 'elite' university? One strand of study explores the methodology used by the various rankings of such HEIs: notably the league tables issued by the *Times Higher Education Supplement*, by Shanghai Jiao Tong University, by *US News and World Report*, and by *Newsweek International*, as analysed and critiqued by Marginson (2007a: ch 3), by Usher and Savino (2007), and by Watson (2007: 24–46). See also Roberts and Thompson (2007) who explore the link between the research score of UK HEIs and their ability to recruit top-performing school-leavers, and who review the literature about the various US, UK, German and global rankings (citing, inter alia, Dill & Soo, 2005; Michael, 2005; and Turner, 2005). A key issue for the methodology behind all such rankings is the almost exclusive emphasis on research output, and citations of it, in English as the lingua franca of academe, leaving universities that do not routinely function in English arguably at a disadvantage (as discussed in detail in Marginson and van der Wende, 2007a; hence the former in Marginson, 2007b, cites with approval the system for comparing universities developed by the German Centre for Higher Educational Development). The (mis)use of such 'highly condensed indicators of quality' by employers recruiting graduates from supposedly 'Top 20' UK universities by way of perceived 'reputation' is explored in Morley and Aynsley (2007), who see such employment practices as leading to 'a reinforcement of a graduate elite, with the labour market playing a vital role in social reproduction processes and threatening to produce a reified higher education economy': in essence, 'employers are reinforcing the steepening of university hierarchies by the authority they give to league tables compiled by newspapers and perceptions of reputation'. Another strand of study looks at the measurement and management of research generally within higher education: in the UK context, Shattock (2003: 5–7) comments that 'high quality research, once established, tends to reinforce itself' and notes 'the extent to which [top] universities, irrespective of size and subject spread, perform well in research across the range of disciplines they profess'; see also Bushaway (2003) on the macro issues of managing research across the institution and Leisyte (2007) on the micro aspects at departmental/research unit level.

Others look at the competition for research funding as one of many markets within higher education: Teixeira et al. (2004) across a range of countries (see also Slaughter & Leslie, 1997; Slaughter & Rhoades, 2004), and Geiger (2004) on research universities in the USA. The latter sees the research market as 'beautifully efficient', and one that has 'shaped American universities' in terms of how they have responded to 'the academic research marketplace' that encourages their expansion of research activity 'because the payoffs are greater to those who do it best' (2004: 249–254). Kirp (2003) also analyses the US HE market, including a case-study of Berkeley that explores its links with industry over science research; while Marginson and Considine (2000: ch 6) consider the commercialization of science research in Australia. More polemical on HE and the marketplace is Washbourne (2005), who argues that market forces do not mix happily with the carrying out of disinterested science/medical research; but Bok (2003: chs 4, 8) provides a more measured review of the possible risks to academic integrity and the potential conflicts of interest arising from the commercial funding of science research and related technology transfer. See also Marginson (2007a) on market competition in HE; Marginson's work is discussed below.

Similarly, and again in a US context, Brewer et al. (2002) explore the strategic positioning of HEIs using an industrial economics model and where strategy is determined according to the particular institution's focus either on recruiting students by offering customer-oriented vocational teaching and by being firmly embedded within their locality/region (Watson, 2007) as a way of developing *reputation*, or alternatively on research funding and research output as a means of enhancing institutional *prestige* as measured by the rankings and tables referred to above. They comment: 'Prestige is costly to build and maintain [89] ... the pursuit of prestige is expensive and risky [134]'; and add that such 'prestige-seeking' can force 'a reduction in resources allocated to other uses', citing as a prime example those for teaching undergraduates (135). All in all, they conclude that pursuing a prestige strategy 'requires substantial and successful investment for an uncertain payoff [135]', not least because it is a zero-sum game ('when one institution gains, another loses [144]'). Kirp (2003: 4) refers to prestige as 'the coin of the realm among the leading universities and liberal arts colleges', and comments that such prestige-seeking means 'more than bragging rights for trustees and alumni' since it brings 'tangible benefits'. Gilbert (2007) offers a case-study in prestige-building: the University of Manchester and its 'transformational agenda' aimed at getting it to 'the first rank of international research-led universities by 2015' (within the 'Top 25' globally). Stensaker (2007) usefully reminds us that achieving a successful brand as an HEI is far more than merely hatching a good marketing plan; it is a much deeper and long-term exercise in developing the HEI's own unique and distinctive organizational identity and culture, and certainly not doing so simply by copying other HEIs in, say, building a shiny new student learning center in an infrastructure arms-race.

Given the cost of becoming and remaining a 'world-class' university, it is not surprising that such institutions are at present concentrated in the wealthier nations – the USA, the UK, Japan, Australia, Canada – and to a much lesser extent in a few European countries beyond the UK. Nor is it at all odd that public policy (even in some such wealthy nations and certainly in those countries that aspire to develop one or more 'global players') increasingly seeks to concentrate the taxpayer financing of research in fewer better-funded and larger critical-mass institutions, explicitly or implicitly differentiating them from less research-active or teaching-only HEIs within the national system. Watson (2007: 45), however, warns that 'even the most powerful institutions cannot really go it alone' since 'the dialectic between competition, collaboration and complementarity in HE is a complex one', and hence the apex needs the pyramid for support, just as the pyramid needs the apex to set it off architecturally. Altbach and Balan (2007) consider the research university in terms of such public policy-making in China, India, South Korea, Brazil, Chile and Mexico. They note that everywhere the research university 'is a central institution of the 21st century' as being 'at the nexus of science, scholarship, and the new knowledge economies' (1), and also how over the past two or three decades 'policymakers engaged almost exclusively with meeting mass higher education demand, largely ignoring the research role of universities' (3). Now, however, Altbach and Balan argue that 'research universities generate growing enthusiasm worldwide' (2) and hence the key policy issue is how the national higher education system incorporates, and more generously finances, one or more of these complex, specialized and costly research universities within its differentiated range of HEIs. Moreover, the question will also arise as to whether the nation is politically comfortable with an explicit recognition that HEIs should have 'diverse missions, structures, and patterns of funding' and that there will be at the pinnacle or apex of the system one or more of these institutions as flagships. They comment that such national systems 'often evolve during the massification of higher education' (6), and indeed the very theme of this book is how mass HE systems across the globe are interacting with the concept of the elite university given that in order nationally 'to allow research universities to flourish requires a way to differentiate them from other types of postsecondary institutions, provide funding at a higher level, and legitimize the idea that these institutions are indeed special and serve a crucial role in society' (6).

That said, the definition of a research university used by Altbach and Balan does not mean that all such HEIs are or need to be world-class: 'All world-class universities are research universities, without exception. But not all research universities are world-class, nor should they be' (7); and, might one add, nor could they be? Nor are the research or flagship universities within a national system the only HEIs, or indeed institutes or agencies, at which research will be conducted. But research universities all around the world, whether also world-class universities or not, have certain features in common. According to Altbach & Balan:

- they are very largely government-funded (other than the likes of Harvard, Yale, Princeton and Stanford in the USA, and Waseda in Japan);
- they are complex, with a range of subject areas, although they are not necessarily the largest HEIs in their respective systems;
- they are 'multiversities' (Kerr, 2001), having a multitude of missions within which research and graduate degrees dominate;
- they are expensively resource intensive; and
- they recruit students and faculty nationally and, if also world-class, internationally.

And they face similar challenges: of sustaining and increasing their income, of wrestling with the pressures of privatization, of balancing pure research with commercial research (of their public good mission with the private market that may reward them better but also constrain their academic freedom), of maintaining their autonomy while being accountable for their use of taxpayer monies, of functioning in the ever-more global and competitive science environment, and of offering their academics both academic freedom and job security within 'a cosmopolitan academic environment' (Altbach & Balan, 2007: 26) and doing so in the potentially threatening context of constant appraisal of the individual's research contribution to institutional earnings and prestige (Hall, 2003; ch 4, where the point is well made that in the culture of HE university traditions of 'collegiality' fit uncomfortably with the idea of 'managing for performance' and 'give rise to tensions at a conceptual and practical level' (77)). Similarly, Watson (2007: 42) is clear that, at macro-level, the State is not able simply to 'manage' some of its HEIs to world-class status; instead it is necessary to *trust* the academic community 'to do the right thing (that is, to pursue its core mission of knowledge creation, testing and use, without fear or favour)': creating a world-class HEI is 'a long-haul proposition' where taxpayer money helps but HEI autonomy and faculty academic freedom is crucial.

Mohrman et al. discuss the Emerging Global Model (EGM) of the research university, arguing that the really elite universities around the world have more in common with each other than they do with most of the HEIs in their national system in terms of the recruitment packages and research infrastructure they need to offer to prospective graduate students and to academic staff whom they compete for internationally:

> These top universities look beyond the boundaries of the countries in which they are located to define a transnational scope. Their peers span the globe ... there may be only a few dozen fully developed EGM universities but they are the institutions that head virtually every list of leading universities worldwide.
>
> (2007: 146)

These EGMs are even more concentrated in even fewer countries, and, of course, overwhelmingly in the USA and to a lesser extent the UK.

Such EGM universities are characterized by eight key features that they all have in common (although other research universities within national systems may have a few of these features, but not all):

- they have a truly global mission transcending the nation-state in which they are located, with highly mobile and international student and faculty populations;
- they are increasingly research intensive, especially in 'Big Science' and also in the context of being 'a knowledge conglomerate' (Geiger, 2004), but where the prime emphasis is on research activity rather than the teaching and wider service/civic-engagement missions;
- their academics are more team-oriented, cross-disciplinary and

internationally-networked, working on research contract projects and consulting for business ('They are busy commercializing their knowledge … on EGM campuses, entrepreneurial activities have been institutionalized' (Mohrman et al., 2007: 151–152); see Etzkowitz (2007) for a case-study of MIT and Stanford, Good (2007) on the Cambridge-MIT link-up, and Clark (1998) on entrepreneurial universities generally);

- they have <u>massive and hugely diversified funding streams,</u> needed to finance the heavy cost of competing globally;
- there are <u>constantly shifting relationships among these universities</u> and government agencies and business;
- they <u>recruit students and academics on a global basis</u> from a highly mobile international talent pool;
- they evolve ever-more <u>complex mechanisms for managing their research activity,</u> such as interdisciplinary centres, science parks and incubator units, technology transfer, patenting, spin-out companies, joint venture funding; and
- they collaborate on a global basis and operate within, and through, various international university associations that offer 'a form of validation of international stature, providing significant prestige to member universities' (158).

The EGM is a response to the process of internationalization and globalization that was increasingly to be found throughout late-twentieth century economic activity of every kind, including HE which, at the elite end, is now increasingly subject to global-referencing (Marginson, 2007a; Marginson & van der Wende, 2007b). This leads to 'new policy dilemmas for national governments' (Mohrman et al., 2007: 159) in the context: of the expansion ('massification') of HE; of the privatization of HE as the taxpayer retreats and governments introduce and hike student tuition fees as a cost-sharing strategy, and as some countries encourage the proliferation of private, commercial HE to meet demand; and of the increased diversification of HE systems. And so:

> The EGM can be described as a super-research university at one end of a continuum of institutional types reflecting different missions and different emphases on research, teaching, application, and service to the area in which the institution is geographically located.
>
> (2007: 164)

Thus, not surprisingly:

> there are tensions between the EGM and other priorities within higher education.
>
> (166)

...the EGM can pit international research prestige against mass education demands.

(168)

... the worldwide reach of the EGM forces uncomfortable, even impossible, situations as nations and universities want it all: playing in the international knowledge game while at the same time providing tertiary education for as many people as want and can benefit from a college degree.

(169)

Indeed, as Mohrman et al. conclude and advise:

Before deciding to develop an internationally competitive research university, policy makers should be clear about why they wish to make this investment ... [since] allocation of resources to high-level research could detract from more general educational goals of the higher education system ... there are other models of excellence in higher education.

(2007: 173–174)

They predict, however, that 'more and more institutions will become full-fledged EGM universities' (adding, 'although not every institution can be or should be an EGM institution'), where these global universities will form 'an elite subset in a larger universe of higher education institutions' (175).

Marginson (2006) considers the dynamics of national and global competition in HE, seeing the two areas as distinct but feeding each other. The research university aims to maximize its prestige as the producer of positional goods, here research performance and the education of highly employable students who then achieve high social status and high earnings (and often donate or bequeath generously to their alma mater!). The 'elite research university' within the national market can carefully select highly qualified students since applicant demand exceeds the supply of student places, not least because expansion of the institution is deliberately constrained to maximize status and to avoid brand-dilution. Given the growing global role of some of these elites, there is the issue of the 'disembedding' of such elites from their national system, of them becoming 'global player' universities that are in the business of producing 'global public goods' (Marginson, 2007a: ch 2; and Marginson, 2007c). Other HEIs operate within their national market as public or for-profit/commercial 'teaching-focused' place-fillers and expanders that are student-volume and student-revenue driven, with a tendency to indulge in hyper-marketing while shaving costs/quality. A third group of HEIs are intermediate between the two ends of the HEI spectrum as 'aspirant research universities' (but with little chance of breaking into the charmed circle of the 'elite research universities').

The elite university within the global positional market relies on the prestige of its research output and the high-value brand of its degree: Marginson sees this 'world market of elite universities' as being essentially the US top twenty, centered on the Ivy League, and the UK's Oxbridge. Next are 'exporting national research universities' in the UK, Canada, Australia, Europe and Japan that are prestige-driven at national level, but may also operate foreign campuses as a profit-making business. Then, also within this global HE market, there are 'teaching-focused export institutions' that offer a lower cost/quality product to foreign students; and, next, there are 'nationally-bound research universities' that have local prestige and are competitive with 'exporting national research universities' in recruiting students nationally, but have insufficient status to do much by way of cross-border activity. The last group within, or segment of, the global market are 'lesser status national/local institutions' that are almost entirely confined within their national borders.

Finally, reference was made above to the complexity of managing, or rather facilitating, research in the EGM (Mohrman et al., 2007) or the Super Research University, SRU (Baker, 2007). This has been explored by Taylor (2006), who studied institutions in Canada, Australia, the UK, and the USA, all of which 'would be immediately recognizable as among the leading research-led universities in the world'. While conceding that research 'does not lend itself to control and management' (citing Hogan & Clark, 1996), he argues, as they and others do, that it can certainly be facilitated: 'The key issue is how to manage effectively in such a way as to maintain an appropriate working environment within which research can thrive.' Taylor sees the key characteristics of 'leading research universities' as: the presence of pure and applied research; the delivery of research-led teaching; a breadth of academic disciplines; a high proportion of graduate research degree programs; high levels of external income; and an international perspective.

From his case-studies he seeks to identify common features of research management in these EGM/SRU institutions:

- they all follow a management style of 'encouraging, supporting and monitoring' rather than 'directing and controlling' (*but* 'There was, in reality, no question of "laissez faire"…'; on 'leadership' in HE governance management, see Palfreyman (2008) and the references within that Paper);
- their aim is 'to release the drive and imagination of talented, ambitious members of staff', in that they are collegial rather than managerial institutions as Shattock (2006, 2007) would view it (the concept of HE collegiality is explored broadly in Tapper and Palfreyman, forthcoming; and in relation to Oxford specifically in Tapper and Palfreyman, 2000, second edition forthcoming);
- their organizational structures vary, and 'there is clearly not a right

or wrong model' providing the management support to the research mission gives speed of response and flexibility on funding opportunities, on costing and pricing procedures, on legal and intellectual property issues, and on a code of best practice for conducting research (half the sample even provided 'professional application writers' to assist academics in bidding for research funds!);

- all these HEIs have financial incentives on offer to departments/ schools and individual academics for encouraging research;
- all have a diversity of funding sources;
- all possess a tolerance of risk when investing in new research areas;
- all give access to central funds from which new ventures could be pump-primed; and
- all have developed 'a deep awareness of cost', and especially recognize the need for research bids to cover indirect costs if the sheer success of research activity is not to bankrupt the entire university.

And all these 'leading research universities' are, in varying degrees, skeptical about the value of detailed institution-wide research plans and of a 'University Research Committee', as opposed to having such plans at the level of the academic units where the research action is to be found: see Bolton (2000); also Bushaway (2003: ch 5) who stresses the importance of ensuring 'resources for research are allocated directly to the research groups or units where successful research is carried out as measured by objective and externally referenced benchmarks…' (145). Hence they also all carefully monitor research performance at departmental/unit level to achieve constant and rigorous self-assessment (Watson & Maddison, 2005), systematically using a range of metrics and indicators that provided benchmarking against competitor institutions nationally and internationally.

These HEIs aim at 'fostering an intensely competitive ethos' and at creating 'managed internal peer pressure' that together will ensure research targets are met across the HEI (with the threat in most of the sample of 'external peer review' of any under-performing unit). The group puts a strong emphasis on human resource development, with highly selective recruitment policies and a wide range of staff development programs linked to research (Bushaway, 2003, ch 7; Partington & Stainton, 2003: ch 5). Incidentally, not one had an employment contract that specified hours of work for academic staff, recognizing that active research faculty are self-motivators. Interestingly, given the tension in allocating academic staff time between the competing demands of teaching and research, all these EGMs/SRUs emphasized both undergraduate and graduate teaching alongside research and there was, in theory, 'a strong philosophical commitment to the integration of teaching and research in the institution to the mutual benefit of both activities'. Partington and Stainton (2003) make the related point that 'managing staff development for research and scholarship entails recognizing the tensions that exist between teaching and research, in particular in relation to the primacy afforded research and its currency in the context of promotion' (102).

In conclusion, the elite universities that are the focus of this book are certainly all of those that would belong to the EGM or SRU category referred to above; they incorporate Taylor's 'leading research universities' and also Marginson's 'world market of elite universities' together with many of his next segment of 'exporting national research universities'. They are as a group for study in this book also, at the very least, the ones, as Altbach and Balan would express it, that are the flagships at the pinnacle or apex of the national systems that are discussed in the book. Moreover, given that quite a few of those systems have yet to generate an EGM/SRU institution (but will surely soon do so in the case of Germany and China – as noted above, Watson (2007: 42), however, is skeptical that the State can just 'buy' world-class states for a few of its HEIs), there are within the group from this selection of countries some that will perhaps be only in Marginson's lesser segment of 'nationally-bound research universities'. And, of course, our concept of elite HEIs for the purposes of this study will include, for example, the French *grandes écoles* and the US top liberal arts colleges that do not appear on the landscape of the research-oriented taxonomies discussed above (Cowen (2007) provides another interesting typology). In all the national case-studies, however, the value of the comparative research exercise that is the theme of the book lies in exploring whether these different mass and diverse HE systems recognize (explicitly or implicitly) and accommodate (especially by way of additional funding) their own, relatively elite HEIs. The OECD (2008) Report on HE globally calls for, *inter alia*, nations to 'ensure the coherence of the tertiary education system where there is extensive diversification', while stopping short of recommending just how diversified the system should be, still less where elite HEIs might fit within a policy of 'extensive and flexible diversification'. In the UK, for example, there was once talk of imposing an explicit R–X–T (Research, Mixed, Teaching) categorization of HEIs, and there is currently talk of HEIs being either 'research-intensive' (and probably liberal arts oriented) or 'business-facing' (and presumably focused both on vocational degrees that involve 'employer engagement' and also on the 'widening participation' agenda); often, however, such a seemingly attractive neat stratification of HEIs leaves rather too many wallowing around within 'the squeezed middle'! Or whether their national systems find the existence of elite HEIs politically embarrassing in egalitarian terms while also being attractive for their contribution to the knowledge-based economy, as well as perhaps being commercially useful as flagships whose wake of prestige other reputation-oriented HEIs in the national system (as Marginson's segment of 'teaching-focused export institutions') can utilize to recruit lucrative fee-paying overseas students...

One further, and final, thought on the character of global-player elite HEIs: in considering the league tables and rankings referred to at the start of this piece and while recognizing the various weaknesses in their methodologies, it has to be acknowledged that, currently, the top end of such international tables is uniformly and absolutely dominated by a dozen or so US universities, most of which are private institutions. The key characteristics of such institutions are: first, relative freedom from government interference in the form of, say, an equivalent of the UK's HEFCE, RAE and QAA where ever-increasing central bureaucracy is driven by a damaging fixation with a new national zeitgeist of audit, accountability and risk management (Power, 1999. 2007; Amann, 2003) – instead these US private 'elites of the elite' have merely a mild form of accreditation that vets their overall credibility and an audit trail that monitors their use of Federal research grants. Secondly, openly fierce rivalry and competition for the best faculty and graduate research students, with no pretence that there is, or can be, a comforting homogeneity across the wide range of institutions now loosely labeled 'university' within massified HE systems; and, thirdly, not only vast but also greatly diversified funding, notably, compared with public HEIs, by way of the ability to levy high tuition fees and to command continuous substantial alumni donations to already huge endowments. Indeed, it is this widening gap between the financial wealth of the private Ivy League (now reinforced by Stanford and MIT) and of certain historically well-funded public research-intensive elites, such as Berkeley, Michigan and Virginia, that gives rise to recent talk of the 'privatization' or 'floating-off' of such state HE flagships as 'charter' institutions and to a debate about 'the crisis of the public university in America' (Duderstadt & Womack, 2003; Ehrenberg, 2006; Priest & St John, 2006). It will be interesting, therefore, to see if, over time, the enhanced public funding of now explicitly identified and labeled 'top' HEIs in China, Korea, Japan and Germany (similarly Norway and Finland are currently pondering plans to encourage national elite HEIs, as indeed Denmark is actually implementing such a plan) can create any true global competition for the likes of Harvard, Yale, Stanford, MIT and Princeton, given that the former will still remain essentially public universities more readily subject to the vagaries of political interference. Such intervention also, of course, occurs indirectly, depending on what the Government targets are for research councils or similar entities centrally disbursing taxpayer monies to individual researchers at HEIs. However, the HEI possessing its own sizeable endowment *might* be willing to, and able to, itself fund long-term research that does not fit the shorter horizon expected by a publicly-funded research body under pressure from Government to demonstrate a contribution to the Knowledge-Based Economy.

And it will be equally interesting to monitor whether the UK's global-players can continue to compete with their US counterparts, given that, while they are also theoretically private legal entities (Farrington & Palfreyman, 2006: ch 2), they are in practice public-funded universities subject to increasing political and bureaucratic interference and micro-management in the name of 'best practice' (Tapper, 2007).[1]

Note

1. On the relative funding of Harvard, Princeton, Berkeley and Oxford see the OxCHEPS/Ulanov Partnership Paper (2004); on the hopelessly misguided attempts by HEFCE to 'reform' Oxford and Cambridge by obliging them as collegial organizations to conform to an inappropriate and crude governance code unimaginatively plagiarized from the commercial sector see Shattock (2006: 51–55, 153) and Palfreyman (2007); and, on HEI governance generally, Farrington & Palfreyman (2007: para. 5.02/fn 3) and as expanded at the HE Law Updates page of the OxCHEPS website).

References

Altbach, P.G. & Balan, J. (eds) (2007), *World Class Worldwide: Transforming Research Universities in Asia and Latin America* (Baltimore: The Johns Hopkins University Press).

Amann, R. (2003), 'A Sovietological View of Modern Britain', *The Political Quarterly* 2003: 468–480.

Axtell, J. (2006), *The Making of Princeton University: From Woodrow Wilson to the Present* (Princeton: Princeton University Press).

Baker, D. (2007), 'Mass Higher Education and the Super Research University', *International Higher Education* 49, 9–10.

Berquist, W.H. & Pawlak, K. (2008), *Engaging the Six Cultures of the Academy* (San Francisco: Jossey-Bass).

Bok, D. (2003), *Universities in the Marketplace: The Commercialisation of Higher Education* (Princeton: Princeton University Press).

Bolton, A. (2000), *Managing the Academic Department* (Buckingham: Open University Press).

Brewer, D.J. et al. (2002), *In Pursuit of Prestige: Strategy and Competition in US Higher Education* (New York: Transaction Publishers).

Bushaway, R.W. (2003), *Managing Research* (Buckingham: Open University Press).

Carter, I. (1990), *Ancient Cultures of Conceit: British university fiction in the post-war years* (London: Routledge).

Clark, B.R. (1998), *Creating Entrepreneurial Universities: Organisational Pathways of Transformation* (Oxford: Pergamon).

Cowen, R. (2007), 'Comparing and Transferring: Vision, Politics and Universities', in Bridges, D. et al., *Higher Education and National Development: Universities and Societies in Transition* (Abingdon: Routledge).

de Burgh, H. et al. (eds) (2007), *Can the Prizes Still Glitter? The Future of British Universities in a Changing World* (Buckingham: Buckingham University Press).

Dill, D. & Soo, M. (2005), 'Academic Quality, League Tables, and Public Policy: a cross-national analysis of university ranking systems', *Higher Education* 49, 495–533.

Dougill, J. (1998), *Oxford in English Literature: The Making, and Undoing, of 'The English Athens'* (Ann Arbor: University of Michigan Press).

Duderstadt, J.J. & Womack, F.W. (2003), *The Future of the Public University in America: Beyond the Crossroads* (Baltimore: The Johns Hopkins University Press).

Duke, A. (1996), *Importing Oxbridge: English Residential Colleges and American Universities* (New Haven: Yale University Press).

Ehrenberg, R.G. (ed.) (2006), *What's Happening to Public Higher Education?: The Shifting Financial Burden* (Baltimore: The Johns Hopkins University Press).

Etzkowitz, H. (2007), 'The University as Crucible of Enterprise: The MIT/Stanford Model', in de Burgh et al. (eds) as listed above.

Farrington, D. & Palfreyman, D. (2006), *The Law of Higher Education* Oxford: Oxford University Press).

Florida, R. (2005), *The Flight of the Creative Class* (New York: HarperBusiness).

Florida, R. (2008), *The Rise of the Creative Class* (New York: Basic Books).

Geiger, R.L. (2004), *Knowledge & Money: Research Universities and the Paradox of the Marketplace* (Stanford: Stanford University Press).

Gilbert, A. (2007), 'The Manchester Merger: Stretching the Golden Triangle', in de Burgh et al. (eds) as listed above.

Golden, D. (2006), *The Price of Admission: How America's ruling class buys its way into elite colleges – and who gets left outside the gates* (New York: Crown Publishers).

Good, D. et al. (eds) (2007), *University Collaboration for Innovation: Lessons from the Cambridge-MIT Institute* (Rotterdam: Sense Publishers).

Hall, A. (2003), *Managing People* (Buckingham: Open University Press), ch 3 contributed by Middlehurst & Kennie.

Hogan, J. & Clark, M. (1996), 'Postgraduate and Research Organization and Management', in D.A. Warner & D. Palfreyman (eds), *Higher Education Management: The Key Elements* (Buckingham: Open University Press).

Karabel, J. (2005), *The Chosen: The Hidden History of Admission and Exclusion at Harvard, Yale, and Princeton* (Boston: Houghton Mifflin Company).

Keller, M. & Keller, P. (2001), *Making Harvard Modern: The Rise of America's University* (Oxford: Oxford University Press).

Kerr, C. (2001), *The Uses of the University* (Cambridge, MA: Harvard University Press).

Kirp, D.L. (2003), *Shakespeare, Einstein and the Bottom Line: The Marketing of Higher Education* (Cambridge, MA: Harvard University Press).

Lang, D.W. (2005), 'World class or the curse of comparison', *Canadian Journal of Higher Education* 35(3), 27–55.

Leisyte, L. (2007), *University Governance and Academic Research: Case Studies of Research Units in Dutch and English Universities* (Twente: CHEPS/UT).

Marginson, S. (2006), 'Dynamics of national and global competition in higher education', *Higher Education* 52, 1–39.

Marginson, S. (ed.) (2007a), *Prospects of Higher Education: Globalisation, Market Competition, Public Goods, and the Future of the University* (Rotterdam: Sense Publishers).

Marginson, S. (2007b), 'Global university rankings: implications in general and for Australia', *Journal of Higher Education Policy and Management* 29(2), 131-142.

Marginson, S. (2007c), Paper given at the Beijing Forum, University of Peking, November 2007.

Marginson, S. & Considine, M. (2000), *The Enterprise University: Power, Governance and Reinvention in Australia* (Cambridge: Cambridge University Press).

Marginson, S. & van der Wende, M. (2007a), 'To rank or to be ranked: the impact of global rankings in higher education', *Journal of Studies in International Education* 11(3/4), 306-329.

Marginson, S. & van der Wende, M. (2007b), *Globalisation and Higher Education* (Paris: OECD).

Michael, S.O. (2005), 'The Cost of Excellence: the financial implications of institutional rankings', *International Journal of Educational Management* 19(5), 365–382.

Mohrman, K. et al. (2007), 'The Emerging Global Model of the Research University', in P. Altbach & P. McGill Peterson, eds, *Higher Education in the New Century: Global Challenges and Innovative Ideas* (Rotterdam: Sense Publishers).

Morley, L. & Aynsley, S. (2007), 'Employers, Quality and Standards in Higher Education: Shared Values and Vocabularies or Elitism and Inequalities?', *Higher Education Quarterly* 61(3), 229-249.

OECD (2008), *Tertiary Education for the Knowledge Society* (Paris: OECD).

OxCHEPS/Ulanov Partnership (2004), 'Costing, funding and sustaining higher education: a case-study of Oxford University', *Higher Education Review* 37(1), 3–31; also as Item 13 at the Papers page of the OxCHEPS website (http://oxcheps.new.ox.ac.uk/).

Palfreyman, D. (ed.) (2001), *The Oxford Tutorial* (Oxford: OxCHEPS); second edition 2008.

Palfreyman, D. (2007), 'Sustaining Oxford as World Class', in de Burgh, H. et al. (eds) as listed above.

Palfreyman, D. (2008), A Comparative Historical Perspective on 'Leadership' in Higher Education, Item 34 at the Papers page of the OxCHEPS website (http://oxcheps.new.ox.ac.uk/).

Partington, P. & Stainton, C. (2003), *Managing Staff Development* (Buckingham: Open University Press).

Power, M. (1999), *The Audit Society: Rituals of Verification* (Oxford: Oxford University Press).

Power, M. (2007), *Organised Uncertainty: Designing a World of Risk Management* (Oxford: Oxford University Press).

Priest, D.M. & St John, E.P. (eds) (2006), *Privatisation and Public Universities* (Bloomington, IN: Indiana University Press).

Proctor, M.R. (1957), *The English University Novel* (Berkeley: University of California Press).

Roberts, D. & Thompson, L. (2007), *Reputation Management for Universities: University League Tables and the Impact on Student Recruitment* (London: The Knowledge Partnership).

Rothblatt, S. (2008), 'Integrity', in Beretta, M. et al., *Aurora Torealis: Studies in the History of Science and Ideas in Honor of Tore Frängsmyr* (Sagamore Beach, MA: Science History Publications).

Salmi, J. & Saroyan, A. (2007), 'International university ranking systems and the idea of university excellence', *Journal of Higher Education Policy and Management* 29(3), 245-260.

Shattock, M.L. (2003), *Managing Successful Universities* (Buckingham: Open University Press).

Shattock, M.L. (2006), *Managing Good Governance in Higher Education* (Maidenhead: Open University Press).

Shattock, M.L. (2007), 'The Management of Universities: Managerialism and Management Effectiveness', in de Burgh et al. (eds) as listed above.

Showalter, E. (2005), *Faculty Towers: The Academic Novel and its Discontents* (Oxford: Oxford University Press).

Slaughter, S. & Leslie, L.L. (1997), *Academic Capitalism: Politics, Policies and the Entrepreneurial University* (Baltimore: The Johns Hopkins University Press).

Slaughter, S. & Rhoades, G. (2004) *Academic Capitalism and the New Economy: Markets, State, and Higher Education* (Baltimore: The Johns Hopkins University Press).

Soares, J.A. (1999), *The Decline of Privilege: The Modernization of Oxford University* (Stanford: Stanford University Press).

Soares, J.A. (2007), *The Power of Privilege: Yale and America's Elite Colleges* (Stanford: Stanford University Press).

Stensaker, B. (2007), 'The Relationship between Branding and Organisational Change', *Higher Education Management Policy* 19(1), 1-18.

Tapper, T. (2007), *The Governance of British Higher Education: The Struggle for Policy Control* (Dordrecht: Springer).

Tapper, T. & Palfreyman, D. (2000), *Oxford and the Decline of the Collegiate Tradition* (London: Woburn Press) – second edition forthcoming (Dordrecht: Springer).

Tapper, T. & Palfreyman, D. (forthcoming), *Oxford and the Evolution of the Collegiate University* (Dordrecht: Springer).

Taylor, J. (2006), 'Managing the Unmanageable: the Management of Research in Research-intensive Universities', *Higher Education Management and Policy* 18(2), 1–25.

Teixeira, P. (2004), *Markets in Higher Education: Rhetoric or Reality?* (Dordrecht: Kluwer).

Turner, D. (2005), 'Benchmarking in Universities: League Tables Revisited', *Oxford Review of Education* 31(3), 353–371.

Usher, A. & Savino, M. (2007), 'A Global Survey of University Rankings and League Tables', *Higher Education in Europe* 32(1), 5–15.

Washbourne, J. (2005), *University Inc: The Corporate Corruption of American Higher Education* (New York: Basic Books).

Watson, D. (2007), *Managing Civic and Community Engagement* (Maidenhead: Open University Press).

Watson, D. & Maddison, E. (2005), *Managing Institutional Self-Study* (Maidenhead: Open University Press).

13

Elite Higher Education in France
Tradition and Transition

Cécile Deer

When considering the enduring dual nature of the organization of higher education in France and its structural and social origins, it is difficult not to refer to Pierre Bourdieu's seminal and comprehensive work on the subject. The arguments he has developed remain compelling and any less complex approach runs the risk of appearing naïvely factual or theoretically narrow. Anyone with a deep interest in these issues should grapple with the complexity of Bourdieu's analyses in order to access a challenging understanding not only of the reproductive social mechanisms at work in education and, in particular, in its elite component in any regional/national setting, but also to gain a more specific knowledge of the underlying sociological logic at work in the French context. Here I will adopt a less complex approach than that of Bourdieu to facilitate an understanding of recent evolutions in the French higher education system. However, a large part of the following story is consistent with the understanding proposed by Pierre Bourdieu (Bourdieu & Passeron, 1970; Bourdieu, 1989; Lazuech, 1999).

Elite Higher Education in France: Some Necessary Clarifications

At undergraduate and masters level, higher education in France is split into two strands: the university sector which is by law[1] non-selective at entrance to its first year (but selective in each of the ensuing years) and the selective sector which is made up of many different higher education institutions with diverse official legal statutes. The type of tuition on offer in the selective sector is often vocational in scope with strong direct links to the job market. This selective sector is in turn made of two very distinct strands: the more strictly vocationally oriented and relatively recently created strand comprises diverse technical higher education institutions such as the *Instituts Universitaires de Technologie* (IUT) or the *Sections de Techniciens Supérieurs* (STS), which are located in upper secondary schools (*lycée*), and the traditional elite institutions commonly referred to as the '*grandes écoles*'. These are small higher education institutions with competitive entrance exams offering either four- or five-year courses directly after the *baccalauréat* or three-year courses after two years of *classe préparatoire* (preparatory class), during which students prepare for the entrance examinations to the *grandes écoles* in broad selected areas of specialization.[2]

Inspired by Jesuit colleges, the first *classes préparatoires* were set up by Vauban to prepare students for the examination for chartered engineers. Today most *classes préparatoires* are located in the *lycées* and admission is based on academic performance during the last two pre-baccalaureate years as well as on merits and distinctions obtained at this examination. Not all the baccalaureates carry equal weight in selection for the *classes préparatoires*. It is essentially the general scientific baccalaureate, especially those majoring in mathematics, which provides the best chances of access, paradoxically even to those *classes préparatoires* specializing in Arts and Humanities. Qualitative and quantitative success rates for applications to the *grandes écoles* examinations, which are organized at national level, can vary dramatically according to the various *classes préparatoires* with some prestigious *lycées* in Paris and in France's main regional cities not only obtaining very high success rates in general but also more specifically at entrance to the most prestigious *grandes écoles*. Any student failing to make the grade after two or three years of preparation can apply for the second year of a university degree.

Historically the task of the *grandes écoles*, most of which remain engineering schools to this day, has been to select, educate and groom the nation's elite, society's future leaders in strategic areas such as engineering, state administration, business, and education. Both the *Ecole des Ponts et Chaussées* and the *Ecole des Mines*, founded in 1747 and 1778 respectively, were set up before the Revolution to remedy the shortcomings of the French universities. The 1789 Revolution and post-revolutionary period reinforced the prominence of the *écoles* as opposed to the universities, which were considered too traditional and too close to the *Ancien Régime* (Verger, 1986). With growth in new sciences and technologies came the setting-up and development of new specialized technical schools outside the universities, such as the *Ecole Polytechnique* for military and civil engineering in 1794. Around the same period, the *Ecole Normale Supérieure* was set up for the training of a small intellectual elite that would then go on to lead the teaching profession. Over the years, the intellectual and professional success of the students of the *grandes écoles* has fed back into the prestige of these highly selective institutions which only accepted and qualified a few dozen students each year.

These elite specialist institutions have held an influential role in the past and present organization of both higher education and of government and society in France (Suleiman, 1978). This influence is fully embodied in the notion of *Corps de l'Etat*, whereby the graduates of a handful of *grandes écoles* (*Polytechniques, Ecoles des Mines, Ecoles des Ponts et Chaussées, Ecole Normale d'Administration*) have enjoyed a quasi-monopoly over certain positions in the 'Colbertist' French state apparatus, often as civil servants, according to their ranking at the end of their studies. The *Société des Agrégés* may be seen as the equivalent for the teaching profession of what the *corps* represents for civil servants.

However, if there is a clear legal definition for the universities, there is no such thing for the group of higher education institutions commonly, but vaguely, referred to as '*grandes écoles*'. The term itself has no strict meaning and the institutions have no specific unitary legal statutes. Besides the most prestigious institutions there are many other '*écoles*' that could be given the qualification '*grandes*'. The *grandes écoles* are therefore characterized by the heterogeneity of their administrative structures. Some are state-maintained (the majority of engineering schools), others are private institutions (many business schools). Among those which are state-funded, most are financed by the Education Ministry, and in particular the *Ecole Normale Supérieure* (ENS), but some are financed by the Defence Ministry (*Polytechnique*), others by the Agriculture Ministry, while the *Ecole Normale d'Administration* (ENA) is directly funded by the Prime Minister's Office. Some are closely linked to a university, others are not.

The *Conference des Grandes Ecoles* is a not-for-profit association that represents those *grandes écoles* which are recognized by the State and deliver national diplomas after at least five years of post-baccalaureate studies. It has some 181 member institutions, all of which cater for a very small number of students. The largest (*Polytechnique, HEC, Centrale, Arts et Métiers* or *INSA*) have around one thousand students each. The number therefore of students

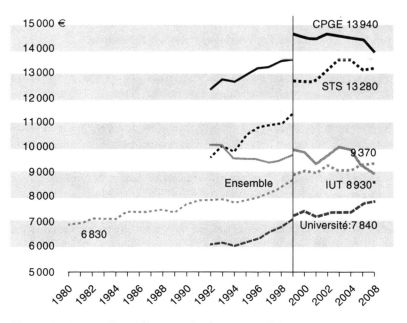

Figure 13.1 Average Expenditure per Student at 2006 Prices.

in the *grandes écoles* represents only a small percentage of the total number of students in higher education. This percentage is slightly higher when taking into account the number of students in the *classes préparatoires aux grandes écoles* (CPGE) but remains below 10%. Despite this, they receive close to a third of the higher education budget, a point to which we will return later.

Traditionally the *grandes écoles* were conceived as teaching institutions and, as such, have had little inclination and incentive to do research. In sociological terms, it is tempting to liken the role of the CPGE and *grandes écoles* in relation to the French higher education sector to that of the leading private schools in the British secondary school sector (though most of the most historically prestigious *grandes écoles* are publicly financed), in that they have set the benchmark against which academic excellence has been encouraged, geared, measured and rewarded. In the French context the picture would not be complete without also referring to the parallel dualism that exists in the organization of research. Here the organizational and administrative separation has been between research activities carried out in the universities and elite *research* centres and institutions, with the Centre National de la Recherche Scientifique (CNRS) and other specialist research institutions (such as INSERM for medical research) playing a key role since the end of the Second World War. The picture which emerges from this quick overview of the situation is one where the universities sit uneasily between two separate worlds of academic excellence, one designed for the teaching of the future elite in key professional areas, the other for the development of cutting edge research.

The *Grandes Ecoles* and the Expansion of Higher Education: A 'Segregated' Democratization?

Academic excellence in France has long been measured by the stringency of the selection process of its elite constituents. In 1998, the Attali Report commissioned by the government to report on the state and future of higher education in France noted that, whilst the number of students in the universities had multiplied by 40 since 1900, the number of students in the engineering *grandes écoles* had only multiplied by 15 over the same period (Attali, 1998). In raw quantitative terms, this can only suggest a strong reinforcement of selective access to the elite institutions. Over the last three decades, processes of educational elitism and social reproduction via academic selection have remained remarkably unchanged and have even become more pronounced throughout the 1980s and 1990s. This has been partly due to unfavorable economic and job market environments combined with expansionist reforms at upper secondary schools and their knock-on effect on the non-selective higher education sector (i.e. the universities), which in turn have played an important role in the well-documented entrenchment of academic and sociocultural advantages in the selective parts of the higher education sector

(Albouy & Wanecq, 2003). The centrality and influence of the *grandes écoles* in these processes has been acknowledged but only recently has it been genuinely questioned.

The higher education reforms of the early 1980s – the early years of the Mitterrand presidency – left the CPGE and *grandes écoles* system largely untouched, though one of François Mitterrand's pre-electoral pledges had been a unified system of education. Clearly what Mitterrand and the new left-wing republican government had in mind was less a unified higher education system than a unified school system. The Third Republic concept of education still prevailed and it was the religious schools that were considered to be potentially more socially divisive than the *grandes écoles*, which were still largely conceived, in particular by the ruling elite, as a meritocratic model of academic and intellectual excellence that was so well suited to the recruitment and training of the French elite, whether administrative (*Ecole Normale d'Administration*), technical (*Polytechnique, Mines, Ponts*), academic (*Ecoles Normales Supérieures*) or managerial (*Ecole des Hautes Etudes Commerciales*), that it could hardly be called into question.

In many respects, this conception of 'Republican elitism' was carried forward in the ministerial decision to create selective three-year diplomas (*magistères*) within the universities, accessible two years after the baccalaureate, to run as competitors but also in parallel with the CPGE/*grandes écoles* system. The *magistères* were designed both with reference and in opposition to the *classes préparatoires/grandes écoles* courses in an attempt to provide an alternative yet selectively recognizable form of higher education excellence in the university. There were a small number of students selected annually (30 per *magistère*) but selection was based on previous achievements and personal interviews; there were close links with industry but in relation to emerging job specializations and needs; there were demanding programs of study but there was flexible pedagogy as opposed to the traditional cramming of the *classes préparatoires* and the well-known ensuing tendency of students to free wheel once they arrived in the *grandes écoles*. The creation of the *magistères* was a limited attempt at generating a small elite within the university sector (60–70 *magistères*) by providing and promoting an updated model of higher education excellence. Unfortunately, the *magistères* were not nationally recognized diplomas but accredited university diplomas, which, in the French context, represents a significant handicap in terms of attractiveness and recognition. In many respects, the setting-up of the *magistères* was a premature attempt at giving more autonomy to the universities for the development of selective elite qualifications. On the other hand, the *Ecole Normale Supérieure*, which does not deliver diplomas of its own, saw an opportunity to develop its activities in this direction.

The 1984 Savary Higher Education Law was essentially concerned with reforming governance structures in the universities and left the organization of the CPGE/*grandes écoles* largely untouched. Significantly, however, despite the large autonomy of action they have traditionally enjoyed, the *grandes écoles* have not been placed outside the remit of the National Evaluation Committee for Higher Education that was set up at the time. This implies that they too could be the object of evaluation procedures, a form of external accountability previously unknown to these institutions (CNE, 1995, 1997, 2002, 2005). Like the university sector, the publicly funded *grandes écoles* have also had to produce strategic mission statements and enter into contractual funding agreements with the central and regional authorities.

Like most higher education systems in Western democracies, since the end of the Second World War higher education in France has been characterized by sharp increases in rates of access and participation, particularly since the beginning of the 1980s. In the French context, this expansion has been far from evenly distributed across the sector, whether quantitatively or qualitatively (i.e. social origins of the students, type of upper secondary education attended, gender representation). Whereas in 1950, 29% of the students in the top four *grandes écoles* (*Polytechnique, ENA, ENS, Centrale Paris*) came from lower social backgrounds, they formed less than 10% of the recruitment by the end of the 1990s though they still represented 68% of the age cohort (Attali, 1998, p. 21). Expansion has taken place essentially in the universities (underfunded and non-selective at the point of entry) whereas growth in the selective and elite part of the sector represented by the CPGE – and the *grandes écoles* to which they give access – has lagged far behind. This has reinforced the screening effect of the *grandes écoles* diplomas in what is a persistently tight job market for young people. Between 1985 and 2005, students from lower social backgrounds (parents who were manual workers or lower-middle class employees), who make up close to 60% of the 20–24 age group, have been increasingly successful in securing access to the universities, where they make up one quarter of the student population. However, during the same period, this category has lost ground in the *classes préparatoires* for the *grandes écoles* (CPGE) where they represent less than 15% of the students. Students from higher social backgrounds (15% of those aged 20–24) are disproportionately represented (over 50%) in these *classes préparatoires* and *grandes écoles* (MEN, 2007a; MEN, 2007b,c).

In a provocative oxymoron, Pierre Merle calls this the 'segregative democratization' of education (Merle, 2000; Merle, 2002). This 'social segregation' occurs at an early stage, at secondary school level with the type of baccalaureate taken. Between 1985 and 2000, the proportion of baccalaureate holders in a class age has risen from 30% to 60%. However, only since 1997 has data collected by the *Direction de l'Evaluation, de la Prospective et de la Performance* (DEPP) allowed the analysis of the higher education path of baccalaureate students according to their social background (Sautory, 2007). This has confirmed that near-universal access to upper secondary education has not been translated into an equalization of the chances of accessing the higher education elite. Children from higher social backgrounds are to be found largely in the scientific baccalaureates, which in France is the logical upper secondary path to the higher education elite (also embracing non-scientific disciplines), whereas children from lower socio-economic backgrounds are over-represented in the technological and vocational baccalaureates, which hardly provide the best chance to be considered for admission to the selective higher education sector. If we combine this with the fact that, for example, of those entering lower secondary education in 1989, 85% of those from higher social backgrounds passed the baccalaureate as opposed to only 52% of children of manual workers and 34% of those whose parents were unemployed, it shows that increased participation and staying-on rates at upper secondary school level throughout the 1980s and 1990s have not resulted in a genuine democratization of access to the upper secondary level (Kieffer & Duru-Bellat, 2000) and *a fortiori* to higher education and its elite component.

By the mid-1990s, the expansion of higher education that had taken place essentially in the non-selective sector of higher education (i.e. the universities) led to further reforms of this part of the system as it was becoming obvious that the quantitative expansion in terms of the sheer numbers entering higher education had not been matched by a qualitative expansion in terms of an equalization of academic chances, which in France is particularly strongly correlated with employment opportunities, life chances and earnings (MEN, 2007a, pp. 34–35; OECD, 2006). In 1991, Claude Allègre, the Education Minister in the Jospin Government, had already set up by decree selective university institutes (*Instituts Universitaires Professionalisés*) in a further attempt to provide another credible alternative selective vocational route within the universities whilst rationalizing and clarifying the vocational qualifications on offer. Parallel to this, Allègre also initiated an interesting reform of the *classes préparatoires* by setting-up new types of scientific *classes préparatoires*, and the modernization of the study programs so that the specialization on offer (mathematics, experimental science and engineering science) would fit better with the reforms initiated at secondary school level. For a short period, this allowed for a greater representation of non-scientific general baccalaureate holders until the end of the 1990s, when further reforms at upper secondary school level with fewer types of baccalaureate and modified contents resulted in a further closure of the CPGE to non-scientific baccalaureate recruits as these reforms were perceived as academically suspicious. The situation has remained unchanged since, with an increase in the number of *classes préparatoires* students reflecting a general trend at baccalaureate level rather than any greater proportion of baccalaureate holders (9.2%) gaining access to these *classes préparatoires* (MEN, 2007b).

It is worth noting that much of this increase has occurred in fee-paying private *classes préparatoires*, where admissions criteria can be less demanding but tuition fees substantial. This illustrates two phenomena. The first is the development of a private market of cramming courses and institutions spawned by the *grandes écoles'* fierce academic selection. The same phenomenon has occurred in relation to the extremely selective examination at the end of the first year of medical studies. The second is the persistent inequalities in public provision across France in the face of growing demand.[3] This has increasingly undermined claims that selection practices are objective and the overall process is meritocratic.

All this had little impact on the actual social recruitment in the elite streams of higher education. In 1998, the Attali Report on a European model of higher education commissioned by Claude Allègre denounced in polite but inescapable terms the sharp social inequalities that existed behind the French embracing of 'meritocracy'. Noting that the vast majority of recruits in the top *grandes écoles* came from a dozen *classes préparatoires*, he provocatively suggested that it might be possible to trace this elite back to between 100 and 200 nursery schools (Attali, 1998, p. 20). Acknowledging the difficulties in generating clear data, the report also pointed to the sharp and widening funding differential in the unit of funding per university student and per CPGE and *grandes écoles* student (Attali, 1998, p. 66).

The more immediate solution that was put forward was that until such time as the *classes préparatoires* could be brought closer to the universities, at least more of the former should be set up in socially deprived areas and specific selection mechanisms should be put in place to increase the presence of students with a technical educational background in order to redress some of the social imbalances in recruitment. The report also suggested reforming the most prestigious *grandes écoles*, in particular by diversifying the sources of their recruitment (opening admissions to technological baccalaureates and to university students) and by reducing their stranglehold on the State apparatus. It was also suggested that selection should gradually move away from strict written and oral examinations to make way for assessment based on previous achievement, course work and interviews. The study programs of the *grandes écoles* would have to be harmonized with those of the universities and, more generally, the universities and the *grandes écoles* should try to co-ordinate more of their activities by bringing their students, staff and technical and scientific resources together. The perennial question remains that of the possibility of setting up *classes préparatoires* within the universities. Like most reports which lay out such radical proposals, the Attali Report set the public debate in motion but was rapidly shelved, although not without suffering the traditional accusations of seeking to sacrifice French higher education to market forces and undermining academic excellence. The Attali Report was, however, a guiding document for the reforms of higher education that have taken place since, and provides a guideline for future policy.

As essentially teaching institutions, the élite *classes préparatoires/grandes écoles* have traditionally favoured academic precocity (e.g. the age limit for the entrance examination at the *Ecole Normale Supérieure* was removed in 2005 as part of a general reorganization of this ancient institution). Further attempts at democratizing and diversifying recruitment in the *grandes écoles* have therefore consisted of establishing limited parallel selective entrance processes for those who, for lack of information, motivation or self-deselection, have missed the *classes préparatoires* route. The management schools have been quicker to act and have been far more pro-active in this direction.

The question of gender is almost an irrelevance as far as access to the *grandes écoles* is concerned or at least it is an issue which is so skewed in the French context that it needs to be understood and acted upon in a very specific way (CGE, 2002). Most *grandes écoles* are engineering schools in which women – as in most Western European countries – represent only a small proportion of the students: 10% to 20% on average. The picture is different when one considers the management school sector where the participation of women has made great progress in recent decades. However, middle to lower ranking management schools are not on a par with similarly ranked engineering schools in terms of prestige. This situation again reflects what has happened at upper secondary school level where participation has increased because of the higher staying-on rate of pupils and, in particular, of girls across the board (Baudelot & Establet, 1992). However, the increase has not taken place in equal proportion in the various types of baccalaureates and crucially in those baccalaureates that open doors to the selective stream of higher education (Duru-Bellat, 2002; MEN, 2007b).

For reasons that are the object of much debate and theorizing, most girls opt for baccalaureates majoring in Arts and Humanities or in Economics and Social Sciences, which, as things stand, can only give them elite access to their narrow respective specializations on high previous academic achievements and merits. On this issue of gender equality, the example of the *Ecole Normale Supérieure*, which only became officially co-educational in the mid-1980s when the historical division by gender was replaced by a division by subjects (Sciences/Arts), may be used as a good example of the difficulties of achieving real equal opportunity of access to the elite (Ferrand, 2004). Meanwhile, the *Ecole Polytechnique féminine* has had to open its doors to male students – in 1994 – as it did not have enough recruits.

It is not currently possible to assess changing access patterns in terms of the ethnic origins of the students as has been the case in Britain or in the United States. Until now this has been considered to be a non-constitutional type of social monitoring. However, the *Zones d'Education Prioritaire* (Education Action Zones) are located in areas where there is a significant concentration of ethnic minorities from first- or second-generation immigrant families.

Therefore, throughout the 1980s and 1990s, the political attempts at reforming the *classes préparatoires/grandes écoles* apex of academic excellence in France in the midst of rapid developments in the higher education sector have been limited and half-hearted. Crucially, they have stopped short of questioning the logic and modalities of stringent types of narrow academic selection (Vasconcellos, 2006) and in particular the pre-eminence of mathematics and of 'make-or-break' competitive entrance examinations as opposed to more diversified approaches and routes to elite institutions. This has allowed further closure of the system to occur which has reinforced a well-documented social and cultural reproduction of the elite. There have been attempts to set up alternative selective vocational routes in the universities but the most important reform has been that of the *classes préparatoires*, initiated by Claude Allègre in the mid-1990s. Even more recently, various crises have forced the country to take stock and 'do some soul-searching' about its educational system: its purposes, practices and achievements. With growing social inequalities and repeated incidents of youth unrest involving upper secondary students worried about their future, university students unhappy with the deterioration of conditions offered in the universities and young people in different communities rejecting the educational system altogether, the role of education as a social 'elevator' (*ascenseur social*) with, at its apex, the elite component as the ultimate neutral republican device for social mobility, has come under increasing scrutiny.

In the wake of repeated unrests that have developed in recent years in the suburbs of most big French cities, the *Institut d'Etudes Politiques de Paris* (Science Po) decided to develop and promote its special relations with some upper secondary schools in the Parisian suburbs (Descoings, 2007). Until now, this is as much as has been attempted at implementing some sort of positive discrimination. The initiative was praised by some as a worthy and overdue move and criticized by others who saw it as a public relations stunt, or as an 'elitist democratization' which did not genuinely address the systemic inequities of French higher education, whilst running the risk of diluting the diploma and reputation of the institution. The recent report of the *Comité National d'Evaluation* on *Sciences Po*, which has been prominent in the French higher education landscape since its creation after the Prussian victory in 1870, provides an insight into the ambiguous and mixed reception which that institution's initiative has received (CNE, 2005). On the whole, however, the *Conference des Grandes Ecoles* has become increasingly aware of the difficulty in maintaining and justifying the status quo (CGE, 2004) and of the proactive role that elite higher education has to play in the promotion of fairer access and equal opportunity, as part of the overall debate on the educational system in France, if that sector aims to retain some sort of legitimacy. However, it also rightly points to the fact that a socially skewed distribution of access is not the preserve of the *grandes écoles* and that this is also to be found in the third cycle of university education, which leads to the doctorate. In 2004, the *Conference des Grandes Ecoles* announced that equality of opportunity would be among its main strategic priorities for the coming years as it acknowledged its significance for social cohesion (CGE, 2004). The following year this led to the signing of a charter to this effect with three ministries (Education, Employment, Integration). Meanwhile, in the face of persistent social inequalities of access to, and participation in, the *classes préparatoires* and *grandes écoles*, the temporary remedy originally proposed in the Attali Report is in the process of being implemented with the planned setting up of CPGE in the *Zones d'Education Prioritaire* (Hénart, 2007), which is accompanied by a burgeoning debate and discourse about positive discrimination (Bourgarel, 2006)

The Parisian Elite: Regional and European Dynamics

The political and administrative power structures of the French higher education system are strongly centralized, which holds true when compared to most other European countries. The most prestigious *grandes écoles* – as institutions whose rationale and organization remain eminently grounded in a hierarchical and centralized educational system devised by and geared to the needs of the Republican State – have been historically located in or around Paris. This has been epitomized in the well-known *esprit de corps*, whose meaning is only partially translated in the English expression 'old boys' network' because it is strongly related to the centralized organization of the French State. This centralization has also been true for the organization of the universities (Charle, 1994). The original Napoleonic imprint goes some way towards explaining the persistence of the situation. The direct translation of this centralization with regard to the university elite is that the most prestigious university postgraduate programs remain largely based in Paris.

This being said, those who have not closely investigated the recent evolution of the French higher education landscape could be forgiven for having missed the subtle decentralizing evolutions which have taken place since the second half of the 1980s (Deer 2002; Musselin, 2001) and their gradual impact on the historical centralization of power and academic excellence. These evolutions may be interpreted in three overlapping chronological stages: regionalization, Europeanization and internationalization.

The regionalization of higher education has its roots in the 1982 decentralizing laws after the election of François Mitterrand combined with a reorganization of the central administration at the Education Ministry (Musselin & Friedberg, 1993) towards the end of the 1980s and the implementation of tripartite contractual agreements between central government, the newly created regional authorities and the higher education/research institutions (University 2000 Plan; Harfi, 2004). With a European and global context less sympathetic to strong government intervention in the national economy, along with the internationalization of exchanges in higher education accompanied by the recent emergence of new players the size of India and China, the traditional links between the economic, political and intellectual elite at central State level in France have had to be reconsidered and 'modernized', though the changes that have occurred so far appear to be no more than a start. Highly symbolic was the reform of the *Ecole Normale d'Administration* (Silguy, 2003), which came into effect in 2005, and the relocation of activities of the School in Strasbourg on the grounds of the necessary decentralization of the French administration. However, the need for the future French administrative elite to acquaint itself with the institutions of the European Union was actively resisted for a long time by the students and the teachers of the School who felt that this would remove them from the Parisian epicenter of decision-making power.

The relocation (started in the mid-1980s, completed in 2000) of the *Ecole Normale Supérieure* to Lyon, the third largest French city and the ancestral counter power to the capital city, seems to have been politically a smoother move. It is telling to read the report of the *Comité National d'Evaluation,* which concludes that the school has in a way been able to reinvent itself through the regional branching out of its activities (CNE, 1997). With the modernization of the regional universities gathering pace towards the end of the 1990s, some of the Parisian engineering *grandes écoles* have also relocated part of their activities and/or reinforced their links with regional elite institutions so as to increase their visibility while still remaining very selective in their intake of students.

However, any increase in the regional presence of the Parisian *grandes écoles* is less significant than the creation since the 1990s of European poles of excellence with the aim of fostering synergies between higher education institutions in broad regional areas, and cooperation between these clusters and the regional and local authorities. This regionalization of higher education activities, in which the *grandes écoles* outside the capital have been strongly encouraged to take part, also reflects the evolutions that have taken place in France as a result of the increased impact of wider European influences. Broadly speaking it is also a policy well suited to an age-old preoccupation of French governments, the *aménagement du territoire* (territorial planning and development). However, some *écoles* have been wary of entering too closely into such agreements for fear of losing part of their managerial and pedagogical autonomy. Fifteen years on, higher education poles of excellence are being revived with an emphasis on joint research activities, whereby the *grandes écoles* are encouraged to develop specific research agreements with universities in their vicinity and/or area of specialization.

This trend raises the question of the impact on the *classes préparatoires* and *grandes écoles* of the development of what is commonly referred to as the European Higher Education Area (EHEA), more particularly the reforms that have very recently been set in motion in the universities with a view to bringing their study programs and qualifications into line with the harmonizing principles of the Bologna Process: organization of the three-stage degree structure of Undergraduate Degree-Master-Doctorate, division of the academic year into semesters and the generalization of the European Credit Transfer System. In order to facilitate the opening up of their recruitment to European students (Erasmus, Socrates), and to reinforce their visibility in the European Higher Education Area, the *grandes écoles* have had to modulate part of their admission criteria to account for the educational diversity of European and, more generally, foreign recruits, which, given the centrality of competitive examinations for the selection of French students, has represented something of a cultural shock. On the other hand, this cultural shock has been a shared experience for European/foreign students studying in the French *grandes écoles* as life and studies in these institutions remain characterized by some age-old idiosyncratic practices[4] and terminology.

For the *grandes écoles*, more than any socio-political pressures to open up their recruitment criteria, the real step towards a greater widening of the criteria for student recruitment has come from the European impulse: the need to be recognized as significant elite players, to accept that academic excellence can come in many guises and has to be accommodated rather than formatted. As a further step in this direction, the management schools are fast developing three-year Bachelor's programs open to students immediately after the completion of upper secondary school. However, this does not signal the end of the *classe préparatoire* since the management schools' favoured option is to run diverse admission processes in parallel.

Elitism: Global Challenges and Financial Pressures

The elitist *grandes écoles* model and the current situation of the *grandes écoles* themselves taken individually are also being questioned in many respects by the internationalization of higher education (Lazuech, 1999): the pressure to redefine what constitutes 'excellence', the need for greater visibility on the world stage in terms of institutional status (France is one of the few countries where the higher education elite lies outside the university), and number of students. Furthermore, there are the financial pressures involved in being located at the top of an increasingly competitive world of higher education whilst remaining accountable to the public paymaster through contractual agreements or scrutiny by the *Comité National d'Evaluation*.

In France, the definition of higher education excellence has traditionally been based on the cramming of knowledge that takes place in the *classes préparatoires* to prepare for entrance to the selective teaching-orientated vocational *grandes écoles* with subsequent preferential access to positions and occupations of high status. In opposition, the way academic excellence has been measured and compared internationally has been increasingly influenced by the American model, which does not sit easily with that of the French *grandes écoles*. In the 2003 Shanghai University's Academic Ranking of

World Universities, only two French higher education institutions appeared in the top 100. These were two Parisian universities: Paris VI (sixty-fifth) and Paris XI (seventy-second). The first *grande école* – the ENS Paris – ranked only one hundred and sixth, and by 2007 the situation has not improved much: Paris VI came thirty-ninth, Paris XI was fifty-second, the *Ecole Normale Supérieure Paris* ranked eighty-third, and a regional university, Strasbourg, came ninety-ninth, well before the *Ecole Polytechnique*, which has always been seen as the jewel in the crown of the engineering *grandes écoles*. The regular OECD *Education at a Glance* reports do not show the performance of France as outstanding in the overall matter of higher education, pointing in particular at the lack of investment in the university sector. Widely reported in the national and influential regional press in the run-up to the presidential elections, the poor showing of French higher education in this ranking and, in particular, the poor performance of the *grandes écoles*, sent shockwaves through the country, and not least through the establishment and the elite institutions (Harfi & Mathieu, 2006). Of course, like any other such ranking (and PISA is a case in point), it has been easy and probably justified to question the assessment criteria. It has been argued that many *grandes écoles* were badly positioned because 'on paper' (i.e. officially) they did not have any systematic and well-developed research activities of their own. However, the *grandes écoles* have developed their research capacities over the last twenty years, not only in-house, but also by setting up doctoral-level programs, sometimes in collaboration with the universities as many *grandes écoles* are not entitled to deliver doctoral qualifications, and by developing collaboration with various specialist research institutions. Nevertheless, these efforts remain insufficient when compared with elite higher education institutions around the world.

The response of the *Ecole des Mines* has been particularly interesting as it decided to publish its own ranking according to its own criteria. Whereas the Shanghai league table takes into account essentially academic criteria such as the quality of teaching staff in terms of prizes won (Nobel Prizes, Field Medals, peer recognition, research publications in major academic journals and citation index performance), the alternative ranking devised by the *Ecole des Mines* puts the emphasis on the number of former students who are in key managerial positions in the 500 biggest international companies according to Fortune Magazine. The aim is to evaluate the professional performance of its former students. When taking into account this criteria, five of the top French *grandes écoles* figure in the top ten in Europe. The counter-ranking produced by the *Ecole des Mines* clearly highlights different definitions of academic excellence and exemplifies how such rankings, either national or international, can be no more than self-fulfilling prophecies. One wonders, in particular, to what extent the *Ecole des Mines*' own league table is skewed by the quasi-monopoly enjoyed by the graduates of a handful of *grandes écoles* in securing the top managerial positions in some of the largest French companies, which remain largely closed to foreign-educated managers.

Nevertheless, this counter-ranking does clearly show the different approaches to evaluating elite higher education: via academic processes and outputs or via graduate output and job market criteria. In matters of international ranking, one group of *grandes écoles* seems to be better positioned, namely the management schools, as shown in the latest European league table of masters in management published by the Financial Times. Most of these *grandes écoles* are private fee-paying institutions, which for a long time now have had to be far more responsive to the national, European and global evolutions in their sector.

Increased competition needs appropriate funding levels and if public funding for the *grandes écoles* has so far been forthcoming, with considerably higher units of funding per student than in the universities, one may wonder whether this will always be the case. Since the publication of the Attali Report, and the launch of the U3M plan for the Parisian universities in 2000, the unit of funding per student in the *classes préparatoires* and *grandes écoles* has started to decrease whilst funding for university students has increased. With higher education institutions encouraged to reorganize their activities so as to concentrate their resources (for example libraries and research facilities), the *grandes écoles* have also come under financial pressure to become more efficient. For example, the ENS experienced financial difficulties when its allocated budget did not meet the costs of its delocalization.

Even the 29 management schools are feeling under pressure. With costs spiraling (10,000 to 11,000 euros per year per student) and tuition fees having reached a significant level (7,000 euros on average) they are emphasizing the role they have played in recent decades in the modernization of French higher education. As part of their contribution to the national effort they are now requesting the government to take measures to facilitate further evolution, such as greater decentralization so as to increase regional funding, tax relief for companies which provide higher education with financial support, the development of publicly subsidized saving plans (*Plan épargne*) for education, the use of part of the *taxe professionnelle* to modernize and develop bursarships based on academic achievement, and tax relief on tuition fees or the creation of a borrowing fund guaranteed by the State (*fond de garantie d'emprunt*) to help students from poorer economic backgrounds.

At another level, the international dimension is increasingly integrated in the study programs of the *grandes écoles*, in particular with periods of study or work placement abroad as a result of bilateral agreements and partnerships with foreign higher education institutions. The importance of learning foreign languages is being increasingly emphasized. Since the end of the 1980s, the *Conférence des Grandes Ecoles* has been very active in signing contractual agreements with foreign counterparts (CGE, 2005b). This internationalization has been essentially organized to provide opportunities for French students to gain experience abroad as part of their studies. However, the possibility that the *grandes écoles* might actively promote their activities in order to maximize their recruitment of high-flying foreign students remains remote. There are also a few examples of delocalization of activities but it seems that the priority has been to satisfy the positional advantage of the French students on the French job market (CNE, Centrale Paris) rather than to develop academic links and exchanges.

The *Aggiornamento* of the French Elite: Different Expectations but a Similar Role

Until recently, there had been little genuine questioning of the *grandes écoles* model in France. Little was known about them as objects of study (Lahire, 1997; Suleiman, 1978). Opinions about them have been polarized between those who – in the wake of Bourdieu's analyses (Bourdieu, 1989) – saw them as the epitome of the academic justification of reproduction and social domination, and those who hailed them as the only true meritocratic model of academic excellence that others, including other countries, could not help but envy. In between were many who – more or less consciously – were too busy playing the system according to its rules to pause and think about its pertinence and adequacy. Since the 1990s, this situation has changed in several ways but the changes have not been radical. They are much more the acceleration of a trend which has gathered pace throughout the 1990s: the regionalization, Europeanization and internationalization of higher education; there has been a slow, inevitable evolution in which everyone is taking part, even the universities.

At the time of writing, there is a sense that this cautious evaluation is quickly going to be overtaken by current developments. In preparation for, and in the wake of the 2007 presidential elections, the *grandes écoles* system has come under increased scrutiny as part of, and parallel to, the reforms proposed for the universities. Recent months have seen an accumulation of signs that the issue is now coming to the fore. Influential national newspapers have published supplements on these matters including many leaders/expressions of opinion from key players in the sector. Several seminars and research projects have been organized on the question of the French elite, elite formation and equality of access. A number of books have been published on the subject, which is a new phenomenon as traditionally very few books are written on higher education in France and even fewer on the *grandes écoles*.

Exposed and criticized for their inability to promote and guarantee fair access to the elite at national level, the *grandes écoles* have lost a large part of their meritocratic moral justification. Throughout the 1980s and 1990s, their small size, highly selective practice and autonomous managerial structure gave them a temporary competitive advantage over the universities when the latter had to open their doors unprepared and underfunded to welcome an influx of baccalaureate holders. Caught resting on their national laurels, the *grandes écoles* overlooked the significance of wider international developments in higher education. In order not to be marginalized and sustain their elite status, they now have to evolve quickly to make up for the ground they have lost both nationally in terms of equality of opportunities, and at the European and international levels both as ambassadors of French higher education excellence but also as fully fledged higher education institutions recognized for types of excellence which may not always have been part of their tradition.

Notes

1. Any questioning of this non-selectivity has been a key aspect of student unrest since 1968.
2. Mathematics and Physics, Biological Sciences, Arts and Humanities, Business/Management, Veterinary Science.
3. The *Institut d'Etude Politique de Lille* has just announced the setting up of a free distance learning *classe préparatoire* with the aim of serving the needs of those students who cannot afford such a course in terms of maintenance funds.
4. In 1998, the practice of *bizutage* (practical jokes played on first-year students by older students), which in some engineering schools could take the form of year-long forms of bullying was forbidden by law, though there was criticism that political correctness had gone too far.

References

Albouy, V. and Wanecq, T. 2003. Les inégalités sociales d'accès aux grandes écoles. *Economie et Statistique*, 361, pp. 27–52.

Attali, J. 1998. *Pour un modèle européen d'enseignement supérieur*. Rapport de la Commission présidée par Jacques Attali, Paris.

Baudelot, C. & Establet, R. 1992. *Allez les filles: une révolution silencieuse*. Paris: Seuil.

Bourdieu, P. & Passeron, J.C. 1970. *Reproduction, élément pour une théorie du système d'enseignement*. Paris: Editions de Minuit. (Bourdieu, P. & Passeron, J.C. 1990. *Reproduction in education, society and culture*. London: Sage.)

Bourdieu, P. 1989. *La noblesse d' état, grandes écoles et esprit de corps*. Paris: Editions de Minuit. (Bourdieu, P. 1996. *The State Nobility*. Cambridge: Polity Press).

Bourgarel, A. 2006. Chronique de l'éducation prioritaire 2003–2005. *Diversité*, 144, pp. 141–154.

CGE. 2002. *Initiatives et propositions à l'intention de l'amont pour améliorer l'égalité filles-garçons*. Paris: Conférence des Grandes Ecoles.

CGE. 2004. *Grandes écoles et enseignement supérieur: éléments de stratégie*. Livre blanc. Paris: Conférence des Grandes Ecoles.

CGE. 2005b. *Les grandes écoles et l'international*. Paris: Conférence des Grandes Ecoles.

CNE. 1995. *L'Ecole Nationale Supérieure d'Arts et Métiers*. Paris: Comité National d'Evaluation.

CNE. 1997. *Ecole Normale supérieure de Lyon*. Rapport d'Evaluation. Paris: Comité National d'Evaluation.

CNE. 2002. *L'Ecole Centrale de Paris*. Rapport d'évaluation. Paris: Comité National d'Evaluation.

CNE. 2005. *L'Institut d'Etudes Politiques de Paris*. Rapport d'évaluation. Paris: Comité National d'Evaluation.

Charle, C. 1994. *La république des universitaires: 1870–1940*. Paris: Seuil.

Cour des Comptes. 2006. *La carte universitaire d'île de France: une recomposition nécessaire. Rapport public thématique*. Paris: Cour des comptes.

Deer, C. 2002. *Higher education in England and France since the 1980s*. Oxford: Symposium.

Descoings, R. 2007. *Sciences Po, de la Courneuve à Shangaï*. Paris: Presses de Sciences Po.

Duru-Bellat, M. 2002. *Les inégalités scolaires*. Paris: Presses Universitaires de France.

Ecole des Mines, PariTech. 2007. *Classement international professionnel des établissements d'enseignement supérieur*. Paris: Mines Paris, Paristech. http://www.ensmp.fr/Actualites/PR/defclassementEMP.pdf, accessed November 26, 2007.

Ferrand, M. 2004. La mixité à dominance masculine: l'exemple des filières scientifiques de l'École normale supérieure d'Ulm-Sèvres. In Rogers, R. (ed.), *La mixité dans l'éducation. Enjeux passés et présents*. Lyon: ENS Éditions, pp. 181–193.

Goux, D. and Maurin, E. 1997. Démocratisation de l'école et persistance des inégalités. *Economie et Statistique*, 306, pp. 27–39.

Harfi, M. 2002. *La France dans l'économie du savoir: pour une dynamique collective*. Paris: Commissariat général du Plan.

Harfi, M. 2004. *Les Universités en mutation: la politique publique de contractualisation (1984–2002)*. Paris: Conseil national de l'évaluation-Commissariat général du Plan.

Harfi, M. & Mathieu, C. 2005. *Étudiants et chercheurs à l'horizon 2020: enjeux de la mobilité internationale et de l'attractivité*. Paris: Commissariat général du Plan.

Harfi, M. & Mathieu, C. 2006. *Classement de Shanghai et image internationale des universités: quels enjeux pour la France? Horizons Stratégique*. Centre d'analyse stratégique, n°2.

Hénart, L. 2007. *Rapport sur la sur la mise en application de la loi n° 2006-396 du 31 mars 2006 pour l'égalité des chances*. Rapport parlementaire n° 3615. Paris: Commission des affaires culturelles, familiales et sociales.

Kieffer, A. & Duru-Bellat, M. 2000. La démocratisation de l'enseignement supérieur en France: polémiques autour d'une question d'actualité. *Population*, 1, pp. 51–79.

Lahire, B. 1997. Les manières d'étudier. *Cahier d'observation de la vie étudiante*, 2. Paris : La Documentation Français.

Lazuech, G. 1999. *L'exception française. Le modèle des grandes écoles à l'épreuve de la mondialisation*. Rennes: Presses Universitaires de Rennes.

Merle, P. 2000. Le concept de démocratisation de l'institution scolaire: une typologie et sa mise à l'épreuve. *Population*, 1, pp. 15–50.

Merle, P. 2002. *La démocratisation de l'enseignement*. Paris: La Découverte.

MEN. 2007a. *The State of School*. Paris: Ministère de l'Education Nationale.

MEN. 2007b. *Les étudiants en classes préparatoires aux grandes écoles. Année 2006–2007*. N° 07–37. Paris: Ministère de l'Education Nationale Direction de la Prospective et de la Performance.

MEN. 2007c. *Repères et références statistiques sur les enseignements, la formation et la recherche*. Paris: Ministère de l'Education Nationale.

Musselin, C. & Friedberg, E. 1993. *L'Etat face aux universités en France et en Allemagne*. Paris: Anthropos.

Musselin, C. 2001. *The long march of French universities*. New York: Routledge.

OECD. 2006. *Higher Education: Quality, Equity and Efficiency*. Meeting of OECD Education ministers. Background report. Paris: OECD.

Sautory, O. 2007. La démocratisation de l'enseignement supérieur: évolution comparée des caractéristiques sociodémographiques des bacheliers et des étudiants. *Éducation & formations*, 74, avril, pp. 49–64.

de Silguy, Y-T. 2003. *Moderniser l'Etat: le cas de l'ENA*. Ministère de la fonction publique, de la réforme de l'Etat et de l'aménagement du territoire. Paris: La Documentation française.

Suleiman, E. 1978. *Elites in French Society: the politics of survival*. Princeton: Princeton University Press.

Vasconcellos, M. 2006. *L'enseignement supérieur en France*. Paris: La découverte.

Verger, J. 1986. *Histoire des universités en France*. Toulouse: Privat.

14
The Elite Public Universities in Australia

Simon Marginson

Introduction

Since the colonial foundations of Australian higher education in the nineteenth century, beginning with the Universities of Sydney in 1853 and Melbourne in 1854, membership of the elite grouping of institutions has been constant through all of the vicissitudes of mission, modernization, policy, funding and system structure. When new institutions emerged during the publicly financed system building between the 1950s and the 1970s, the first universities in the main capital cities maintained a dominant position; and they continued to do so during the abolition of the binary system in 1987, the turn to the New Public Management (NPM) mode of governance in the 1980s and 1990s, the attenuation of public funding; the growing importance of global trade in student places, and the emergence of world university rankings. The elite grouping has formally established itself at the national level as the 'Group of Eight' (Go8).

On most indicators of resources and performance, especially research-related areas, there is a significant gap between the Go8 and its competitors. Increasingly, however, universities are not just locally and nationally referenced but globally referenced; and the Australian institutions, which in a commercial way have become highly internationalized, will be shaped by global developments. However, here the position of the Australian Go8 is more ambiguous. Part I of the chapter investigates the historical roots of the Go8 universities in Australia. Part II situates the hierarchy and the present mechanisms of its reproduction in more detail. Part III brings the full global setting into the picture and considers the future.

Evolution of the Group of Eight

The elite layer of higher education institutions in Australia is often called the 'sandstones'[1] though that tag strictly applies only to the six pre-World War I universities created in each of the British colonies, which have sandstone in their core buildings. Five of the six founding universities achieved principal status: the Universities of Sydney, Melbourne, Queensland, Adelaide and Western Australia. Architecturally the University of Tasmania was also a sandstone but the economy and demography of the state were too small for its university to achieve front rank. After a long period of colonial cringe and under-funding, when many leading families sent their children to be educated in Britain, the Murray Report (1957) laid the basis for federal government policy and in the 1960s the Australian Universities Commission created a modernized system of higher education and facilitated mass participation. Between 1960–1961 and 1975 public spending on education in Australia multiplied by almost five times, with the most rapid increase in higher education. The five 'sandstones' were transformed, acquiring research and doctoral programs across all fields of study, and new institutions were opened (Marginson, 1997; Martin, 1964).

The other three universities that achieved elite status all emerged in the first fifteen years after World War II. The Australian National University (ANU) began in Canberra in 1946 originally as an institution solely devoted to research and graduate studies. The second university in Sydney, the University of New South Wales (UNSW) began as the NSW University of Technology in 1949 and acquired its present title in 1958. The Act to found the second university in Melbourne, Monash University, also passed in 1958 (Department of Employment, Education and Training – DEET, 1993). The ANU continued to receive additional research funding after undergraduate programs began and became the leading center for basic research. Strong in both physical and life sciences, it also developed special expertise on the Asia-Pacific region, reflecting Australia's geography, housing more experts on China and on Indonesia than any university in North America. Science, engineering and medicine at UNSW and Monash became as strong as at the sandstones. They also led the nation in legal education, and like ANU they emphasized research on East and Southeast Asia. The three institutions played the key role in Australian foreign aid training of regional leaders under the Colombo Plan. At all three there was a sense of excitement and innovation, and a less British and more nationalist feel (Marginson, 2000). They supported Australian arts. In the life sciences there was a pronounced interest in the Australian biosphere. UNSW moved early to link research to industry and later became an administrative model for the whole sector.

Another eight universities were founded between 1964 and 1975. All did exciting things, using innovative, sometimes experimental organizational designs. For a time, in many disciplines, one or another of these institutions was the place to be. But in the end none were strongly funded in basic research for long enough so as to rival the older foundations. Still less did any of this group secure enough support from leading families in their city to outdo the leading eight in social status, which would have required them to sustain not just research strength but leadership in professional training in law and medicine for a generation or more. Only two of the post 1961 group had a medical faculty prior to 2000.

In effect, therefore, after Monash opened its doors in 1961 the first eight institutions achieved closure. In the late 1960s and early 1970s at Melbourne, and from the 1980s at Sydney, many felt the second university in each city was moving ahead of the first. Such judgements turned out to be nearer the mark with respect to Sydney than to Melbourne. The University of Melbourne reformed its administration and strengthened its medical faculty, staving off the Monash challenge.

In 1976 the annual growth of public funding of higher education was suddenly halted. No more federally funded universities were created until the University of the Sunshine Coast in Queensland two decades later. When the expansion of funding stopped, with it was ended the prospect of a change in the hierarchy driven directly by state investment. As it turned out, the turn to quasi-market competition as the principle of system organization, instead of opening the system to upward mobility on the basis of intellectual merit and executive acumen, reinforced the closure. Amid the heightened material scarcity associated with the NPM, there was less potential for academic innovations at a scale sufficient to provide the basis for upward institutional mobility. Universities gained strategic freedoms but competition tended to recycle the pre-existing disparities in resources and status.

The Dawkins Reforms and After

In 1985, following the creation of a fee-paying international education market in the UK, international education in Australia was reframed along similar lines. Between 1987 and 1992 under the federal Labor Minister for Education, John Dawkins, the structure and financing of the national system were transformed (Dawkins, 1988; Marginson and Considine, 2000). Student charges were introduced, mergers and university entrepreneurship were encouraged and the old binary distinction between research-intensive universities and colleges of advanced education was abolished. The Dawkins reforms triggered a marked shift in funding. In 1986, 85 percent of the total revenues of higher education institutions were from government sources. In 1996 that proportion was at 58 percent and by 2006 it had fallen to 44 percent (Department of Education, Employment and Workplace Relations – DEEWR, 2007a).

Many saw the absorption of the colleges of advanced education into a unitary university sector as an opportunity to secure a more egalitarian order. However Dawkins simultaneously introduced mixed public and private funding, and lowered the funding rate for all universities whether old, merged or new. Though the elite universities now faced downward pressure on their basic research capacity they continued to draw on the research infrastructure previously established and could transfer resources from teaching into research and doctoral education. Class sizes increased and purse strings tightened but they maintained the research-intensive mission and with difficulty sustained resilient academic cultures (Marginson and Considine, 2000). In a regime with a common funding formula; fee-based markets where status was a key determining variable; and a partial shift from research support via basic grants to competitive bidding, and hence to research funding directly determined by capacity and track record; the prior market leaders held most of the cards.

The universities founded between 1964 and 1975 lost out particularly badly. They had always been overwhelmingly dependent on public funding and had lesser prospects of private earnings; and their research intensity was only partly established. The bold innovations of the 1960s and early 1970s looked less exciting and more risky as time went on and they tended to revert back to conventional practices. Later in the 2000s when most of this new group formed an organization they chose the title 'Innovative Research Universities' (IRU) but their faculties were no longer organized on the basis of interdisciplinary themes and social problems, and their governance no longer ran through participatory assemblies.

The five leading universities of technology in each mainland state always had solid public standing and gained traction from the designation 'university' and the right to bid for research grants and offer doctoral programs. Curtin and RMIT Universities, and the University of South Australia became major players in the international degree market. Organized as the Australian Technology Network (ATN) the group came to sustain a clear national profile. But despite a crafted research evolution in targeted areas, especially at Curtin and the Universities of Technology in Sydney and Queensland, none had the basic research capacity or the medical faculties to underpin a serious challenge for elite status.

A measure of the dominance of the top eight universities is that they have all sustained elite status regardless of organization or strategy; though these factors have affected the pecking order within the group. Queensland and Melbourne overhauled administration and used financial drivers and propagation of a performance culture to secure a more effective relationship between the executive centres and disciplines. UNSW achieved a similar outcome in more top-down fashion. Western Australia followed more quietly, while ANU benefited from having lively academic communities open to global influences. In the outcome Melbourne achieved the leading status position, Queensland's stocks rose even more markedly and Western Australia gathered strength as well. In the last decade Queensland has been particularly effective in building life science research and attracting enhancing support from Atlantic philanthropies, industry and state government. The University of Melbourne (2007) has now restructured its degree programs to establish US-style liberal first degrees underneath postgraduate professional training, a bold departure from the British practice that shaped the Australian system. It is designed to position the university more favorably vis-à-vis the worldwide sector, providing more portable degrees of higher quality.

In contrast Adelaide, and to a lesser extent Sydney, struggled to modernize. Despite this, Sydney, the peak institution in the largest, wealthiest and most globally connected Australian city, remains a top four university under all measures, and one relatively strong in basic research. Within its own smaller city the position of Adelaide has always been unchallengable, commanding nearly all of the first preferences of high achieving students and second to Western Australia in research income per full-time academic.

The trajectory of Monash has been more ambiguous. A pioneer in the 1990s and a sector leader in internationalization, it nevertheless found itself at the bottom of the Go8. Monash moved hard to exploit the Dawkins policy settings. It grew to more than three times in size, including 15,000 international students; acquired seven campuses beyond its core at Clayton, including sites at Malaysia and South Africa; and built the corporate and commercial side of activity. It combined research intensity at Clayton, and elite social status in law and medicine, with non-elite missions like an Australian ATN university. Monash leant further than the other Go8 institutions towards the mass and commercial side of higher education, and partly away from the autonomous academic pole of the field.

Even so Monash did not lose its footing in the elite group. Though research was not its main developmental priority, after 1987 the University remained fourth or fifth in Australia in terms of aggregate research output. Even the high growth path had something in common with others in the Go8. Melbourne, Sydney, UNSW, Queensland all combine the research mission with a student body akin in size to the land-grant sector in the United States, plus a large international student enrollment more like that of a mid-ranking British institution; and Monash was respected within the group for its commercial acumen. As the level of subsidy applied to public places declined, its burgeoning number of domestic students became a handicap, creating pressures for quantity/quality tradeoffs. Nevertheless on most indicators Monash remains well ahead of the first competitor outside the Go8, Macquarie.

The Dawkins template was uni-dimensional. The blueprint for all institutions was a public university with a comprehensive mission in teaching and research, providing degrees at all levels and across most fields of study, and active in both professional programs and general degrees in the arts/humanities, business and science and/or technological disciplines. Nearly all had over 10,000 students, many more than 20,000, and all enrolled what was by world standards a large number of fee-paying international students. Not only was there no other kind of elite institution, such as the liberal arts colleges in the USA, there were no specialized institutions of the kind other nations maintained in medicine, engineering, business studies, media or the arts. Under the hegemony of a singular comprehensive mission with all institutions competing on the same ground, the stratification of a national system becomes transparent and a league table view seems like common sense. Newer universities tend to produce themselves as inferior copies of the elite institutions, and are seen as such. Thus the Go8 have found it straightforward to maintain their inherited position.

Under the federal Labor government in power until 1996, the explicit identification of segments was discouraged. Under the coalition Liberal–National Party government of 1996–2007, 'diversity' was more openly proclaimed as a positive value. However, the definition of 'diversity' was never made fully explicit. Despite some rhetorical emphasis on the value of diversity of mission little was done to achieve it. The common funding rate and uniform regulatory formulae were maintained. Government policy statements also emphasized diversity in the sense of a market hierarchy, with variable prices and values, but its one attempt to introduce variable tuition costs for subsidized domestic student places was stymied when the whole of the cash-strapped sector adopted the highest level of charge (much the same thing happened in the United Kingdom). However, in this climate it became more acceptable for the elite universities to organize openly and the self-defined Group of Eight was formed (Go8, 2007). The Go8 established its own secretariat for lobbying purposes. Later ATN and IRU secretariats emerged. These processes were encouraged by the Liberal Party federal minister Brendan Nelson (2002–2006), who no doubt preferred to deal with fewer competing agencies. The Go8 remained members of the umbrella organization of all universities, Universities Australia, formerly the Australian Vice-Chancellors' Committee, but that body became internally fractured.

The one way that horizontal diversity was introduced was through privatization. From 2005 onwards approved private institutions have been eligible for subsidized student loans for tuition. Growing rapidly from a small base the private sector commands about 10 percent of enrollments. Notre Dame University in Perth recently received funding to open a medical school in Sydney. However it will be another generation before any private institution is in a position to compete strongly for high-scoring school leavers and global standing against the institutions in the Go8, and research parity might take even longer. In 2006 there were 984,156 students enrolled in accredited higher education institutions in Australia of whom 943,384 (95.6 percent) were in public higher education institutions. Just 24,238 (2.5 percent) were in the three private universities offering doctoral programs in a range of fields: the multi-site Australian Catholic University, Bond University in Queensland, and Notre Dame University in Western Australia (DEEWR, 2007a).

The Dynamics of Reproduction

What marks out the elite group and sustains its historical trajectory? Throughout the developed world mass higher education systems share similar dynamics, though the balance between elements may differ. In Australia one sign of the elite segment is the concentration of student demand, as indicated by the presence of high-scoring school leavers and a surplus of applications over places. Four Go8 institutions are overwhelming leaders in their states in securing school leaver preferences: Western Australia, Adelaide, Queensland and Melbourne. Sydney and New South Wales are relatively equal, but with Sydney ahead. Both face competition from Macquarie and the University of Technology, Sydney only in certain program areas. ANU is less focused on first degree supply, and being isolated from the large population centres is less of an undergraduate demand magnet. Monash falls behind Melbourne in Victoria.

But student demand is only one of a number of factors. Elite reproduction is maintained also by the status of the leading universities in the eyes of the professions, government and international higher education; and by the concentration of research capacity and outputs. In addition, though price differentiation plays a negligible role in the sector, except in international student places and executive MBA programs, the leading universities carry stronger assets and human capital and have a superior capacity to generate private and public revenues in competitive settings.

These elements will now be examined. They tend to feed into each other. Universities with strong student demand and esteem in industry tend to have a better resource profile. The accumulation of economic capital feeds into both entrepreneurial initiative and research capacity, in turn generating more status and wealth. However, if there is one single element that is the royal road to status in Australian higher education, it is research. Research is not the only factor in the reproduction of elite institutions – it plays a negligible part in prestigious law and business programs – but it is the largest single factor. Long-term research outcomes are crucial to securing high-scoring undergraduates, and top doctoral students and academic staff; and in reproducing the domestic esteem in which institutions are held. Research is even more decisive on the global plane. While the domestic histories of universities cut little ice outside the nation unless the university is Harvard or Oxford, research performance is readily measured by a common scale.

The Incentive Structure

Nevertheless, while elite reproduction is a broadly similar process everywhere and research is the principal common element, elite reproduction is also articulated through the particular conditions of each national system. Here Australia is best understood as a nation where the NPM reforms of the 1980s and 1990s were thoroughgoing, and successfully created a stable quasi-marketized system, one with distinctive strengths and weaknesses. Once almost entirely government funded, in 2004 Australian higher education had the equal third highest dependence on non-government funding among the Organization for Economic Cooperation and Development (OECD) nations.

That year Australia allocated 0.8 percent of GDP in *private* funding of tertiary education. The OECD average was 0.4 percent. Other high private investors were the United States (1.9 percent), Korea (1.8 percent) and Japan (0.8 percent) but all three had a long history of high private funding.

In 2004 Australia allocated 0.8 percent of its GDP to *public* funding of tertiary education, below the OECD average of 1.0 percent and equal twenty-fifth of the 28 OECD nations providing data. The US rate of public investment was 1.0 percent. Between 1995 and 2004 Australia was the only nation to reduce total public funding of tertiary education, the key to basic research capacity, by 4 percent in real terms. The average OECD country increased public funding by 49 percent in real terms. Australian student numbers rose by 31 percent meaning that public funding per student dropped a sizable 28 percent (OECD, 2007). For university vice-chancellors the main game in town for the last two decades, much more pressing than building a stellar research performance, has been to plug that funding gap.

As noted, the decline in public funding per student in the elite universities began with the Dawkins restructuring. It was institutionalized on an annual basis by the abolition of full indexation of grants in 1995 which meant public funding covered an ever-decreasing share of total costs. There were additional reductions in the real rate of funding in 1997–2000. A 2005 increase in the funding rate for subsidized places, and extra monies allocated on a continuing basis in 2007, restored the 1997–2000 cuts but did not compensate for the Dawkins changes or the accumulated effects of de-indexation, which continued. A one-off increase in research support was announced in 2001 and phased in over the next five years; but the largesse was confined to research project funding and there was no repeat of the exercise. One means of coping, as in other nations, was to allow the material conditions underlying teaching to deteriorate. The average student-staff ratio rose from 12 to 1 in 1985, to 21 to 1 in 2005. Casual labor was used for a growing portion of teaching. Even with these expedients the total funding of subsidized places (the public subsidy plus the student contribution under the Higher Education Contribution Scheme, HECS) fell below real costs. This meant domestic students had to be part subsidized from market incomes.

Given that the number of subsidized domestic students, and their tuition costs, were capped throughout the period, universities had five sources of discretionary income: research funding, donations, the sale of services, full-fee domestic student places and full-fee international student places. All pursued research funding but for the most part this was a zero sum game. Individual institutions at best could achieve moderate increases this way; and research performance was inhibited by the material constraints. Donations, sale of services and domestic fee-charging were all pursued with vigor by most institutions but by themselves proved insufficient to sustain core operations. By the mid 1990s it was apparent that only international education could fill the funding gap. In this manner the Australian higher education system as a whole, including six of the eight Go8 universities, was driven to attract large numbers of international students (Marginson, 2007a).

From the point of view of government this structure of incentives has had the double policy virtue of generating export dollars for Australia and reducing the fiscal load on the higher education budget. For the institutions, fee-based education has been a main driver of university strategies; a principal theatre of competition within the domestic system and on a world scale, and a factor that has further opened the institutions to global influences. It has also affected elite reproduction, both through the kinds of infrastructure and activities it creates, and its negative effects on other possibilities and potentials such as research.

Only two of the Go8 have avoided full-scale mass education in the international student market. In that respect most of the elite institutions in Australia have been on a different trajectory to the peaks of higher education in the USA and the UK. The cases, exceptional in Australia but more normal in the developed world, are: the ANU, protected by its advanced research funding and mission; and the University of Western Australia (UWA) which from early in its history benefitted from a large private endowment and enjoys a level of private income larger than the Australian norm. UWA has deliberately remained smaller than other capital city universities. Despite the geographical isolation of Perth the university is a strong performer in the Australian context.

In all institutions the level of dependence on federal funds for teaching and student HECS payments has fallen, but more so in the Go8 than most other universities. In 2006 all Australian universities together received 42.2 percent of income from the federal government and 2.0 percent from state governments, with 38.7 percent in student charges for tuition. Of the last input, the main components were 11.7 percent in deferred student charges under the HECS and 14.9 percent from international student fees, totalling $2.4 billion (DEEWR, 2007a). The system-wide proportion of funding from HECS-based places in 2006 was 37.8 percent. However in the Go8 institutions, that proportion was significantly less, ranging from 31.6 percent at the University of Queensland down to 23.6 percent at Melbourne.

The Go8 exhibit higher than average earnings from research and, in most cases, from sources such as international students, domestic postgraduate students, domestic full-fee undergraduates, short non-award courses and services to industry and community, and consultancy. These revenues are determined by market power and entrepreneurial effort. For the most part the Go8 outperform other institutions. The ATNs can replicate or exceed the entrepreneurial effort of the Go8, but the Go8 institutions tend to employ higher quality support staff as well as better academic staff, and their brand is stronger. The Go8 also had much higher than average levels of income from bequests and from their own investments; and where they opt to do so they perform strongly in the Australian and international markets for full fee places. These areas will now be examined in turn.

Research Capacity and Resources

The Go8 universities secure a higher proportion of their income from research than do other Australian universities. The system average is 10.3 percent. Go8 dependence on research varies from 17.2 percent at Adelaide down to 14.4 percent at Sydney and Melbourne and 12.2 percent at Monash.[2] Seven of the newer pre-1987 universities also draw above average levels of income from this source, but they have much lower incomes from student fees, investments and donations than the Go8, boosting the proportional role of research. The ATNs draw 4.8 to 7.3 percent of income from research (DEEWR, 2007a).

Nowhere is the distinctive mission and position of the Go8 more apparent than in the data on research income and performance, as Table 14.1 shows. One indicator is the allocation of Research Infrastructure Block Grants (RIGB), which reflect performance in national competition for research project monies allocated by peer review. The Go8 scooped 73.5 percent of all RIGB monies on offer in 2005.[3] The highest performer outside the Go8 was the University of Tasmania, the other 'sandstone', with 2.7 percent. The ATN group commanded just 4.7 percent RIGB monies between them (DEEWR, 2007b).

The Go8 also received 63.9 percent of research performance-based allocations under the Institutional Grants Scheme in 2005. The most telling indicator of the concentration of capacity in leading-edge research is the distribution of Australian Research Council Discovery Grants. This scheme is

Table 14.1 Non-Current Assets and Income from Investments and Donations, 2006

Institution	Non-current Assets, 2006	Income from Investments, 2006	Donations and Bequests, 2006
	$s Million	$s Million	$s Million
Melbourne	3,613	104.3	22.6
Sydney	3,590	116.1	26.5
ANU	2,273	105.6	8.4
Monash	1,867	35.0	18.1
Queensland	1,784	23.5	24.1
UNSW	1,744	47.1	6.7
Western Australia	1,438	59.7	13.1
Adelaide	789	14.6	5.1
Total Go8 institutions	*17,098*	*505.9*	*124.6*
Other 31 institutions	*16,532*	*192.7*	*34.7*

Source: DEEWR, 2007a

highly competitive with a success rate of 20 percent. In 2007 the Go8 secured 597 of the new Discovery Grants for projects commencing in 2008, 68.3 percent. The other eleven pre-1987 universities secured 20.3 percent of grants; the five ATN universities 7.3 percent; and the other 15 institutions, 4.0 percent (ARC, 2007).

All Australian universities enroll doctoral students but PhD programs play a larger part in the Go8. Each have over 1,500 PhD students and they enroll half the national total between them. At all Go8s except Monash, PhD students exceed 6 percent of total student numbers, which may seem low to some but is research intensive in the Australian context, with the highest levels 14.1 percent at ANU and 9.3 percent at Western Australia (DEEWR, 2007a).[4]

A further indicator of the distribution of research capacity is university-determined research-only academic posts. This is not a precise indicator because staffing policies vary, but the number of research-only posts is growing rapidly, probably because of external pressures to concentrate and lift research output. Between 1996 and 2006 total research-only staff increased by 50.4 percent while staff in teaching-research posts increased by just 7.3 percent. In 2006 there were 12,944 research-only academic staff with 8755 (67.6 percent) in Go8 institutions. The largest concentrations were Queensland 1,424; ANU 1,414; Melbourne 1,414; Monash 1,324; UNSW 1,138; and Sydney 1,074 (DEEWR, 2007a).

Non-Market Private Incomes

Income from investments and donations provides resources that on the whole are subject to a higher measure of discretion than government-source funds, industry funding or student fees. Table 14.2 indicates that in 2006 the Go8 institutions between them took the lion's share of income from investments, and from donations and bequests – more than two and a half times as much as all other 31 higher education institutions combined.

As these data suggest, and Table 14.2 demonstrates, the Go8 enjoy stronger asset bases than the other institutions. The asset data include the notional value of land and buildings, commercial property, and financial holdings such as shares and continuing bequests. All of the Go8 institutions except Monash are located on prime inner-city land, and Monash has a large suburban acreage. The differences between Go8 asset bases partly reflect differing capital city property values, and are also affected by financial assets and non-university property. However, it should be noted that public universities in Australia have a limited power to leverage the value of their land to secure borrowings and often require Acts of Parliament to sell it.

Table 14.2 Research Standing, Incomes and Outputs, Selected Indicators

Institution	Share of Monies Distributed for Research Infrastructure Block Grants,[a] 2005	Institutional Grants Scheme Allocations[b] from Federal Government, 2005	New Australian Research Council Discovery Grants, 2008	Institutional Ranking in Shanghai Jiao Tong Ranking, 2007	Number of Discipline Groups in Shanghai Jiao Tong Top 100, 2007
	%	$s million			
Melbourne	13.7	32.8	112	79	4
Sydney	11.6	30.0	98	102–150	1
Queensland	9.4	29.1	71	102–150	3
UNSW	8.9	23.8	87	151–202	1
ANU	7.9	16.7	78	57	3[c]
Western Australia	7.6	16.2	35	102–150	2[d]
Adelaide	7.5	16.3	41	151–202	0
Monash	6.9	20.9	75	203–304	0
Total Go8 institutions	73.5	185.8	597	8 in top 304	14
Other 31 institutions	26.5	104.8	277	9 in top 508	1[e]

Sources: DEEWR, 2007b; ARC 2007.

Notes
a   Research Infrastructure Block Grants are allocated according to the institution's share of national academically competitive research funding.
b   Institutional Grants Scheme monies are top up federal grants based on research performance as measured by total income for research (60%), government-funded academically selected research student load (30%) and publications output (10%).
c   Includes Science 38, Life Science 44.
d   Includes Life Science 37.
e   U Newcastle Engineering.

Full-fee Entrepreneurship

In 2006, 152,746 domestic students in Australia were enrolled in full-fee-paying places, mostly at postgraduate level. Though several universities inside and outside the Go8 are strong in the postgraduate market, Monash and Sydney are the leaders (DEEWR, 2007a). Both postgraduate and undergraduate full-fee places are financed by tuition loans subject to income contingent repayment arrangements, lightening the burden.

Most domestic undergraduate students opt for HECS-based subsidized places but some enroll on a full-fee basis in prestigious fields such as Law that they could not access on the basis of their academic scores. Full-fee domestic undergraduate places tend to concentrate in the Go8 institutions, reflecting in part the positional advantage of those degrees, in part the entrepreneurial energy focused on the supply and marketing of places. In 2006 six Go8 institutions secured more than AU$5 million in revenues from undergraduate full fee places: Melbourne AU$19.3 million, Sydney AU$15.1 million, UNSW AU$10.0 million, Monash AU$9.5 million, Queensland AU$5.4 million and ANU AU$5.1 million. Western Australia chose not to be active and Adelaide was a minor player. The only other public universities generating more than AU$5 million income in this way were RMIT and Deakin Universities in Victoria.

In 2006 there were 733,352 domestic students and 250,714 (25.5 percent) full-fee-paying international students, almost three-quarters onshore in Australia. This was much the highest proportion of internationalized enrollments in the OECD. From 1996 to 2006 the number of international students increased from 53,188 to 250,794 (371.5 percent) while domestic students rose by 26.2 percent.[5] Almost two in five international students are in postgraduate programs, mostly at Masters level, with just 7,658 (3.1 percent of the total) enrolled in doctoral programs. In terms of academic disciplines, 55.8 percent of all commencing international students in 2006 were concentrated in the areas of Management and Commerce and Information Technology (DEEWR, 2007a). The Go8 universities exhibit a broader spread than average but the same concentration in business and technologies is apparent.

Australian universities have developed a distinctive business model of international education designed to maximize revenues, based on high-volume standard-cost medium-quality provision. The curriculum is not varied significantly for international students. The revenues from international education have been concentrated not so much on teaching and learning but on new assets such as buildings; the functions of marketing and recruitment and non-academic student support; and in some universities, although to a lesser extent, assistance with remedial academic English problems (Marginson and Eijkman, 2007). Using this business model Australia has become the fifth largest provider of cross-border places and enrolls more students from mainland China and Hong Kong combined than does the USA

(OECD, 2007). Education is Australia's fourth largest export, generating more than AU$11 billion each year in fees and other spending by students (ABS, 2008).

Table 14.3 shows that in each of five Go8 institutions the number of international students exceeded 6,000 in 2006. Only at Monash, with 17,087 international students, more than one third in transnational programs and distance education offshore, is the international student proportion above the national average. However six of the Go8 exhibit significant financial dependence on revenues from this source: Monash AU$190.7 million (18.1 percent of income in 2006), Melbourne AU$191.6 million (16.1 percent), UNSW (14.4 percent), Adelaide (12.4 percent) and Sydney (12.2 percent). Monash's profile in international education, like the ATNs RMIT, Curtin and the University of South Australia, is characterized both by high volumes and a significant transnational presence. The other Go8s mostly focus on onshore education where quality is more readily maintained. There are few offshore international students at Sydney, and even fewer at ANU, Queensland, UNSW and Melbourne.

At Melbourne and Monash the proportion of income obtained from international education exceeded that obtained from the federal government for teaching domestic students in 2006, as was the case also at RMIT, Curtin and Central Queensland University. Most Go8 universities are mass educators of international students but elite educators of domestic students. There is tension between these roles. When the international market tightened in the mid 2000s, some universities found the academic quality of their marginal international students was lower than that of their marginal domestic students.

Both international student numbers and financial dependence are significantly lower at the ANU and Western Australia, where the volume-building imperative is less demanding, than the other Go8 universities. ANU has a high number of international students relative to its size, although many of them are on scholarships. There is a strong international presence in the ANU doctoral program. Outside ANU Australia provides few scholarships to international students. In 2002 only 1.6 percent of international students received this kind of support, mostly via foreign aid to Southeast Asia and the Pacific (DEEWR, 2007a). Individual universities leverage their international revenues to sustain a handful of scholarships but they have more pressing needs for those revenues.

As a result the large-scale Australian international program is one-dimensional, largely focused on first degrees and vocational Masters programs to the exclusion of research. This contrasts markedly with the USA, where two-thirds of that nation's annual intake of foreign doctoral students is supported by scholarships, foreign research students play key roles as graduate research and teaching assistants, and about half the international doctoral

Table 14.3 International Education, 2006

Institution	International Students, 2006	Proportion of All Students	International Students in Off-shore Locations, 2006	Proportion of International Students	Income from International Students, 2006	Proportion of All Income
		%		%	$s million	%
Melbourne	10,376	23.9	99	0.9	191.6	16.1
Sydney	9,680	21.1	620	6.4	148.1	12.2
ANU	3,246	22.3	0	0	41.8	4.8
Monash	17,087	31.2	6,007	35.2	190.7	18.1
Queensland	6,607	17.6	0	0	107.7	11.5
UNSW	8,788	21.3	72	0.8	119.6	14.4
Western Australia	3,421	19.3	1,122	32.8	44.2	7.8
Adelaide	4,903	25.4	698	14.2	58.6	12.4
Total Go8 institutions	64,108	23.4	12,823	20.0	902.3	12.7
Five ATN institutions	58,877	31.7	27,384	46.5	483.7	20.6
Other 26 institutions	127,809	24.4	27,968	21.9	989.4	15.4

Source: DEEWR, 2007a.

graduates stay and swell the American knowledge economy. It also contrasts with the UK, which like Australia provides international education on a commercial basis but adds talent-attracting scholarships; and Singapore and China which are also moving to attract foreign research talent. All of these nations regard elite universities as key institutions in the competition for high skill and research labor. In order to ensure the business success of international education in the late 1980s, Australian policy markets largely eliminated the potential for subsidized places. Now, when a change of policy is overdue, they find it difficult to pluralize the objectives of the program. Australia remains highly successful in the fee-based global market business terms in but is locked into a narrow mission profile that leaves it partly decoupled from the global competition for top-end talent.

The Global Position

Globalization has changed the game in two respects (Marginson and van der Wende, 2007). First, distances have been reduced and geographical locality has become more decisive. The Australian sector is located on the edge of China, India and Southeast Asia and the student traffic into Australia brings its neighbours closer. Second, instant communications have abolished time barriers and while nations survive, the old insularity of outlook that characterized national education systems is disappearing, with the signal exception of the USA (Marginson and van der Wende, 2007). Higher education, especially in elite institutions, is increasingly subject to global referencing. Because this cuts across national hierarchies it has more potential than before to disrupt the cycle of elite reproduction. For example ANU was long rated below the Melbourne and Sydney universities in Australia. But its superior position in global research rankings has pushed it up; and in the first systematic Australian rankings it was equal top in 2006 and top in 2007 (Williams, 2007).

If the new potency of global factors means that the supremacy of the Go8 within Australia is no longer guaranteed, it must be said they have started the new race from the front of the grid. However, the global position of the Go8 is more problematic.

Australia's commercial presence onshore and offshore has helped to build university reputations and in turn has helped to deliver excellent rankings in the *Times Higher*, which in 2007 elevated all eight members of the Go8 into its world top 100. The Australian National University (ANU) was at 16, remarkably ahead of Stanford at 19 and Berkeley at 22. According to the *Times*, the ANU and Melbourne enjoy the same academic peer ranking as Harvard, Cambridge, Oxford and Yale (*Times Higher*, 2007). But *The Times* exercise is methodologically flawed, and in such a manner as to unduly favour Australian (and British) institutions. *The Times* peer review survey secures a response rate of 1 percent of the questionnaires sent to academic staff worldwide and the pool is heavily overweighted by returns from the nations where *The Times* has iconic status, notably the UK and Australia (Marginson, 2007b). The Australian universities also benefit from the inclusion of international student enrollments in the index.

The annual <u>Shanghai Jiao Tong University</u> Institute of Higher Education's measures of research performance are sounder, and research performance is more important than commercial presence in forming sustainable reputation in higher education. <u>Australia had 17 universities in the Jiao Tong top 500 in 2007, an excellent result for a nation of its size, but just two universities in the top 100: ANU (57) and Melbourne (79).</u> Three more are in the Jiao Tong top 150: Sydney, Queensland and Western Australia. Canada, the nation most similar to Australia in size, history, geography, polity and economy, has two universities in the first 36, Toronto and British Columbia (SJTIHE, 2007). In the Shanghai Jiao Tong discipline rankings the Australian universities have just three discipline groups in the top fifty, two at ANU; though Melbourne has four in the top 100 (Table 14.2).

Tellingly, Canada has sustained public funding but avoided the advanced forms of state intrusion and commercialization, which have taken root in Australia. The Canadian case also points to the key role played by the public funding of research in sustaining elite status in developed nations, as also do the cases of Switzerland, Sweden and the Netherlands. Even in the USA where private exceeds public funding by three to two, federal research grants play a central role in supporting (and stratifying) the sector. In Australia the national effects of the NPM mode of governance contrasts with its global effects. The shift from public funding to mixed funding, in the context of hyper-scarcity, probably strengthened the competitive position of the Go8 universities within Australia, but weakened their competitive position at the world level because of the negative effects on research capacity, and the narrowing of cross-border mission.

Because of its special research funding, ANU has partly avoided the general malaise affecting Go8 global research performance. This suggests the way forward for some or all of the rest of the Go8 is the introduction of special research grants on the ANU model. After a long history of system management via uniform formulae, it is difficult for policy makers to single out some Australian universities for enhanced research development. The key obstacle is not a deep national commitment to equality of resources and status – as noted, the Go8 have always held the dominant position in the Australian system – it is the difficulty of making decisions on the basis of expert judgment rather than the apparent equities of uniform mission and process. Nevertheless, working in a national tradition more genuinely egalitarian than the Australian one, policy makers in Germany *have* managed to single out certain universities for augmented research funding. It can be done.

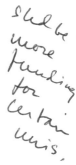

National Positioning Strategy

There are fundamental issues of national positioning at stake here, larger than fiscal policy or export revenues. Arguably, the fact that Australian international education competes on a business model *qua* business, rather than a distinctive approach to teaching and learning, has its roots in Australia's origins as a nation recently created by European settlers. It suggests both the settler-state's gift for improvization and the derivative character of its culture and identity. To simplify, the Australian claim for its international education in Asia is 'we do British and American business education. We do it as well. We are closer, friendlier, and cheaper'. This is not an adequate basis for a sustainable competitive advantage. Most educators and opinion makers outside Australia see education and knowledge as more than a business. In particular, they expect elite universities to stand for a larger, more enabling set of values.

Arguably the optimum long-term positioning strategy for the Go8 is to maintain strong networks in the main global knowledge centers, while integrating closely with the nations in East and Southeast Asia, and perhaps South Asia, that provide many of the students and skilled migrants coming to Australia. This integration should be anchored in a more innovative and culturally sensitive approach to teaching/learning, more Australian students taking a semester or two offshore, and a stronger Asian languages program. Correspondingly, Australian universities could focus more effort on building partnerships with the emerging science nations in Asia, Singapore, China, Taiwan China and Korea and on recruiting high-quality doctoral students and post-doctoral scholars from those nations. The strategic objective should be a central role in university research in the Asia-Pacific. There is much scope here for government to shape the course of development with targeted subsidies. The election of a new Labor government in November 2007 with a Prime Minister, Kevin Rudd, fluent in Putonghua (Mandarin) and committed to an 'education revolution', allows the issues to be reconsidered. There is no question there will be a continued elite sector in Australia. Most of the present Go8 are certain to maintain their national status. What is less clear is whether Australian universities will maintain or change, enhance or lose their global reputations and missions. Much will depend on whether Australian strategy is determined by British history or by Asian geography.

Notes

1. This label slipped into general usage after an article I published in 1997 where it was applied to the top five older universities. This contrasted with the 'redbrick' universities of the ANU, New South Wales and Monash, which are more modernist in design, in architecture, in organizational culture, and in a more post-colonial spirit. Very occasionally, we who research and write about the sector actually coin a term that enters the public language (some might say that it is the only time we produce a useful output!) This was my one time. Inevitably though, 'sandstone' slid out from under the architectural category and was expanded to admit the 'redbricks' with scarcely a stone building between them. I have had to debunk its use (Marginson, 1997; Marginson and Considine, 2000: 175–232).

2. The ANU draws a much higher proportion of total income from research than the others; internal university estimates range up to four-fifths of all income; but ANU data comparable with those obtained for all other institutions are unavailable.

3. Note the performance of ANU, Western Australia and Adelaide is stronger that the table implies, as they are smaller than the other five universities.

4. The only other institutions where PhD students, as a proportion of all students, exceeds 4 percent are Tasmania, Flinders, Wollongong and Macquarie (DEEWR, 2007a).

5. A series break in the DEEWR student data means the longitudinal comparison is imprecise.

References

Australian Bureau of Statistics, ABS. *International Trade in Goods and Services, Australia*, ABS Catalogue number 5368.0. Canberra: ABS, 2008. http://www.abs.gov.au/AUSSTATS/abs@.nsf/mf/5368.0. Accessed July 25, 2008.

Australian Research Council, ARC. *Discovery Projects Funding Outcomes*, 2007. http://www.arc.gov.au/ncgp/dp/dp_outcomes.htm. Accessed September 30, 2007.

Dawkins, J. *Higher Education: A policy statement*. Canberra: Australian Government Publishing Service, 1988.

Department of Education, Employment and Workplace Relations, DEEWR. *Selected Higher Education Statistics*, 2007a, various years. http://www.dest.gov.au/sectors/higher_education/publications_resources/statistics/publications_higher_education_statistics_collections.htm. Accessed December 31, 2007.

Department of Education, Employment and Workplace Relations, DEEWR. *Higher Education Report 2005*. Canberra: DEEWR, 2007b.

Department of Employment, Education and Training, DEET. *National Report on Australia's Higher Education Sector*. Canberra: Australian Government Publishing Service, 1993.

Group of Eight. Website, 2007. http://www.go8.edu.au/. Accessed December 18, 2007.

Marginson, S. *Educating Australia: Government, economy and citizen since 1960*. Cambridge: Cambridge University Press, 1997.

Marginson, S. *Monash: Reinventing the university*. Sydney: Allen and Unwin, 2000.

Marginson, S. 'Global position and position-taking: the case of Australia.' *Journal of Studies in International Education* 11 (1) (2007a): 5–32.

Marginson, S. 'Global university rankings.' In *Prospects of Higher Education: Globalization, market competition, public goods and the future of the university*, edited by S. Marginson. Rotterdam: Sense Publishers, 2007b.

Marginson, S., and Considine, M. *The Enterprise University: Power, governance and reinvention in Australia*. Cambridge: Cambridge University Press, 2000.

Marginson, S., and Eijkman, H. *International Education: Financial and organizational impacts in Australian universities*. Report prepared for the Monash Institute for the Study of Global Movements. Melbourne: Monash University, 2007. http://www.cshe.unimelb.edu.au/people/staff_pages/Marginson/Marginson.htm.

Marginson, S., and van der Wende, M. *Globalization and Higher Education*. Paris: OECD, 2007. http://www.cshe.unimelb.edu.au/people/staff_pages/Marginson/Marginson&van_der_Wende2006OECD.pdf.

Martin, L. *Tertiary education in Australia*, Volume 1, Report of the Committee on the Future of Tertiary Education in Australia. Melbourne: Australian Universities Commission, 1964.

Murray, K. *Report of the Committee on Australian Universities*. Canberra: Commonwealth Government Printer, 1957.

Organization for Economic Cooperation and Development, OECD. *Education at a Glance, 2007*. Paris: OECD, 2007.

Shanghai Jiao Tong University Institute of Higher Education, SJTUIHE. *Academic Ranking of World Universities*, 2007. http://ed.sjtu.edu.cn/ranking.htm. Accessed November 15, 2007.

Times Higher Education Supplement. *World University Rankings*. 9 November, 2007.

University of Melbourne. *The Melbourne Model*, 2007. http://www.futurestudents.unimelb.edu.au/courses/melbmodel/. Accessed September 30, 2007.

Williams, R. *Ranking Australian Universities: Controlling for scope*, 2007. http://melbourneinstitute.com/publications/reports/uniscope/mainpaper.pdf. Accessed December 18, 2007.

15
(Post-) Mass Higher Education and Japanese Elite Universities

Fumi Kitagawa

Introduction

The Japanese higher education system moved into what is generally called the 'mass' stage of development in the 1960s, a period characterized by rapid economic growth for the country and the development of a large private higher education sector. In his critical examination of Japanese higher education in relation to the 'capitalist developmental state', McVeigh (2005) argues that Japanese universities have strayed from their teaching and learning mission in the process of being driven by the demands of economic growth, becoming institutions geared primarily for producing official qualifications, certificates and credentials. Government spending on Japanese higher education is often said to be the lowest among advanced nations.[1]

Prevailing global perceptions hold that Japanese universities are inferior to their Western counterparts in terms of research, just as most advanced research in Japan is widely believed to occur not in universities, but in the research laboratories of leading private firms (Fransman, 1999). While Japan boasts a powerful manufacturing sector supported by a very vigorous national innovation system (Freeman, 1988), it has a low number of 'world-class universities' and few Nobel laureates when compared to other countries (Moodie, 2006). The role played by universities thus far in the Japanese national innovation system has been a matter for speculation. Japanese participation in international research collaborations is limited and the relative impoverishment of Japanese academic science has only recently begun to be addressed by the government (Nakayama and Low, 1997). However, in terms of research outputs such as the number of publications and citation, Japanese top universities have performed rather well in the Asia Pacific region.[2]

This chapter provides a historical perspective on the notion of 'elite universities' in Japan. Elite universities were established under specific historical and social contexts, preserved and transformed through time. Many of the current elite universities originate from the traditional 'imperial universities' of the late nineteenth century. There were seven former imperial universities which were historically treated as 'elite institutions' by the government. These seven, along with a small number of other distinguished national universities

257

and research-intensive prestigious private universities, constitute what are currently referred to as the 'top research universities'. Official recognition of certain institutions as elite 'imperial universities' ceased in 1949. Since then the Japanese government, at least officially, has treated universities equally, while they have sought to protect top research universities from the 'massification' of higher education (Yonezawa, 2007).

In recent years, the awarding of special status to a limited number of higher education institutions has become a widely recognized strategy in East Asia as well as in North America and Western Europe. Countries such as China and Korea, which are seeking entry into the exclusive club of top global universities, are doing so by establishing a small number of extremely well-funded research-intensive universities. South Korea has the 'Brain Korea 21 (BK21)' scheme to develop such research-intensive universities, while China has launched the 'Project 211 and 985'. These countries are said to be emulating California's long-established master plan. The Japanese government, following these trends, has also strengthened its 'world-class university' policies since the late 1990s (Yonezawa, 2003). In all these examples, the focus is on fostering research trends that will drive national economies in the future, that will keep the brightest students at home and attract the best from overseas, and on the development of prestigious institutions to rival the world's top universities such as Harvard and Stanford in the United States, Oxford and Cambridge in the United Kingdom, and the French *grandes écoles*.

It appears that the model for the American 'super research university' (Baker, 2007) has become attractive not only in the United States but also one increasingly admired by many research universities throughout the world. Considerable financial resources are now being allotted by governments in North America, Asia and in Europe, to create top research universities. Policymakers and institutional managers have identified factors similar to other national contexts, including faculty working conditions, competitiveness-based governmental support for research, a large private sector, and so forth. However, as Baker points out, what is frequently missing in this approach is the exceptional 'societal support' the United States has been able to generate for education, and particularly higher education. Such societal support for higher education has enabled the development of a symbiotic relationship between massification and super research universities in the United States (Baker, 2007). This is a point worth considering when analyzing present-day Japanese higher education.

Trow (1976, 2006)[3] illustrates the transformation of higher education systems in three stages: *elite, mass* and *universal*. Higher education in Japan today is facing financial as well as demographic constraints, which may be indicative of a *'post-massification'* stage.[4] University reforms since the beginning of the 1990s have to be seen as part of a wider transformation of Japanese social as well as education systems. Basic social trends affecting Japanese universities today include a declining birth rate coupled with greater rates of participation in higher education.[5] The population of 18-year-olds is expected to decrease even further, although the continued rise in the proportion of the population attending university would offset negative demographic trends affecting university programs in the short term. However, over the long term, the combination of almost universal middle-class university education with a declining population of prospective students means that an increasing number of institutions will fail to meet their admissions targets (Hada, 2005). The impact of demographic trends in Japan has an acute effect on the very large number of private institutions, especially the less prestigious ones, some of which have already closed their doors. Consequently, 'compete or perish' is the prevailing mood of the Japanese higher education sector today.

What is distinctive in the Japanese higher education system is the coexistence of three higher education systems (national, private and local public) within the sector with different marketization forces and varying degrees of state control at work. Furthermore, several for-profit universities have recently been approved by the government.[6] As of 2006, there were 568 private universities, 87 national universities and 89 public (municipal and prefectural) universities with degree awarding power (MEXT, 2006). National universities are established and primarily funded by the national government, but their legal status since April 2004 is that of 'National University Corporations' (NUCs), with greater autonomy than before. Public universities are established and primarily funded by local authorities at either the municipal or the prefectural level, with some of these institutions now changing their legal status to 'Public University Corporations'. Private universities are non-state educational institutions run by 'school corporations' (*gakko hojin*) (see the next section for details). The majority of government expenditure for higher education is distributed to national universities, whereas a relatively small amount of money is provided to private universities in spite of their larger number of students. According to Akabayashi and Naoi (2004), national universities offer far higher quality education, at least in terms of expenditure, than private universities.

It has been observed that Japanese higher education is going through 'the biggest higher education reforms in more than 100 years' (Goodman, 2005). Eades (2005) points out the changing division of labor between the three sectors of HEIs: up to 1998, the tripartite division between national, public and private universities was that 'national universities should meet the needs of the nation, public universities should meet the needs of the local communities that established them and private universities should be mainly responsive to the market'.[7] Arguably, such a division is becoming more complex through 'deliberate erosion' (Eades, 2005) of the difference between the three sectors as the pace of university reform accelerates.

This chapter presents a broad-brush picture of recent reform processes in Japanese higher education, and addresses the following principal questions: What is the role of the elite university in a changing social and demographic landscape, especially in the post-massification stage? In what ways is the relationship between teaching and research changing at Japanese elite universities? What is the cost of emulating 'world-class university' policies to create and maintain elite higher education in the post-massification stage? These questions need to be located in the specific structural and policy contexts in which the current Japanese higher education system is embedded.

This chapter is structured as follows. Following this introduction, the second section gives an overview of the historical background of 'elite institutions' in the Japanese higher education system. The third section describes recent higher education reform processes and policy instruments that aim to create research-intensive top universities. The fourth section of the chapter describes the manner in which the current top Japanese research universities' institutional missions, perceived challenges and future strategies, and relationships with the government are conditioned by the changing characteristics of the national research and mass higher education systems.[8] The concluding section sums up the discussion, critically examines tensions within the system and problems caused by recent policy reforms, and identifies possible new directions for the Japanese higher education system.

Historical Background of 'Elite Institutions' in Japan

Imperial Universities: Japan's Original Elite Universities

The Japanese higher education system was created by the Meiji government in the late nineteenth century. The University of Tokyo was established in 1877 as the first and only university in the country at that time. The university was founded by amalgamating older government schools for medicine and western learning. It was renamed the 'Imperial University' (*Teikoku daigaku*) in 1886, and then Tokyo Imperial University (*Tokyo teikoku daigaku*) in 1887 when the imperial university system was created. The Meiji government's Imperial University Ordinance of 1886 (*Teikoku daigaku rei*) describes the main priority of universities as 'the teaching of, and fundamental research into, arts and sciences necessary for the state'. The main aim was to meet the needs of the state and contribute to national strength (Okada, 2005). In 1898, the Education Minister stated that:

> Tokyo Imperial University is a place where people study basic principles and increase their knowledge in response to the needs of the state ... they are then supposed to apply what they have learned, diligently and sincerely, making the utility of science apparent.
>
> (Bartholomew, 1978: 253)

Nine imperial universities were founded by the Empire of Japan between 1877 and 1939; seven in Japan, one in Korea and one in Taiwan.[9] These universities were run by the imperial government until the end of World War II. Many of the imperial universities started as elite teaching institutions. This was done through hiring foreign university teachers from countries such as Britain, Germany, France and the United States to import Western academic knowledge. From the end of the nineteenth century to the early twentieth century, imperial universities developed their research and development capacity, which contributed to the rapid modernization of Japan throughout this period (Bartholomew, 1989; Kamatani, 2006).

The University of Tokyo has been an elite institute in Japanese society since its founding. The roots of the University can be traced back to a small government academy, created within the *Tokugawa Shogunate*, devoted to the study of foreign languages and the translation and analysis of imported writings on the West (Cutts, 1997). The *Tokugawa Shogunate* had settled on the modern university system as a means to enable Japan to meet new foreign challenges. The University of Tokyo acted as Japan's leading 'window for the importation of Western knowledge' and gradually developed as a center for research as well (Bartholomew, 1989). Throughout its history, the University has produced a large number of elite government officers, professionals as well as top researchers.

The second imperial university, later to become Kyoto University, was established in 1897. Following this, the government established five more imperial universities: Kyushu in 1911, Hokkaido in 1918, Tohoku in 1907, Osaka in 1931 and Nagoya in 1939. Apart from the imperial universities, several polytechnics in Tokyo with prestigious reputations became universities and colleges. These include the Tokyo Institute of Technology in 1929 and Hitotsubashi University in 1920; both eventually were granted national university status. The government concentrated higher education investment in the imperial universities and a select few prestigious national universities, which maintained an elevated status distinct from other universities and higher learning institutions. Along with strengthening the elite institutions, the government established a number of specialized medical colleges, teacher training colleges, and colleges of commerce across the country to train skilled professionals and build national human resource capital.[10]

Elite Private Universities

The history of private higher education is as long as that of the imperial university system. Many private universities were established by visionary individuals, with specific social missions and enterprising spirits. For example, Yukichi Fukuzawa established Keio Gijuku as a Dutch language school in 1858, with Keio calling itself *daigaku* (university) by 1890. Shigenobu Okuma established a private polytechnic in 1882, which later became Waseda *daigaku* (university) in 1902. In 1919 and 1920, the Japanese government officially recognized ten private universities.[11]

Amongst a number of prestigious private universities in Japan today, Keio and Waseda have assumed leading positions and are seen as research-intensive private universities. Long, prestigious histories and a large number of alumni wishing to remain as instructors at their own universities have enabled these institutions to develop active research faculties (Yonezawa, 2007). However, even these top private universities receive a relatively small share of public research grants. As of 2005, Keio, the highest-ranked among the private universities, ranked tenth among all the universities in terms of grant amounts, receiving only approximately 12 percent (2.5 billion yen) of the Scientific Grants in Aid awarded to the University of Tokyo (20 billion yen) (see Tables 15.1 and 15.2). Waseda, which ranks fifteenth overall, and second among the private universities, received 1.7 billion yen (Asahi Newspaper, 2007). Waseda and Keio have kept their leading elite status mainly through market competitiveness, attracting outstanding students, providing prominent human resources and leaders to the business world, and have managed to receive relatively large amounts of external funding (see Table 15.3).

Private universities in general have had to develop much more specific and focused institutional strategies and strategic management mechanisms than have national universities due to limited support from the government and fierce market competition. Research-oriented, prestigious private universities are facing fierce competition from newly 'corporatized' national universities, which are still supported heavily by the government. For example, following the corporatization of national universities in 2004, Waseda University has implemented a number of organizational reforms of their own, based on the perception that there will be even fiercer competition with new NUCs.[12] Similarly, Keio University recently announced a strategic merger with a specialized pharmaceutical university, Kyoritsu Yakka *Daigaku*.

Post-imperial Elite Universities

McVeigh (2005) categorizes the development of post-imperial Japanese higher education into the following periods: 1) democratization (1945–1955); 2) expansion (1956–1974); 3) quality improvement (1975–1982); and 4) the second expansion period (1983 to the present). The main structure of the current higher education system in Japan was established in 1949, with the upgrading of various types of higher and post secondary institutions into the university system.[13] This resulted in a very diversified and hierarchical system embracing different sets of institutions. The existence of a large private sector helped to absorb the pressures for the massification of the higher education system.

Under the American military occupation, the Japanese government established at least one comprehensive university in each of the 46 prefectures

(Okinawa became the forty-seventh prefecture in 1972) designated as a 'national university'. Local governments (prefectures and municipalities) also established local public universities, and these universities were expected to serve local communities' needs by providing specialized education in community care, medical studies, local public policy, arts and communication and so forth. Many local public universities focus on teaching as their resources are limited, although a few of these universities are strong in research.

In 1949, the former imperial universities lost their special official status, and all universities – national, local public and private – were henceforth to be treated as equal under the law. However, financial treatment by the national government remained differentiated between the former imperial universities and other national institutions. There have also been funding differences between national, public and private universities. As of the 2007 fiscal year, government subsidies to all NUCs amounted to 2.2 trillion yen while government subsidies to private universities (including four-year and two- to three-year institutions) (*shigaku zyoseikin*) amounted to 320 billion yen (Torii, 2007).[14]

Allegedly, the existing hierarchical structure in both the public and private sectors has resulted in a rather 'rigid domestic ranking' of higher education institutions, in terms of both undergraduate enrollment and research activities. The relatively stable government funding mechanism has protected this hierarchical structure. The government has concentrated resources in top elite institutions 'to the extent that these institutions have been kept from being adversely affected by the massification of higher education in the country' (Yonezawa, 2007: 487). Until recently in Japan, based on both support from government and the wider society, massification along with the preservation of national 'elite institutions' seem to have been mutually supportive and to have re-enforced one another (for further discussion on this point, see Trow, 2006).

Japanese University Reform and the Idea of Research Excellence

Geiger (2004) illustrates how profoundly the fundamental task of contemporary research universities to create, process and disseminating knowledge has been affected by market forces. In the Japanese context, recent higher education reforms by the government seem to reinforce such processes. A number of international studies have revealed how different micro-decisions and micro-incentives generate perceptible differences in institutional behaviour (Geuna and Martin, 2003). The degree of concentration of national science research funding and the pattern of the research funding allocation have also had major impacts, which will be examined in detail in this section.

Rising competition with other Asian nations and their universities has forced the Japanese government to place higher education high on the national policy agenda in order to maintain strategic competitiveness. Recently, the Japanese research system has been subject to widespread reform. This includes changes to the role of key ministries, changes to the decision making structures for science and technology as well as wide ranging reforms to the governance of Japan's national universities in 2004. Reform issues have centered on changing the legal governance structures of national universities into 'corporate' entities, to promote increased independence and entrepreneurialism, as well as to foster institutional diversification and efficiency. Based on the 1995 Science and Technology Basic Law, the development of a new research system throughout the 1990s seems to have led to the emergence of new systems of innovation in which universities play more significant roles as *economic resources*.

Japanese university reform since the beginning of the 1990s has reinforced the differentiation between institutions. New types of budgetary funds and project-based research funds established during the 1990s (Asonuma, 2002) served to strengthen competition among universities by creating a mechanism for differentiated financial allocation which is justifiable to both universities and society. Hicks (1993) argues that the system has been evolving in directions more favorable for university research excellence. During the 1990s, the government reorganized the top national universities to strengthen graduate schools at both the doctoral and master levels (*daigakuin jutenka*). In 2003, professional graduate programs (*senmonshoku daigakuin*)[15] were newly introduced by the Ministry of Education, Science, Culture and Sports (MEXT) to respond to changing skill needs in the so called knowledge-based society (Ushiogi, 1997). As a result, all former imperial universities and some other top universities separated faculties from departments (at the undergraduate level) and faculties were located in graduate schools. This is seen as a way to separate the research and teaching functions of research universities, and seven former imperial universities were given priority to go through with this reorganization.

In 2004 a 'radical' change (Yamamoto, 2004) was introduced to Japanese national universities through the National University Incorporation Law (2003), which granted them more autonomy from government (see Box 15.1; for details of the process, see Hatakenaka, 2005; Oba, 2005; Watson and Ohmori, 2005, and Yamamoto, 2004). This Law intends to promote more active and socially engaged institutions with greater organizational diversity and distinctiveness, and may also indirectly promote inter-university competition (Woolgar, 2007). Since 2004, the 89 newly established National University Corporations (NUCs) have received two types of grants from the national government: grants for operating costs, and subsidies for capital expenditures.[16] NUCs have full discretion to use the grant, while the flexibility of the capital subsidy is constrained. The government announced in 2006 that operating grants will be reduced by 1 percent each year for all NUCs.[17] Each

---

Box 15.1 Japanese Reform Processes and Legal–Institutional Frameworks Towards University Corporatisation

1995 Enactment of the Science and Technology Basic Law

1998 The University Council report, 'The Image of Universities in the 21st Century'

1999 Creation of the National Institute for Academic Degrees and University Evaluation (NIAD-UE)

2001 Introduction of reform plan for universities known as 'Toyama Plan'

2002 Center of Excellence scheme (COE 21)

2003 Enactment of The Incorporatisation Law

2004 Incorporatisation of national universities

2007 Global COE program

---

institution is expected to develop supplementary income sources which may or may not include increases in tuition fees, competitive research funding and income from industry. The government encourages universities to generate such external incomes.

In 2001, with the Toyama Plan,[18] MEXT announced in its basic policy target to select the top 30 universities in the country for special treatment, which evolved into the '21st Century Centers of Excellence' (COE21) program. The initial idea was to select the 'top 30' universities; however, it was widely felt that the seven former imperial universities would have an unfair advantage. During implementation, a more flexible system evolved in which individual departments and research units in any university could compete equally for research incentive funds, whether national, local public or private universities (Eades, 2005).

The selection for the scheme was based on performance and research potential,[19] with 274 COE units from 97 universities selected in the three consecutive fiscal years of 2002, 2003 and 2004 (JSPS, 2006).[20] The main activities supported under this program include an invitation to top overseas researchers to work in Japan, support for young researchers (doctoral and post-doctoral fellowships), collaboration with foreign research groups, symposia and workshops and for the provision of new equipment and space for research. The emphasis is on 'strategic research training' and 'competition', particularly at the graduate level in the sciences and engineering, and medical research, which played to the strengths of national universities.

The launch of the COE 21 project can be seen as a marked shift in Japanese higher education policy regarding the status of its elite institutions. The changing policy rationale to designate policies to strengthen elite universities can be summarized as follows: '... *invisible differentiation* is becoming more difficult, and justification through *visible evidence of performance* is becoming more influential' (Yonezawa, 2007: 491; emphasis added). However, one of the problems is that the Japanese competitive funding system does not have sufficient built-in management mechanisms.[21] There are a number of intrinsic cultural issues to be considered as the process of reforms and further penetration of 'audit culture' (Strathern, 2000) into Japanese higher education accelerates. For instance, it is observed that there is a distinctive difference between scientific fields and humanity fields in terms of the level of performance of research activities, different levels of internationalization and the different nature of evaluation systems (Eades, 2005).

Rankings among the top universities based on the number of selected COE research units merely reinforced the existing hierarchy of Japanese higher education institutions. Table 15.1 shows the top ten institutions in terms of the number of COE 21 projects. These comprise the former seven imperial universities, the Tokyo Institute of Technology and two research-intensive private universities (Keio and Waseda). It is interesting to see how closely the ranking based on the COE projects correlates with results based on ranking by research grants and external income. Table 15.2 shows the top ten Japanese universities based on the research grants (Scientific Grants in Aids as of 2005). The top ten consist of the seven former imperial universities, the Tokyo Institute of Technology, the University of Tsukuba,[22] and Keio University. The Universities of Tokyo and Kyoto receive 20 percent of the total grant, the former seven imperial universities receive 43 percent, and the top ten universities 49 percent of the total grant (Doi, 2007).

In Japan, just as in many other countries, policy makers and university administrators have eagerly embraced the discourse surrounding 'entrepreneurial universities' (e.g. Clark, 2001) and have sought to further promote university–industry links as a means to stimulate economic growth, and the 'service function of universities' (Cummings, 1998) has received growing attention. Following the 1995 Basic Law, the number and scope of recent university reforms have accelerated to encourage further development of university–industry links which had hitherto been legally and structurally constrained in Japan (Woolgar, 2007). Research commercialization and income from industry through knowledge transfer activities still remain peripheral to many academic communities in Japan, where 80 percent of R&D is performed in the industry sector. However, recently, there has been steady growth in income through the commercialization of research from universities and through collaboration with industry.

Table 15.3 shows the top ten Japanese universities with the highest research income from external sources (joint and commissioned research[23] with industry and other organizations). Again, these consist of the seven

Table 15.1 COE 21 University Ranking by Number of Projects and Grants Received (in million yen)

	Institution	Total # of Projects	2002	2003	2004	Grants Received in Total (million yen)
1.	University of Tokyo*	28	11	15	2	4,339
2.	University of Kyoto*	23	11	11	1	3,374
3.	University of Osaka*	15	7	7	1	2,470
4.	University of Nagoya*	14	7	6	1	1,786
5.	University of Tohoku*	13	5	7	1	1,955
6.	Tokyo Institute of Technology**	12	4	5	3	1,781
6.	University of Hokkaido*	12	4	6	2	1,755
6.	Keio University***	12	5	7	0	1,751
9.	Waseda University ***	9	5	4	0	1,037
10.	University of Kyushu*	8	4	4	0	1,266

Sources: Japan Society for the Promotion of Science (JSPS)http://www.mext.go.jp/a_menu/koutou/coe/05041401/003.htm access 03/10/07; Eades, 2005; Yonezawa, 2007).

Notes

*   Former Imperial University (NUC).

**   National University Corporation (NUC).

*** Private University.

Table 15.2 Top Ten Japanese Universities in Terms of the Amount of Scientific Grants in Aid Received in FY2005 (million yen)

1.	University of Tokyo*	20,112
2.	University of Kyoto*	13,115
3.	University of Tohoku*	9,479
4.	University of Osaka*	8,929
5.	University of Nagoya*	6,455
6.	University of Kyushu*	5,683
7.	University of Hokkaido*	5,614
8.	Tokyo Institute of Technology**	4,544
9.	University of Tsukuba**	3,020
10.	Keio University***	2,486

Source: Ministry of Education, Science, Culture and Sports (MEXT) http://www.mext.go.jp/b_menu/houdou/17/08/05083006/005.htm access 03/10/07.

Notes
*Former Imperial University (NUC).
**National University Corporation (NUC).
***Private University.

Table 15.3 Top Ten Japanese Universities with Highest Income from Joint and Commissioned Research with Industry and Other Organizations in FY2004 (in million yen)

1.	University of Tokyo*	21,151
2.	University of Kyoto *	9,868
3.	University of Osaka *	9,595
4.	University of Tohoku*	5,895
5.	Waseda University ***	5,270
6.	University of Kyushu*	4,952
7.	Keio University***	4,852
8.	Tokyo Institute of Technology**	4,076
9.	University of Hokkaido*	4,038
10.	University of Nagoya*	2,760

Source: MEXT, 2006 http://211.120.54.153/b_menu/houdou/17/06/05062201/001.htm access 03/10/07.

Notes
* Former Imperial University.
** National University Corporation (NUC).
*** Private University.

former imperial universities, the Tokyo Institute of Technology and two private universities, Keio and Waseda.

The Japanese government's efforts to foster world class research have been accelerated by the establishment of new support programs. In 2007, the Global COE program replaced the COE 21 program, with the number of selected Global COE research bases now much smaller than those of COE 21, while the amount of grant to each research base is expected to increase substantially. In terms of selection criterion, the potential sustainability of research beyond the program and the emphasis on educating and training young researchers (thus 'research bases' (*kenkyu kyoten*) rather than 'project units') were highly regarded.[24] Adding to this, in September of 2007, MEXT announced the 'World-Top-Level Research Center (WTL) Program' to support five research bases for the next 10 to 15 years, with approximately 500 million to 2 billion JPY per base annually (MEXT, 2007).[25] Four former imperial universities, namely, Tohoku, Tokyo, Kyoto and Osaka, and the National Institute for Materials Science (NIMS) were selected.

It is important to be aware of the detrimental effects of the current policy emphasis on research, increasing competition for research funding, and the strengthening of graduate schools as distinct from undergraduate education. In order to complement the policy emphasis on research and competition, MEXT has introduced a number of instruments to support education and societal roles of higher education institutions. According to a senior MEXT official:

> ...while declining operating grants draws much public attention, it is important to understand that many national universities are making use of Special Education and Research Grants such as COE 21 and the Good Practice in University Teaching (GP) Programs, and manage to secure sufficient resources for teaching and research. For national university corporations, it is important to utilize corporatization, be responsible for managing the organization, activate the university, and combine competitive and non-competitive grants to secure resources. It is important to enhance healthy competition and collaboration, with a division of labour among institutions and alliances between universities.[26]

At the institutional level, it should be remembered that specific mechanisms to implement the missions of each university effectively must change by taking into account various factors that surround the university. It is up to each institution how to formulate their own missions and implement innovative institutional strategies. In this respect it is interesting to note that some of the elite universities once led the discussions about educational innovation in the early 1990s. The University of Tokyo carried out fundamental curriculum reforms of its undergraduate liberal arts program in 1993. Keio University set up a new campus in 1990 whereby interdisciplinary approaches and problem-based learning was seen as the core of their educational activities. Today, in response to increasing market competition, there seems to be a widespread effort to develop innovative educational programs. A group of prominent non-research-intensive universities has emerged, with strong profiles in educational innovation. For example, Ritsumeikan University, one of the top private universities set up a branch university, Ritsumeikan Asia Pacific University, in 2000, with strong international programs taught in English and Japanese. Akita International University, a local public university incorporated (Public University Corporation), is building its reputation for its global liberal arts education taught in English.

There have been collaborative efforts to innovate research and education across institutions. For example, the University of Gifu (NUC) and Gifu Pharmaceutical University (*Gifu Yakka Daigaku*), a local public university specializing in pharmaceutical science established by Gifu City, agreed to form the United Graduate School of Drug Discovery and Medical Information Science in December, 2006, which was formally approved in April, 2007. This is seen as a new and innovative approach to inter-university collaboration across sectoral (national and local) boundaries. While not an institutional merger, the two universities have agreed on a number of organic collaborative activities.[27] The process has created opportunities for university departments to talk to each other, identify priority research areas and to strengthen their capacity for research excellence with support from a private firm. These universities are not 'elite' institutions in the traditional sense, but they are creating research excellence through collaboration, by appropriating the rapidly changing policy environments they are in and by building partnerships through which they can gain wider societal support.

Institutional Strategies of Top Research Universities

A new group of top research universities seen as *elite* universities seems to be emerging in Japan. In what ways are these institutions responding to new policy and institutional landscapes? How do these changes affect their organizational management and teaching and research activities? What are the perceived tensions?

Many of the old elite universities, both national and private, used to have strong academic autonomy. This is gradually changing with the introduction of new governance structures characterized by a top-down leadership style and a growth in the number of external stakeholders influencing university decision making processes. It is becoming evident that the new and the old ways are not always easy to reconcile.

The scope of this paper is limited to a discussion of three of the national elite institutions, namely, the University of Tokyo, the University of Tohoku and the University of Kyushu, all of which were former imperial universities, became part of the national university system in 1949, and are now NUCs. The focus is on their new identities, the influence of corporatization, the governance and management of each institution in terms of managing teaching and research, external funding, and how respective internationalization agendas have been influenced by growing international linkages and competition.

The University of Tokyo

In the case of the University of Tokyo, an NUC and the top research university in Japan, the total operating budget was 188 billion yen as of 2005. Of this sum, 51 percent was from the national government (including operating grants), 29 percent was from the University's own revenues (including 17 percent from a university hospital and 9 percent from tuition fees), 20 percent was from external revenue (including commissioned research funds and donation).[28] The University had 1,595 joint and commissioned research projects with industry which brought 21 billion yen in income in 2004. Figure 15.1 shows the recent increase in joint research with industry and other organizations.[29] In order to increase financial autonomy from the central government, the University established the University of Tokyo Foundation in 2004, through which the University is able to engage in long-term borrowing.[30]

Since corporatization, the University has introduced measures to increase efficiency and cost-effectiveness in management and has changed internal funding allocations (Yokoyama, 2006). Corporatization is seen as a trigger which has provided the University with the opportunity to build its identity as a national university and the autonomy to manage its own organization; however, its president has said that the speed of higher education reform has been detrimental to the university's teaching function.[31]

The University of Tokyo has been considered as the leading university in almost every field of study throughout its history. The University recognizes its position as being the best in Japan, and has taken strong leadership to

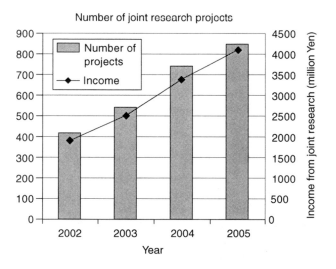

Figure 15.1 University of Tokyo External Income (joint research with industry and other organizations).

achieve a better global reputation through its 'action plan'.[32] The University recently opened a new campus in Kashiwa in Chiba prefecture near Tokyo, and aims to promote truly international research excellence by attracting top foreign researchers. In order to strengthen links with other Asian nations, the University has set up a liaison office in Beijing and is planning to increase such offices in other countries both within the region and beyond. Tokyo University participates in the International Alliance of Research Universities (IARU)[33] along with other top research universities worldwide: ETZ Zurich, the National University of Singapore, the University of Beijing, the Australian National University, the University of California (Berkeley), Yale University, Copenhagen University, and the Universities of Oxford and Cambridge. The University is also strengthening its undergraduate education, based on its liberal arts education tradition at the College of Arts and Sciences, which is developing linkages with universities and colleges throughout East Asia to promote liberal arts education.

The University of Tohoku

In March, 2007, the University of Tohoku (one of the former imperial universities) revealed its new strategic plan, the 'Inoue Plan' (named after its then president), and announced the University's aim to become a 'world top 30 University' in ten years' time.[34] Inoue, in 'The Challenge of Becoming a World Class University' (Inoue 2008), identifies the University's strategies and action plans through five principal pillars: research, teaching and learning, social contribution, campus environment, and organization and management. These five pillars set the overall vision of becoming a world-class university. The University has hosted 13 COE 21 research projects, and has won four research bases under the Global COE program.

To nurture top-level young researchers, the 'University of Tohoku International Advanced Research and Education Organization'[35] was launched in April 2007. This initiative is based upon the achievements of the already existing COE Program, encompassing a wide area of academic fields, namely, the natural sciences, the humanities, and the social sciences. It aims to create inter-departmental curricula and provide selective, high-level interdisciplinary graduate education.

Tohoku also maintains strong research institutes of international excellence in the material and fluid sciences. The Institute of Material Research has close links with the University of Cambridge's Department of Material Science and Metallurgy, and has set up offices in Cambridge, Stockholm, Stanford and Beijing. The University's Institute of Fluid Science has set up offices in the USA, Australia and South Korea. Since corporatization, the University of Tohoku as a whole has assumed a proactive international strategy, and has opened international offices in Australia, France, Russia, and South Korea.

The University has been very active in collaborating with industry, having recently entered into comprehensive organizational agreements to work with five specific business partners. Targeting post-doctoral fellows and doctoral students, the University offers specially designated courses providing transferable skills to make graduates employable within a high-skills society.

The University of Kyushu

The University of Kyushu, NUC and a former imperial university, has a distinctive orientation to work within the Asian region. In the University internationalization strategy, developing links with Asia, building the Center of Excellence in Research, establishing international university–industry links and developing these international links in partnership with local authorities and industrial associations are explicitly identified as the main strategic activities of the University. The University of Kyushu's Intellectual Property Management Center is working collaboratively with Shanghai Jiao Tong University in China to promote university–business links in Kyushu and Shanghai, matching business needs and university expertise. The University is also working closely with Taiwan's Industrial Technology Research Institute (ITRI) in developing international knowledge transfer.

Prior to corporatization, the University of Kyushu had started its long-term strategic planning and organizational reforms along with its relocation to a new campus.[36] The University of Kyushu was one of the earliest universities to establish a new organizational structure to divide teaching and research functions. Since 2000, all academic staff members belong to the 'research faculty' (*kenkyuin*) while graduate students are attached to graduate schools (*gakufu*) and undergraduates belong to departments (*gakubu*). Some research faculties are organized across disciplines to enhance the ability of academics to conduct interdisciplinary research, while most of the graduate schools are organized by discipline to train graduate students. Academic staff still teach undergraduate students in the departments, but the new system is based on the explicit organizational division of teaching and research.[37] This can be seen as a response to the government's policy of strengthening the research capacity of research-intensive universities, especially at the graduate school level. Other research-intensive universities are strengthening their graduate education, but the University of Kyushu is the only one with such an explicit organizational structure.

Its president evaluates the corporatization process for the University of Kyushu very positively, especially in building up the following areas of activity: strategic thinking, speed of action, public relations activities targeting stakeholders, dissemination of information, creation of a university with its own character, and development of an internationally competitive education and research base. As in all institutions, there have been some negative consequences of corporatization caused by a misunderstanding of the process.

Corporatization should not be merely about introducing competition or creating profits, nor does it necessitate neglecting basic research. Therefore, the president believes that an accounting system which suits the wider purposes of the university is required.[38]

Conclusion: Japanese Elite Universities in the New Era

Japanese elite universities and the higher education system are in a process of rapid transformation. This chapter has provided a historical background to Japanese elite universities, followed by an overview of recent policy changes transforming Japanese higher education and innovation systems.

Elite universities have transformed themselves throughout history. Following the Meiji Restoration in 1868, a key role for the universities was promoting the industrial development of the nation. During the early development of universities in Japan, the contribution of elite universities to society seems to be more explicit than that of today. The old elite status of former imperial universities was transformed into the idea of 'research excellence' as the Japanese higher education system expanded after World War II. This elite status has been strengthened through recent policy changes which include increases in total research funding, the introduction of competitive research funding (combined with the decrease in basic funding in the form of operating grants), increases in external funding, and the strengthening of graduate schools along with their research and training function.

Two fundamental challenges faced by the current Japanese higher education system have been identified: declining demographics and financial constraints from the public sector, particularly for less prestigious institutions. The Japanese higher education system today is in the 'post-massification' stage, having moved from *elite, mass* and moving towards a *universal* system. The series of legal, institutional and financial reforms which have affected national universities in the last decade has changed the higher education system radically. Recent reforms have affected the 'state–university relation' (Kaneko, 2005). National universities, since becoming corporate organizations, cannot rely on government protection and supervision to the extent they used to; they have to plan and manage their finances and human resource policies, be 'entrepreneurial' in order to receive more external funding, and compete nationally and internationally.

There are a number of growing tensions within Japanese post-mass higher education at the system level. National universities have accumulated knowledge and experience throughout the decade's reform processes, while many private universities and local public universities are on a precipice with declining numbers of young people and facing financial constraints. There are increasing tensions between prestigious and less prestigious private universities. There is also a very strong sense of crisis among 'non-elite' national universities in peripheral areas, and the perception of a growing gap between institutions in urban and rural areas both in terms of student enrollment and research capacity. Indeed, the growing economic gap between urban and rural areas (or centers and peripheries) is a sensitive issue in current policy debates in Japan.

Within the university, there is a growing tension between the humanities and sciences, between applied and non-applied sciences, and between undergraduate basic education and specialized education at the graduate level. Increasing support from the government for high-level research, both through established research funding channels and new programs such as COE initiatives, accelerates these tensions and gaps within the Japanese higher education system.

There is a cost to pay in pursuing world-class university policies if these policies are implemented without paying sufficient attention to societal realities. The careful designation of elite research universities, with balanced public investment and competition as an integral part of the 'post-massification stage' of the higher education system is required. This has to be located in the changing national innovation system, in light of the increasing influence of the global economy and international competition.

Japanese society has been able to sustain a unique mix of elite and non-elite national universities, a large number of private universities with a few exceptional research-oriented institutions, as well as public local universities. The diverse and differentiated higher education system has been a driving force behind the postwar socio-economic development of the country. As pointed out earlier, the development of a new research system in Japan throughout the 1990s is proving to be a basis for the emergence of new innovation systems in which universities play more significant roles as *economic resources* (Kitagawa, 2005). However, this should not be understood as following a linear model of one-way knowledge transfer from academic science to industry, nor as following global competition to create world class universities as 'nation-positioning' institutions (Bleiklie and Henkel, 2005: 2).

Gibbons argues, 'Much innovation, and hence economic development, depends less on original discoveries and more on the timely take-up, modification and marketing of knowledge solutions that already exist but need to be adapted to local environments' (2004: 97). Japan has been the prime exemplar of such incremental innovation throughout the 1980s; such innovation is no more likely to emerge from the elite research institutions than from any others (Moodie, 2006). In the twenty-first century, a wider spectrum of innovation, not only in high tech and manufacturing but also in the service sector and public sector, will be required. The existing diversity of the higher education system which provides a wide range of human resources and skills is a formidable societal asset for the Japanese tradition of innovation.

To create an authentic, internationally competitive post-mass higher education system, the creation of world-class top research universities is only part of the solution; there are other approaches worthy of emulation and exploration. Historically, Japan has developed institutional diversity within its system, partly supported by family investment in education in the form of private tuition fees. This diversity needs to be further encouraged both by educational innovation and institutional change, combined with wider societal support. To create such an environment, not only public support from the central and local governments, but also increased private support from stakeholders such as individual citizens, business, alumni, foundations, charities, communities and so forth should be encouraged. A wide range of policy instruments is necessary to promote such conditions, including the possibility of further incentives such as tax exemptions for donations. Entrepreneurial activities and the financial management of universities need to be strengthened but with careful risk assessment.

The title of *top research university* may not, in fact, be a synonym for *elite university*. Today, however, these two characterizations are used interchangably, in Japan as well as elsewhere. Universities have become 'places of expectations' but also they should constitute 'spaces for reflection' (May and Perry, 2006). Elite universities are not only about being entrepreneurial and gaining research grants, but they should act as civic partners in society. The importance of wider societal support for higher education needs to be addressed. At the same time, the societal role – obligation – of universities as mechanisms for social critique should not be forgotten.

Notes

1. In terms of the expenditure on tertiary education institutions as a percentage of GDP as of 2003, Korea and the United States spend 2.6 and 2.9 percent of their GDP respectively on tertiary institutions, and these two countries have the highest proportion of private expenditure (2.0 and 1.6 percent respectively) on tertiary education. Japan spends 1.3 percent (0.5 percent from government expenditure and 0.8 percent from private expenditure) (OECD, 2006).
2. According to the 2007 Shanghai Jiao Tong University ranking, 'Academic Ranking of World Universities', six out of the top ten Asia Pacific universities are Japanese: Tokyo (1), Kyoto (2), Osaka (5), Tohoku (6), Nagoya (8) and the Tokyo Institute of technology (9).
3. During Japan's period of rapid growth following World War II, Japanese researchers of higher education showed great interest in Trow's ideas. Two of Trow's works on higher education transformation (1976 and 2000) have been translated into Japanese (1998). Amano (1998) argues that such popularity derived from the simple assumption that Japan would soon follow the transformation happening in the US.
4. Arimoto (1996) introduced the concept of the 'post-massification stage' to explain the specific transformation from a mass to universal higher education system in Japan.
5. The number of 18-year-olds in the Japanese population fell from 2,049,000 in 1993 to 1,500,000 in 2003, while the total number of university students rose from 2,389,648 in 1993 to 2,803,901 in 2003 (Hada, 2005).
6. For-profit universities mainly target the adult professional education market, such as legal professionals, business executives, and creative industry professionals.
7. See how these roles are delineated by MEXT (2005).
8. The sources of information include academic literature, policy surveys, secondary literature surveys (including results of a 2006 questionnaire survey conducted with university

presidents), institution websites, various communication with university academics and officers of the Ministry of Education.

9. The Japanese Imperial Universities established in Korea and Taiwan catered to the needs of the Japanese residents in the colonies more than the colonized natives (Kim, 2007).

10. The author would like to thank Mr. Shuichi Tsukahara, Head of the Department of Higher Education, National Institute for Educational Policy Research (NIER) for helpful comments on these points.

11. In 1919 the University Order (*Daigaku rei*) was enacted, recognizing some private colleges as universities. Before 1920, some private universities such as Waseda and Keio had called themselves universities, although their legal status was 'specialized college' (*senmon gakko*); only imperial universities had been officially recognized as universities (*daigaku*).

12. Organizational changes include increased leadership of department heads, the establishment of a governing body at the center of the university, inclusion of administrative staff in governing bodies, the introduction of efficiency and cost-effectiveness in management and better links between departments, faculties and research centres (Yokoyama, 2006).

13. In 1951, the Provisional Reform Discussion Committee suggested a return to the pre-war, two-layered system: newly formed universities would focus on research, while two- or three-year specialized universities would provide practical training in engineering, commerce, agriculture and education. In 1961, a revision of the School Education Law was made for 'colleges of technology' (*koto senmon gakko*), specifically designed for 'industrial education' (McVeigh, 2005).

14. Enacted in December, 2006, the reformed Basic Education Law states that the central and local governments must promote private education in light of its public nature and the fact that private education has an important role to play in schooling and university education.

15. These include legal studies, accounting, medical studies, public policy, intellectual property management, technology management, public health and teachers' training.

16. Operating grants amount to 1.2 trillion yen; subsidies for capital expenditure amount to 1 trillion yen.

17. The total amount of grants for operating costs for national universities as of FY 2007 is 1.2 trillion yen, reduced by 17 billion yen from FY 2006. The decision, called 'Basic Principles 2006 for economic and fiscal management and structural reforms', is known as the *Honebuto* (solid) Policy.

18. Three major changes were proposed by the Toyama Plan: First, the reorganization of national universities, including the merger of some institutions; second, the introduction of putative business methods to national universities through a process of 'incorporatization', and third, the introduction of competitive mechanisms into the university sector, including national, public and private universities (Yamamoto, 2004).

19. See Currie (2002) and Eades (2005) for details of evaluation and criteria.

20. Each program would receive an average of around 100 million yen per year for five years (the annual budget ranged from 26 to 330 million yen), with the budget for the final three years dependent on an interim progress review after two years (Eades, 2005).

21. For example, the number of peer reviewers per project funded by Japanese Grants in Aid is only 0.05, while with the US NSF, the number is 6.1. (Takeuchi, 2007).

22. Tsukuba University is a research-intensive NUC, established in the 1970s and located in Tsukuba Science City.

23. Commissioned research includes contracted research by the state and local authorities, and certain research programs contracted by Japan Science and Technology Agency.

24. In total, 63 research bases (32 research bases from former imperial universities) from 28 universities (21 national, 4 private and 3 local public universities) have been selected. http://www.jsps.go.jp/j-globalcoe/data/shinsa/sinsakekka.pdf, accessed September 30, 2007.

25. 'World-Top-Level Research Center' (WTL) program, http://www.mext.go.jp/a_menu/kagaku/toplevel/shiryo/07022804/005.htm, accessed September 30, 2007.

26. Comments by the Head of NUC support unit, MEXT, recorded in *Ronza* (2006: 207).

27. Gifu University NUC formed similar 'united graduate schools' with other NUCs, including: the United Graduate School of Agricultural Science (Shinshu University, Shizuoka

University and Gifu University), and the United Graduate School of Veterinary Science (the Obihiro University of Agriculture and Veterinary Medicine, Iwate University, Tokyo University of Agriculture and Technology, and Gifu University).

28. http://www.u-tokyo.ac.jp/fin01/pdf/H17kessannogaiyou.pdf, accessed October 3, 2007.
29. http://www.u-tokyo.ac.jp/res01/d04_04_h14_j.html, accessed October 3, 2007 The level of joint research stayed low from the 1970s to the 1990s. Other industrial funding such as scholarship donations and contracted research increased in the 1980s and 1990s respectively (Hatakenaka, 2003).
30. The University Foundation aims to receive 13 billion yen in donations by the end of FY 2007. This is rather small compared with Keio University, which has 36 billion and Waseda University with 24 billion. These numbers are far less compared with US research universities such as Harvard, Yale and Stanford.
31. Comments by President Komiyama, the survey report recorded in *Ronza* (2006: 206).
32. According to the THES World University Rankings (2005, 2006), University of Tokyo was ranked 16 in 2005, and 19 in 2006 alongside the National University of Singapore. According to Shanghai Jiao Tong AWUR, the University of Tokyo ranked 20 in 2007.
33. http://www.iaruni.org/, accessed November 26, 2007.
34. According to the THES in 2006, the University of Tohoku is ranked as 168. According to Shanghai Jiao Tong AWUR in 2007, Tohoku is ranked as 76.
35. http://www.iiare.tohoku.ac.jp/e/, accessed November 10, 2007.
36. http://www.kyushu-u.ac.jp/university/change/gakufu/research04.php, accessed October 27, 2007.
37. http://www.kyushu-u.ac.jp/university/data/gaiyou18jpn/H18kyudai_gaiyo_p-09.pdf, accessed November 26, 2007.
38. Comments by President Kajiyama, recorded in a survey in *Ronza* July 2006: 202.

References

Akabayashi, H. and Naoi, M. (2004) Why Is There No Harvard Among Japanese Private Universities? http://repec.org/esFEAM04/up. 30196.1080739062.pdf, accessed November 26, 2007.
Amamo, I. (1998) Higher Education Research in Japan, *The Horizon of Higher Education Research*, 1, pp. 7–28. Tokyo: Japanese Society for Research in Higher Education. (in Japanese).
Arimoto, A. (1996) Cross-National Study on Academic Organizational Reforms in Post-Massification Stage, *Research In Higher Education*, 25, pp. 2–22.
Asahi Newspaper (2007) *Daigaku Ranking* 2007. Tokyo: Asahi Newspaper, *Daigaku* Editorial Office.
Asahi Shinbun Publications (2006) Survey Results of the Presidents of National Universities, *Ronza*, July.
Asonuma, A. (2002) Globalisation and Higher Education Reforms: the Japanese Case, *Higher Education*, 43, pp. 127–139.
Baker, D. (2007) Mass Higher Education and the Super Research University, *International Higher Education*, 49, pp. 9–10.
Bartholomew, J. (1978) Japanese Modernization and the Imperial Universities, 1876–1920, *Journal of Asian Studies*, 37(2), pp. 251–271.
Bartholomew, J. (1989) *The Formation of Science in Japan: Building a Research Tradition*. New Haven: Yale University Press.
Bleiklie, I. and Henkel, M. (eds) (2005) *Governing knowledge*. London: Springer.
Clark, B. (2001) The Entrepreneurial University: New Foundations for Collegiality, Autonomy, and Achievement, *Higher Education Management*, 13(2), pp. 9–24.
Cummings, W. (1998) The service university in comparative perspective, *Higher Education*, 35, pp. 1–8.
Currie, W. (2002) Japan's Top 30 Universities, *International Higher Education*, Winter, pp. 23–24.
Cutts, R. (1997) *An Empire of Schools: Japan's Universities and the Molding of a National Power Elite*. New York: M.E. Sharpe.
Doi, R. (2007) Structural analysis of universities' competitive environment for teaching and

research. RIETI Policy Discussion Paper Series 07-P-003 (in Japanese). http://www.rieti. go.jp/jp/publications/pdp/07p003.pdf, accessed November 26, 2007.

Eades, J. (2005) The Japanese 21st Century Center of Excellence Program: Internationalisation in Action?, in *The 'big bang' in Japanese higher education: the 2004 reforms and the dynamics of change* (pp. 295–323), edited by J.S. Eades, R. Goodman and Y. Hada. Melbourne: Trans Pacific Press.

Fransman, M. (1999) *Visions of Innovation*. Oxford: Oxford University Press.

Freeman, C. (1988) Japan: a new national system of innovation?, in *Technical Change and Economic Theory* (pp. 330–348), edited by G. Dosi et al. London: Pinter Publishers.

Geiger, R. (2004) *Knowledge and Money: Research Universities and the Paradox of the Marketplace*. Stanford: Stanford University Press.

Geuna, A. and Martin, B. (2003) University Research Evaluation and Funding: An International Comparison, *Minerva*, 41, pp. 277–304.

Gibbons, M. (2004) Globalisation, innovation and socially robust knowledge, in *The university in the global age* (pp. 96–115), edited by R. King. Houndsmills: Palgrave Macmillan.

Goodman, R. (2005) W(h)ither the Japanese University? An Introduction to the 2004 Higher Education Reforms in Japan, in *The 'big bang' in Japanese higher education: the 2004 reforms and the dynamics of change* (pp. 1–31), edited by J.S. Eades, R. Goodman and Y. Hada. Melbourne: Trans Pacific Press.

Hada, Y. (2005) Postgraduate and Professional Training in Japanese Universities: Causes and Directions of Change in *The 'big bang' in Japanese higher education: the 2004 reforms and the dynamics of change* (pp. 219–241), edited by J.S. Eades, R. Goodman and Y. Hada. Melbourne: Trans Pacific Press.

Hatakenaka, S. (2003) *University-Industry Partnerships in MIT, Cambridge, and Tokyo: Story-telling Across Boundaries*. London: RoutledgeFalmer.

Hatakenaka, S. (2005) The Incorporation of National Universities: The Role of Missing Hybrids, in *The 'big bang' in Japanese higher education: the 2004 reforms and the dynamics of change* (pp. 52–75), edited by J.S. Eades, R. Goodman and Y. Hada Melbourne: Trans Pacific Press.

Hicks, D. (1993) University-industry research links in Japan, *Policy Science*, 26(4). pp. 361–395.

Inoue, A. (2008) Inoue Plan 2007, Tohoku University Action Plans (revised for 2008), http://www.bureau.tohoku.ac.ip/president/open/plan/Inoue_Plan_2007.pdf, accessed July 25, 2008.

JSPS (2006) *The Achievements of the 21st Century Center of Excellence Program*, http://www.mext.go.ıp/a_menu/koutou/coe/06092116/all.pdf (available in Japanese), accessed November 26, 2007.

Kamatani, C. (2006) University-Industry Cooperative Research in Japan: from Meiji Era to Second World War (in Japanese). *NIER Research Bulletin*, 135, pp. 57–102.

Kaneko, M. (2005) Higher Education Reform in Japan and Germany: Are we heading for the same direction? CRDHE Working Paper Vol. 1, *Higher Education Reform in Japan and Germany: Transformation of State-University Relation*, http://www.he.utokyo.ac.jp/pdf/workingpaper200505.pdf, accessed November 26, 2007.

Kim, T. (2007) Old Borrowings and New Models of the University in East Asia, *Globalization, Societies & Education, Special Issue: Globalization*, 5(1), Special Issue: Changing Nature of the State and Governance in Education, pp. 39–52.

Kitagawa, F. (2005) Constructing Advantage in the Knowledge Society – Roles of Universities Reconsidered: The case of Japan, *Higher Education Management and Policy*, 17(1), pp. 45–62.

Kitamura, K. (1997) Policy Issues in Japanese Higher Education, *Higher Education*, 34, pp. 141–150.

May, T. and Perry, B. (2006) Cities, Knowledge and Universities: Transformations in the Image of the Intangible. *Social Epistemology* 20(3/4), Special Issue: Universities in the Knowledge Economy: Places of Expectation/Spaces for Reflection? pp. 259–282.

McVeigh, B. (2005) Higher Education and the Ministry: The Capitalist Development State, Strategic Schooling and National Renovationism, in *The 'big bang' in Japanese higher education: the 2004 reforms and the dynamics of change* (pp. 76–93), edited by J.S. Eades, R. Goodman and Y. Hada. Melbourne: Trans Pacific Press.

MEXT (2005) *Wagakuni no Koto kyoikuno Shoraizo* [*The Future of Japanese Higher Education*], http://www.mext.go.ip/b_menu/shingi/chukyo/chukyo0/toushin/05013101.htm, accessed July 25, 2008.

MEXT (2006) *Gakko kihon chosa.* http://www.mext.go.ip/b_menu/toukei/001/06121219/002/001/001.htm, accessed November 26, 2007.

MEXT (2007) *World-Top-Level Research Center (WTL) Program,* http://www.mext.go.ip/a_menu/kagaku/toplevel/shiryo/07022804/005.htm, accessed September 30, 2007.

Moodie, G. (2006) Research to excellence, *Griffith Review,* 11, pp. 32–38. http://www.griffith.edu.au/griffithreview/campaign/apo/apo_ed11/moodie_ed11.pdf.

Murasawa, M. (2002) The Future of Higher Education in Japan: Changing the Legal Status of National Universities, *Higher Education,* 43, pp. 141–155.

Nakayama, S. and Low, M.F. (1997) The research function of universities in Japan, *Higher Education,* 34, pp. 245–258.

Oba, J. (2005) The Incorporation of National Universities in Japan: Initial Reactions of the New National University Corporations, *Higher Education Management and Policy,* 17(2), pp. 105–125.

Okada, A. (2005) A History of the Japanese University, in *The 'big bang' in Japanese higher education: the 2004 reforms and the dynamics of change* (pp. 32–51), edited by J.S. Eades, R. Goodman and Y. Hada. Melbourne: Trans Pacific Press.

OECD (2006) *Education at a Glance.* Paris: OECD.

Shanghai Jiao Tong University (2007) *Academic Ranking of World Universities 2007,* http:/www.arwu.org/rank/2007/ranking2007.htm, accessed July 25, 2008.

Strathern, M. (ed.) (2000) *Audit Cultures: Anthropological Studies in Accountability, Ethics and the Academy.* London: Routledge.

Takeuchi, A. (2007) Weakness of the Japanese Research Systems: Allocating research funding in favour of 'Imperial Universities', *Shukan Toyo Keizai,* October, pp. 48–49. (in Japanese)

The Times Higher Education Supplement (THES) (2005) World University Rankings, http://www.topuniversities.com/worlduniversityrankings/results/2005/top_200_universities, accessed July 26, 2008.

The Times Higher Education Supplement (THES) (2006) World University Rankings, http://www.topuniversities.com/worlduniversityrankings/results/2006/, accessed July 26, 2008.

Torii, Y. (2007) Towards the New Era of Higher Education Financial Responsibility *IDE,* 492, pp. 4–10. (in Japanese)

Trow, M. (1976) *The University in the Highly Educated Society: From Elite to Mass Higher Education* (*Kogakureki shakai no daigaku: Elite kara Mass he*) (in Japanese). Translated by I. Amano and K. Kitamura. Tokyo: Tokyo University Press, 1998.

Trow, M. (2006) Reflections on the Transition from Elite to Mass to Universal Access: Forms and Phases of Higher Education in Modern Societies since WWII. in *International Handbook of Higher Education* (pp. 243–280), edited by J Forest and A. Philip. New York: Springer.

Ushiogi, M. (1997) Japanese Graduate Education and its Problems, *Higher Education,* 34, pp. 237–244.

Watson, D. and Ohmori, F. (2005) A tale of two countries: higher education "incorporation" in the UK and Japan, A Daiwa Anglo-Japanese Foundation Lecture, February.

Woolgar, L. (2007) New Institutional Policies for University-Industry Links in Japan *Research Policy,* 36, pp. 1261–1274.

Yamamoto, K. (2004) Corporatization of National Universities in Japan: Revolution for Governance or Rhetoric for Downsizing?, *Financial Accountability and Management,* 20(2), pp. 153–181.

Yokoyama, K. (2006) Entrepreneurialism in Japanese and UK universities: Governance, management, leadership, and funding, *Higher Education,* 52, pp. 523–555.

Yonezawa, A. (2003) Making World Class Universities: Japan's Experiment, *Higher Education Management and Policy,* 15(2), pp. 9–24.

Yonezawa, A. (2007) Japanese flagship universities at a crossroads, *Higher Education,* 54(4), pp. 483–449.

16
The Ivy League
Roger L. Geiger

On November 20, 1945, the presidents of eight northeastern institutions signed the "Intercollegiate Agreement," pledging to field football teams that were "truly representative of the student body" and to abide by common standards of eligibility and financial aid. This was the first formal affiliation among a previously ill-defined group of institutions that sports writers of the 1930s had started calling the "ivy league." At the heart of this initiative were the Big Three – Harvard, Yale and Princeton (HYP). They had absolutely dominated collegiate football from its invention until the formation of the National Collegiate Athletic Association in 1905. When dominance was no longer possible, they concluded a Three Presidents Agreement after World War I to manage the rules of engagement among themselves. As World War II drew toward a close, they wished to step back further from an expected resurgence of big-time athletics, but they no longer felt they could do so alone. They inaugurated discussions leading to the Intercollegiate Agreement among "a few of our other natural rivals and friends" – Brown, Columbia, Cornell, Dartmouth and the University of Pennsylvania (Bernstein, 2001: 180, 177). It would take subsequent assertions by the Big Three to create a definitive moat between Ivy League amateurism and the games played by other major American universities, and a full decade before true league play was begun. However, the "ivy colleges" as they first called themselves were the Big Three writ large; and this was true as well of the symbolic Ivy League that associates the eight universities of the athletic conference in a collective identity.[1]

Indeed, there is a curious parallelism between the formal athletic conference and the more encompassing unity of the Ivy League. Just as they had once represented domination in football, Harvard, Yale, and Princeton represented the highest level of attainment in undergraduate qualifications, institutional wealth, and academic excellence – all qualities that the other Ivies wished to be associated with. And, as in athletics, they sought to make the rules for themselves. But unlike athletics, where the Ivies felt that they could not and did not wish to compete with other major universities, in these other areas they far outstripped all but a handful of rivals.[2] Always standing above and apart from American mass higher education, their advantages have never been greater than in the twenty-first century.

In the *U.S. News* rankings for 2008, HYP occupied their accustomed top three spots (in this case PHY), and the Ivies claimed eight of the top fourteen. HY have the largest endowments in the country (Princeton is fourth), and HYP lead on a per-student basis. The other Ivies are among the twenty richest universities. In peer ratings of research and graduate programs, the category where competition is stiffest, five Ivy schools were among the ten highest overall ratings (see Table 16.1). Perhaps most important, HYP have remained associated with social-economic-political elites who have consistently provided political and cultural leadership to the nation.[3] Yale historian George W. Pierson sought to demonstrate this point in *The Education of American Leaders*, where he compiled the colleges and universities attended by acknowledged leaders over time in a variety of fields. The primacy of Harvard is striking, followed by Yale, Columbia (when professional degrees are included), and Princeton. For the nineteenth century, the Ivies produced more leaders than all other colleges combined; and for the first half of the twentieth century these institutions led all others (Pierson, 1969).

This paper seeks to explain how this group of institutions assumed and maintained primacy in educating social and intellectual elites, how they amassed their extraordinary wealth, and how they sustained a leading role in learning. It looks first into the historical foundations for this primacy, examining the preponderant role of HYP, but also showing how the other Ivies related to these same developments. It next asks how the Ivies surmounted the major challenges presented by the evolution of a modern mass system of higher education. Finally, it explicates the conditions responsible for their growing advantage in the twenty-first century and the challenges that has entailed.

Despite the common Ivy identity, these eight institutions differ greatly from one another. HYP are most similar in the recruitment and socialization of undergraduates, but as universities, Harvard hosts a multitude of graduate and professional schools and Princeton few, with Yale somewhere in between. Columbia and Penn are sprawling urban conglomerates, but of quite different character. All are colonial foundings except Cornell, a land-grant institution, coeducational from the outset, that remains partly public. Dartmouth shares with Cornell a rustic isolation, but takes fierce pride in its resolutely collegiate character, despite recent growth in research. Traditionally less rigorous than neighboring Harvard and Yale, Brown made a virtue out of laxity in 1969 with an undemanding New Curriculum, which then attracted the Ivies' largest number of applicants for the next two decades.

Nineteenth-Century Foundations

Harvard was the first and the foremost colonial college, and although its academic leadership has since been challenged, it has never really been relinquished. Declared in 1780 to be a university by the Massachusetts state constitution, it had by far the largest and most learned faculty in the early nineteenth century and called itself "the university at Cambridge" (Geiger, 2000). However, the most fateful development of these years was the growing identification of Harvard College with the upper class of the Boston region (Story, 1980). Whether old merchant families or newer recruits, the "Boston Brahmins" forged a shared culture – conservative in politics and liberal in religion – through domination of cultural institutions, principally Harvard. They controlled the governing body, the Harvard Corporation, and enrolled their sons. Harvard College was open to all qualified students, but it charged the highest tuition outside the South, and student lifestyles raised the cost of attendance far more. As prospective students favored a handful of preparatory schools, standards of admission rose as well. The panoply of student organizations assured the transmission of the mores and folkways of their class.[4]

An increasing flow of private donations by mid-century added to the wealth of Harvard and to a growing list of scientific appendages. The obvious aristocratic drift provoked increasing political opposition, which centered on the composition of the Board of Overseers. An impasse of sorts was only resolved during the Civil War, when legislation replaced publicly appointed Overseers with representatives elected by Harvard Alumni. Thus, in 1865 Harvard became a fully private institution. Alumni influence served directly to reform a rather raggedly run institution. In 1869 the Overseers elected thirty-five-year-old Charles W. Eliot to be president (1869–1909). Joining Brahmin culture with academic excellence, over the next forty years he put Harvard in the forefront of the reforms that produced the modern American university (Morison, 1936: 323–99; Story, 1980: 175–80).

While Harvard developed on an affluent regional base, Yale achieved its eminence as a national university. Under president Timothy Dwight (1795–1817), it became a leader in the Second Great Awakening of evangelical Christianity, which pervaded much of the country until at least the Civil War (Dobkin Hall, 1984: 104–113 & passim; Geiger, 2000). Governed narrowly by trustees drawn from Connecticut Congregational ministers, Yale nevertheless spearheaded the most important developments in American colleges throughout the nineteenth century. It was instrumental in establishing theological seminaries as post-graduate institutions and spreading their influence through the American Education Society. When the college curriculum was challenged in the 1820s, it produced the hugely influential Yale Reports of 1828, which not only defended the classical course, but defined it as intellectual and character preparation for professional studies – as undergraduate education. When demands for wider curricula arose in the 1840s, Yale developed the first scientific school, the most successful mid-century model for both advanced and applied scientific studies. In 1861 Yale awarded the first American Ph.D.s. Yale graduates dispersed across the expanding nation as ministers, educators, and mostly lawyers. They assumed positions of leadership and sent their sons and other promising youths back to New Haven to drink from the same nourishing waters. Until after the Civil War, Yale was the largest American college and a university in all but name.

At the end of the 1860s Yale faced the same choices as Harvard. "Young Yale" – a movement led by successful Wall Street alumni – demanded modernizing reforms, an end to clerical control, and a voice in governance. But complacent Yale held them off, conceding a minority of alumni trustees but choosing conservative Noah Porter (1871–1886) as its new president (Dobkin Hall, 2000: 196–220; Leverque, 2007: 29–66). Yale's academic development was slowed for the rest of the century, but it still led the country in another important respect. Yale students developed the most exuberant extracurriculum, including perfecting the rules and tactics of American football. Strenuous competition in a multitude of student activities and organizations shaped highly successful graduates, who found their way in increasing numbers to the New York financial hub. After Yale elected a "modern" president in 1899, their loyalty and generosity produced a burgeoning flow of gifts for their alma mater (Geiger, 2004).

Unlike Harvard and Yale, Princeton struggled in the nineteenth century. The premier college of the American Revolution and the American enlightenment, it was thrown into turmoil as the values underlying these movements waned. It reacted by embracing a rigid Presbyterianism, a legacy that modern Princetonians prefer to forget. From its nadir in the 1820s, the college gradually expanded enrollments and academic rigor. By the end of the century, its alumni too asserted greater influence and sought academic modernization. Their champion was Woodrow Wilson (1902–1910), who shaped modern Princeton during his brief presidency (Axtell, 2006). Its graduates too grew wealthy in the canyons of Wall Street, and increasingly supported the development of the college.

Challenge 1: The Academic Revolution

The emergence of the American university in the 1890s involved a transformation of curriculum, teaching, and university organization. The most far-reaching changes were establishing the academic disciplines as the knowledge base and adopting the advancement of disciplinary knowledge, through graduate education and research, as a primary institutional mission. New endowed universities, notably Johns Hopkins, Stanford, and Chicago, were premised on these principles, but for others the challenge was to integrate this new curriculum and new mission with the traditional roles of the colleges. For the Ivies, increasingly dependent on alumni who related almost exclusively to their colleges, this was a ticklish task. Two forms of prestige were at stake: national and international recognition for learning and the advancement of knowledge; and more local social expectations for educating and replicating social elites.

In 1910, journalist Edwin Slosson published remarkably insightful portraits of the fourteen *Great American Universities*. These institutions were the leaders and the victors in the academic revolution, and all the Ivies, save Brown and Dartmouth, were among them.[5] Harvard and upstart Columbia, along with the University of Chicago, were the academic leaders of that era. Cornell and Yale were close behind in scientific prowess. Penn excelled in medicine, and Princeton (along with Yale) uneasily mixed scholarly excellence with powerful collegiate traditions.

President Eliot probably recognized better than anyone that the academic and social ideals could and should be reconciled: the highest intellectual distinction in academic learning bestowed a priceless patina on the university's graduates, no matter how remote from their own classroom experience. Eliot instituted a curriculum of free electives that allowed the scholars he recruited with Harvard's growing wealth to teach and develop their areas of expertise. Slosson found that Harvard "offers more courses in a greater variety of subjects than any other American university. It has not only the largest faculty, it has also the most eminent (Slosson, 1910: 8)." Students were free to partake or not of these riches. But student culture fragmented despite the college's numerous clubs and organizations. Brahmin students lived apart and maintained direct social ties with the Boston upper class. The advanced studies of professors and graduate students were the business of academic units and controlled by the faculty. Eliot's formula would be deemed too liberal by some contemporaries and by his successor, but it allowed Harvard to succeed emphatically as a research university.

Columbia for much of the nineteenth century was a small college with high standards that served established professional families of New York City. In 1890–1910 it underwent a remarkable transformation, moving to a new campus at Morningside Heights and becoming an academic giant. In the process, the college gradually lost its Knickerbocker constituency, even as the university added numerous new units, some affiliated or associated, and including a large graduate school. By 1910, Columbia was the only Ivy school to have more graduate than undergraduate students. The college, the university, and its supporters were oriented toward graduate and professional studies, and the donations that drove its relentless expansion came chiefly from New York family fortunes. More than even Harvard, Columbia was an educational conglomerate, adept at exploiting its New York base to pursue excellence in graduate and professional education (Geiger, 2004: 52–53; McCaughey, 2003: 259–263; Slosson, 1910: 442–473).

Cornell was a true pioneer of the academic revolution. Founding president Andrew Dickson White (1868–1885) was a Yale graduate and a professor at Michigan under Henry Tappan, an early university advocate. With Ezra Cornell's benefaction and the income from the New York State land grant, he sought academic distinction as well as practical studies. Hailed initially as a democratic Mecca, its strength in science and engineering soon began to draw the sons of wealthy manufacturers. When Slosson visited the campus he sensed "a spirit of caste and exclusiveness" much like other Eastern universities, centered particularly on the fraternity system. Women students chiefly came from more humble circumstances and were scorned for that reason (Slosson, 1910: 312–343; 328 for the quote). Cornell's academic prestige was its strongest currency from the outset, and it translated to social prestige by the twentieth century.

The University of Pennsylvania had long harbored academic strengths. The foremost American medical school for most of the nineteenth century, it pioneered schools for dentistry and veterinary science. It possessed renowned research institutes for biology and archeology, which were exceptional for that era. These strengths were reflected in its output of Ph.D.s. But in other respects Penn differed from its putative reference group. Slosson found an "extremely diversified student body" drawn from ethnic Philadelphia and from the non-affluent hinterland – not an admired trait among Ivy schools. The large Wharton School of Finance, though developing new social sciences, had decidedly low status. And, with a modest endowment, Penn was largely a tuition-driven institution. The university drew what support it received from Philadelphia but failed to build a sustaining relationship with that city's fragmented elite (Slosson, 1910: 344–372, 361 for the quote; Geiger, 2004: Appendices).

Yale and Princeton sought high academic standards and had sufficient wealth to achieve them, but both schools had difficulty reconciling research with social reproduction. Yale's achievements in research and graduate education were largely due to its scientific school. However, having been first to establish one, Yale was last to abolish its anachronistic separate status, which Slosson compared to the Austro-Hungarian Dual Monarchy. When a partial unification was achieved in 1919, the sciences were actually weakened by the hegemony of Yale College. Yale's growing affluence nevertheless allowed the provost and the graduate school to build a distinguished research university parallel with the college (Geiger, 2004: 203–207; Slosson, 1910: 34–74). At Princeton, president Wilson held an aversion for "Germanic scholarship" and admiration for the Oxonian ideal; but even the latter was difficult to sell to the alumni, who defended a social regime based on exclusive eating clubs. To accommodate graduate students Princeton built an isolated residential college in ornate gothic style. There the graduate dean held court with carefully screened students at teas and high table. Yet, Princeton was soon recognized for scholarly distinction. Graduate students numbered fewer than the faculty, permitting each to work closely with professors. Princeton became the most bifurcated university: a "country club" for undergraduates, in the words of both Wilson and F. Scott Fitzgerald, it also developed leading programs in mathematics and theoretical physics (Axtell, 2006: 378–394; Geiger, 2004: 200–203; Slosson, 1910: 75–109).

Challenge 2: Mass Higher Education

For most of American history the largest institutions of higher education were also the best. This was especially true following the academic revolution, when scale was imperative for covering the disciplinary curriculum and offering doctoral studies. In 1900, the six Ivies just reviewed enrolled almost 10 percent of students in higher education (Geiger, 2004: Appendix A). All these institutions grew irregularly, as they tinkered with admissions requirements and added new units. Enrollment growth accelerated after 1900, especially for state universities. However, it was not until the aftermath of World War I that the U.S. experienced what Martin Trow (1973) later characterized as the transition from elite to mass higher education.[6] Faced with more applicants than they could, or wished to, accommodate, and from groups that had never before attended in more than small numbers, the Ivies had to decide how they would choose their students and how they would sustain relations with their elite constituencies. First confronted in the 1920s, these issues challenged these institutions for the rest of the century. The admissions challenge nevertheless passed through three stages: improvising selection in the 1920s; confronting meritocracy in the 1950s; and achieving racial diversity after 1970. This section considers the first two stages, while the third is part of their current predicament.

The first school to develop procedures for selective admission was Dartmouth, where enrollment had always been limited by the availability of living accommodations in Hanover. Dartmouth in 1920 was by no means an elite school, drawing its students from all social strata of northern New England and dispersing graduates to Boston, New York, and beyond. It inspired fanatical devotion in its alumni, epitomized by one alumnus's deathbed statement that for him Dartmouth had been religion enough. President Ernest Hopkins (1916–1945) achieved his position through alumni work without previous academic appointment. Dismissive toward "professional scholarship," Hopkins supported rigorous undergraduate teaching and the ideal of the "liberal college," which was popularized by Alexander Meiklejohn, President of Amherst College. Dartmouth alumni supported this vision and were accorded a large role in running the College (Widmayer, 1977: 236–249, 168–170).

In 1921 Dartmouth adopted the "Selective Process for Admission." Four criteria were employed: scholastic record, other activities, a personal rating by the student's principal or headmaster, and a personal rating from an interview by an alumnus. Hopkins hailed this approach as promoting an "aristocracy of brains." He also claimed it gave a better chance to the "well-rounded" boy who was not a top scholar, although rival colleges suspected Dartmouth of using this rationale to recruit athletes. Hopkins further averred that the Selective Process increased diversity; preference was given to sons of alumni and residents of New Hampshire, but also to applicants from the South and West. The Selective Process probably raised the academic qualifications of Dartmouth students, but nearly all came from similar WASP, upper-middle class backgrounds (Levine, 1986: 137–146; Widmayer, 1977: 61–65).

Selective admissions at the other Ivies – especially at HYP and Columbia – were more consciously designed to hold down the numbers of Jewish students and to preserve the social character of the colleges. A large literature has minutely described how this was accomplished (Geiger, 2004: 129–139; Synott, 1979; Weschler, 1977). Personal data was required to assess "character" and to flag socially undesirable applicants; sons of alumni were virtually automatic admits; and wider geographical recruitment was instituted to identify more "well-rounded boys" of the right sort. Discrimination in admissions had to be reconciled with faculty preferences for academic ability. Harvard president Abbott Lawrence Lowell (1909–1933) was repudiated when he attempted to establish a Jewish quota, and he had to proceed less overtly through the selective process. Social selection was rationalized by invoking the criteria for Rhodes scholars – character, scholarship, athletics, and leadership. Discrimination in the Ivies was never completely exclusionary, although nearly so at Princeton, but was instead a massive tilt toward the social constituencies of these institutions. The proportion of alumni sons at Yale doubled during the first decade of selective admissions; private school graduates rose from 70 to 80 percent. And alumni reciprocated. In addition to a huge expansion of campus facilities, the endowments of Harvard and Princeton tripled from 1919 to 1939, and Yale's quadrupled.

Once institutionalized, discrimination persisted through the 1930s despite far less enrollment pressure. Only the upheavals of the war and the GI Bill suppressed these practices, or drove them underground. By the 1950s, HYP appeared to lead the ascendancy of academic merit as qualification for college admission.

Recent scholarship by Jerome Karabel and Joseph Soares has shown that the popular image of increasing meritocracy obscured the persistence of strong ties with existing social constituencies (Soares, 2007; Karabel, 2005).[7] Through the 1950s and 1960s the Ivies benefited from a rising tide of applicants with better and better credentials. The qualifications of entering classes naturally rose but, ironically, the more qualified the applicant pool became, the more admission decisions were based on personal qualities. This was accomplished by emphasizing certain criteria. For academic achievement, greatest weight was placed on the verbal SAT score, which correlates closely with socio-economic status. Candidates were further scrutinized and given scores for personal qualities, frequently determined in alumni interviews. These evaluations probed for evidence of character and leadership, as well as passing judgment on physical attractiveness and vigor. At Yale, statistical analysis showed that alumni interviews carried the greatest weight in admission decisions. Alumni sons, not surprisingly, were far more likely to be admitted. These results were not due to chance. At HYP in particular, the intellectual, psychological, and physical qualities of applicants and students were the most rigorously studied aspect of university operations. The bias in admissions was precisely what was intended.

After 1965 both Harvard and Yale began efforts to diversify their student bodies. Harvard actively recruited students from minority and disadvantaged groups. A new admissions director at Yale recruited more widely and, to the growing consternation of alumni, reduced the advantage of legacies. At the end of the decade, an internal study at Harvard identified 69 selective institutions – those receiving more qualified applicants than they could accommodate. When these schools were stratified into six groups, Harvard and Yale placed only in the second tier; Brown, Cornell, Penn, and Princeton were in the fourth; and Columbia and Dartmouth were even lower (Soares, 2007: 40). The Ivies paid a price in academic qualifications for their proclivities for potential leaders, athletes, and alumni sons.

Challenge 3: Revolution in Research

Research in American universities was greatly advanced during the 1920s and 1930s through support from the great philanthropic foundations. The scientific distinction of HYP made them major beneficiaries. The fact that these same colleges produced the largest number of foundation trustees and officers could not have hurt (Geiger, 2004: 140–245; Pierson, 1969: 127). However, the real challenge occurred during and after World War II when the federal government became the chief patron of academic research. To be a successful research university and academic leader now required universities to compete for these funds and to engage in Big Science.

For three of the Ivies, the postwar setting was a welcome opportunity to expand scientific prowess. Columbia had been the fourth largest performer of wartime research, and it moved most aggressively to attract continuing federal support. Cornell too continued defense research and also assembled one of the strongest teams in theoretical physics. Penn's Moore School of Electrical Engineering built the first electronic computer (Geiger, 2004a: 6–61; McCaughey, 2003: 356–364). HYP, in contrast, had misgivings. Although Harvard's James Conant (1933–1953) had led the scientific mobilization during the war, the university resolved not to continue its large wartime laboratories in radar countermeasures and underwater sound. Although deeply committed to research, postwar Harvard sought, somewhat quixotically, to confine itself to basic research and to eschew federal entanglements. Yale was most aloof from wartime research, but eventually concluded that it had to make significant investments in atomic physics if it were to maintain its academic standing. Princeton was the most apprehensive of the perils of federal support, but the momentum of scientific projects soon brought a major facility for fusion research. As late as 1962, a report by future provost and president, William G. Bowen, found much to fear from possible federal control; but the report concluded that federal support for research had benefited science and education at Princeton, and enhanced its prestige (Bix, 1993: 9–52, Geiger, 2004a: 47–57, 81–92).

Indeed, after the Soviet launch of Sputnik in 1957, an outpouring of federal support for all aspects of university research emanated from civilian rather than defense agencies. These new funds supported basic research, graduate education, and scientific facilities. There is no need to describe the unprecedented growth of academic research as funding quadrupled during the 1960s. All six of the Ivy research universities partook of this cornucopia. At Dartmouth and Brown research commitments followed in the 1970s. This "golden age" presented challenges of a different sort: how much research was too much? How far could the Ivies expand science, engineering, and graduate education on a limited undergraduate base? Hard choices only came at the end of the decade, when federal research funding ceased to grow and support for research infrastructure disappeared.

The 1970s were difficult times for the Ivies and for most of U.S. higher education. Despite their wealth and innate advantage, the Ivies faced the alienation of much of their alumni base due to ugly confrontations with student radicals and controversial efforts to diversify their students. Endowments were pummeled by the stock market collapse, mounting inflation, and a drought of alumni giving. Commitments to research and graduate education appeared extravagant in retrospect, but scaling them back threatened the wellsprings of academic prestige. In sum, the Ivies faced three imposing challenges: 1) to restore the financial strength on which other aspirations depended; 2) to find a balance in college admissions between the diversity demanded by American society and the access expected by their traditional social base, who were vital for resolving the first challenge; and 3) to support research and graduate education sufficiently to bolster academic standing and institutional prestige. Other American universities faced similar issues, but the Ivies would show the way toward their resolution.

The (Re-) Ascendancy of the Ivy League

Three inter-related developments allowed the Ivies to transcend the predicament of the late 1970s. A readjustment of admissions practices allowed these schools to protect relations with their traditional constituencies even while broadening their applicant pool. The emergence of differential pricing as the standard practice for private colleges yielded substantial increases in tuition income. Following closely, a pronounced rise in demand for admission to selective institutions inflated the currency of the Ivy League. As these developments focused institutional concerns on undergraduates, universities became

more tentative in their commitments to research. Most private colleges benefited from these trends, but none more than the Ivies.

The recruitment of minorities, the admission of women, and the egalitarian spirit of the late 1960s roiled the admissions patterns of the Ivies. Tentative efforts to enroll more minority students in the mid-1960s were soon
challenged as inadequate. The demands of militants for increased numbers
were actually strongly supported within the universities, given the intense
concern for social change and the racial crisis gripping the nation. Despite the
scarcity of minority students fitting the Ivy profile, by 1970 minority students
exceeded 10 percent of incoming classes at HYP. By then, Yale and Princeton
were also admitting women, and Harvard was integrating the women of Rad-
cliffe. Original plans called for about 20 percent female students and no
reduction in the number of male students, but this sexist vision proved
chimerical in the face of subsequent pressure from women's groups. By mid-
decade HYP struggled to resist demands for a 50–50 split. The resolution was
sex-blind admission which, given the preponderance of male applicants, produced classes with 60 percent or more males – a temporary male advantage
that soon shrank to parity. Women actually strengthened the applicant pools:
their academic records tended to be better; many also came from alumni
families; and, unlike minorities, they made slight demands on the student aid
budget. However, there were now fewer slots for the hypothetical future male
leaders that HYP had always sought (Karabel, 2005: 349–448).

Alumni reacted to this development with predictable dismay. Although
Princeton kept the acceptance of legacy sons above 50 percent, complaints
were still rampant. The situation was direr at Yale, where alumni sons fell
from over one-quarter of students to under 15 percent, and their acceptance
rates fell below 40 percent. In 1973 the pressure from alienated alumni forced
a change in admissions director and a change of course. The proportion of
alumni sons matriculating rose back to nearly one-quarter in the early 1980s
before resuming a slow, inexorable slide. Most important, HYP survived the
upheavals of the 1960s and 1970s, rebuilt relations with alumni, and kept
their social bases more or less intact. But the old days were gone forever.
Admissions in the era of diversity had become a constricted zero-sum game.
With the "tagged" groups of minorities, athletes, and alumni legacies claiming
more than 40 percent of slots, there was little space for the growing hordes of
applicants from the rest of American society.

Differential tuition pricing could be called a "social invention"; that is, an
innovation with partly unforeseen consequences that evolves into a widely
adopted practice due to the conjunction of other factors. In this case, Harvard
sparked the process, while federal policies and changing demand accelerated
it. HYP had long set the tuition ceiling for private colleges, but in the 1970s
they believed they lacked pricing power because of a weak (for them) supply
of applicants and competition from the public sector. In 1978, Harvard, with

the strongest applicant pool, nevertheless boosted tuition 18 percent, from $4,450 to $5,265. For the next ten years its tuition increases averaged $840 each year, and Yale and Princeton were quick to follow (Geiger, 2004b: 161–84). Over three decades the cost of attendance rose nearly tenfold, more than tripling in constant dollars.

The Ivy League had always provided scholarship aid for needy students, but Harvard made its tuition hikes more palatable by increasing institutional financial aid. However, the power of this aid was magnified by the existence of new forms of federal student aid. Legislation in 1972 had created federal grants for low-income students, but in 1978 additional legislation made federal student loans available to the middle class. Now there were three sources for meeting costs of attending college: student/parental contribution, federal grants and loans, and institutional aid. A private college could thus extract the maximum amount from parents (following guidelines for expected contributions) and from federal student aid, and then make up the difference with institutional aid. Often called tuition discounting, the result was a different price for each aided student. Most important, by charging each student only what he or she could afford (and borrow), differential pricing removed price resistance to higher tuition. As the Ivies and their ilk escalated tuition, a system of "high-tuition/high-aid" emerged, which now prevails in private and much of public higher education.

High-tuition/high-aid had long been considered more equitable by economists because it reduced the subsidy received by wealthy students. But its effects in practice were more complicated. Because federal forms of student aid are means tested and capped, this source of funds could not be inflated with tuition. Instead, as tuition rose institutional aid had to cover the growing shortfall, or "unmet need." For private colleges in general, the tuition discount has continued to creep upward and currently claims more than 40 percent of the "sticker price." Hence, the amount of revenue a college actually receives depends chiefly on the amount that students actually pay. Fortunately for the Ivies, the more selective the institution, the fewer students who require student aid. For Harvard in 2007, tuition and fees were about $34,000, and total cost of attendance about $44,000. Prices for the other Ivies were, as always, comparable. More than half of students in the Ivy League paid full price, a certain sign that they came from wealthy families.

In the 1950s, the Yale director of admissions estimated that Yale had historically needed to draw 60 percent of its students from the wealthiest 5 percent of families to ensure adequate tuition income. Despite the turmoil affecting the economy and admissions, Yale appears to have stayed close to that mark throughout the twentieth century and to the present. Moreover, that profile would largely fit the Ivy League: a calculation done for the year 2000 showed that 6–7 percent of families (45–55-year-old heads) could be expected to pay the full cost of attending an elite private college (Geiger, 2004b: 170–171; Soares, 2007:55–67, 162–166).[8]

Differential pricing allowed the Ivies to roughly triple their real tuition prices from 1977 to 2007, and the preponderance of wealthy students allowed them to retain the vast bulk of those increased revenues. The large majority of Ivy League students come from upper and upper-middle income households. Given the staggering cost of attendance, a significant portion of student aid funds must be directed to assisting upper-middle class students. Still, the number of applicants continues to rise, largely as a result of the increasing social demand for places at selective institutions.

"Selectivity sweepstakes" refers to the heightened concern for admission to elite colleges that began to build in the 1980s and has intensified ever since (Geiger, 2004c: 77–83). As the anti-elitist attitudes that characterized the 1970s dissipated, *U.S. News & World Report* published its first ranking of selective colleges and universities in 1983. Although college guides had been published since 1960, the numerical rankings of *U.S. News* had a greater impact; they democratized what had formerly been largely tacit knowledge of the elite college pecking order. Part artifact and part agent, college rankings propelled public preoccupation with the prestige and assumed advantages of these institutions. This naturally favored the Ivies, which stood near the front of the pack.[9] Moreover, as a kind of self-fulfilling prophecy, high rankings encouraged more and better applicants. And under the emerging system of high-tuition/high-aid, that translated into greater tuition revenues. However, underlying this apparent fashionable trend, more fundamental social processes were at work.

Economist Caroline Hoxby has provided the most cogent analysis (Geiger, 2000a: 93–108; 2004c: 80–81; Hoxby, 1997; Hoxby and Long, 1999). Since 1950, U.S. higher education has experienced persistent geographical integration. As some institutions recruited more widely, stronger students gravitated toward colleges that spent more and offered better programs. This phenomenon caused increasing differentiation by academic ability – average student quality rose at stronger colleges and dropped at weaker ones. However, smart students are themselves an important input to educational quality because of their influence on peers. Thus, colleges with higher expenditures received an additional boost to academic quality from the increased quality of their students. Hoxby documented these developments with abundant data. For students, seeking a selective high-spending college paid off in an apparently superior education and greater career earnings. For institutions, higher expenditures attracted better students, yielded superior educational results, and boosted prestige.

Neither students nor university leaders read Hoxby's academic studies, but they act as if they had. From 1985 to 2005 the number of first-year applicants to the Ivy League rose from 90,000 to 155,000. The average combined SAT scores of matriculants increased by 100 or more points. The Ivies – and other elite private colleges and universities – operated in a virtuous cycle where increased revenues and expenditures produced higher quality, greater prestige, more and better applicants, and increased revenues and expenditures.... Critics likened this to an arms race that demanded ever greater spending and where unilateral disarmament was impossible. Seen from within the institutions, these consequences took some time to develop.

Despite the favorable trends just noted, the Ivies felt that they were struggling for much of this period. At Yale, financial improvements were not sufficient to avoid severe budgetary strains stretching into the early 1990s, when the closing of departments was seriously considered. Both Yale and Princeton were unhappy with admissions and particularly sought to raise their "yield rate" – the percentage of admitted students who matriculated (Karabel, 2005: 514–535). Affluent by any reasonable standard, they judged their status by their own tiny reference group. There, Harvard was indubitably superior in just about every meaningful category. And now Stanford had risen to the level of the Big Three, able to compete as well or better in these same contests. In the face of these severe standards Yale, Princeton, and the rest of the Ivies found much cause for worry as late as the mid-1990s.

Financial uncertainties seem to have led to a de-emphasis of externally funded research. Elite private universities remained committed to high quality in their scientific departments, but were reluctant to expand faculty or facilities to match the growing volume of research funding. All the Ivies (save Dartmouth, initially the smallest performer) had a smaller share of academic research in 2000 than in 1980 (Geiger, 2004c: 155–159, Appendix B). This trend did not affect medical research, which is remote from undergraduate colleges and depends almost wholly on NIH funds. The outlook for federal support for academic research was dismal during the early and mid-nineties. In these years Penn may have been alone in assuming an aggressive posture toward research. Only at the end of the decade did the Ivies and other private universities realize that substantial investments were needed to keep abreast of, let alone maintain distinction in, the revolutionary advances taking place across scientific fields. By then, the favorable financial tendencies generated by differential pricing and the selectivity sweepstakes seemed to coalesce into an unanticipated financial gusher.

From 1995 onward the economy moved steadily upward, and the financial markets, in "irrational exuberance," soared. This enormous creation of wealth benefited, above all, holders of financial assets, including endowed universities. The Ivies, and elite private institutions generally, were triple winners: donations poured in from well-off alumni in ever increasing sums; endowments grew with the general rise of financial markets; and, through the employ of sophisticated money management, their endowments grew faster than the market in good times and declined less in bad ones. In 1993 the endowments of all eight Ivies totaled $18 billion; in 2007 Harvard and Yale each surpassed that figure, and the Ivy total was $81 billion.

The Stewardship of Wealth

The great good fortune of the Ivies has been accompanied by mounting criticism and increased scrutiny. Harvard has been accused of being a hedge fund, and Congress has threatened to impose spending rules on university endowments, like those previously imposed on foundations. Harvard responded to these pressures in 2007 by offering more generous student aid packages, eliminating tuition for students with family income below $60,000 and reducing it for families earning up to $180,000. Yale announced voluntary guidelines for spending a larger percentage of its endowment, hoping to ward off a government mandate. And the other Ivies (and elite competitors) have fallen in line. For institutions in the public sphere, being very rich carries a heavy responsibility to use that bounty in ways that are consistent with the public good. But even the public can seldom agree on what contributes to the public good.

Indeed, the embarrassing success of their financial model has incited a kind of hostile envy. Although the Ivies, given their current secure positions, might wish to exhibit social responsibility, such steps as strengthening departments by hiring star professors or luring exceptional middle-class students are lambasted in the media as unfair and detrimental competition for less fortunate institutions, particularly the public sector (and even *Business Week* finds this wealth disturbing – November 29 2007). Yet, the ways the Ivies have chosen to spend their surplus wealth probably poses the greatest danger to the delicate balance of the stressed admissions system that undergirds their prosperity.

Which students deserve to benefit from the abundant resources that Ivy colleges now offer is a perplexing question. Here the zero-sum era has degenerated into political gridlock. A former admissions officer testifies:

> the pressures on the admission office from various special interest groups ... faculty, alumni, coaches, parents, school principals and headmasters ... all [lobby] against each other in competition for a set number of places.... [E]ven a slight dip in one year brings a kind of pressure that pushes up that measurable item the next year at the probable expense of some other variable.
>
> (as quoted in Karabel, 2005: 545)

The political clout of these groups weighs heavily on the admissions policy and only encourages additional groups to mobilize, as Asian-Americans did in the 1980s to overcome glaring under-representation. This struggle has exacerbated the paradox noted earlier, whereby the more selective admissions becomes, the more it relies on personal rather than academic factors. When Princeton announced that it would increase enrollment in the college by 500, it argued that this would *raise* the academic qualifications of incoming classes

– a confession that its preoccupation with tagged groups was forcing it to pass over a good deal of academic talent.

There is no consensus over a socially optimal approach to elite college admissions, or even what difference it makes. Do graduates of these schools possess advantages in terms of career advancement, earnings, and future leadership positions? The schools believe and act as if they do. Social scientists have taken great interest in this question. The preponderance of research indicates that these advantages are real, although it is less clear why that is the case. It is difficult to determine to what extent advantage is due to admissions offices selecting students for personal traits conducive to future success, to the influence of talented peers, to integration into social networks forged through the school, or to the provision of a superior education. Probably all these factors play a role, but the first three depend critically on who is admitted to study at these schools (Soares, 2007: 129–135). However, this situation presents a policy dilemma: if the selection process favors students from privileged classes who also achieve superior personal performance, altering the admission process to reduce their presence would diminish the very advantages that were intended to be redistributed.

Still, the current admissions regime has many drawbacks. The sheer energy and resources consumed by this process have become excessive, including large marketing expenditures by institutions and an industry of college consultants to coach affluent students. All this generates great anxiety among prospective students and their parents, in addition to unnatural behavior to gain comparative advantage. The technical details of the process have become the object of heated controversy over their impact on particular constituencies, with early, binding admission being the latest example. Furthermore, the admissions process is the principal driver of the arms race (Geiger, 2004c: 115–131).[10]

The present system is clearly a problem for institutions, both in crafting a class and in confronting the pressures from their constituencies. Karabel concludes that these institutions (namely, HYP) have scaled back their deference toward old elites in favor of expanding participation of newer social elites. The sons and daughters of professors are now nearly as numerous as the children of business people. But this still leaves these institutions overwhelmingly populated by affluent students and those possessing an abundance of cultural capital. What seem like sensible correctives to critics do not appear feasible to university leaders. Diminishing the number of athletes or reducing further the acceptance of alumni children, as Karabel and Soares recommend, would irritate groups (no longer just old Eastern money) that have generously supported these institutions. Affirmative action for middle-class students carries huge problems of selection, as well as colliding with the zero-sum conundrum. De-escalating the demands of the admissions process scarcely seems possible given the high stakes that prospective students and their parents believe to be riding on these decisions (Karabel, 2005: 550–555; Soares, 2007: 196–201).

Moreover, the steps taken to spend more of their wealth and improve their public image – namely, eliminating tuition for middle-income students – may exacerbate the problem. What high-achieving student would not jump at the chance for a free Ivy League education? Or one costing less than a state university? But the last thing these institutions need is more highly qualified applicants. The crush of applications that is sure to follow is likely to spawn unwelcome consequences. For the Ivy universities (and few outsiders would sympathize with them) the zero-sum gridlock of appeasing the tagged groups will become that much more difficult in the face of additional, academically superior applicants; and the resulting disparity between the two groups of students may widen. Actual admissions decisions, faced with the impossibility of discriminating on academic ability, will become even more driven by personal characteristics. As the Ivies claim more top students, the screening value of admission is likely to increase more than the intrinsic educational value. And, the perceived advantage of elite institutions will become more exaggerated, with negative implications for American democracy. Of course, actual consequences will depend on who is chosen among the throngs of additional applicants, but by offering powerful inducements to well-off families the new schemes are ill-suited to alter the socio-economic skew.[11]

Perhaps a different approach would be more consistent with the stewardship of wealth. Making their ample resources available to greater numbers of people would be a clearer path to serving the public good. One way in which the Ivies have been doing this is through increased investments in the advancement of knowledge. One of Yale's first initiatives with its burgeoning endowment was to commit $1 billion to bolster research equally on its medical and regular campuses. Yale has also exerted leadership in stimulating the growth of the biotech industry in and around New Haven. Penn too has combined expansion of its research capacity with community development in Philadelphia. Investing in science at this juncture means participating in the revolutionary transformation of fields like biotechnology and nanotechnology, which require major investments in interdisciplinary institutes and related infrastructure. Harvard also committed to this kind of investment in planning for a new campus at nearby Alston. After a global inquiry, it identified thirteen cross-disciplinary areas of emphasis (Geiger and Sá, 2008: chapter 5). From 1998 to 2005 the Ivies slightly increased their share of total academic research, although HYP continued to shrink (Table 16.1). Conspicuous gainers were Penn, Columbia, and Dartmouth.[12]

A more radical way to enhance the public good would be to increase enrollments. Until now, the Ivies have basically pursued a strategy of concentrating increasing resources on each student. The marginal benefits of this approach long ago surpassed any reasonable rate of return, and must now

Table 16.1 Ivy League Data

	Undergrad Enrollment ('06)	Freshman Applicants ('06)	Acceptance Rate ('06)	SAT 25%–75% Range ('06)	US News Rank ('07)	Endowment ('07) 000's	Graduate & Professional Enrollment ('06)	Research Expenditures ('05) 000's	Research Share ('06)	NRC Ratings ('95)
Brown	6,010	18,316	13.80%	1,350–1,530	14	$2,166,633	2,115	$138,203	0.33	3.52
Columbia	7,318	14,665	11.21%	1,330–1,540	9	$5,937,814	14,999	$535,424	1.11	4.08
Cornell	13,562	28,098	24.70%	1,280–1,490	12	$4,321,199	6,077	$606,804	1.36	4.15
Dartmouth	4,085	13,938	15.70%	1,350–1,550	11	$3,092,100	1,668	$179,094	0.42	2.95
Harvard	9,968	22,645	8.90%	1,390–1,590	2	$28,915,706	15,810	$447,196	0.95	4.6
Princeton	4,790	17,564	10.20%	1,370–1,590	1	$13,044,900	2,295	$202,380	0.39	4.35
Pennsylvania	11,922	20,483	17.60%	1,330–1,530	5	$5,313,268	11,821	$654,982	1.42	3.89
Yale	5,332	19,451	9.70%	1,390–1,580	3	$18,030,600	6,083	$431,618	0.96N	4.28

Notes

Author created from Integrated Postsecondary Education Data System; US News and World Report; National Science Foundation; The Chronicle of Higher Education, Almanac Issue, 2007–2008.

have diminished to the vanishing point. A greater social return would be achieved by making their abundant assets available to greater numbers of students. Princeton took a step in this direction when it committed to add an additional 500 students, although, characteristically, it did so entirely on the basis of internal considerations. A significant enlargement of undergraduate enrollments would benefit society by allowing more students to enjoy a high-cost, subsidized educational experience. It would alleviate at least some of the pressure on the zero-sum gridlock; and it would make it easier for these institutions to add social diversity to their predominately affluent clientele.

Increasing enrollment would also cause consternation across the selective sector of higher education: every additional blue-chip recruit drawn to the Ivies would be one less for their competitors. But the same growth logic is even more compelling when applied to the entire selective sector. Expanding and diversifying is costly, high-quality higher education should benefit American society by making more of these places available to low- and middle-income students. True leadership would be required to break the current tacit rules and to move higher education toward this goal. Is such leadership possible from the institutions that claim to educate American leaders? In the past, a combination of vision and institutional interest has occasionally moved these institutions to break with tradition and launch significant reforms. Today, however, a myopic preoccupation with inter-Ivy competition and a comfortable affluence make it unlikely that the Ivies are capable of challenging the current regime.

Acknowledgments

I would like to thank Bruce Leslie, Ted Tapper, and Pat Terenzini for helpful comments.

Notes

1. The Ivy League is officially known as the Council of the Ivy Group Presidents and has offices at Princeton University.
2. Today one can identify a comparable group of non-Ivy elite private universities: Stanford is considered a peer of HYP; Chicago, MIT, and Caltech are at the pinnacle of academic distinction; Duke, Northwestern, Washington University, and Johns Hopkins fall within the Ivy distribution of academic excellence and US News & World Report rankings. It should be noted that comparable forms of excellence can be found in the leading state universities and, for undergraduate education, a similar number of liberal arts colleges.
3. In 2004, President George W. Bush defeated fellow Yale grad John Kerry, after besting Harvard grad Al Gore in 2000. Since 1980, a Yale grad has been on the presidential ticket in every election. The only family repeats to hold the presidency are graduates of Harvard (John Adams/John Quincy Adams; Theodore Roosevelt/Franklin D. Roosevelt) and Yale (George Herbert Walker Bush/George W. Bush).
4. These attitudes included anglophile envy of Oxbridge: Anthony Trollope flattered Harvardians in 1862 by noting that Harvard "is to Massachusetts ... what Cambridge and Oxford are to England. It is the ... University which gives the highest education to be attained by the highest classes in that country": quoted in Story (1980: 133).
5. The others: Chicago, Stanford, Johns Hopkins, and the public universities of California,

Michigan, Wisconsin, Minnesota, and Illinois. These are the same institutions featured by Laurence Veysey, *Emergence of the American University* (Chicago: University of Chicago Press, 1965).

6. Trow, surveying postwar Europe, placed the tipping point between elite and mass higher education at a 15 percent participation rate, the level reached in the U.S. in 1940. However, the characteristics of mass higher education appeared in the 1920s in urban universities with part-time students, teachers colleges and junior colleges: David O. Levine, *The American College and the Culture of Aspiration* (Ithaca, NY: Cornell University Press, 1986).

7. The discussion of admissions that follows is indebted to these studies. HYP and the other Ivies found different ways to do the same things when it came to admissions, hence the examples from individual institutions represent general practices.

8. Harvard reported in 2007 that one-half of its undergraduates came from families earning more than $180,000 per year, roughly the top 5 percent of incomes.

9. In 1987, HYP ranked after Stanford (#2, 3, 4); Dartmouth was #6, Brown #10, Cornell #11, Columbia #18, and Penn #19: *U.S. News & World Report* (October 26, 1987: 53). See Table 16.1 for current rankings.

10. These liabilities have been exacerbated by stupid public policy. For decades the most selective eastern institutions, led by the Ivies, met to compare admissions decisions in what was known as the Overlap Group. The purpose of the group was to maintain a common need-blind policy for financial aid and avoid competitive bidding for students that would drive up costs and distort student decisions. In 1991 the federal government sued the Overlap Group under the Sherman Antitrust Act, and the group dissolved. This action destroyed the only means for collective action on admissions, and with it any hope for dealing effectively with tuition escalation and the arms race.

11. Harvard extended free tuition from families earning $40,000 to $60,000. For the 35 percent of families earning $60,000–120,000, Harvard will now be less expensive than a state university; for the 10 percent of families in the $120,000–180,000 tranche, Harvard will be less expensive than most private institutions. See Donald E. Heller, "How Harvard Foils Its Own Good Intentions," *Chronicle of Higher Education: Today's News* (December 17, 2008).

12. Generally, the Ivies strive for academic excellence rather than volume of research, but in biomedical fields, which encompass much of the Ivies' research, quality and quantity reinforce one another.

References

Axtell, James (2006) *The Making of Princeton University: from Woodrow Wilson to the Present* (Princeton: Princeton University Press).

Bernstein, Mark K. (2001) *Football: the Ivy League Origins of an American Obsession* (Philadelphia: University of Pennsylvania Press).

Bix, Amy Sue (1993) "Backing into Sponsored Research: Physics and Engineering at Princeton University, 1945–1970," *History of Higher Education Annual*, 13: 9–52.

Business Week (2007) "The Dangerous Wealth of the Ivy League," November 29.

Dobkin Hall, Peter (1984) *The Organization of American Culture, 1700-1900: Private Institutions, Elites and the Origins of American Nationality* (New York: New York University Press).

Dobkin Hall, Peter (2000) "Noah Porter Writ Large: Reflections on the Modernization of American Education and Its Critics, 1866–1916," in Roger L. Geiger (ed.), *The American College in the Nineteenth Century* (Nashville, TN: Vanderbilt University Press), 196–220.

Geiger, Roger L. (1984) "Reformation of the Colleges," in Peter Dobkin Hall (ed.), *The Organization of American Culture, 1700–1900: Private Institutions, Elites, and the Origins of American Nationality* (New York: New York University Press).

Geiger, Roger L. (2000) "The Reformation of the Colleges in the Early Republic, 1800–1820," History of Universities, 16, 2: 129–182.

Geiger, Roger L. (2000a) "Markets and History: Selective Admissions and American Higher Education Since 1950," *History of Higher Education Annual*, 20: 93–108.

Geiger, Roger L. (2004) *To Advance Knowledge: the Growth of American Research Universities, 1900–1940* (New Brunswick, NJ: Transaction Publishers).

Geiger, Roger L. (2004a), *Research and Relevant Knowledge: American Research Universities Since World War II* (New Brunswick, NJ: Transaction Publishers.

Geiger, Roger L. (2004b) "Market Coordination of Higher Education: the United States," in Pedro Teixeira et al., *Markets in Higher Education: Rhetoric or Reality?* (Boston: Kluwer), 161–84.

Geiger, Roger L. (2004c) *Knowledge and Money: Research Universities and the Paradox of the Marketplace* (Stanford: Stanford University Press).

Geiger, Roger L. & Creso Sá (2008) *Tapping the Riches of Science: Universities and the Promise of Economic Growth* (Cambridge, MA: Harvard University Press).

Heller, Donald E. (2007) "How Harvard Foils Its Own Good Intentions," *Chronicle of Higher Education: Today's News*, December 17.

Hoxby, Caroline M. (1997) "The Changing Market Structure of U.S. Higher Education," Harvard University, mimeo.

Hoxby, Caroline M. and Bridget Terry Long (1999) "Explaining Rising Income and Wage Inequality among the College Educated," *NBER Working Paper 6873.*

Karabel, Jerome (2005) *The Chosen: The Hidden History of Admissions and Exclusion at Harvard, Yale and Princeton* (Boston: Houghton Mifflin).

Levesque, George (2007) "Noah Porter Revisited," *Perspectives on the History of Higher Education,* 26: 29–66.

Levine, David O. (1986) *The American College and the Culture of Aspiration* (Ithaca, NY: Cornell University Press).

McCaughey, Robert A. (2003) *Stand Columbia: a History of Columbia University in the City of New York, 1754–2004* (New York: Columbia University Press).

Morison, Samuel Eliot (2003) *Three Centuries of Harvard* (Cambridge, MA: Harvard University Press).

Pierson, George W. (1969) *The Education of American Leaders: Comparative Contributions of U.S. Colleges and Universities* (New York: Praeger).

Slosson, Edwin E. (1910) *Great American Universities* (New York: Macmillan).

Soares, Joseph A. (2007) *The Power of Privilege: Yale and America's Elite Colleges* (Stanford: Stanford University Press).

Story, Ronald (1980) *The Forging of an Aristocracy: Harvard and the Boston Upper Class, 1800–1870* (Middletown, CN: Wesleyan University Press).

Synott, Marcia Graham (1979) *The Half-Opened Door: Discrimination and Admissions at Harvard, Yale, and Princeton, 1900–1970* (Westport, CN: Greenwood Press).

Trow, Martin A. (1973) *Problems in the Transition from Elite to Mass Higher Education* (New York: Carnegie Commission on Higher Education).

Veysey, Laurence (1965) *The Emergence of the American University* (Chicago: University of Chicago Press).

Wechsler, Harold (1977) *The Qualified Student: A History of Selective Admissions in America* (New York: Wiley).

Widmayer, Charles E. (1977) *Hopkins of Dartmouth* (Hanover, NH: University Press of New England).

17
Oxbridge
Sustaining the International Reputation

Ted Tapper and David Palfreyman

Introduction: the Oxbridge Conundrum

A limited number of national groupings of higher education institutions have a brand name that conveys an image of international excellence: the Sandstones of Australia, the *grandes écoles* of France, the US Ivy League, the former Imperial universities of Japan, and Oxbridge. The historical link between the University of Oxford and the University of Cambridge is their collegiate identity. Whatever else may divide them it is this core characteristic that continues to bind them together.

However, any analysis of the reputation of higher education institutions quickly runs into the problem of separating out cause and effect. Thus Sheldon Rothblatt has written: 'It is difficult to imagine the success of Oxford and Cambridge without the beauty of buildings and gardens' (Rothblatt, 2007: 69); and he reinforces the point with reference to the uplifting locations of several continental and American elite institutions. But does the architectural beauty and gracious spaces contribute to success? Or are they rather manifestations of that success? Thus elite universities take steps to ensure that they project a positive aura. Indeed so much of the architecture and manicuring of Oxford and Cambridge is dependent upon their identity as collegiate universities. There is a protective looking-inwards to secure privacy and solace as well as to enhance esteem. These are as much ways of preserving a valued self-image as projecting an aura to enchant the outside world.

The analytical problem is that almost everything associated with the collegiate universities can be seen as contributing to Oxbridge's success: buildings, gardens, polite porters with ties if not uniforms and bowler-hats, relatively easy access to London, civilized dining, the great age of many colleges, and – perhaps more plausibly – additional financial resources (generous founders, grateful alumni and, for a long time, a deferential state). And, from the perspective of the universities it is hopefully a spiralling interactive process: success begets tangible benefits that buttresses success, which ensures more largesse, and so on.

This chapter is constructed around the proposition that historically Oxbridge's pre-eminence has depended essentially upon the relationship it has forged with state and society. It is Oxbridge's continuing ability to make itself indispensable to the dominant interests in state and society that accounts for its elevated status in the higher education hierarchy – it has always been at the apex of 'the pyramid of prestige' to use Halsey's evocative phrase (Halsey, 1961). Although the central proposition around which this chapter is structured provides more of an organizational framework for the empirical evidence than a theory of institutional dominance, it represents an attempt to move the analysis of developments in higher education beyond the descriptive level in which they are invariably trapped.

The changing relationship between Oxbridge and the dominant interests in state and society has gone successively through three broad stages: Oxbridge as part of a network of interacting institutional interests (the cement binding 'church and state'), Oxbridge and the reproduction of class interests and national culture, and Oxbridge at the leading edge of the production of world-class research. The chapter will conclude by analysing Oxbridge's position within the contemporary system of British higher education as well as by reflecting upon what future there is for the idea of collegiality given the dominance of the research imperative.

Oxbridge: The Changing Relationship to State and Society

From Institutional Symbiosis to Class Reproduction

Prior to the latter half of the nineteenth century, for many undergraduates Oxbridge was little more than a finishing school, part of the rite of passage for those of a certain class. It was an experience in character formation with subsequent careers dependent more on class background (assuming the role of a country gentlemen) and patronage (the army, the navy, a political career and service to the state – with the colonies providing outdoor relief for the less exalted members of the upper class) than acquiring a degree. Oxbridge was important less for the quality of the educational experience it had to offer and more because it was part of the structure of elite national institutions and social networks. It was enmeshed in the fabric that bound those institutions together, reinforcing those social networks already created by the great public schools. Historically, successfully completing the degree program was essential for those who wanted to enter the church (Curthoys notes that before 1850 three-quarters of those graduating from Oxford and Cambridge entered holy orders – 1997: 482) but for few other careers.

This is a world that was steadily eroded by economic forces (the creation and expansion of the nation's manufacturing base), political change (the tentative steps towards establishing a democratic polity and the growth of the central state) accompanied by social and occupational evolution (the decline in influence of the established Church, the emergence of the proletariat and the expansion of the bourgeoisie). It took political intervention, by way of royal commissions in the 1850s and 1870s, to lever Oxbridge into the nineteenth century, and there is little doubt that if there had not been a positive, if belated, response to the expanding interests in society then Oxbridge's national influence would have slowly withered on the vine. But once the response had been made then an Oxbridge education was extremely attractive to the burgeoning ranks of the bourgeoisie. There was the traditional allure of an Oxbridge education (its national reputation and the highly valued experience of residence in college – so significant in English eyes) but without the perception of its entrapment in institutions that were wedded irrevocably to the declining interests of the past. The challenge posed by the emerging civic universities (and for medical education, the Scottish universities) could be repulsed. Indeed, as Barnes notes, two approaches to professional education could co-exist,

> ...one that was connected with the national elites of politics, administrations, business, and the liberal professions and designed to mould character, the other aimed at providing the provincial middle class with utilitarian training in preparation for careers in the newer technological and professional occupations....
>
> (Barnes, 1996: 289–290)

But if this can be described as a bourgeois revolution then it was a revolution with an exceedingly long fuse. The gilded youth did not disappear overnight, the established career paths changed but slowly, and then there was the alleged antipathy of Oxbridge graduates to employment in the expanding manufacturing industries (a dominant theme in the work of both Barnett, 1972 and 1986, and Wiener, 1986, which receives some support from the careful scholarship of Rothblatt, 1968; Coleman, 1973; and Perkin, 1989). Patronage may have been in terminable decline but few professions established access routes suggesting that these were careers 'open to all the talents'. Moreover, some career avenues even in terms of public service remained more inaccessible than others. Rothblatt refers to the Foreign Office and the Diplomatic Corps as 'closed preserves' (1968: 161). Moreover, the significance of family background did not disappear overnight, for some professions required would-be entrants to pay a financial premium to secure access and paid salaries that were initially little more than a pittance (Curthoys and Howarth, 2000: 292–295). But what did change was the importance of a university degree. It was scarcely worth one's while studying for the new Cambridge Natural Science Tripos (Macleod and Moseley, 1980) with the intention of becoming an industrial chemist and then failing to complete the course.

Therefore entry into the professions required the appropriate qualifications whilst the civil service (with perhaps the Indian Civil Service providing the best example) began to impose competitive entrance examinations. However, the changes are suggestive of an accommodation of values strongly influenced by Oxbridge's collegiate traditions. While expertise became more important it was the cultivated man, rather than the narrowly trained expert, who replaced the traditional gentleman. In the nineteenth century struggles for the soul of Oxbridge – embracing Newman, Pattison and Jowett – it was Jowett who triumphed (Halsey, 1992: 27–33). This critical process of change in the latter half of the nineteenth century, so stylishly traced by Rothblatt for Cambridge (1968) and Engel for Oxford (1983), was crucial to the regeneration of both Oxford and Cambridge. The contention is that this distinctive cultural style, stressing public service over entrepreneurialism, facilitated access to key leadership roles in Britain (and thus the critiques of Wiener and Barnett). A new model of the gentlemen is created – '...efficient, responsible Christian gentlemen rather than effete aristocratic rakes and loungers' (Perkin, 1989: 367).

Whilst in recent years Oxbridge has undoubtedly been more heavily criticized for its failure to remove the barriers to access than for any of its other supposed shortcomings, this has not been a threat to its reputation until comparatively recently. Indeed, it could be argued that until around 1945 the access barriers were either irrelevant in the determination of status, or even helped to enhance it. The evolution in the basis of Oxbridge's national reputation was dependent upon a prolonged shift from its enmeshment in a network of interests bound together by patronage in which the broadly defined educational experience (besides the creation of Cambridge's Natural Science Tripos there is also the example of Oxford's Philosophy, Politics and Economics – PPE – degree) tied it into the promotion of bourgeois interests. Moreover, given the considerable growth of the private sector of schooling in the later half of the nineteenth century (with the links to Oxbridge reinforced by the fact that dons became schoolmasters and vice versa), it is scarcely surprising to discover that the scholarship systems and access routes of the two universities were closely linked to the interests of the private schools, and thus of their clientele. Indeed, it has been argued that the nineteenth-century reform of the scholarship system of the private schools in fact undermined the educational opportunities of 'poor and needy' pupils (Tapper, 1997: 28–53).

There were closed scholarships to Oxbridge colleges many of which were restricted to the pupils of named fee-paying schools; invariably, open scholarships were such that it was impossible to contemplate winning one unless one had been educated privately; and the entrance process was controlled by the colleges, whose procedures would have loomed as a minefield to the uninitiated. And then there were the college interviews (allegedly a context for the exchange of social and cultural capital) with some preparing to follow in their fathers' footsteps, whilst others were entering alien territory. The strength of the links between Oxbridge and class interests were self-evident.

In his angrily perceptive *The University in Ruins*, Readings (1996) has argued that until comparatively recently the primary purpose of universities, as powerful national institutions, was to embellish and sustain national culture. However, what Oxbridge achieved was the steady fusion of two different class cultures to create not so much a new national culture but rather a cultural style (including core values) that cut across class boundaries (the upper class and the more elevated ranks of the middle class), which shaped distinctive individual cultural mores for the most powerful members of society.

The Triumph of Meritocratic Values and the Protection of Oxbridge's Elitism

Post-1945 the challenge to Oxbridge's reputation has come not so much from the mobilization of excluded class interests (as in the nineteenth century) but rather from a combination of pressure from the state (which post-1945 underwrote almost all the costs of British higher education, although some of the Oxbridge colleges continued to have considerable independent financial resources), accompanied by a steady realignment of the central purposes of the two universities. A critical part of the story has been the drive to make meritocratic values central to the functioning of British higher education with the issue of undergraduate access generating the most intense value conflict. Thus the widening participation agenda was set in train, which has found its sharpest challenge in the exclusion of the white, English working-class from higher education generally and from the elite universities in particular.

Although the pressure for widening participation may have been driven by the state, it was the demography of admissions that first placed access firmly on the political agenda. And it was demography that impacted upon the interests of the middle class as well as stimulating those political forces that were concerned at the gross under-representation of students from working-class families. The University of Oxford's Franks Commission noted that: 'Before 1945 admissions presented no particular problem for Oxford or for any other British university; but the increase in the number of those wanting a university education has changed the picture' (University of Oxford, 1966: 65). And in evidence to the Commission a potent personal reflection from Sir Maurice Bowra, the then Warden of Wadham College, revealed: 'Until 1945 suitable entries seldom exceeded the actual places available. The colleges, with very few exceptions, took almost anyone who was thought good enough to get some sort of degree and able to pay his way' (University of Oxford, 1965, Part 1V: 17). The implication of Bowra's observation is that Oxford (and there is no reason to presuppose that Cambridge was very different) provided a relatively undemanding means of securing or sustaining middle-class status as long as you possessed the requisite financial means and you were considered able 'to get some sort of degree'! Once demand for places exceeded supply then the situation changed dramatically. The Pandora's admissions box was opened and the annual scrutiny of who was admitted (and, even more point-edly, who was excluded) began in earnest. An elite higher education was widely perceived as the route to securing and sustaining middle-class status in a society supposedly increasingly dominated by meritocratic values.

In this context it was to be expected that entry routes enabling privileged access to particular social groups (mainly students who had been privately educated) would come under pressure, and we have seen the demise of closed scholarships, of open entrance scholarships and of college examinations, but not of interviews that are still used by some universities (or certain depart-ments within universities) that have an excess of supply over demand. But to match the procedural changes it was necessary to develop an ideological defence against the charge of persistent social bias in access. This has been found in the idea that entry is now determined by meritocratic criteria, which has meant constructing an appropriate definition of what constitutes merito-cratic entry and then measuring the extent to which it has been achieved. There is a range of evidence to suggest that in recent years there has been sub-stantial movement in the desired direction. Thus Halsey and McCrum held as 'good news' the fact that Oxford was moving towards accepting proportionate numbers of students educated either privately or in the state sector who had been awarded 30 points in their A-level examinations. They also noted that this state-sector deficit declined 'from 1994–1995 systematically in subsequent years', and was in the process of being eliminated (Halsey and McCrum, 2000: 23).

Of course the apparent declining discrimination against academically high-flying state school applicants does not negate the question of how meri-tocratic entry is to be measured. Do we compare, for example, state and pri-vately educated applicants and acceptances only after first controlling for the respective standards of pre-university entrance qualifications? However, besides providing a counter to external criticism of Oxbridge's entry proce-dures, the embracing of the meritocratic principle has the advantage of shift-ing the focus of attention for explaining why higher education, and the elite universities in particular, are socially unrepresentative. If increasingly it is less the fault of the universities (as they strive to remove discriminatory proce-dures and to increase their appeal to traditionally under-represented groups) then where does responsibility reside? It is now fashionable to direct attention elsewhere. Should not the widening participation agenda shift its focus because higher education institutions can scarcely be expected to compensate for failure at school? And, if there is little cultural support for higher educa-tion in certain social groups, what are the obligations of the universities to address this issue? What, therefore, is the appropriate point of intervention if inequality in access to higher education is to be effectively tackled?

But equally it is important to remember that academic merit is not a socially neutral possession. As Ball's *Class Strategies and the Education Market*

(2003: 88–92) argues the unequal access to social and cultural capital will impact upon the individual's struggle to secure academic capital. Thus if entry to elite higher education is to be dependent upon meritocratic criteria, defined essentially in academic terms, then the distribution of those who possess it will be socially skewed. This is a framework within which the more affluent and culturally aware members of society can work to secure their goals – the reproduction of their class status and its concomitant rewards. Moreover, they can do so in the knowledge that this is a highly realistic strategy given the regard in which leading companies still hold Oxbridge graduates.

The reforms of the nineteenth century enabled Oxbridge to respond to the changing societal context that kept the two universities in tune with established dominant class interests (there were claims well into the twentieth century that they had an obligation to educate the nation's future leaders regardless of their ability to profit in an academic sense from an Oxbridge education – see Curzon, 1909) as well as providing an education for the emerging bourgeoisie. There was a shift of values from ascription to merit (although, as Rothblatt noted, recruitment into the Foreign Office and Diplomatic Corp was slow to change), but money still counted in terms of university access and pursuing a professional career. What really changed was the importance of securing a degree within the context of a collegial environment that emphasized the values of service and manliness.

Since 1945 academic criteria have steadily become more significant in securing access, which besides helping to broaden somewhat the social base of Oxbridge has intensified the competition within the middle class for undergraduate places. Undoubtedly it is this broader spreading of middle-class entry into higher education (not all can hope to study at either Oxford or Cambridge) that has helped in part to account for the emergence of a stratum of universities (for example: Durham, Bristol, Exeter, York, Warwick, London School of Economics, Imperial College and University College London) that are considered to be particularly prestigious in England with respect to undergraduate education.

However, although meritocratic criteria have undoubtedly become more significant in determining both entry to Oxbridge and recruitment into the British establishment over time, it can be argued its impact has been more upon the mode of access rather than the social basis of recruitment. Today the meritocratic criteria engender genuinely fierce competition, whereas before 1945 (in spite of competitive entry into many public and professional posts) they were designed more to ensure that minimum standards should be met. However, no one should be deluded into believing that a level playing-field has been created in terms of class competition for limited places. But perhaps that is more of a problem for state and society at large than for the universities in particular.

Research: Higher Education as an Economic Resource

In a very powerful passage Rothblatt makes the following acute observation:

> When universities in Britain were essentially teaching institutions, the intellectual reputation of tutors, lecturers and professors was secondary. Universities were close to church and state in England or community in Scotland and suppliers of educated men for elite positions, but they were not national institutions with global commitments linked to every existing knowledge domain and vigorously creating new ones.
>
> (Rothblatt, 2007: 72)

Nonetheless, it should not be forgotten that embedded within both Oxford and Cambridge there have always been eminent scholars who have pushed back the boundaries of knowledge. Moreover, in spite of all the apparent commitment to undergraduate teaching (built around the highly esteemed tutorial – often seen as Oxbridge's 'jewel in the crown' – Tapper and Palfreyman, 2000: 96–124), the nineteenth-century 'revolution of the dons' gave the college don a part to play in the promotion of scholarship and research as well as establishing his role at the centre of teaching and examining. There was a keen desire to differentiate the college don from the schoolmaster as well as recognition of the potential drudgery of a role centered on teaching alone.

However, it is evident that the balance between the commitment to teaching and research in the responsibilities of the Oxbridge don has tilted steadily, even sharply in recent years, in favour of the latter. Contemporarily it is the research record of the two universities that gives them their world-class status and enhances their national reputations. Moreover, it should not be forgotten that the foundation of this research record owes much to annual public funding instigated in 1919. A reputation for high-quality teaching would at best impart little more than a local reputation, commanding the respect of your students, and perhaps fellow tutors. It may be gratifying to be remembered with affection by past students but this counts for little when it comes to establishing a powerful academic reputation. Moreover, promotion and the ability to move up the university pecking order are increasingly dependent upon the quality and depth of the individual's research. Research competence undoubtedly carries more weight than teaching quality in evaluating both individual and institutional reputations.

If Oxbridge, therefore, wanted to maintain its elevated reputation, both nationally and internationally, it had to move beyond the functions it performed in sustaining the dominant socio-cultural interests in Britain. Critically, the periodic assessment of research in British universities is not simply about the conferring of academic status but also a mechanism for the selective distribution of considerable sums of public money. Consequently, a record of high achievement leads to the acquisition of disproportionate resources that, if used intelligently, should enable the recipient institutions to enhance their reputations. Moreover, this has occurred in a context in which undergraduate student numbers have increased whilst the unit of resource (the teaching income per student received from the funding councils) was for some years in steady decline (Greenaway and Haynes, 2000).

In terms of the outcomes of the Research Assessment Exercises (RAEs – the periodic evaluation of university research outputs in the UK) the record is unequivocal. In a composite table of results from 1986 to 2002 Cambridge heads the list on each occasion with Oxford in second place in 1986, 1989 and 1992 and in third place in 1996 and 2001. The record is particularly impressive given the breadth of their 'knowledge domains', much more broadly based than several other high-ranking institutions such as the London School of Economics (LSE) and Imperial College (Shattock, 2003: 6). And the distribution of resources is consequently (and purposefully) very selective: 'It is clear that ... the vast majority of funds go to a small number of universities' (HEFCE, 2000: Annex E, 2), and '75 percent of HEFCE research funds went to 26 HEIs' (HEFCE, 2000: 15). Furthermore, within this select band the Universities of Oxford and Cambridge, in the company of two of London's colleges, Imperial and University, stand out.

There are two league tables (constructed by the Institute of Higher Education of China's Shanghai Jiao Tong University and *The Times Higher Education Supplement*) that claim to rank the world's leading universities. And, although not surprisingly, they have been subjected to considerable criticism (for the best reflective overview see Usher and Savino, 2006) they have also received enormous publicity. At the top end of both sets of tables there is a strong representation of US and British universities, with Oxford and Cambridge (even more so) accorded elevated rankings. In 2007 Cambridge, Oxford and Yale were ranked equal second (with Harvard University first) in the ranking list constructed by *The Times Higher Education Supplement*, while in 2006 Shanghai Jiao Tong's rankings put Cambridge second and Oxford in tenth place (with again Harvard in first place).

The Shanghai Jiao Tong's ranking list is almost exclusively dependent upon research reputation (as measured by alumni and/or staff who win Nobel Prizes or Field Medals, or are 'highly cited' researchers) and research output (published articles and listings in citation indexes – with the larger size, in comparison to Oxford, of Cambridge's scientific base giving it particular strength in the science citation index). Nonetheless, whilst *The Times Higher Education* rankings are constructed on a broader base (which may explain why British universities appear to perform better), research reputation/output (also relying on citation indexes) remains a critical input. Furthermore, one suspects that 'peer review' scores (which contribute the largest input, 40 percent, into the rankings) will also be strongly influenced by research reputations.

The historical basis of Oxford and Cambridge's reputations was dependent on their relationship to the dominant national interests, more specifically their links to the key institutions of state and society. As the socio-economic structure of Britain changed they became an indispensable part of the process of elite recruitment, proving themselves capable of sustaining this role within the post-1945 context of an ever more demanding interpretation of merito-cratic ideology. The current situation points to another critical shift: reputa-tion is now based on research output rather than the links between an Oxbridge undergraduate education and recruitment into the more elevated occupational ranks of state and society.

Although even a cursory analysis suggests that academic judgement plays a very significant role in determining reputations based on research, in the case of Britain's RAEs it is a process organized by the state (effectively under the control of the funding councils) and is not immune to direct government intervention. Moreover, the projected move towards a metrics assessment model after RAE 2008 will considerably lessen direct academic involvement in, and management of, the process. Furthermore, it is interesting to note the role that journalists have played in constructing league tables (Usher and Savino, 2006: 5–7), which suggests there is a broad public interest in the rela-tive status of higher education institutions. And, of course, in constructing the tables they have selected the criteria that in their eyes determine institu-tional status.

Significantly, the change reflects not so much the authority of the academy to define its own purposes but rather the widely shared political sentiment that research development is central to creating and sustaining an economy that can compete effectively in an increasingly global market. Whilst the selective allocation of research resources, via the RAEs, may have been led by a powerful science lobby intent on preserving the scientific infrastructure by concentrating it in the leading universities, the case was strongly reinforced by the claim that the nation needed a critical research mass if it were to remain at the cutting edge of research that led to technological and scientific development. And, not surprisingly, there has been a persistent effort to relate that development to the enhancement of the economic base. The stress with respect to teaching embraced the importance of the acquisition of transferable skills. Thus a sophisticated economy needed not so much – with certain key exceptions (technical and professional skills) – a nar-rowly trained labor force but one with the qualities that could be readily adapted to the needs of the labor market, including the ability to respond flexibly to economic change. In parallel fashion, although pure research was seen as highly prestigious, it was equally (if not more) important to translate research into enhancing commercial activities. Indeed, many universities engage in significant entrepreneurial ventures – including both Cambridge and Oxford – with much academic labor devoted to turning intellectual capital into commercial profit. Accompanying the expansion of research has been an inevitable shift in the balance of the student base – from undergraduates pursuing broad degree programs to postgraduates engaged in specialist research.

Primus Inter Pares

The shift from teaching to research in determining the reputation of Oxbridge is paralleled by an apparent decline in the relative importance of the two universities in steering entry into the highest status stratum of the labor market. Morley and Aynsley write, 'The hierarchy of opportunity in the labor market appeared to correspond to a highly stratified education sector', and that 'The long-term implications of these patterns could be a closer fit between social hierarchy, educational hierarchy and employment opportunities' (2007: 239, 247). But research by the Sutton Trust, whilst not contradicting this possibility, demonstrates that within the top-end of the 'highly stratified education sector' the potency of Oxbridge as the pathway to prestigious jobs has experienced a decline over the past twenty years (Blair, 2007: 34; Sutton Trust, 2007). In the context of a more broadly defined elite stratum of universities in the UK (that is, the Russell Group), this development is none too surprising. The demarcation of an elite higher education sector provides an opportunity for employers to look beyond Oxbridge in order to broaden their recruitment net without taking undue risks. Moreover, although there may be a relative decline in these terms of the impact of an Oxbridge education, it remains exceedingly influential.

Undoubtedly the move towards greater selectivity in the distribution of research resources (with selectivity more pronounced in England than in Scotland and Wales) benefited the public funding of Oxbridge. However, given that resource distribution is at stake, this is an issue that has generated considerable political tension. Few higher education institutions want to exclude themselves from the research assessment exercises regardless of the fact that they know the financial returns for the weaker research universities are paltry. Moderately successful departments argue that cuts in funding lessen their chances of improving their research output, thus allegedly undermining the expansion of research excellence nationally. And moves towards a funding model that would concentrate all research resources in a small number of institutions are regarded with anathema in most quarters (but perhaps not in those quarters that will ultimately determine the outcome of this struggle). Such a move would result in a very hierarchical model of higher education.

In a review of Rothblatt's *Education's Abiding Moral Dilemma*, which pits the values of the author against the values of the reviewer, Watson writes,

Finally, like Trow, he has no time at all for the work of the Dearing Committee (National Committee of Inquiry into Higher Education of 1997–1999), not least in its attempt to maintain a controlled and mutually respectful diversity within the UK system.

(Watson, 2007: 411)

Watson is implicitly supporting a structural model of the university system that has much in common with Halsey's 'pyramid of prestige': there will be institutional differences (but it will be a rather flat pyramid) and universities will be bound together by mutual respect or at least mutual interests as they seek to develop common policy fronts. But there is the possibility (for some the danger) that a diversified system of higher education would mean a hierarchical model with the institutions forming mutually exclusive prestige layers based on the fact that each served different purposes – stratification with a vengeance.

Currently the UK's model of higher education is changing quite rapidly but a reasonably shallow pyramid appears to be emerging with the development of soft and overlapping layers within the pyramid. The main divisions can be loosely associated with the three organizational groupings: the Russell Group, the 1994 Group and Campaigning for Mainstream Universities – CMU (which has recently rebranded itself as the Million+ Group). However, with the exception of Oxbridge and London's University and Imperial Colleges, few universities demonstrate research excellence (as measured by the Research Assessment Exercises) across a broad front with many higher education institutions containing a mix of both strong and weak research-oriented departments. But, at least as measured by the ranking lists constructed by *The Times Higher Education Supplement*, a number of British universities have reputations that put them towards the top of the world-class league table. And, as noted, a wider range of universities now appear to assist entry into the higher reaches of the British occupational structure.

Whilst the current model will undoubtedly evolve with the pyramid probably becoming steeper over time, it is difficult to imagine (given the current alignment of higher education and political interests) that a few institutions (or even just Oxford and Cambridge) will be able to detach themselves from the pyramid as self-contained elite institutions with at least pretensions of world-class status or that, alternatively, a stratum of detached 'sub-universities' will appear. The expansion of higher education through the creation of two-year Foundation degrees can be undertaken in the further education colleges rather than the universities, although a few are pursuing this opportunity. Such developments, certainly at the apex of the pyramid, require the development of stronger market forces, a more concentrated distribution of public funding (especially for research), and a more pronounced interlocking (formally and informally) of the internationally prestigious institutions of higher education. At present further shifts in the structure of the overall system are in abeyance. However, the fact that the CMU is reported to have renamed itself the Million+ Group because it wants the post-1992 universities to have a more effective and distinctive policy voice (Newman, 2007: 4), coupled with the impending review of student fee levels (2009), suggest that this is just a lull before institutional differentiation is further solidified.

Whither the Collegiate Universities?

Oxbridge remains a brand image of considerable repute, with the prestige of the two universities extending beyond the traditional boundaries of higher education (note the strength of their publishing houses and the immense prestige of the Oxford English Dictionary). Whilst it may be more accurate to describe their position as *primus inter pares* with reference to a comparatively small number of elite British universities, nonetheless they remain at the apex of Halsey's 'pyramid of prestige'.

But the retention of reputation does not come without a price. The historical prestige of Oxford and Cambridge was in part dependent upon the fact that they were collegiate universities. Whether residence in college, or college tutorials, had a significant causal impact upon sustaining Oxbridge's position in the network of elite national institutions or securing access to top jobs is debatable. However, what is not debatable is that the increasing dominance of research in determining national and global reputations has reshaped the collegial tradition within the two universities. Increasingly it appears that the universities rather than the colleges are the dynamic forces that will sustain Oxbridge's international reputation. This is not to say that the colleges are immune to, or unwelcoming of, change – including some incorporation of the research dynamic (although somewhat too tentatively in the eyes of some – Harrison, 2001), but the impression is more of colleges responding to change than initiating the process, a role which inevitably has been delegated to the universities as they grapple with the pressures of the state, and increasingly the market.

Thus one can see changes in the character of Oxbridge that are suggestive of a shift in the balance of power within both universities. University leadership is now more forceful and more prominent, the web of university administration is more extensive and pervasive, the state's intervention (research assessment, quality control and student fees) increases the leverage of the university juxtaposed to the colleges, and academic appointments in Oxford have come more under the control of the University (Soares, 1999: 216–218; 234–240). These developments occur within a context that weakens the traditional undergraduate teaching role of the colleges: the growth of postgraduate numbers, the expansion of a cadre of research fellows who are often on temporary or rolling contracts and have marginal collegial loyalties, academics who relate to their colleges pragmatically rather than out of a sense of loyalty, and tutors for whom their departments provide their most significant ties to the collegiate university and who, moreover, are more engaged by their research than their teaching. In effect the concept of collegiality is in the process of being redefined. It is not that it will disappear but the federal principle, which is at the heart of the collegial tradition (and especially its expression as a mode of governance), is under considerable pressure. Given that this may be the price Oxford and Cambridge must pay if they are to retain their positions as universities with world-class reputations, it could be worth paying. However, it is a moot point for how long Oxford and Cambridge can continue to be defined as collegiate universities if the internal balance of power moves inexorably in one direction.

Conclusion

Oxbridge has retained its reputation for excellence over time because of the way it has related to dominant societal interests, and as those interests have changed so Oxbridge has responded accordingly. To express the point in Harvie's terms, the sustaining of reputation is dependent upon the development of 'a new integration of university and society' (Harvie, 1997: 698). Whilst powerful social interests within British society intent on maintaining the privileges that have accompanied their status may still help to sustain Oxbridge's national reputation, its world-class brand name is now based on its burgeoning research reputation. It is this reputation that ensures the continuous presence of Oxbridge at the elevated end of the two world-class league tables that this chapter has drawn upon.

However, whilst the evidence continues to place Oxbridge at the top of the national pecking order there is no suggestion that they have broken away from the system of British higher education to form their own small, self-contained club. At both the national and international levels there are a number of British universities with powerful, and broadly based, research reputations. And, moreover, with respect to the facilitation of access to the highest status jobs, Oxbridge's potency appears to have declined somewhat. A comparatively small number of British institutions of higher education (with mixed identities) are becoming a more clearly identifiable elite stratum over time – not necessarily sharply separated from the stratum below but with distinctive characteristics.

Whilst the British model of higher education may not be rigidly stratified, at the international level what appears to be emerging is an elite stratum of universities that are beginning to form a separate 'world-class' league (Marginson, 2007). If this is the case then one would expect their closer interaction over time: the movement of students and faculty, co-operation in major research projects, the sharing of administrative expertise (including personnel transfer), and the creation of institutional links that result in regular formalized interaction to discuss matters such as the purposes, means and desired outcomes of higher education. The emerging culture would be constructed around the maintenance of a particular idea of the university with at its core an expanding endeavour to produce new research that could be translated into useful knowledge, accompanied by the training of students destined to occupy not simply the commanding heights of national institutions but also of those international and regional bodies that embrace politics, economics, and the key cultural organizations. And, not surprisingly, the world-class universities would be intent on ensuring their own replication by drawing predominantly from 'the brightest and the best' to be found within their own ranks.

In his justly famous *Science as a Vocation* (Gerth and Mills, 1948: 129–156), Weber pointed to three encroaching developments within the then system of German higher education: the increasing dominance of state funding and policy control, the bureaucratization of university governance, and the casualization of the academic workforce (academics as proletarians!). What this overview of Oxbridge's continuing pre-eminence points to is a more complex contemporary picture: the critical need to secure both state and market funding, the importance of retaining academics who are considered to be pre-eminent in their fields (although this may be accompanied by the expansion of faculty who have short-term contracts), and a real desire to sustain some of the values of the collegiate university that retains authority in the hands of the dons and resists the incorporation of 'outsiders' in the governance of either the universities or the colleges.

Whilst Oxbridge may have sustained its international reputation by responding to dominant national and international interests (with the state playing an important role in assisting that response through the nineteenth century commissions of enquiry and financial support for the expansion of the research infrastructure post-1918), it has also fought to maintain its own understanding of what gives it merit. Thus it has to accommodate pressure but is pro-active in determining how it will respond to that pressure, and whilst it reshapes its practices it attempts to retain what it considers to be of real value. And perhaps this is the true merit of its reputation and should remain so? Maassen and Stensaker (2005) have argued that when theorizing about change in higher education it is critical to look at the input of various institutional actors. The historical perspective developed in this chapter has been built around a broad structural approach to change in which the collegiate universities responded to the evolving demands of state and society. However, it should not be forgotten that the universities and their colleges were, and continue to be, far from passive actors in this process. They are not simply instruments either for politically determined policy agendas or service enterprises responding to the demands of competitive markets but, nonetheless, they ignore the dominant forces in state and society at their peril.

Thus the structural perspective of this chapter, which is broadly sympathetic to the line taken by Halsey and Harvie, needs to be related to the work of Perkin, Rothblatt and Barnes with their emphasis on institutional (and even individual) behaviour to give a more rounded understanding of how Oxbridge has sustained its reputation. While the process of change in higher education is undoubtedly complex, it is our contention that without being in tune with the dominant social, economic and political forces of the day both the institutional and individual inputs are doomed to failure.

References

Ball, S. (2003) *Class Strategies and the Education Market*, RoutledgeFalmer, London.

Barnes, S. (1996) 'England's Civic Universities and the Triumph of the Oxbridge Ideal', *History of Education Quarterly*, 36(3), 271–305.

Barnett, C. (1972) *The Collapse of British Power*, Eyre Methuen, London.

Barnett, C. (1986) *The Audit of War*, Macmillan, London.

Blair, A. (2007) 'Oxbridge losing its appeal as a finishing school for the elite', *The London Times*, June 28, 34.

Coleman, D.C. (1973) 'Gentlemen and Players', *Economic History Review*, Second Series, 26(1), 92–116.

Curthoys, M.C. (1997) 'The Careers of Oxford Men', in M.G. Brock and M.C. Curthoys (eds) *The History of the University of Oxford: Volume VI, Nineteenth Century Oxford, Part 1*, Clarendon Press, Oxford, 477–510.

Curthoys, M.C. and J. Howarth (2000) 'Origins and Destinations: The Social Mobility of Oxford Men and Women', in M.G. Brock and M.C. Curthoys (eds) *The History of the University of Oxford: Volume VI, Nineteenth Century Oxford, Part 2*, Clarendon Press, Oxford, 571–595.

Curzon, Lord (1909) *Principles and Methods of University Reform*, Clarendon Press, Oxford.

Engel, A. (1983) *From Clergyman to Don: The Rise of the Academic Profession in Nineteenth Century Oxford*, Clarendon Press, Oxford.

Gerth, H.H. and C. Wright Mills (1948) *From Max Weber: Essays in Sociology*, Routledge and Kegan Paul, London.

Greenaway, D. and M. Haynes (2000) *Funding Universities to Meet National and International Challenges*, The Russell Group, London.

Halsey, A.H. (1961) 'A Pyramid of Prestige', *Universities Quarterly*, 15(4), 341–345.

Halsey, A.H. (1992) *The Decline of Donnish Dominion*, Clarendon Press, Oxford.

Halsey, A.H. and N.G. McCrum (2000) 'The slow but certain arrival of equality at Oxford University', *The Times Higher Education Supplement*, November 17.

Harrison, B. (2001) 'Arts Research and the Colleges', *Oxford Magazine*, 188, 4–6.

Harvie, C. (1997) 'Reform and Expansion, 1854–1871', in M.G. Brock and M.C. Curthoys (eds) *The History of the University of Oxford: Volume VI, Nineteenth Century Oxford, Part 1*, Clarendon Press, Oxford, 697–730.

Higher Education Funding Council for England (2000) *Review of Research*, HEFCE, Bristol.

Maassen, P. and B. Stensaker (2005) 'The Black Box Revisited: The Relevance of Theory-Driven Research in the Field of Higher Education Studies', in I. Bleiklie and M. Henkel (eds) *Governing Knowledge: A Study of Continuity and Change in Higher Education: A Festschrift in Honour of Maurice Kogan*, Springer Press, Dordrecht, 213–226.

Macleod, R. and R. Moseley (1980) 'The 'Naturals' and Victorian Cambridge: reflections on the anatomy of an elite, 1851–1914', *Oxford Review of Education*, 6(2), 177–195.

Marginson, S. (2007) 'Higher Education in the Global Knowledge Economy', in *Social Change and University Development*, Beijing Forum Organizing Committee, Beijing, 110–146.

Morley, L. and S. Aynsley (2007) 'Employers, Quality and Standards in Higher Education: Shared Values and Vocabularies or Elitism and Inequality', *Higher Education Quarterly*, 61(3), 229–249.

Newman, M. (2007) 'Post-92 group heralds latest rebranding', *The Times Higher Education Supplement*, November 16.

Perkin, H. (1989) *The Rise of Professional Society: England since 1880*, Routledge, London.

Readings, B. (1996) *The University in Ruins*, Harvard University Press, Cambridge, MA.

Rothblatt, S. (1968) *The Revolution of the Dons*, Faber and Faber, London.

Rothblatt, S. (2007) *Education's Abiding Moral Dilemma: merit and worth in the cross-Atlantic democracies, 1800–2006*, Symposium Books, Oxford.

Shanghai Jiao Tong rankings (2006) http://ed.sjtu.edu.cn/rank2006/.

Shattock, M. (2003) *Managing Successful Universities*, Open University Press/SRHE, Maidenhead.

Soares, J. (1999) *The Decline of Privilege: the Modernization of Oxford University*, Stanford University Press, Stanford.

Sutton Trust (2007) http://www.suttontrust.com/news.asp#a038.

Tapper, T. (1997) *Fee-paying Schools and Educational Change in Britain*, Woburn Press, London.

Tapper, T. and D. Palfreyman (2000) *Oxford and the Decline of the Collegiate Tradition*, Woburn Press, London.

Times Higher Education Supplement (2007) 'World University Rankings', October 9.

University of Oxford (1965) *Commission of Inquiry, Evidence: Part IV*, Clarendon Press, Oxford.

University of Oxford (1966) *Report of Commission of Inquiry, Volume 1*, Clarendon Press, Oxford.

Usher, A. and M. Savino (2006) *A World of Difference: A Global Survey of University League Tables*, Educational Policy Institute, Toronto.

Watson, D. (2007) 'A review of Sheldon Rothblatt's Education's Abiding Moral Dilemma: merit and worth and the cross-Atlantic democracies, 1800–2006', *Higher Education Quarterly*, 61(3), 409–412.

Wiener, M.J. (1986) *English Culture and the Decline of the Industrial Spirit, 1850–1980*, Cambridge University Press, Cambridge.

18
Conclusion
Converging Systems of Higher Education?
Ted Tapper and David Palfreyman

Structural Adjustments to Mass Higher Education

This volume has documented – sometimes in very striking language – the issues that have been generated by the arrival of mass higher education. It is a development that has led to a range of tensions as established systems have been forced to come to terms with the new realities. These are tensions that demonstrate contrasting levels of concern. In nations with historically deeply ingrained and narrow interpretations of the meaning of higher education, there has been considerable public questioning of whether we are witnessing the expansion of higher education or its destruction (what remains truly 'higher' about higher education). If there is no choice but to follow the expansionist road because the pressures that drive it forth are overwhelming, then how are systems supposed to adjust? Do the established models simply expand and incorporate greater numbers? And, in the process do they sustain their established degree programs or create new programs of study? Or do they acquire different institutional layers that either compete or, at least informally, harmonize with one another? How are the costs of expansion to be underwritten and, if these fall upon the public purse, what are the appropriate accountability mechanisms? The funding issues inevitably bring us into the realm of institutional regulation. Should there be state regulation and, if so, what form should it take? Can market mechanisms be relied upon to ensure the provision of quality products at a fair price? How do the HEIs adjust to these pressures? What is their decision-making autonomy in the context of market and state pressure?

Besides documenting the emergence of these issues, the volume has also shown the complexity of the response pattern, not only in terms of differences in the national patterns but also in the oscillation of responses within individual countries and regions (coupled with the occasional attempt to produce politically expedient fudges). Moreover, it should not be forgotten that responsibility for higher education policy, like other areas of social policy, is often shared between levels of governance. In Germany, India, the United States and the Nordic countries, for example, one sees the pull of either local structures of governance and/or the push of regional socio-economic pressures. Indeed, it could be argued that in each of the countries and regions that make up this book, it is the national governments that are experiencing the greatest difficulty in sustaining their policy influence as their systems of higher education respond increasingly to global forces (it is possible to analyse higher education as a product that is increasingly traded in a global marketplace) or find their salvation in offering better services to their local communities.

Accepting the fact that it is dangerous to generalize about national and regional patterns of change what, nonetheless, have been the responses to the key issues driven by the pressures of rapid expansion? With respect to the value conflicts stimulated by expansion it is undoubtedly the United Kingdom, and particularly England, that has experienced the greatest self-doubts. It is not that there is widespread opposition to the expansion of education in England but rather whether all that is now on offer should be called higher education. The English embraced professional education in the universities, witnessed by the expansion of medical and legal education in the nineteenth century, but have been more loathe to accept the proposition that non-professional vocational training merits the label of higher education, so sustaining a distinction between liberal education and the vocational training of undergraduates.

But such peculiarly English qualms are either more muted, or non-existent, elsewhere. In France, for example, the *grandes écoles* incorporated a powerful applied science perspective (engineering courses as not only demanding but also intellectually rigorous) and similarly, few Americans question the merits of their great business schools. Thus the Netherlands, the Nordic countries, France, India and several Latin American countries have developed higher education structures which have the equivalent status of universities, with programs that can compete effectively for students. Of course, to some considerable extent the proliferation of the idea that higher education is both a valuable cultural and also a crucial economic resource gives rise to inexorable pressures for expansion that systems find it impossible to resist: it is almost a universal article of faith that the expansion of higher education is one of the key prerequisites of economic growth. It would seem ludicrous, given this perspective, to downgrade the significance of vocationally oriented courses that are geared to meet the labor demands of specific sectors of the economy. No government has been keener than successive British governments to push a widening participation agenda and also to persuade HEIs of the need to develop close contacts with industry. The call may be for diversity, that institutions should develop their particular strengths, but it is a diversity founded on the idea that higher education has key social and economic roles to fulfil and this is an obligation that has to be shared universally.

Structural differentiation has therefore been a critical dimension in the expansion of higher education; it is one of the key – if not *the* key – feature of contemporary systems of higher education. Moreover, it has been accompanied by a more generous understanding of the meaning of higher education: its purposes, who should be incorporated, how it is to be delivered, and its relationship to the wider society. The concept of the university as an ivory tower is long dead.

Although the bulk of the focus on structural change within the various case studies has been directed at the traditional, essentially state-funded, models of higher education, there have been repeated references to the emergence of new privately funded sectors in, for example, Central Europe, Latin America, India and even China. Moreover, these are not necessarily institutions designed to fulfil a public purpose (although they may do that) but rather they aim to be profit-making bodies. They are businesses, with, of course, their parallels in Western Europe and North America (with the University of Phoenix and Kaplan University aiming also to establish an international market), dependent upon their ability to attract sufficient student numbers (their clientele) who will pay the fees that they calculate will enable them to generate profits.

Although to date this may not be a major structural shift because of its comparatively limited scope, it does represent a significant challenge to the more traditional understandings of the purposes of higher education and those institutions responsible for its delivery. The United States, with its long history of a pluralist system of higher education mixing public and private funding and serving very diverse purposes, appears the natural home for such a development. However, within the United States the concern for diversity within higher education has not meant a desire to create a competitive profit-making sector but rather delivering social, economic and cultural goals. And at the prestige end of the market, the Ivy League universities would most definitely see themselves as fulfilling public purposes: providing high quality teaching, enhancing scholarship, promoting research and thereby serving, if indirectly, the community at large.

An accompanying radical structural shift, which has not been much reflected upon in the chapters, has been the provision of higher education outside the formally defined sector of higher education. Interestingly, it is the United Kingdom, which arguably has had one of the most clearly defined understandings of higher education, which provides perhaps the best example of this development. Thus links, often formal links, develop between institutions of higher education and further education colleges in which the latter act as feeder institutions for the former, which may well mean covering the initial year of a degree program. There is now also the prospect of two-year 'foundation degrees' modelled along the same lines but with the further possibility that companies will be granted degree-awarding powers in relation to their staff development programs. The obvious model for this has been the United States with its junior/community colleges linked in California to the state universities and the varying branches of the University of California, the so-called Master Plan.

There is a powerful body of academic opinion (we have drawn upon the work of Trow) holding that a mass system of higher education is only viable if it permits elite institutions to flourish within it. Thus in this model there is no contradiction between the concepts of elite and mass; the model is composed of mutually reinforcing segments. The elite institutions are supposedly only viable if there is also a thriving mass. The links between the segments (which effectively make up a pyramid of prestige regardless of the soothing ideological balm that may envelop it) are constructed out of the possible flow of students: from junior/community colleges to state universities to complete an undergraduate degree program, and then on to the University of California for post-doctoral research or professional training. But the world is never that simple as students compete to finish (even commence) their undergraduate degrees at the campuses of the University of California (especially the most prestigious at Berkeley or the University of California at Los Angeles – UCLA), and the state universities vie to construct graduate programs that will appeal to their own graduates and even attract some from other campuses. On paper it may appear a harmonious structural model but in reality it is marked by powerful underlying tensions.

The move in the United Kingdom towards developing higher education programs in colleges of further education was clearly part of the government's 'widening participation' agenda, that is to attract into higher education a broader social intake (meaning in the English context mainly – although not exclusively – more students from state schools, working class social backgrounds and from families with no prior experience of higher education). Thus it would seem to be an idealistic policy initiative to broaden the social base of access to higher education. While there is no intention of questioning the policy's good intentions, it is important to point out its structural implications. Higher education is expanding outside its traditional institutional base. It is not just a question of diversity but also one of differentiation. Moreover, it is a strategy that to some extent helps to protect further those universities where demand for places exceeds supply. Students with foundation degrees may be eligible to apply for any university place, but they are being directed towards those universities that run such programs or have formal links with colleges where they are in place.

The conundrum of the relationship between kinds of higher education institutions, which was so elegantly addressed in Sheldon Rothblatt's Foreword, has been a constant theme in most of the chapters in this book. The tension is particularly noticeable in the United Kingdom because of its traditionally narrower understanding of the idea of the university. Thus Scott, in his chapter on the United Kingdom, has argued in favour of a model embraced by shared values and purposes and, moreover, has claimed that, in spite of all the pressures to the contrary, the United Kingdom still retains the essential ingredients of this model. In their chapter examining the changing basis of Oxbridge's reputation, the volume editors have taken a more ambivalent position. They have argued that, while there is not an explicit hierarchical structure, there is institutional differentiation marked by both shared and contrasting purposes, different strategies of development, and contrasting relationships to state and society. Specifically with reference to the distribution of public resources for research (and most notably the sharing out of the research income of the funding councils), they describe Oxbridge's position as primus inter pares. And, of course, there are those who would argue that University College London (UCL) and Imperial College are on the same pedestal as Oxbridge. Similarly in the United States (see Roger Geiger's chapter), the Ivy League consists of eight institutions, but it should be remembered that there are both public and private institutions in the United States that would see themselves as belonging to the same elite club while still (especially if they are public institutions) in touch with the base.

It has proven impossible to consider the emergence of mass systems of higher education without analysing the input of two related variables: the governance of higher education and its funding. As predominantly state institutions (even if it should be the 'local' state as in Germany, India and the US), structural evolution is inevitably entwined in a political process. There is a general recognition, which has been a strong theme in the recent literature and reinforced by our authors, that states have sought to evolve new forms of governance in higher education. With respect to system governance the move has been from state control (with the perception of HEIs as part of the state apparatus) to state steering (which will be the central theme of the next volume of the series, which is edited by Jeroen Huisman). Consequently, responsibility for policy development has been downloaded to the institutional level with governments expecting much firmer institutional management, often under the direction of a governing body dominated by an internal leadership cadre working closely with prominent outsiders.

But, at least in terms of structural change (indeed with reference to all broad policy directions) whether these new patterns of institutional governance are very influential is debatable. The new structures in higher education and degree programs are effectively the product of state action, as seen in France, Norway, the Netherlands and Germany. Although the ideas for change may also emerge from below in response to the broad social pressures (in this case the increasing demand for higher education), policy implementation nevertheless still requires state intervention. The United Kingdom has experienced the publicly sanctioned movement from a binary model of higher education to a unitary model and, according to many observers, we are now witnessing the emergence of a carefully stratified unitary system thanks to government policy. Within the structural parameters institutions may adopt strategies that enable them to be more or less successful but it is success and failure inside a framework within which they have little choice but to function. Of course there is the possibility that institutions can declare independence from the state structures (by going private) but this is a high-risk strategy. It is one thing to sustain a private sector that already functions effectively, but quite another to create one from scratch. Risk is a mightily constraining break on radical innovation.

In a critical sense the arrival of mass higher education has in fact broadened the range of state intervention in the affairs of higher education, notwithstanding the general move from control to steering modes of governance. Expansion, especially when fuelled by state expenditure, has intensified accountability pressures. Is mass higher education, especially when embracing new programs and structures, capable of delivering quality? If the public purse underwrites expanding costs, what guarantees are there that the institutions are offering value for money? Thus quality assurance regimes have either emerged, or become part of the higher education discourse, from India to Latin America to Europe. The development of the European Higher Education Area (EHEA) has moved from schemes designed to encourage student and faculty interchanges, to the regulation of degree programs, to the consideration of quality assurance procedures. While the intrusion of the national state may be resisted and reshaped (as is certainly the case with respect to quality assurances procedures in the United Kingdom) the supranational state has started to exert its influence. And this is not a movement that has bypassed the United States, although the stimulus for concern may be not so much fears about the quality of higher education (the US adjusted to a mass system of higher education some decades ago) but rather its spiralling costs. While market choice may be effectively exercised at the point of entry into higher education, it can be difficult for the student to change institutional base (credit transfers notwithstanding) once in the system. Changing college is not like changing your automobile.

The most significant structural change resulting from the emergence of mass higher education, with a number of subtle ramifications, has been its impact upon funding. If the state was prepared to underwrite expansion with the same level of resources with which it had supported an elite system then one could expect that not a great deal would change. But with the possible exception of the Nordic countries, this has not been the case in terms of the national systems examined in this book. It has been argued that prior to the emergence of mass higher education there was a slack in the system and expansion could occur without significantly impacting upon the quality of provision. But over time as funding per student declined this was an increasingly difficult argument to sustain. The continental European models became more untenable as time passed, while the United Kingdom refused to confront seriously the issue of funding with governments deluding themselves that the supposed margin of slack could be whittled away by what were euphemistically called 'efficiency gains'. And there were always those higher education systems, both in Latin America and in India, which had to compete for scarce resources against the argument that expenditure on schooling was a more viable way of alleviating social difficulties and enhancing economic growth.

Although the movement towards charging students economic fees (fees that cover more than costs) has been tentative, with resistance particularly strong in countries such as France with traditions of open access and the embedded belief that students should not be required to pay fees, there has been a general shift in the direction of cost-sharing between student/family, and taxpayer/government. For most students their higher education remains highly subsidized but the wheels of change have been set in motion. Moreover, this has been coupled with the emergence of what Burton Clark has called 'the entrepreneurial university'; that is universities seeking to augment their resources through marketplace activities so shifting the relative balance of their state and market incomes. Clark draws his examples from England, the Netherlands, Scotland, Sweden and Finland. And our chapter on Japanese higher education provides powerful examples of the same cultural shift. The possibility arises, therefore, of HEIs possessing more resources to control their own development. Although located within structures that have been created by public policy, institutions can manoeuvre to create for themselves particular niche markets. Consequently, within the formal structures different institutional groupings emerge. In the United Kingdom, for example, there is considerable variation amongst both the 'traditional' universities and those acquiring the university label as a result of the 1992 Further and Higher Education Act, a variation that is expressed in both formal and informal links.

From Elite National to World-class Universities

This book has examined, within the context of the emergence of mass higher education, the fortunes of elite universities. There was an implied assumption (not altogether verified by the evidence) that rapid growth would inevitably lead to structural change and that elite universities, especially within systems underwritten mainly by public funding, would find it difficult to hang onto their reputations. We were aware that Trow had argued to the contrary, that elite institutions were protected by the wider expansion of higher education. It is almost as if expansion released a safety-valve, the increasing pressure for higher education could be met without providing a direct challenge to elite institutions. The elite institutions would expand but they could do so without having to change their values and practices. Naturally in numerical terms they would become a smaller part of their national systems, which – ironically – made them even more elitist institutions. But Trow's prognosis was developed in relation to US higher education with its mixture of private and public funding with the elite stratum in relative terms much more dependent upon private funding that the system as a whole. The question, therefore, is how widely applicable is Trow's prognosis?

Perhaps the most striking quality of the elite institutions of higher education is their proven ability to survive fundamental changes to the broader environments in which they are located. Following its cataclysmic defeat in World War II, Japan experienced massive political and cultural change and yet, as our chapter on Japanese higher education shows, the former Imperial universities (in spite of the formal termination of their status) remain some sixty years later at the very pinnacle of the national system. Although the time span in both cases is more limited, much the same can be said of the elite institutions in Poland and South Africa. Perhaps the South African case is the more surprising of the two given the close association of the elite universities with the interests of white South Africa (notwithstanding the fact that the universities were also predominantly liberal political centers opposed to the apartheid regime). With some of the oldest universities in Europe, the Polish universities were embedded in traditions that were not easily subverted by the post-1945 regime. More generally in Europe, the medieval foundations appear to have sustained their reputations, and many of the great American universities can trace their origins back to colonial times or the early years of the Republic.

Within the Anglo-American world of higher education two particularly powerful national labels have sustained their reputations over time: Oxbridge and the Ivy League. However, this is status perhaps disproportionately based on historical reputation (as opposed to contemporary empirical evidence), and it could be argued that its scope is delineated by well-defined cultural boundaries. Before their destruction by the Nazi regime both German and Austrian universities could lay claim to international status. And it is important not to leave out of the equation the distinguished Scandinavian universities with strong traditions of research, scholarship and professional training.

In recent years we have seen an increasing interest (much of it stimulated by journalists) in the development of so-called world-class university league tables. The focus has moved from national to international status, and from historically established reputation to measured world-class league position. Simon Marginson has presented a powerful critique of the methodology upon which such tables are based, but his chapter on the Australian Sandstones demonstrates the significant impact they have had upon shaping institutional decision-making. Although the two best-known tables, constructed annually by *The Times Higher Education Supplement* and the Shanghai Jiao Tong University, illustrate the decisive dominance of US universities (especially Harvard University), in relative terms (the representation of world-class universities within the different national systems) the Australian higher education system performs admirably.

The criteria that determine rankings in the league tables are dominated by the measures of research excellence, indeed in much of Philip Altbach's outstanding work on international higher education there is almost an instinctive linking of research and world-class to construct the concept of 'the world-class research university'. Whereas historically reputation appeared to be broad-based (the social basis of undergraduate recruitment, the academic quality of the faculty, research excellence, the intellectual strength of the degree programs, and the links to the dominant centers of power – economically, politically and culturally), it is now narrowly focussed with the quality of research outputs taking precedence. Our chapters have brought to the fore powerful counter-arguments. Neither India nor the Latin American countries have resource bases that are sufficiently large to enable their universities to compete in these terms. If the variables that determine ranking simply exclude universities in many national systems, then it seems absurd to claim that the tables have a global remit. Furthermore, there are regional and national systems incorporating values which direct higher education towards fulfilling critical social goals with the implication that institutional excellence has to be measured in these terms. For example, in the Nordic countries access to higher education was perceived as critical to securing the broader commitment to social justice, whereas (in parallel fashion) in Latin America the universities were obliged to enhance national culture and a sense of social solidarity.

It is no exaggeration to say that the international league tables have dealt a considerable blow to French national pride. The *grandes écoles* impact upon the league tables by their virtual absence. However, they were not created to be centers of international research excellence (research and development in France has been located in designated research centers rather than in its institutions of higher education) but to channel their graduates into the commanding heights of the French state and dominant positions within French economic and cultural life. And in these terms they have been remarkably successful, although the dice are so loaded in their favor (far more generously financed than the French universities and with little international competition when it comes to filling national posts of prestige and power) it would have been remarkable if they had not been successful. Nonetheless, the example of France forcefully illustrates the point that both criteria and context are critical in determining institutional success.

Yet, notwithstanding the legitimate critique of the methodology of the league tables, of the undue attention they have attracted and of their potentially negative policy messages, they are undoubtedly a powerful force for action in both academic and government circles. Although the universities that top the global ranking lists rarely trumpet their success in public (private muted satisfaction is the usual reaction), there is little sustained institutional criticism. For better or worse the universities appear to be enveloped in the evaluative process. There are two interacting forces that make it difficult for them to do otherwise. The academic profession world-wide has come to value the importance of research over teaching. Academics who do not engage actively in research are in danger of being relegated to a marginalized teaching role. Consequently there are few institutions, certainly in the economically developed world, that purposefully do not embrace a research agenda however marginal that may seem in relation to the world's leading research universities.

But perhaps more significant are the higher education policies pursued by national governments. Several governments (in this volume we have paid particular attention to China, Japan and Germany) have decided to pursue policies that will explicitly augment the research income of a selected number of their institutions of higher education. For Germany this is a startling development given that it is an initiative led by the Federal government (constitutionally higher education institutions are the responsibility of the regional governments), and so blatantly challenges the established norm of a level playing field with respect to the distribution of funding. The central state is making the resources available that it hopes will enable some selected universities to expand and enhance their research agendas. The explicit intention may not be (as is the case with the Chinese government) to ensure more German universities acquire an elevated world-class status but rather to ensure that Germany remains at the cutting-edge of research development in the belief that this is essential if it is to compete effectively in the global economy. However, it may be assumed that the ranking lists will be looked at keenly to see whether the policy appears to be succeeding! Within this context (and the United Kingdom has its own research assessment exercise that determines the selective distribution of a large proportion of the public resources allocated to research) it is very difficult for institutions to swear a vow of abstinence and refrain from competing. It is not simply a question of purposely denying the institution access to public resources but also sending out the message that your institution lacks the capacity to be a world-leader in cutting edge research.

Thus it is difficult for national systems and individual universities of national repute to resist the pressure for change, and even the egalitarian and social goals associated with the universities of the Nordic countries and Latin America are under pressure. If they fail to go down this route will their status steadily decline with those who can afford the costs sending their children overseas to receive a higher education? Or – and more significantly – will the research capacity they currently possess disintegrate as increasing numbers of their leading researchers and best graduate students gravitate towards those universities that bear the 'world-class' stamp of approval? And it is of some significance that France's *grandes écoles* have started to enlarge their research capacity.

What the analysis of the world-class league tables demonstrates is the interesting interaction between international, national, local and institutional pressures. The structural development of higher education systems occurs through an interactive process that embraces these differing levels. National governments make resources available that they believe are vital to sustaining the research of their higher education institutions, and which they also assume is critical to their future economic performance in the global economy. In many countries there has been a significant regional and local input into shaping the character of higher education. What happens to these traditional forces in view of national responses to global pressures? Does a stratum of higher education emerge which is embedded locally or regionally? Are there some universities that, in order to sustain themselves, have to straddle different roles? The evidence suggests that, since there are no neat answers to these questions, more complex internal structures of higher education will steadily emerge, which is one of the messages embedded in the chapters of this book. But undoubtedly elite national institutions, like those with a global ranking, will endeavour to hold on to their reputations. Moreover, the struggle for global recognition will become more intense as national governments provide the resources that will allow their elite institutions to compete more effectively in the global research market.

Concluding Observations

The evidence of our chapters suggests that there is a measure of convergence embracing national and regional systems of higher education. They are moving towards the US model in the sense of becoming much more pluralistic, although the relative weight of the various dimensions that make up the pluralist whole will vary considerably: for example, at least in the short run it is unlikely that any Indian universities will gravitate towards the top of the world-class league table, but India has an elite stratum of universities some of which could develop some cutting-edge research in a selective number of fields. Indeed, this may be the way forward for many developing countries including those in Latin America, which are far from being amongst the world's poorest nations. And for the elite South African universities this is an option with considerable viability, especially given the sophisticated development in certain segments of its economy.

We have seen how the emergence of mass higher education has resulted in a general trend from public to private funding. But the shift is clearly more marked in some countries than others. Moreover, even institutions that are predominantly privately funded invariably attract a stream of public monies that supports some of their critical functions. The research that elite national institutions rely upon to propel them into the ranks of the world-class universities is underwritten in most national systems by considerable inputs from the public purse, augmented by research funding from organizations that have (state-regulated) charitable status. Moreover, in some countries the state has adopted a purposeful role in the regulation of research in higher education, as evidenced in the competitions for additional funding that both the Japanese and German governments set in motion. Indeed in Scotland, for example, the national government went so far as to put into place procedures that would concentrate certain research fields (chemistry and physics) in particular universities. The idea, therefore, that there is a worldwide trend towards a declining state role in the affairs of higher education needs to be carefully refined. The role may be different, and it may be differently organized, but nonetheless it remains potent on a wide national front.

In relation to the funding of research in higher education, and more specifically the development of world-class research universities, the following broad differences have emerged, although it should be stressed that they are ideal types:

1. The state identifies a limited number of universities for additional funding designed to enhance their research profiles (a top-down strategy currently pursued in China).
2. The state invites universities to compete for additional research funding and selects a limited number on the basis of a selective competitive process (Japan, France and Germany).
3. The state distributes public resources for research funding through a combination of periodic reviews of institutional research quality, and the evaluation, usually by peer review, of individual applications to research funding bodies (the United Kingdom, Australia and New Zealand).
4. The state invites competitive applications for research funding (again evaluated mainly by peer review) through two main public channels: research funding organizations and government departments (United States and South Africa).

Furthermore, models 2, 3 and 4 do not preclude universities from seeking additional funding from (mainly) charitable bodies and private corporations. Balán has written 'China's reform is probably the most daring experiment ever in reshuffling a large-scale higher education system' (2007: 292). But, as all the chapters in this volume illustrate, change is the norm for national and regional systems of higher education worldwide. The strategies may differ and the degree of internal opposition will vary but there is an inexorable shift towards greater structural differentiation of which the drive to create world-class research universities is but a part, and by no means a move that commands universal support.

It is interesting to hypothesize that structural change in higher education within individual nations is following one of three main tracks: the shift towards the public/private model embraced by the United States; a European model developing under the auspices of the European Higher Education Area in which there is stronger role for centralized state (even supra-national) planning; and a mixed pattern emerging elsewhere (even mixed within individual nation states) that will develop in response to local cultural traditions, the input of international organizations (such as the World Bank, which will be a central theme in the third book of the series edited by Roberta Bassett and Alma Maldonado-Maldonado), regional alliances and the patterns of cross-national institutional interaction (for example, the links between US universities and those in Latin America).

Although, as we have seen, the so-called world-class universities have developed in the context of their national settings, this may be a situation that is in the process of changing. There is a possibility that the next major structural shift will be international in scope: the world-class universities become increasingly entwined in a network of relationships that separates them from their national bases. In this book several chapters emphasized the inevitable interaction between elite institutions and the base of the national systems in which they were set: the elite institutions relied on the base for replenishment, and were protected by it as it expanded in response to the pressures for widening participation. In the emerging world in which higher education is a global commodity, the leading universities may increasingly be tied into an international network with interlocking responsibilities for research, patterns of elite recruitment (of staff as well as graduate, and even undergraduate, students), the creation of cultural values and – of course – their own reproduction. They feed off each other rather than their national bases.

Reference

Balán, J. (2007) 'Higher Education and the Research University' in P. Altbach and J. Balán (eds) *World Class Worldwide: Transforming Research Universities in Asia and Latin America*, The John Hopkins Press, Baltimore, 286–308.

Index